CONSUMERS IN THE ECONOMY

D. Hayden Green, Ed. D.
Oak Park and River Forest High School
Oak Park, Illinois

Published by

SOUTH-WESTERN PUBLISHING CO.

H46

CINCINNATI   WEST CHICAGO, ILL.   DALLAS   PELHAM MANOR, N.Y.   PALO ALTO, CALIF.

Copyright © 1983

by South-Western Publishing Co.

Cincinnati, Ohio

ISBN: 0-538-08460-X
Library of Congress Catalog Card Number: 81-86433

2 3 4 5 6 7 8 K 9 8 7 6 5 4 3

Printed in the United States of America

Preface

In periods of prosperity and during times of shortage, you face the question of "how to live well." In order to get maximum satisfaction from your resources, you need to study consumer and economic education. No other course is more deeply rooted in the real world or more relevant to everyday living than consumer and economic education.

This textbook centers on the four topics of concern to all individuals: *decision making, resource management, money management,* and *citizen participation.* The unit on decision making emphasizes attitudes, values, choice making, and the problems facing the consumer. The unit on resource management deals with purchasing and conserving goods and services. The unit on money management covers borrowing, saving, investing, paying taxes, and insuring your life, health, and property. The unit on citizen participation includes consumer protection, laws and regulations, consumer redress procedures, and the responsibilities of individuals in the American economic system.

The objectives for *Consumers in the Economy* were developed from a review of curriculum guides for states that require consumer and economic education for high school students; from *Classification of Concepts in Consumer Education*, a national study funded by the U.S. Office of Consumers' Education; and from national research about the objectives for consumer and economic education. The subject matter of *Consumers in the Economy* is arranged according to a plan that provides for the development of important consumer and economic concepts. You start by identifying the role of the consumer in the marketplace. You progress by studying resource management, money management, and finally, the consumer's role in the economy.

Consumers in the Economy is multidisciplinary in its approach. The concepts and skills taught in this textbook come from business, economics, sociology, psychology, anthropology, political science, mathematics, business education, and home economics. The content, however, always emphasizes you as a consumer.

After studying *Consumers in the Economy*, you will realize that being a consumer means more than buying "things." You will have an opportunity to come face to face with your own values, goals, dreams, and priorities before you become caught up in the adult concerns of bills, mortgages, marriage, children, and taxes. Throughout this course you will have opportunities to consider such questions as "What is the good life?" "What are my priorities?" "What is my definition of living well?" and "What commitments am I willing to make to achieve my priorities?"

The ultimate goal of *Consumers in the Economy* is to help you become a competent consumer. Competent consumers are aware of their values; they know how to establish priorities and can act efficiently in the marketplace.

D. Hayden Green

CONTENTS

Unit 1

CONSUMER
DECISION
MAKING

Chapter 1

Consumers in the Marketplace

We are a nation of consumers. From the cradle to the grave we are users of goods and services. We consume products and services 24 hours a day, 168 hours a week. We spend 12 to 16 years learning to earn a living, but we spend little time learning how to be competent consumers. That's what this book is about—becoming a competent consumer in the American economy. In this chapter we will identify the consumer, discuss consumer decision making, and examine the *marketplace*—that is, the environment where consumers make decisions about the use of their money.

THE CONSUMER

Who is a consumer? A *consumer* is any individual who uses or acquires goods or services for personal or family purposes. More simply stated, a consumer is a user of goods and services. Think about the "things" or services which you may be using at the present: books, desk, pen or pencil, and perhaps the help of a teacher. But being a consumer is more than using or acquiring "things." Following is a broader view of the consumer.

How we consume is how we live. As consumers, we spend our incomes to achieve a certain way of life. Most of us, however, seldom have enough income to satisfy all our wants. As a result, consumers must make choices. In the past, consumers often focused on which brands to purchase, which stores to buy from, and the like. But being a consumer today means making decisions not only about individual *resources* (such as money, time, property, savings, and talents), but also about world resources. In the decade of the eighties, consumers must deal with the problems of using limited natural resources as well as satisfying personal needs and wants.

Decisions, Decisions

The consumer is a decision maker in the marketplace. A *decision* is the act or process of making a choice. In the process of decision making the consumer *establishes a goal, gathers and evaluates the information, compares alternatives and considers consequences,* and *makes a decision* that results in the taking of action or no action. For example, you as a consumer may want to reduce the amount of time you spend doing routine math calculations. Your goal, then, would probably be to get an electronic calculator. You may talk with your parents or friends to gather information. In addition, you may read *Consumer Reports,* a magazine which reports information about products and product testing, to evaluate the calculators on the market. Then, you probably will compare different calculators at various stores. The next step is to consider the consequences of the decision. That is, if you spend your money on the calculator, the result will be faster, more accurate calculations and less money to spend on something else. Once the process is complete, you decide to buy or not to buy a calculator.

The amount of time spent in the process of decision making varies with the amount of money involved in the purchase and the meaning and importance of the purchase to the consumer. The amount of time spent on a decision also will be affected by previous experiences with the product, the need for a product, and the expected results and consequences of the purchase. In other words, sometimes consumers' decisions are simple, such as deciding to go to a movie or a basketball game. Other decisions are complex, such as choosing a career or a college. Decision making becomes even more complicated as we begin to realize the consequences of our actions on society, our families, and ourselves.

Life-style. Consumer decisions play a large part in choosing a *life-style*. What is a life-style? It's your typical way of life as influenced by your resources, roles, needs and wants. It includes where you live, what you eat, how you dress, and the friends you have. Your life-style also includes the intangibles of life — things that are not readily visible to others — such as your spiritual or emotional needs. Your life-style may include eating out regularly, traveling, jogging or playing tennis, reading books, or developing spiritually. The sum of your consumer decisions determines your life-style, and your life-style is your personal standard of living.

Social Costs. The impact of individual decisions and actions, when considered collectively (or as a whole), is known as a *social cost*. The results of 225 million consumer decisions in this country are enormously important to our society and to the world. Consumer spending accounts for about two-thirds of the total economic activity in the United States each year. According to the U.S. Department of Commerce, consumers spent over $1,626.6 billion on products and services in 1980. To see the full effect of consumer decisions, we should examine their influence on our energy, resources, and environment.

Energy. Two thirds of all energy used in America goes to personal consumption. That is, one third goes directly for propelling cars, heating homes, and running appliances. Another one third is used for the manufacture, transportation, and processing of the goods consumers use.

Resources. Annually, consumers in the United States use 290 million tons of forest products, 140 million tons of metals, 1.9 billion tons of fuel minerals, and 2.1 billion tons of other materials.

Environment. We discard 160 million tons of waste materials each year, or approximately 4.5 pounds per person every day of the year. Such waste includes 4.8 billion cans (250 per person), 26 billion bottles and jars (135 per person), 65 billion metal and plastic caps and bottle tops (338 per person), plus more than a half billion dollars worth of miscellaneous packaging materials.

As stated earlier, consumers can no longer make decisions only on the basis of personal costs. Decisions need to reflect both personal costs, as measured in terms of dollars spent, and social costs, as measured by the amount of energy used, the effect on the environment, and other social considerations. Consumers are becoming aware that being a consumer involves more than just making decisions about the best use of personal resources — that their decisions also have an impact on society as a whole.

Consumer Choice

In the United States consumers have freedom of choice. This means we are free to make personal decisions on the basis of our values. Our values are the ideas which we as individuals or as members of a group or society consider correct, desirable, and important. We make choices to accomplish our goals. *Goals* are the specific aims or objectives which reflect a set of values. The most immediate consumer goals reflect the needs and wants of human existence. *Needs* are those things considered essential to human existence. *Wants* are those things which are desired by individuals but which are not essential to human existence. In other words, the goal of most consumers is survival and satisfaction.

People do not really need things like television sets, music, or newspapers. But people want these things and get satisfaction and fulfillment from them. We also get satisfaction from making improvements to our basic needs. For example, our homes have rooms for eating, entertaining, and sleeping because people want a house with more than one room. Likewise, we may need only the most basic nutritional requirements, but as human beings we want more. Therefore, we have a variety of foods available to us at the supermarket and many different types of restaurants to choose from when we eat out.

Our wants are unlimited and complex. That is, the products, services, and living conditions we seek often include the product and something else. For instance, we want a product plus convenience, or a product plus atmosphere, a product plus safety, or a product minus any health hazards.

Our society is made up of all the things we want. We all have an image of the kind of life we want to live. It may be called our *mental standard of living*. The thing that largely determines the quality of living that consumers achieve is the nature of our wanting. If our mental standard of living is shaped by helplessness or ignorance of the marketplace, we may settle for a meager level of living. If, on the other hand, we have a vision or idea of the many possibilities that are available to us, we can achieve the best and richest life from our resources. This is not to say that a lot of consumption results in satisfaction. Sometimes what we choose not to buy or use adds more to the quality of our lives. To repeat, it is the nature of our wanting that is the most significant factor in our lives as consumers.

The Competent Consumer

In today's society individuals must learn to be competent consumers, that is, to act efficiently. Competent consumers are aware of their values, they know how to establish priorities, and they are able to act efficiently in the marketplace. Every consumer choice consists of two parts. The first part involves the consumer's values and tastes. Quite simply, the characteristics of a product make it preferred by one person but not by another person. For one consumer, satisfaction may require a product plus status or a product plus beauty. For another consumer, satisfaction may require a product plus durability or a product minus any health or safety hazards. We sometimes use the expressions "it's a matter of taste" or "those are their values" to describe the first part of consumer choice.

The second part of consumer choice involves how the "preferred product" can be obtained economically or as efficiently as possible. For example, you may want product X, brand Y. A friend may want product X, brand Z. We can say that the different choices are a matter of taste. But when you and a friend both want product X, brand Y, and you pay $12.95 and your friend pays $15.95, you are acting efficiently while your friend is being wasteful or inefficient.

A very good tool which consumers use in making choices is the *opportunity cost* principle. Consumers often have only a vague notion of this concept, but all consumers use it. The opportunity cost principle helps to establish priorities. In order to understand the principle, it is necessary to know that the word "cost" does not mean "the price in dollars." Perhaps a better name for the opportunity cost concept would be "the either/or cost." That is, we know that if we have a limited amount of money and if we buy one thing, we cannot buy something else. We can spend our money *either* on this product *or* on that product. For example, assume you have $20 and want to buy jeans, buy wall posters, and go to a movie. If you buy the jeans, you probably will have to do without one or both of the other items. Whatever you must do without is the opportunity cost. By using the opportunity cost principle, either knowingly or unknowingly, we consumers attempt to make decisions which reflect our priorities.

Throughout this textbook we use the term "competent consumer" to describe consumers who

   —are aware of their values and goals
   —know how to establish priorities
   —are able to act efficiently

Chapter 2 examines how values influence our consumer decisions and Chapter 3 presents the decision-making process in more depth. But now the consumer's environment—the marketplace—will be examined.

THE MARKETPLACE

We have already identified the marketplace as the environment where consumers operate, but look at this word more closely. The root of the word — market — means a place where buyers and sellers meet. It may be a department store, a roadside vegetable stand, or a salesperson at the front door. Markets are local, regional, national, and international. There are markets for every type of product and service; for example, the housing market, or the grocery market. In addition, the act of buying and selling is governed by laws, customs, and rules. Therefore, "marketplace" is a word used to cover the different markets in various locations which are governed by laws, rules, and customs. The term "marketplace" is used in its broadest sense to refer to all buying and selling of goods and services.

In the marketplaces of the United States, consumers are free to make their own choices. Individual consumers decide what they want and achieve both satisfaction and dissatisfaction as a result of their choices. Producers are also free to offer products and to influence the consumer. The characteristics of this marketplace are presented below.

A World of Alternatives

There has never been a marketplace so large, so complex, and so abundant with goods and services as the present American marketplace. The number of products available boggles the mind. Consumers can buy products ranging from the most essential to the most extravagant — from mopeds to limousines, from plastic forks to gold-plated toothpicks, from sleeping bags to water beds, and from golf carts to snowmobiles. A modern supermarket now stocks more than 10,000 different items. There are so many different things inside a large supermarket that if you stopped to look at each one for just 30 seconds you would not get out of the store for nearly 11 days.

The marketplace of today is vastly different from the one of just 50 years ago. It has changed from local manufacturers to huge impersonal corporations; from small stores and shops owned and operated by local residents to chain supermarkets and department stores; from small family-run corner diners and restaurants to franchised fast-food chains. "Plastic money" (credit cards) has become more commonplace than cash as a means of payment. The number and complexity of products often make consumers feel as if they need training in chemistry, food science, medicine, law, and finance.

A Marketplace Philosophy

A close examination of the marketplace until 1960 would show that the relationship between buyers and sellers was governed by the ancient philosophy, *caveat emptor,* which means "let the buyer beware." If buyers wasted their money or bought a product that was worthless, or even harmful, it was considered merely the result of the buyers' ignorance.

As the marketplace changed, the relationship between buyers and sellers changed. The relationship has become one of the amateur buyer against the professional seller; the individual against the corporation. A new marketplace philosophy emerged with large-scale industrialization, advancements in technology, and an abundance of products. By the beginning of the 1960s, a new market philosophy, *caveat venditor,* "let the seller beware," began to emerge. This new marketplace philosophy can be seen in the consumer laws and federal regulations that have been passed; examples include the Truth-in-Lending Law, Fair Credit Reporting Act, and National Traffic and Motor Vehicle Safety Act. It is also reflected in the *Consumer Bill of Rights* which was proclaimed by President Kennedy in a message before the Congress of the United States in 1962. Presidents Nixon and Ford each affirmed and added to these basic rights of all consumers. These rights now include the following.

—*The Right to Safety.* To be protected against the marketing of goods which are hazardous to health or to life.
—*The Right to be Informed.* To be protected against fraudulent, deceitful, or grossly misleading information, advertising, labeling or other practices, and to be given the facts needed to make informed choices.
—*The Right to Choose.* To be assured, wherever possible, access to a variety of products and services at competitive prices; and in those industries in which competition is not workable and government regulation is substituted, an assurance of satisfactory quality and service at fair prices.
—*The Right to be Heard.* To be assured that consumer interests will receive full and fair consideration in the formulation of

government policy and fair treatment in its administrative agencies.

—*The Right to Redress or Remedy.* To be assured that buyers have ways to register their dissatisfaction and to have complaints heard when their interests are badly served.

—*The Right to Consumer Education.* To ensure that consumers have the assistance necessary to plan and to use their resources to their maximum potential and for greatest personal satisfaction.

Consumer Power

The phrase, "the consumer is king," is an expression often used to describe the role of the consumer in the marketplace. The view that the consumer is king suggests that the sellers who provide the goods and services must give consumers the products and services they demand or want. Some economists even go further and contend that consumers ultimately control and guide production by their buying decisions. This concept is called consumer sovereignty.

Consumer sovereignty means that consumers have the power to decide how society uses its resources. Those who hold this opinion believe that consumer decisions are like "dollar votes" being cast in favor of production of a good or service. In other words, consumer decisions direct production and determine what products will succeed and which styles or models will be available. It is generally held that if a consumer decides not to buy something or not to use a service, the sellers who provide the good or service will either go out of business or change the product or service to suit the consumer's demand.

The opposite view of the consumer's role in the marketplace is that consumers are mere puppets or pawns who are easily manipulated. This idea holds that manufacturers do not attempt to satisfy the wants of customers. Instead, manufacturers create the demand for the products which they produce.

These two different theories of the consumer's role in the marketplace pose a major question: Are the products in the marketplace the result of actual consumer demand or of created demand? The answer is that neither the "consumer is king" view nor "the consumer is a puppet" view is correct. The truth lies somewhere in between. Producers determine what products will be on the market;

yet consumers are powerful. Consumer power stems from the consumer's ability to say no to shoddy merchandise, unethical business practices, and deceptive schemes. But there is still the problem that was mentioned earlier: in the marketplace as it exists, consumers are amateur buyers. When making decisions consumers often act with limited information and rely on common sense and hunches. Also, consumers often do not know of their rights in the marketplace. In order for consumers to exercise their power effectively, they should be equipped with the information, skills, and knowledge needed to operate in the marketplace. This is one purpose of consumer education.

CONSUMER EDUCATION

This course may be your first introduction to consumer education. Perhaps you are asking, what is consumer education? Who needs it? Why should anybody study consumer education? Let's look at these questions.

What Is It and Who Needs It?

Consumer education is a dynamic subject which equips people with the knowledge and skills needed to operate in the marketplace. It is the study of the knowledge needed to choose, to spend, and to conserve resources, goods, and services. Who needs it? That's simple. All consumers!

Why Study It?

Why should anyone study consumer education? All consumers need to know how to buy, how to use reliable sources of information, how to compare alternatives, and how to consider the consequences of their consumer decisions. All consumers need to know about laws which give them rights and responsibilities. If consumers encounter dishonest business practices, they should know how to obtain help. Consumers in the future will need a broad range of behaviors for dealing with economic conditions, with scarce resources, with the environment, and with achieving the life-styles they desire. What are these behaviors which consumers must learn?

They include coping, questioning, planning, purchasing, conserving, participating, and influencing.

Below is a brief look at each of the behaviors which consumers use to successfully function in the U.S. marketplace.[1]

1. *Coping* means being able to deal with existing conditions. It includes such things as trying to avoid stress and mistakes, recognizing emotional advertising claims, dealing with insufficient time, and responding properly to heavy sales pressure.

2. *Questioning* is an important consumer behavior which encourages self-reliance and a think-for-yourself attitude. Consumers need to ask questions before purchasing and to challenge misinformation and fraud. Asking questions prevents unnecessary and unwise purchases. Questioning includes voicing a complaint and seeking remedies more actively when dissatisfied with a product, a service, or a business practice.

3. *Planning* is the process of making arrangements in advance to manage financial resources. This is done after considering goals, needs, and values. Planning applies to earning income as well as to spending, saving, investing, borrowing, protecting, and paying taxes.

4. *Purchasing* is putting into practice the decision-making process. Purchasing involves seeking and using information, considering alternatives and consequences, and selecting a product or service. This behavior results in consumers buying a greater number of their products and services from sellers who make information available and who offer evidence of quality, durability, and efficiency. At the same time, this consumer behavior means refusing to buy products that are potentially harmful to health or environment.

5. *Conserving* is the consumer's action or decision to preserve or use resources efficiently rather than wastefully. Our natural resources are limited and the use of these materials also must be limited.

6. *Participating* is the consumer's involvement in the decisions of business, government, and community services which

---

[1]Adapted from *Classification of Concepts in Consumer Education*, by Rosella Bannister, Charles Monsma: U.S. Office of Consumer Education.

affect consumers. Consumer participation includes questioning, analyzing, and suggesting alternative solutions to consumer issues and problems. Without consumer-citizen participation, programs, products, and services are far less responsive to the consumer's interest. Participating means leaving behind the passive role of being a recipient and taking on the active role of being a participant. Active, informed, and assertive consumer participation is a requirement for a responsive democratic society.

7. *Influencing* requires individuals and groups to raise the consumer's voice to modify the policies of business and government which affect the workings of the marketplace. In order to be influential, consumers must be represented in the debates about legislation, government regulation, and business-consumer affairs.

Caveat Emptor: *To Buy or Not to Buy*

When discussing consumer choice, it is important to recognize that consumer satisfaction is based on individual preferences. Can one person tell another what to prefer or what individual tastes should be? Of course not. Freedom of choice means freedom to make bad, as well as good, choices within the limits of the law. Does that mean that the government or the law decides which consumer products are good or bad? Again, no. The law does put some restrictions and limits on certain products, but each individual must decide which product to buy or not to buy. The evaluation of products is the responsibility of each consumer.

By evaluation we mean that each consumer must determine the worth or appropriateness of a product. One way to begin to evaluate products is to realize that some goods and services promote well-being, that others have harmful effects, and that still others neither promote nor harm well-being. Goods and services which further the well-being of consumers may be called *wealth*. Those which have an effect that harms the consumer may be called *illth*. If they have a neutral effect which neither helps nor harms the consumer, we may call them *nealth*. In Illus. 1-1 are some goods and services classified according to their contribution to the well-being of consumers.

Obviously these classifications are not rigid and objective. For example, not all the food you eat nor all the beverages you drink add to your well being. You may eat or drink too much or too little. In either case the result may be harmful to your health. Remember that freedom of choice means being free to choose products that may be bad for you as well as products that are good for you. Who is to judge? The responsibility is yours. Buyer Beware.

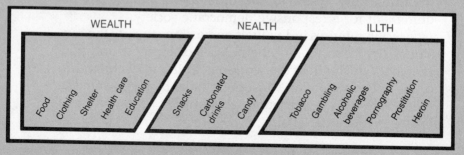

Illus. 1-1

From ECONOMICS FOR CONSUMERS, *Seventh Edition, by Leland J. Gordon and Stewart M. Lee. Copyright © 1977 by Litton Educational Publishing, Inc. Reprinted by permission of Wadsworth Publishing Company, Belmont, California 94002.*

VOCABULARY REVIEW

Marketplace	Opportunity cost
Consumer	Caveat emptor
Resources	Caveat venditor
Decision making	Consumer Bill of Rights
Life-style	Consumer sovereignty
Social cost	Consumer education

QUESTIONS FOR REVIEW

1. Approximately what amount of time does a person spend each day as a consumer?

2. What steps are involved in the consumer decision-making process?

3. What is a person's life-style and how do consumer decisions influence one's life-style?

4. What are the personal and social consequences of consumer decisions?

5. What is a competent consumer as defined in this textbook?

6. How has the United States marketplace changed in the last 50 years? Cite examples.

7. What is the new philosophy of the marketplace?

8. State the six basic consumer rights of all individuals.

9. What is the meaning of consumer power in the marketplace?

PROBLEM-SOLVING AND DECISION-MAKING PROJECTS

1. Mark Dunnet saved $600 from his summer job. He would like to buy a set of speakers, a turntable, and a receiver/amplifier with the money. He also anticipates going to the local community college after graduation from high school. He would like to buy a car when he has enough money saved. What is the opportunity cost of Mark's decision if he saves the money for the car?

2. Assume that Kathy Parker wants to buy a tennis racket. Describe the decision-making process she should use for choosing a tennis racket.

3. Using the definition of life-style as presented in this chapter, write a description of your current life-style. Include such factors as where you live, how you dress, your hobbies and forms of recreation, your eating habits, and your choice of friends. Include, if you wish, any changes you would like to make in your life-style.

COMMUNITY AND HOME PROJECTS

1. Look around your immediate environment and think about your activities during the past 24 hours. Divide your consumer activities into two categories—goods and services. Make a list of the

goods you have used or bought and a list of the services you have used or bought.

2. Young consumers often have some unasked and unanswered questions about money management, marketplace practices, economics, and their roles as consumers. With the permission of your teacher, make a list of three to five questions you would like answered during the course of your study. Submit the questions and allow your teacher to answer them throughout your study of consumer education.

3. Using a magazine, make a list of every item advertised in the issue. Divide these items into three categories—those that contribute to *wealth, nealth, illth.*

Consumer Values and Goals

The decisions you make will determine whether you simply *live* or whether you *live well*. Making a decision does not, by itself, guarantee a happy, satisfying life. You must learn to make the *right* decisions for yourself. Each of your consumer decisions involves not only acting according to your values and goals, but also acting either efficiently or inefficiently.

In this chapter we will see how examining values and establishing goals can help consumers make the right decisions. In Chapter 3 we will examine ways to help consumers act efficiently and economically.

THE ART OF CHOOSING WELL

Making the right decisions can be very hard. The decision-making process may at times make you feel confused, pressured, or unhappy. But making decisions can be easier if you know:

—where you are "coming from"—that is, you understand your values; and

—where you are going—that is, you know your goals

You can set goals that reflect your values, and you can work toward those goals if you know what you believe in and what you want from life. Up to the present, many of the choices in your life have been made for you. Where you live, where you go to school, and how much money you can spend have been decisions outside your control. Soon, however, it will be your responsibility to make these decisions. In the near future you will get the chance to "take control" of your life. You will be on your own. In her book *Welcome to the Real World*, author Annie Moldafsky says:

Before you get on with the business of making your life work for you, you have to articulate what your expectations really are. . . . You have to come face-to-face with your values, goals, dreams, priorities.

Now is the time to ask the important questions: "What are my values? What do I want? Where am I going? How do I fit into the world?" For the consumer, the questions are even more specific: "What kind of life do I want with the resources available to me? What kind of life-style do I want? How am I going to go about getting that life?" When you begin to ask these questions, you have begun to take a look at your values.

Examining Values in Your Life

Every action you take, whether you know it or not, is based on your values. *Values* are the ideas and principles which we as individuals, groups, or societies consider correct, desirable, or important. Table 2-1 shows a list of values which people consider important in their lives. The list could be endless.

Table 2-1

Values

Religion	Economy
Education	Extravagance
Honesty	Maturity
Change	Dignity and Worth of Each
Conformity	Individual
Equality	Financial Success
Freedom	Individual Liberty
Leisure	Saving for the Future
Children	Faithfulness in Marriage
Loyalty	Family Stability
Initiative	Individuality
Obedience	Respect for Authority
Practicality	Democracy
Social Prestige	Beauty
Physical Health	Tradition
Family	

Values determine not only what you want from life, but also how you go about turning your "wants" into reality. In your life as a consumer, values work in the following way. Before you set a goal, you consult your personal system of values. For instance, you may think: "I do not have a college education, and I want one; but I do not have the money needed to attend college now." In this case your value is a belief in the importance of education. Your goal is to earn a college degree. The decision you must face is how to pay the cost of the education you want.

Planning Your Life

The ability to make plans, as well as the ability to examine your values, is viewed as one sign of maturity. The ability to make plans can mean the difference between simply living and living well. A "well-lived" life is usually a life that has been examined and planned.

Just Living. Many people seem to let life just "happen" to them. You may have met some of these people. They drift into college because it's what their parents want. They stay with a job they hate because they are in debt. What's the problem? These people have never examined their lives, never planned, or never asked some important questions about the direction of their lives.

Living Well. Living well is living thoughtfully; that is, you know what you want, why you want it, and how you're going to get it. Thomas Jefferson was talking about living well when he wrote about our rights to "life, liberty, and the pursuit of happiness." He was saying that as citizens of a democracy, we should expect more than just being able to stay alive.

Our nation's laws give consumers freedom of choice — freedom to pursue the things we want. Our responsibility as consumers is not just to want, but to *want well*. The decision-making skills we learn are of no use if we do not know *what's worth wanting in the first place*. Our wants must lead us toward the kind of life-styles that reflect our values. It is the task of each of us to decide what we value and in what order.

DEVELOPING A PERSONAL VALUE SYSTEM

The values of families and society are passed on from generation to generation. Customs, traditions, and prejudices are absorbed by the child before the child is aware that a value system is being formed. The values we learn as children have a particularly strong hold on us throughout life.

As a young adult, you begin to form values of your own. You begin to organize your beliefs and priorities. You may reject some values, or you may make them even more important in your life. The process of "organizing" your value system may bring you into conflict with yourself, your family, and your society.

Priorities, Priorities

Once you have absorbed and accepted certain values, you move to a new level. This new level is called "value rating" or "ranking your values." At this point, you begin to decide what values are of greatest importance to you and which values are of least importance.

Values change in relation to one another as you go through life. Perhaps you put a high value on saving part of your income. You also may value a good time with friends. One Friday afternoon, someone at school offers to sell you a ticket to a rock concert. Many of your friends are going. You turn down the offer. Why? Because you have decided to put a higher value on saving money than on entertainment.

During the next week you read about a new computer course offered at night. You decide to enroll even though it means taking money out of savings. Why? Because you have decided that you want to learn this skill more than you want to save money.

Rating Values. Learning how to "rate" your values will help you make more satisfying decisions. If you act on your values *without* considering how important they are, you may find your life being run by your less important values. For example, say that a consumer places high value on owning a home. This person also likes to travel. If the person spends a great deal of money on traveling, then a down payment for a house may never be possible. This consumer is acting on personal values, but the less important value is in control. Value rating helps to keep your high-priority values in control.

Conflicting Values. Making decisions will often bring you into conflict with your own values. It may be very difficult for you to say: "This *is* more important!" For example, working adults with families may experience a conflict between the desire for time with the family and the desire to further their education in night school. Both values are important and the choice will be difficult.

Commitment to Values

Dr. Gordon Miller, author of the book *Life Choices*, says: "Simply being able to set priorities on your values does not really mean that you actually value what you say you do. The missing component is *commitment.*" It is easier to decide what your value priorities are than it is to act on them. Suppose, for example, that people believe strongly in conserving energy. Does it always follow that these people will act on this belief? No. By their actions, they may show that other values are more important. By continuing to drive a car when public transportation is available, for instance, they "say" that the convenience of automobile travel ranks higher than conserving energy. Making a commitment to follow through on your value decisions is the final stage of value development.

TURNING VALUES INTO GOALS

Knowing how your actions reflect your values is an important step in taking control of your life. You need to set goals. *Goals* are the specific aims or objectives which reflect a set of values. According to Dr. Miller: "One of the biggest stumbling blocks in the decision-making process is the movement from exploring and clarifying your values to a clear statement of your goals in life."

When you set goals, start small. You don't have to plan your whole life at one time. Dr. Miller offers this advice to the "beginning" goal-setter:

1. Think back to your value priorities. Ask yourself: "What will this goal give me that I value?"
2. Be specific. Make a clear statement of your goal, one that is

definite enough to name some specific actions you can take to achieve it.

3. Establish some kind of mental timetable or target date. This will motivate you to action.

4. Select a goal that does not depend on future events or "good luck" to bring it about. If your goal is to achieve a certain style of living, it should be one you can achieve without depending on winning the state lottery.

5. Try not to think about achieving your goal as the ultimate end. Think about how you might feel once you've achieved the goal. What new choices or opportunities will have opened up? What might you do next? Don't see your goals as a "dead end."

Above all, do not forget that you will encounter obstacles as you try to achieve your goals. You may discover that YOU are one of the biggest problems. You may fail to achieve a goal because you lack self-confidence, energy, or time. You may be afraid of making a mistake, of failing, or of what will happen if your life is *really* changed once you reach the goal. For instance, you may plan to lose weight through an ambitious program of diet and exercise. You may not reach the goal because you don't seem to have time to jog every day, or you secretly dread the unhappiness you may feel if your plan fails.

Other people can also be "stumbling blocks" in your path. You may not reach a goal because friends say "that's dumb" or your family says "it's too hard for you." They may be hostile to your plan. For instance, if your goal is to pursue a traditionally male-only career (and you're a woman), achieving the goal may be made difficult because of your family's lack of support. Or you may find your actions limited by competing responsibilities. Your family may take up the time or energy that could have been spent on achieving a goal.

Your social or economic environment also can be an obstacle to achieving your goal. If your goal is in conflict with established custom, you may feel pressured to seek a more acceptable goal. Your actions may be limited by the state of the economy or by the resources available in your community.

When you encounter an obstacle, you must decide whether you will revise your goal or find ways to get around the problems. At that point, you must weigh how much your goal is worth to you.

CONSUMER ACTIONS

The ways in which consumers act on their values are a major force in the direction their lives take. Consumer actions provide a way for consumers to fulfill certain psychological and social needs.

Physical and Psychological Needs of Consumers

Dr. Abraham Maslow, a noted psychologist, has divided human needs into two categories: physical needs and psychological needs. Americans today live in a society in which their basic *physiological needs* (food, clothing, shelter) and the need to feel safe and secure in one's life are usually easy to satisfy. Our *psychological needs* are more complicated and difficult to realize. For example, what psychological need might the purchase of a sweater fulfill? By wearing a sweater, you may experience a stronger sense of *belonging* to a special group at school. As human beings, we need to feel wanted, to feel we belong to a group, and to be accepted by the people around us. If the sweater is unusual, you may be seeking the esteem gained from being a trend setter. *Esteem* is the need for prestige, recognition, and achievement. Your purchase may also be a means of *self-expression*. Perhaps the purchase of a sweater is part of a carefully considered plan to show knowledge about how to "dress for success."

Patterns of Consumption

Consumers make commitments to their personal values each time they make a choice in the marketplace. Dr. Arnold Mitchell, an economist at California's Stanford Research Institute, studies consumer choices. Dr. Mitchell's goal is to find out how consumer buying habits reflect values.

The Stanford research project is financed by 70 large American corporations which are vitally interested in consumer values and life-styles. Corporations want to know about consumer values because our choices and values affect future business. Dr. Mitchell has identified three major consumer groups: need-driven, outer-directed, and inner-directed.

Need-Driven. About 19 million American adults belong to this consumer "class." Forced by low income to buy what they must, need-driven consumers are seldom free to buy what they want. They place a very high value on security and survival. In many ways, need-driven consumers are denied freedom to express values and goals because their lives are filled with the need simply to stay alive.

Outer-Directed. Approximately 110 million adults fall into this consumer class. In general these consumers buy with an eye to outward appearances. Dr. Mitchell identified three types of outer-directed consumers:

1. *Belongers* — These consumers like to fit into a group. They tend to conform to traditional values and place high priority on home life, honesty, and duty. In consumer life, they are not experimenters. Belongers make purchases that strengthen their ties to a group and they catch on to fads only after the fad has become generally accepted.
2. *Emulators* — As the word indicates, emulators are "imitative" consumers. Their consumption is intended to be noticed. Emulators like to spend money on "visible" items like new cars and elegant clothing. They tend to buy products purchased by respected or famous people in order to be part of a "beautiful people" life-style.
3. *Achievers* — Achievers spend money, time, and energy on the "good things" of life. They put priority on being successful, and they are willing to work hard to achieve success. Achievers are the backbone of the luxury-item market and tend to buy top-quality products. Their self-confidence allows them to *begin* consumer buying trends — videotape machines are one fairly recent example.

Inner-Directed. Inner-directed consumers, currently about 26 million adults, buy to meet their own inner needs and wants and not to live up to the expectations of other people. Of all consumer groups, inner-directed consumers are the best educated and the most liberal in their values. They are often motivated by social concerns as well as by personal concerns. From a business point of view, this group is hard to "sell" on a product or service because their values and interests are so varied. Inner-directed consumers may be motivated by desires for such things as personal pleasure, inner understanding, exciting experiences, and achievement of social goals.

Classifying Yourself

At this point in your life, it is very hard to place yourself in any one of these consumer categories. During the teenage years, your consumer values may lead you to behave as an "emulator" in some decisions and an "achiever" in others. In some consumer decisions, you will follow your parents' lead. In others, you will react negatively to their values and patterns. For example, Dr. Mitchell notes that a great many student protesters of the 1960s were children of affluent "achiever" parents. Having seen what they considered the limitations of the achiever life-style, the "younger generation" turned to other values.

During your lifetime, says Dr. Mitchell, you may make radical changes in your consumption patterns as your values and goals grow and change. Changes may come from within you or be caused by changes in society.

VALUES AND GOALS FOR SOCIETY

Obviously your consumer values and goals affect your personal life-style. But when you act out of commitment to certain values and goals, your actions also have great impact on your family, your friends, and your community—in short, on your society.

A society, like a single human being, must think about its values and goals if the society is to "live well." A society that lives well is one which provides maximum possible freedom for each citizen to pursue a satisfying, fulfilling life.

By maximum freedom, we do not mean that societies should disregard laws and allow people to "do their own thing." It means, rather, that society must be so organized as to keep us from blocking each other as we try to reach our goals. Society, in other words, acts as a referee, trying to find the best solution to conflicts among citizens.

Social Priorities

The people of a society determine the values of the nation. Ideally, the votes of individual citizens elect politicians who in turn make laws which reflect the values of the voters. It is unlikely that any society can fully reflect the values of each citizen. Some citizens want more social welfare programs; others call for lower taxes. Still others push for stricter laws to protect the environment. Some citizens believe that government should not regulate or interfere with the operations of businesses.

Democracy, our nation's form of government, is based upon the idea that the values and goals of the *majority* of citizens should be followed. Our society gives every citizen the right to express opinions and to try to persuade others to share the same values. Inevitably the competing values and goals of individuals make "trade-offs" and compromises necessary. For example, one person lives on a fixed income and wants the government to do something about inflation. Or perhaps a neighbor has lost a job and wants the government to put money into the economy. Such action might create more jobs but keep inflation rates high. Our political system tries to balance the conflict between our competing rights and interests. Today the problem of balancing the values and goals of more than 230 million citizens is especially difficult.

Where to, America?

Setting goals for a nation that is experiencing a "values crisis" is hard. In the broadest sense most social observers agree that our national goal has always been to progress. By progress we mean to take a step forward, to move up, to improve, to "get ahead." Our nation's history tells of these efforts to progress in areas such as technology, civil rights, education, and so forth.

In the American marketplace *progress* is defined as the production and consumption of an ever-growing supply of consumer goods and services. In the past progress for consumers meant that each generation could and should reach a higher standard of living than the preceding generation. The *standard of living* is the level of necessities and comforts to which a person or a society may be accustomed or to which they aspire. The expression usually refers to the measurement of the material things in our lives, such as food, clothing, shelter, medicine, transportation, and tools. The energy crisis, as no other event before, jolted our belief that American life would continue to progress or to get better. Consumers have always accepted the benefits of technology and economic development. But now pollution, water contamination, noise, and related problems are making consumers question the results of this technology and

Caveat Emptor: *Materialism vs. Voluntary Simplicity*

Where do the *things* you own fit into your system of values? Materialism has been an important part of American life since the first explorers brought back tales of streets paved with gold. *Materialism* is a belief that comfort, pleasure, and wealth are the highest values and goals in life. The so-called "American Dream" was a dream about freedom and material wealth.

Around the country, a small but fast-growing number of consumers is embracing a life-style often called *voluntary simplicity*. It is a life-style chosen freely and marked by less dependence on material goods. Those who choose the simple life look for durable products to last a lifetime, share ownership of lawnmowers and other products, recycle products, engage in do-it-yourself projects, and become involved with small-scale projects to produce food or energy. By clearing away the "clutter" of overconsumption, these people hope to have more room to create a satisfying inner life.

The decisions to move away from materialism is a personal and a social decision. As future shortages become reality, consumers will be forced to shift their expectations, that is, their "mental standard of living." Consumers will need to learn how to place other values ahead of material consumption. This is your time. You're more alert, more aware than you were as a child. And today you're not yet caught up in many of the problems of bills, mortgages, marriages, children, and taxes. Now is a good time to "come to grips" with what is the "good life" for you. Buyer Beware.

development. Consumers once believed that resources were unlimited, but every day, it seems, the newspapers tell of shortage in another area.

Economists now predict that the standard of living for American consumers is likely to level off during the next decades. We will have to find new ways to think about progress. Some sociologists believe that American consumers are already beginning to change. Consumers are watching their utility bills, eating smaller meals, and putting new soles on old shoes. Many consumers are moving away from the goal of personal consumption and moving toward the goal of improving the quality, rather than the quantity, of their lives—and they are taking pride in their actions. For these people, *progress now means consuming better, not consuming more.* The goal of American consumers in the next decades will probably be *learning to live well in an age of limited resources.* It is a challenge, not a threat.

VOCABULARY REVIEW

Value conflicts

Value priorities

Need-driven consumers

Outer-directed consumers

Belongers

Emulators

Achievers

Inner-directed consumers

Materialism

QUESTIONS FOR REVIEW

1. What are values, and how do they influence consumer decisions?
2. What two questions should consumers ask in order to make the decision-making process easier?
3. What does it mean "to take control" of your life?
4. What is the difference between "just living" and "living well"?
5. How does a person go about turning values into goals?
6. If people say they believe in saving but are always borrowing from friends, what are the people lacking in order to accomplish their stated value?
7. What are the three major consumer groups?
8. Of the three different types of consumers, which is the hardest to sell and why?

PROBLEM-SOLVING AND DECISION-MAKING PROJECTS

1. Make a list of five material possessions you value the most. These do not have to be the most expensive items you own, but only

those you value the most. After each item, explain why it is on the list. In other words, what is it that you value?

2. Imagine that because of a variety of circumstances you can keep only three of the possessions. Which three possessions would you prefer over the others? What values influence your choice? As you consider which ones to give up, what conflicts occur in making your choice?

3. After doing Projects 1 and 2, state a value which you can identify as important to you. Try to recall an action which you have taken that shows some commitment to this value. Now identify a future action which would establish your commitment to this value.

4. Consider the items listed below, and select only one of these items.

(a) Your five favorite TV programs.
(b) Organizations you belong to.
(c) Best gift you ever received.
(d) Best gift you ever gave.
(e) A record of major purchases you made in the past year.
(f) Your photo album.
(g) Your savings account.
(h) Organizations or people you have given money to.
(i) Organizations or people you have worked for (without pay).
(j) Things you no longer use but have not thrown away.

What does this choice indicate about your values and about the commitments you have made to them? Write a brief statement explaining your value commitments.

COMMUNITY AND HOME PROJECTS

1. Keep a journal for at least the length of this course. Jot down value-related thoughts and feelings whenever they occur. From time to time, ask yourself these questions: "Are my values at all different from what they were a week ago?" "a month ago?" "Am I clearer on value issues now than a week or month ago?" "Are some issues more confusing now?" Submit this journal to your instructor at the end of this course.

2. Survey students in your school. Determine if they are "living well"; that is, do they know what they want, when they want

it, and how they're going to get it? Write a report about your findings.

3. Survey people in five different age groups to determine what they think social priorities should be for your community. Consider people in these age groups: 16-25, 26-35, 36-45, 46-64, and 65 or older. Prepare a report on your findings.

Chapter 3

Consumer Decisions

To buy or not to buy, that is the key question for consumers. Decision making is a consumer's principal task. A consumer can act either competently or carelessly. Competent consumer decisions yield high payoffs in terms of increased purchasing power and personal satisfaction. Careless and haphazard consumer decisions result in wasted resources and personal dissatisfaction. In this chapter we will discuss the decision-making process and sources of reliable consumer information.

THE DECISION-MAKING PROCESS

Consumer decision making is a series of deliberations and actions taken to arrive at a choice or to solve a problem. The process works in the following way.

Identify the Goal

Consumers make choices in order to accomplish goals. For example, if we need to get to school or work, then the goal is transportation. But as discussed in Chapter 1, our goals for the products and services we buy often include other satisfactions such as reliability, ease of use, convenience, and status. The first step of the decision-making process, then, is to clearly identify the goal.

Get Reliable Information

Once consumers have a goal, the most crucial step in the decision-making process is to get reliable and accurate information.

In order to act competently, consumers need to know what products and brands exist. They also need to know which products have certain desired characteristics and at what prices. Unfortunately, consumers seldom are able or willing to obtain complete product information, but the more information consumers have, the greater the likelihood of efficient decisions.

Consider Alternatives and Consequences

After consumers get appropriate and accurate information, they need to compare alternatives. Alternatives are the options available when a choice needs to be made between two or more products or courses of action. Comparison of alternatives usually requires information about other products, prices, and stores. It also includes deciding whether to use something you already have, to make something rather than to buy it, to borrow the product from someone else, to rent instead of buy, or to do without.

After the alternatives have been identified, they should be examined and ranked. That is, consumers need to consider the consequences of a decision—to buy or not to buy. This is where consumers apply the opportunity cost decision-making tool discussed in Chapter 1. Consumers are able to rank their priorities according to their values, goals, and resources by considering what must be given up in terms of money or other products. Competent consumers also weigh other consequences of a purchase, such as upkeep, effect on the environment and on personal health, and even the amount of time required to use a product.

Make a Decision and Take Action

Getting information and considering alternatives and consequences enable consumers to select a product or a service or to choose a course of action to accomplish a goal. At this point it is possible for consumers to act efficiently, that is, get the product they want as economically or cheaply as they can. Consumers will be able to enjoy the satisfaction of a product or service while knowing that they have acted competently—or with a minimum expense or waste of resources. In general by following this consumer decision-making process, consumers gain confidence and gratification from the careful and efficient use of personal resources.

SOURCES OF INFORMATION

Numerous sources of information are available to consumers. In fact, consumers are constantly being bombarded with information about products and services. Advertising is one way that sellers communicate information to buyers. But more important to consumers than advertising is objective information. There are three types of objective information: prepurchase information, point-of-purchase information, and postpurchase information.

Prepurchase Information

Prepurchase information, such as manufacturer's pamphlets, product ratings, and product literature, allows consumers to select products or services on the basis of expected performance. Some sources of reliable prepurchase information are discussed below.

Product-Rating Magazines. Two magazines offer consumers reliable information about products. One, *Consumer Reports*, is published by the nonprofit Consumers Union, established in 1936. *Consumer Reports* is distributed to 1.75 million members and subscribers. The magazine reports the results of objective product testing of everything from large and small appliances to frozen foods and automobiles. To guard its independence and to achieve objectivity, Consumers Union accepts no commercial advertising, accepts no free samples for testing, and forbids commercial use of its test results. When testing, Consumers Union conceals, insofar as possible, the identity of each product.

In addition to product information, *Consumer Reports* carries the results of research on such public issues as health and auto insurance, water contamination, and health food advertising. Membership subscription in Consumers Union also supports consumer positions before the courts, Congress, and regulatory agencies.

Consumers' Research, established in 1927, also publishes a monthly magazine. The ratings of products in *Consumers' Research Magazine* are based on the performance of samples studied in engineering examinations or in controlled laboratory tests. Sometimes ratings are based on judgments by qualified unbiased experts. Prices are given, but they do not affect the product's ratings.

Magazines can be a good source of prepurchase information.

Money Management Magazines and Books. Other magazines provide consumers with valuable information about financial and money management matters. For instance, *Changing Times* and *Money* cover a wide range of topics including taxes, insurance, investing, budgeting, and credit. These magazines do not test or rate products but provide a consumer perspective on money management topics.

In addition to magazines there are books available on buying products and services. Examples are *The New Handbook of Prescription Drugs*, Edmund's car price books, and "how to buy" books on topics such as photography equipment, stereo equipment, and camping and sports equipment.

Government Agency Publications. Federal, state, and local governments provide an abundance of useful consumer information. Four times a year the federal government publishes the *Consumer Information Catalog*. This catalog lists booklets from nearly 30 agencies of the federal government. From this source, consumers can find booklets on car repair, health care, energy conservation, and household topics. Many of these government information booklets are free.

Other Sources of Information. Businesses and manufacturers provide factsheets, brochures, and booklets about their products which can be used for comparing the products and product features. Major appliances and electrical products usually come with extensive information about features, maintenance, and energy usage. Some businesses are required to furnish product and service information. For example, each interstate moving company which is asked to give an estimate of the cost of a move is also required to give the customer a copy of its performance report for the prior year.

Another type of business-sponsored aid is the mail-order catalog. Many of the large department stores provide mail-order catalogs to customers and prospective customers. Catalogs offer valuable price information and are a good source of specific information about products. Even the Yellow Pages of the telephone book supply consumers with a list of sellers of almost any product. The telephone is the cheapest means of getting product and price information.

Point-of-Purchase Information

For many of the products which consumers buy, the most readily available information is *point-of-purchase information*. Point-of-purchase information is usually on the package or product label or is displayed with the product. Several types of point-of-purchase information will be presented below.

Product Labels. The product label is the consumer's link to what's on the inside of the package. All containers must bear the following information:

—the brand name
—the common or generic name
—the name and place of business of the manufacturer, packer, or distributor
—the net quantity of the contents

Most labels, however, provide much more than the minimum required information. Most usually contain a detailed description of the product. In the case of food the label contains a list of ingredients. In the case of clothing, instructions which tell how the item should be used and cared for are included.

Warnings. Many packages carry clearly stated warnings about the hazards associated with the product's use. Examples of such warnings are: "Harmful or fatal if swallowed" and "Caution: Combustible mixture—Keep out of the reach of children."

Appropriate Use. Most labels contain valuable information about the appropriate use of the product. An example of appropriate use information is: "Dosage—for adults and children over 12 years, 1 or 2 tablets with water."

Energy Use. Refrigerators, freezers, air conditioners, clothes washers, and furnaces are some of the products required to have labels, such as the one in Illus. 3-1, which indicate energy consumption. Energy labels on appliances must show three types of information: (1) the estimated annual operating cost, (2) a range of estimated annual operating costs for comparable products, and (3) a table showing how the energy cost can vary with a wide range of utility rates. This information allows consumers to determine more easily the actual energy cost of using an appliance.

Quality Seals. One important source of product information available to consumers is a seal. Seals are designed to give buyers some dependable third-party assurance about the quality of the product they are buying. Seals are granted by magazines, independent testing companies, professional organizations, and government agencies. The seals are usually characterized as "tested," "guaranteed," "certified," or "approved."

Consumers often think seals mean more than they do. One research study found that many people think that the agency which grants a seal can be sued if the product is defective. Others think a seal means that a product has met government standards. The paragraphs that follow tell what a seal really means to the consumer.

Magazine Seals. The best known *magazine seal*, the "Good Housekeeping Seal," is a promise by the manufacturer to replace or refund the purchase price of a certain defective product advertised in the magazine within four years of purchase. *Good Housekeeping* magazine does testing and approves products; therefore, its seal reflects the judgment of the staff of the Good Housekeeping Institute. If the product is advertised in the magazine, the advertiser may be licensed to use the seal. Magazine seals do not necessarily certify

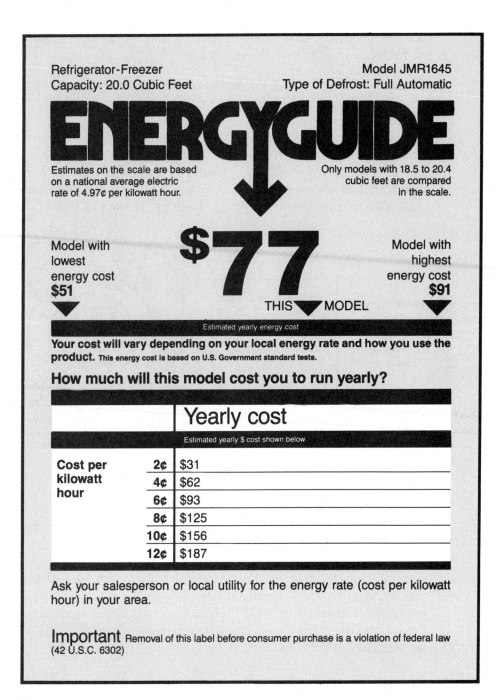

Refrigerator-Freezer
Capacity: 20.0 Cubic Feet

Model JMR1645
Type of Defrost: Full Automatic

ENERGYGUIDE

Estimates on the scale are based
on a national average electric
rate of 4.97¢ per kilowatt hour.

Only models with 18.5 to 20.4
cubic feet are compared
in the scale.

$77

Model with
lowest
energy cost
$51

Model with
highest
energy cost
$91

THIS ▼ MODEL

Estimated yearly energy cost

Your cost will vary depending on your local energy rate and how you use the product. This energy cost is based on U.S. Government standard tests.

How much will this model cost you to run yearly?

		Yearly cost
		Estimated yearly $ cost shown below
Cost per kilowatt hour	2¢	$31
	4¢	$62
	6¢	$93
	8¢	$125
	10¢	$156
	12¢	$187

Ask your salesperson or local utility for the energy rate (cost per kilowatt hour) in your area.

Important Removal of this label before consumer purchase is a violation of federal law (42 U.S.C. 6302)

Illus. 3-1

An energy quide label can show consumers the average annual costs of operating specific models of major appliances.

that the products have been tested by the magazine or that the products are the best on the market.

Safety Seals. Of more value to consumers than magazine seals are *safety seals* provided by independent testing organizations. Safety certifications require extensive research and testing. These seals indicate that equipment, materials, and products meet specific standards of safety and performance. Four safety seals in use are: the Factory Mutual Approval Mark, Underwriters Laboratories (UL), the American Gas Association (AGA), and the Association of Home Appliance Manufacturers. Two of these are shown in Illus. 3-2.

Illus. 3-2

Consumers need to know what seals mean. Some seals are little more than a form of advertising while others are indicators of safety and performance standards.

Source: Factory Mutual Research Corporation and Underwriters Laboratories.

Postpurchase Information

Consumers sometimes experience a great deal of dissatisfaction as a result of product defects, poor product quality, unsatisfactory repair services, and failure of companies to live up to their advertising claims. *Postpurchase information* is an essential part of the decision-making process. Postpurchase information is a statement about the expected responsibilities of both the consumer and the merchant or manufacturer if the product fails to perform properly. Before making a purchase, the consumer should always ask about postpurchase remedies.

Warranties. The warranty on a product is important postpurchase information. *Warranties*, also called guarantees, are promises that a product is free from defects in materials or construction. A warranty informs the consumer of the seller's or manufacturer's responsibility for a product. Sellers and manufacturers offer two basic kinds of warranties — implied and express.

Implied Warranty. An *implied warranty* is an unwritten promise that a product is fit for ordinary purposes for which it is sold. Implied warranties are warranties of merchantability and/or warranties of fitness for a particular purpose. A warranty of merchantability means that the product is in proper condition for sale and will do what it is intended to do. For example, ovens are made to cook food at certain controlled temperatures. If an oven won't heat, or heats uncontrollably, the oven is not salable. A warranty of fitness for a particular purpose is a special type of warranty that arises when a consumer relies on the seller's advice that the product can be used for a particular purpose. For example, a consumer may tell a salesperson that a washing machine is needed to wash 20 pounds of clothes at a time. The salesperson may then tell the customer that a particular model washer will be able to wash that many clothes. If, on the basis of such advice, the customer buys the washer, a warranty of fitness for a particular purpose has been made. The Uniform Commercial Code provides that if a product does not have a written warranty, it is covered by an implied warranty. The code is in effect in all states except Louisiana.

Express Warranty. An *express warranty* usually is a written warranty. The two types of written warranties are full warranties and limited warranties. A *full* warranty includes the following guarantees:

—A defective product will be repaired or replaced free of charge, including removal and reinstallation when necessary.
—The product will be repaired within a reasonable time period after the customer has complained.
—The customer will not have to do anything unreasonable to get warranty service, such as return a heavy product (for example, a piano) to the store.
—The warranty is good for all owners of the product during the warranty period.
—If the product has not been repaired after a reasonable number of times, a customer can get a replacement product or a full refund of the purchase price.

—Implied warranties cannot be disclaimed or limited to the length of the written warranty.

As the name suggests, a *limited* warranty gives the customer less than full warranty protection. Following are some instances of warranty limitations sometimes found in limited warranties.

—The warranty covers parts only; the customer must pay labor.
—The customer must return products to the store for service.
—The warranty is not transferable.
—The warranty covers repairs only, not replacement nor refund.
—Only a partial refund or credit will be provided.
—The warranty is void if a registration card is not returned.
—Implied warranties cannot be disclaimed, but they can be limited to the duration of the written warranty.

Warranties vary from product to product, manufacturer to manufacturer, and seller to seller. Thus, you should read and understand the warranty provisions before you purchase a product. If a warranty is not offered, ask to see a copy of it. According to the Magnuson-Moss Warranty Act of 1975, you have the right to see the warranty before purchasing a product.

Service Contracts. A *service contract* is an optional agreement which provides protection after a warranty has expired. Manufacturers, dealers, and repair shops sell service contracts to customers who purchase such major appliances as video cassette recorders, air conditioners, TV sets, washers, and dryers. A service contract is like an insurance policy. The contract covers the cost of repair if something goes wrong with the product after the warranty period expires. For what seems like a small cost, consumers can insure themselves for future repairs. If the product needs repair, the consumers are protected. If the product doesn't need repair, the consumers waste their money. According to a study by the Center for Policy Alternatives at the Massachusetts Institute of Technology, service contracts tend to be overpriced. The cost of the service contract can be 10 to 16 times the expected cost of repairs.

Return/Refund Policy. Because consumers may need to return a product that is unsatisfactory, they should know the store's return or refund policy. Return/refund policies can cause much dissatisfaction for both consumers and merchants. In most cases, a store is not obligated by law to make refunds or exchanges unless the merchandise is defective or the merchandise was sold through some deceptive means. Consumers should not hesitate to ask about the store's return or refund policy.

Cooling-Off Period. When you buy products from a door-to-door salesperson, you should be made aware of a *cooling-off* or *cancellation period*. Under a Federal Trade Commission rule, a salesperson must tell you your cancellation rights. The rule gives consumers three business days to change their minds about any purchase of $25 or over made in their homes. The consumer signs and dates a cancellation form and mails it to the address of the seller anytime before midnight of the third business day after the contract date in order to cancel the sale. Consumers don't have to give a reason for cancelling. This cancellation privilege does not apply to sales made at the seller's place of business or to sales under $25.

COMPARISON OF STORES, SERVICES, AND PRICES

In today's crowded marketplace all kinds of sellers attempt to get your attention and your money by offering different prices, a variety of services, and a wide range of quality. An important part of pre-purchase information and point-of-purchase information comes from a comparison of stores, services, and prices. When purchasing products over $25, you should compare the cost of the items at three or more stores. You can expect to find considerable price and service variation between the different types of stores. To get the best buy, you need to weigh carefully the advantages and disadvantages of each store before making your decision.

Types of Retail Stores

Retailing involves the sale of goods to the final customer. Most consumers purchase products from retail stores. Retail stores perform the final step in the marketing process, that is, selling products to the consumer. Retailers (or merchants) buy products from manufacturers or wholesalers (dealers who often buy from manufacturers or producers and sell to retailers).

Department Stores. A department store sells a wide variety of goods in many price ranges. Some examples of department store merchandise are clothing, furniture, major appliances, sporting and hobby goods, home improvement goods, auto equipment, toys, garden and workshop tools, and health and beauty aids. In some department stores, such as Sears Roebuck, Montgomery Ward, and J.C. Penney, merchandise carries the store name. Other department stores sell well-known, name-brand goods. Department stores also offer a broad selection of services such as credit plans, service facilities, and liberal return policies. Department stores may be independently owned and operated, or they may be a member of a chain which is owned and operated by a large company.

Specialty Shops. As the name implies, a specialty shop offers a limited number of goods or just one type of product. For example, a specialty shop may sell only major appliances or only televisions. Some specialty stores offer a number of brands, while others sell only one particular brand. Salespeople often are highly knowledgeable about the merchandise and make an effort to provide personal service and attention. Prices at specialty stores may be higher than at department stores handling many different products.

Discount Stores. Discount retailing provides the consumer with the opportunity to save money because of large volume purchases and self-service. Prices for many products are lower at discount stores because these stores buy directly from producers in large quantities (called volume buying). Producers usually charge retailers less for products bought in large volume. They may operate out of a stripped-down warehouse-like building, or they may operate out of showrooms with carpeted aisles and sparkling showcases. Some discount stores sell only well-known, name-brand goods, or they may feature their own private brand products. Discount stores usually offer fewer customer services and have fewer salespeople. Repair services are limited and refund or return policies may not exist. In some discount stores, the merchandise may not be well known. Discounters sometimes sell *knock-offs*. Knock-offs are cheaply made products that look like the name-brand merchandise.

Supermarkets and Convenience Stores. A supermarket is a large departmentalized store that features foodstuffs and is characterized by self-service. Customers assemble their products in carts or baskets and take them to a checkout counter where the products are packaged and payment is made. Supermarkets are expanding their stock. While they remain primarily food stores, many have added other wares such as drugs, hardware, and clothing. Sometimes nonfood items in supermarkets are priced higher than at other stores. For cusomters who wish to avoid the checkout lines at supermarkets, convenience or quick-service stores are available. These stores are small in size and carry limited quantities of most grocery items. However, convenience stores are open extended hours, often 24 hours a day, and generally are more expensive.

Mail-Order Firms. Mail-order businesses let people shop by mail. The largest catalog operations are the ones of the larger chain department stores such as Sears Roebuck or Montgomery Ward. Mail-order catalogs provide the consumer with useful information about products, convenient at-home shopping, and return privileges. Obviously, a disadvantage of mail-order shopping is the lack of opportunity to see a product before buying it.

Customer Service

When deciding to buy a product, many consumers consider customer service an important factor. Customer service includes such services as free delivery of products to the customer's home, installation of appliances, and repair service at the home. Other customer services offered may include check cashing or the availability of credit or a liberal return or refund store policy. Free clothing alterations are provided as a consumer service in some stores, but not in others. For many consumers, a convenient location or late shopping hours are a type of customer service. Generally, the more customer services a store offers, the higher its prices will be relative to stores that don't offer such services.

Price

The price of a product is a major concern for most consumers. Some people use the price of a product as an indicator of quality.

Customer service is an important factor in a consumer's choice of stores.

Source: Louisiana-Pacific Corporation

Caveat Emptor: *Push Money*

Consumers are easily influenced when they lack adequate product information. Unfortunately, in a great number of stores salespeople are mere order takers and are not informed enough about a product to give adequate information. Others may be well-informed, but the consumer has no way of knowing if the salesperson is being paid a *spiff* or *push money*. Push money is a cash incentive given to the salesperson by the manufacturer for each of the manufacturer's products that is sold. Push money is different from a *commission*, which is money paid a salesperson for products sold. Store commissions are given to salespeople for selling all products in the store. A spiff is paid by the manufacturer for the sale of a particular product. For example, if salespeople are pushing Product A this week, the commission may be better than on other products. The next week they may tell you that Product B is superior. Most likely they are getting a spiff, such as $10 per item sold for Product B. Buyer Beware.

This attitude can be seen in the expression, "You get what you pay for." Sometimes consumers assume that a low price means low quality, and a higher price means higher quality. Unfortunately, consumer decision making is not so simple. Prices may reflect the availability of services, a prestigious name, or an expensive location, but not better quality. Therefore, when buying durable products, consumers should seek information about the quality of competing brands before they consider price. After determining the "best product," compare prices at three or more different stores. *Comparative shopping* is comparing prices of identical or similar products or services in order to obtain the best price. This practice helps the consumer to get the best product at the lowest price.

VOCABULARY REVIEW

Prepurchase information	Express warranty
Point-of-purchase information	Full warranty
Magazine seals	Limited warranty
Safety seals	Cooling-off period
Postpurchase information	Knock-offs
Implied warranty	Push money

QUESTIONS FOR REVIEW

1. How does the consumer benefit from careful, deliberate consumer decision making?

2. What alternatives are available to consumers when considering the purchase of a product?

3. What are the three types of information which consumers should seek before buying a product?

4. Name two magazines which provide consumers with reliable information about consumer products.

5. Name two safety seals which indicate that a consumer product has met research and safety standards.

6. What is a service contract and should a consumer purchase one for large appliances?

7. What is one way to obtain the best product at the lowest cost?

8. How does push money affect consumers who are shopping for a product?

PROBLEM-SOLVING AND DECISION-MAKING PROJECTS

1. Assume that you won $100 in a contest. Identify a product which you would buy with your prize money. State the steps you would take in the process of deciding which product to purchase.

2. Assume that you have shopped for a small camera which you want to buy with $20 given to you for your birthday. After shopping you made this list.

Brand A	3rd preference
Brand B	1st preference
Brand C	2nd preference

Brand B	
Department Store	18.95
Specialty Store	19.00
Discount store	16.97

   a. From this information does it appear that a careful, deliberate decision-making process has been followed?
   b. Explain why there is a price variation between different stores.
   c. At which store would you most likely buy the camera? Why?

3. Select a product which costs over $25 which you anticipate buying or would like to buy in the future. Follow the decision-making process suggested in this chapter.

   Step 1. Identify the goal or purpose of the product.
   Step 2. Gather information about the product in *Consumer Reports, Consumers' Research Magazine,* and other sources of information. Determine from this information the best product.
   Step 3. Shop for the identical product in at least 3 different stores to determine the best price.
   Step 4. Decide at which store you would buy the product.

Write a report which summarizes your research. Use the following topic headings: purpose or goal, the best product, the best price, the decision.

4. a. Read at least one article in each of the following magazines: *Consumer Reports, Consumers' Research Magazine, Changing Times,* and *Money.* Write a brief summary of each article.

   b. How do the magazines differ in coverage and usefulness for consumers?

COMMUNITY AND HOME PROJECTS

1. With the cooperation of your teacher, prepare a notebook entitled: Consumer Sources of Information. Obtain samples of the following types of information: Articles from consumer product-test rating magazines, government agency pamphlets or booklets, manufacturers' product booklets, labels and packaging information, warranties, etc.

2. With the permission of your parents, obtain a copy of a full or limited warranty from a product recently purchased. Answer the following questions: Who issues the warranty? Who is covered? What product or part of the product is covered? What is it guaranteed against? Is this a full or limited warranty? What is the duration of the warranty? What does the consumer have to do to get warranty coverage and service?

3. Visit three stores in the community and inquire about the stores' return and refund policy. Write a brief summary of your findings.

Advertising

Why do you eat certain breakfast cereal or use a particular brand of toothpaste? What makes you want to drive a particular type of car? Is your demand for products or services the result of your own wants or needs, or are your wants influenced by advertising? Whether we know it or not, advertising greatly influences our lives as consumers. In this chapter we will examine the role of advertising in the marketplace, present the various types of advertising, suggest some ways consumers can analyze advertising techniques, and discuss the ways advertising is regulated.

INFORMATION OR PERSUASION

Advertisements and commercial messages about products and services are everywhere. Advertising plays an important communication function in our marketplace. For the consumer, it is another source of information. Advertising is information about products, services, or ideas. Through advertising, consumers are provided with information about a wide variety of products and services available from sellers. But advertising is more than information: it is also persuasion. For the merchant, advertising is designed to sell products. It is not unbiased or objective with regard to a product or service being advertised. Advertising, then, both promotes and presents information about goods and services.

Advertising in our society has critics as well as defenders. Critics claim that it:

—Promotes materialism and causes people to buy what they don't need and can't afford.

—Creates artificial wants which result in wasted productive resources.

—Reduces price competition and creates competition that is based on false, insignificant, or nonexistent differences in products.

Want to see lightweight plumbing that won't rust?

Borg-Warner Chemicals supplies plastic for pipes that is lighter, less expensive and easier to work with than the metal plumbing it replaces. That's Borg-Warner today. And there's more to come. In eight major markets, Borg-Warner is a company to watch.

Watch Borg-Warner

For an annual report write: Borg-Warner, Dept. 25, 200 South Michigan Avenue, Chicago, Illinois 60604

Some advertising provides information about products, services, or ideas.

Source: Borg-Warner Corporation

—Promotes unnecessary competition between brands resulting in higher prices.

—Lowers the general level of taste.

—Plays upon consumer emotions and motivations.

—Provides little or no useful information for consumers.

On the other side are the defenders of advertising. For the defenders, advertising is merely a helpful aid in purchasing goods or services. The proponents of advertising claim that it:

—Provides information about new or unknown products and about changes in technology.

—Communicates details on performance or characteristics of existing products.
—Promotes changes in aspirations and living standards by exposing people to goods, services, and new ideas.
—Contributes to more leisure time by promoting time-saving products and services.
—Communicates new ideas and facts.
—Reduces the cost of newspapers, magazines, TV, and radio programs by selling space or time to advertisers.
—Supplies daily price information, including money-saving specials and sales.
—Tells consumers the location of specific sellers, thereby saving consumers time and money in finding products and services.

In today's complex marketplace, advertising is an essential tool of business. Advertising can be useful to consumers if they know what product or service they want and if they can overlook emotional appeals to buy a particular product or service.

TYPES OF ADVERTISING

For the seller, advertising works in four ways.

—By spreading the news to consumers about new products
—By reminding consumers of the existence of products
—By overcoming human inaction, that is, by encouraging consumers to try a product or service
—By adding a value not in the product, that is, by making it look desirable or needed by the buyer

Advertising is often consumer oriented—or aimed directly at the consumer. But there are other types of advertising. *Trade* advertising is sent out to wholesalers and retailers. A clothing manufacturer uses trade ads to introduce a new line of fashions, and hopes that wholesalers and retailers will read the ad and order the clothes. *Industrial* advertising is designed by manufacturers to reach other manufacturers or producers of raw materials. For example, a steel manufacturer may run an industrial ad to interest manufacturers of products using steel (such as automobile manufacturers).

Professional advertising is intended for men and women who provide professional services, including doctors, dentists, teachers, and architects. A drug company will run an ad for its products in a medical journal so that doctors who read the journal will see the ad and prescribe the product for patients.

Institutional advertising is yet another type of advertising. Instead of promoting the product of a particular company, these advertisements promote the products of a business group with a common interest. For instance, the Association of American Publishers tells consumers that "A book is a loving gift"; the florists ask consumers to "Say it with flowers"; and the dairy industry tells consumers that "Milk is a natural."

Public-service advertising is an entirely different type of message. Public-service advertisements promote such causes as public education, safe driving, a clean environment, religion, health, and nutrition.

The most recent type of advertising to emerge is called *public-issue* or *non-product* advertising. Public-issue advertising advocates an idea or position regarding some public concern. Most of the issues have to do with some aspect of living in a complex society such as questions involving corporations, government, business, unions, or political parties. Most public-issue advertising is selling an idea. The American Bus Association used advertising to criticize the amount of taxpayer money spent by the government to subsidize passenger trains.

ANALYZING ADS – PERSUASION, PUFFERY, OR INFORMATION

Advertising is both an art and a science. It is a science of human behavior, and it is an art of persuasion. *Persuasion* refers to the act of influencing a person with an appeal to reason or emotion. Professional persuaders use a variety of techniques to do this. Two common methods of persuasion are *intensifying* and *downplaying* various parts or bits of information being communicated. Intensifying is accomplished by praising, bragging, boasting, emphasizing, or exaggerating the good aspects of a product or idea. Downplaying is accomplished by hiding, concealing, omitting, disguising, or minimizing the bad aspects of the product or idea.

To be useful, an advertisement should provide information about the product. Consumers should learn to look for these three features in every advertisement: (1) the existence of a product or service, (2) where a product or service can be obtained, and (3) a simple statement about the characteristics or qualities a product possesses.

Most ads provide information about the existence of a product and where it can be obtained. However, instead of providing helpful information about the qualities or features of a product, many ads use *puffery*. Puffery is an exaggerated statement about the attributes and value of a product. The words *best*, *greatest*, *purest*, and *perfect* are common examples of puffery used in advertisements. Puffery and statements of the seller's opinion are permitted by the Federal Trade Commission, but such statements should not be taken seriously.

Caveat Emptor: *The Language of Advertising*

Some consumers laugh at ads. Others claim they disbelive and ignore them. And other think ads are harmless nonsense. Regardless of their attitudes, consumers need to know something about the language of advertising. Many consumer decisions are based unknowingly on the appeals of ads. The following chart is a look at the language of advertising.[1]

Claim	Explanation	Examples
Weasel claim	A weasel word is a modifier that makes the statement meaningless. Some commonly used weasel words are: helps, like, virtual, acts, works, can be, up to, as much as, refreshes, comforts, fights, the feel of, the look of.	Helps control dandruff symptoms with regular use. Leaves dishes virtually spotless. Fights bad breath. Looks, smells, tastes like ground-roast coffee.

---

[1]Adapted from Jeffrey Schrank, "The Language of Advertising Claims," *Media & Methods* (March, 1974), pp. 44-48.

Unfinished claim	The unfinished claim does not finish a comparison. The ad claims that the product is better or has more of something but does not finish the comparison.	Our TV gives you more. Twice as much of the pain reliever doctors recommend most. Our creamer gives coffee more body, more flavor. Quieter, smoother ride. More active ingredients than other popular spray oven cleaners.
Unique claims	This claim states that no other product is like the product advertised; it's unique; it has something no other product has.	There's no other mascara like it. Either way, liquid or spray, there's nothing else like it. Our ambassador service – no one else has anything like it.
Same claim	The same claim says something about the product that is true for all brands of the product. It's a claim that can be made about any of the other competing products.	Our coffee is mountain grown. The detergent gasoline. Our radials: made for American cars. Our shoes made for American feet.
So what claim	This claim provides a means of creating an illusion or association of superiority but makes a careful reader say, "So what?" The claim which is made may be true, but it neither offers real information nor gives any advantage to the product.	Our soup gives you not one, but two chicken stocks. Strong enough for a man but made for a woman.

Vague claim	The vague claim doesn't quite make a claim. This claim usually uses colorful but meaningless words and emotional statements which defy proof.	Lips have never looked so luscious. Its deep rich lather makes hair feel new again. Stay on the young side with our cereal. For skin like peaches and cream. The end of meatloaf boredom. Finger-lickin' good.
Endorsement or testimonial claim	A famous person, usually an actor or actress or sports personality, appears to use the product and lends his or her credibility to the product.	"Listen, I love today's western look, right down to the boots," Johnny Cash. What does Brooke Shields have to say about our skin cream? Her skin says it all.
Scientific or statistical claim	This claim uses a scientific proof, data, or a mystery ingredient to establish superiority.	Our breath mints contain a sparkling drop of retsyn. Our cleanser has 33% more cleaning power than another popular brand.
Compliment the consumer claim	This claim says something nice about the consumer.	You pride yourself on your good cooking.
Question claim	One way to avoid making a factual statement about a product is to ask a question which the viewer or listener will answer in such a way as to affirm the product's goodness.	Our model — isn't that the kind of car America wants? Shouldn't your family be drinking our punch? What do you want most from coffee? That's what you get most from our coffee.

Good, better, and best claims	In the language of advertising, best means better, and better means best. In the minds of the advertisers, best means that the product is exactly the same as a number of other products. No one is clearly superior to the others. The word better when used in a claim means that a product is superior to all others.	Our orange juice — the best there is. It's our custom to give you the fastest flight to the East. Our product cleans grease better than any other leading liquid cleaner.
New and improved claims	The word "new" has a magical appeal to it. On a national basis, a product can be called new for only six months. The improved claim does not mean changed for the better. It means changed or different from before. In place of new and improved, watch for words which say new, but don't mean new — introductory, now, today's, announcing, revolutionary, presenting, a fresh way to....	Our new improved dog food with high quality protein. Now it's actually better at helping your dog stay healthy. Now double-protection toothpaste. Fights cavities and freshens breath. New improved furniture polish — now polish as often as you want without the worry of build-up. Our creamer — new jar, new taste.

Buyer Beware.

Many companies advertise by mail.

REGULATION OF ADVERTISING

Advertising comes into the home uninvited. Sometimes the messages contain useful information. Often the messages stir hidden feelings and yearnings. Some ads are brash and offensive. A few ads may be misleading and deceptive. As a result, a threefold system of regulations has developed to protect consumers from dishonest advertising. Regulation of advertising in the U.S. consists of government regulation, self-regulation by the advertising industry, and consumer regulation. Each one of these is discussed below.

Federal Regulation

Government regulations attempt to keep advertising fair, honest, and moral. In 1914 Congress created the Federal Trade Commission and gave it power to deal with abuses in interstate (existing between two or more states) advertising. The criteria used by the Federal Trade Commission to determine if an ad is misleading or deceptive are:

—Tendency to deceive. Proof of actual deception is not essential. If an advertisement has a tendency to mislead or deceive (that is, deception is the natural and probable result), the FTC can act to stop the ad.
—Actual truthfulness. The purpose of the laws against deceptive advertising is protection of the consumer. Nothing less

than literal truthfulness is tolerated. According to the FTC, the important criterion is the impression which the advertisement is likely to make upon the general public.

—Omission of important facts. The FTC has concluded that even though every sentence considered separately is true, the advertisement as a whole may be misleading because factors are omitted that should be mentioned or because the message is composed in such a way as to mislead.

—Double meaning. Because the purpose of the law is to prohibit advertising that has the tendency and capacity to deceive, an advertisement that can be read to have two meanings is illegal if one of the meanings is false or misleading.

Today, the FTC investigates complaints and has the authority to hold hearings and to issue an order prohibiting a company from carrying out an illegal action.

Another federal agency, the U.S. Postal Service, has authority to act on complaints from consumers who have been cheated by mail-order advertising. Also, the Federal Communications Commission is charged with the regulation of advertising on radio and TV stations. These federal agencies do not have the power to prohibit an ad from appearing, but they can force an ad to be discontinued or modified if it is determined to be false or misleading.

Deceptive Practices. The National Advertising Division of the FTC is responsible for enforcing the provisions of the FTC Act which forbid misrepresentation and unfairness in national advertising. Following are some advertising practices which have been found deceptive.

Bait and Switch. A product is advertised at an exceptionally low price, and consumers go to the store to buy the item advertised. Once they are inside the store, they find that the merchandise is not available or is supposedly less desirable than another product. The salesperson then directs their attention to another model that costs more. The "bait" is the advertised low price. The "switch" is the more expensive, nonadvertised item.

Advertised Specials. Stores often advertise specific items on special sale. When consumers arrive, they may be told, "We sold out earlier than we expected." The FTC has ruled that stores ought to have advertised specials readily available at the advertised price during the advertised sale period. Many stores distribute rain checks (a right to the product at the advertised price when it's available) if the merchandise is not available. If rain checks are not distributed voluntarily, ask for them. You have the right to the product at the advertised price. If the store makes a habit of not having items as advertised, complain to the nearest FTC office.

"Buy One — Get One Free." "Free gift." Some ads offer a free gift, but the usual price of the product may have been increased to cover the cost of the gift. The FTC has ruled that a consumer has a right to believe that the merchant will not directly and immediately recover the cost of the free merchandise. When advertisers use the term "free," all the conditions and obligations of the consumer must be stated clearly along with the free offer. For example, if a home demonstration of another product is required in order to receive a free product, this condition must be clearly stated.

False Price Comparisons. "Regularly $19.95; Now Only $14.95." This bargain may not be a bargain at all if the regular price is a false price. The claim of a former (regular) price must be a price at which the product was openly and actively offered for sale for a reasonable period of time; it is a price used in the recent, normal course of business; and it is a price at which sales were actually made. If the former price is an artificial price used to make an appealing comparison, it is a deceptive practice.

False Retail Store Price Comparisons. "Retail Value, $25.95; Our Price, $14.95." When price comparisons are made between one store and others in an area, the advertised price must be based on fact, not on an artificial price. In other words, if the competitive pricing in an area is $16.95 in a number of retail stores, the advertiser cannot claim that a higher price such as $25.95 is a genuine price. An advertiser must be reasonably certain that the price quoted is not more than the price at which substantial sales of the article are being made in the area.

Manufacturer's Retail List Price. "Suggested Retail List Price $24.95; Our Price, $20.95." Many consumers believe that a manufacturer's list price is the price at which an article is generally sold. Manufacturers do provide retailers with suggested prices. Due to competition and widespread disregard for these suggested prices, however, such terms as "manufacturer's retail list price" are not dependable indicators of actual "regular" price. A reduction in a manufacturer's suggested price would appear to be a savings or a bargain. Unless the manufacturer's retail list price is the actual price at which a substantial number of items are sold by retailers in the area, the manufacturer's suggested retail price should not be advertised as the regular price. Today, only rarely are sales of an article made at the manufacturer's suggested retail price. According to FTC guidelines, neither the manufacturer nor the retailer may put price tags on products which make the manufacturer's retail list price appear to be the common price in the area.

FTC Enforcement. The FTC has four tools of enforcement when dealing with advertising that does not meet the FTC's concept of acceptable advertising.

Consent Agreement. When the FTC determines that an advertisement is clearly deceptive or false, it notifies the advertiser of its intent to file a complaint and usually negotiates a consent agreement. A *consent agreement* is a legal arrangement in which the advertiser modifies or discontinues a practice without admitting any violation of the law.

Cease and Desist Order. The FTC has the power to order an advertiser to cease and desist — that is, to stop an act or practice. The advertiser, of course, can appeal the order. As a result, some cases have taken years from the time the original complaint was filed to the time the cease and desist order became final. Ads for Carter's Little Liver Pills kept the word "liver" during a sixteen-year legal battle with the FTC before the company finally had to stop using the reference to "liver."

Corrective Advertising. A firm whose ad is found false must agree to correct public misconception by devoting some portion of its future advertising to admitting past deceptions. For example, one company agreed to run an ad for a year to correct previous misleading nutritional claims:

> If you've wondered what some of our earlier advertising meant when we said our juice has more energy than orange juice or tomato juice, let us make it clear: we didn't mean vitamins or minerals. Food energy means calories, nothing more.

Ad Substantiation. As part of the FTC's regulation of advertising, *ad substantiation* requires advertisers to submit data to support claims about safety, performance, efficiency, quality, or comparative prices. Essentially, ad substantiation is a policy which warns advertisers that they will be regarded as guilty of unfair practices if they make claims without having reasonable proof in their files.

Self-Regulation

Self-regulation refers to attempts on the part of the advertising industry to set standards of practice for members of the advertising business. For example, the American Association of Advertising Agencies has a creative code which sets high ethical standards for its members.

Many companies, as a part of their advertising philosophy, develop guidelines for use in preparing and evaluating their advertising. Before an advertisement is cleared for use, it will be checked and approved by the product research people who verify that the product claim is supported by appropriate research data. It may also be checked by the legal staff, which examines all claims made, to make certain they conform to federal, state, and local regulations.

National Advertising Review Board. An important aspect of the advertising industry's effort at self-regulation is the National Advertising Review Board—a board of 50 men and women who represent industry, the advertising business, and consumers. The NARB, a self-regulatory body whose objective is to maintain high standards of truth and accuracy in national advertising, reviews complaints in this area.

When the board receives a complaint about an advertisement, it refers the complaint to the National Advertising Division (NAD) of the Council of Better Business Bureaus. The NAD staff will ask the advertiser for claim substantiation data. If the data verifies the claims, the person who made the complaint is so advised. When the person who complained is not satisfied, the NARB may be asked to review NAD's conclusion. If the claim is not adequately substantiated, the NAD staff attempts to get the advertiser to make appropriate corrections or changes in the ad. An advertiser who refuses to make the suggested change is referred to the NARB.

If the NARB agrees with the findings of the NAD, the board will try to have changes made in the advertising. When an advertiser refuses to accept the judgment of the board, the board will publicly disclose its position and that of the advertiser and will refer the matter to the appropriate government regulatory agency. Self-regulation by the advertising industry works effectively. There has not been a single case where the verdict of the NAD staff or NARB was defied.

Consumer Regulation

The final judge of the truth of advertising rests with consumers. It is the consumer's responsibility to complain when a product is purchased on the basis of advertised performance claims and it is found that the product's actual performance falls below expectations. In addition, a complaint should be made to the National Advertising Division of the Council of Better Business Bureaus, to the Division of Advertising Practices of the FTC, or to a regional FTC office when a consumer believes that an advertisement makes an untrue or inaccurate claim in its national advertising.

When registering a complaint about an ad, it is important to identify the brand name of the product, the name of the advertiser, when and where the ad appeared, and the reason for the complaint. If possible, supply a copy of the advertisement.

Local Better Business Bureaus receive and act on complaints concerning local advertising. Another means of challenging questionable ads is by talking directly with local TV and radio stations or newspaper advertising managers. Remember that the FTC, as well as local media, rely to some extent on the public for observing and reporting misleading or deceptive ads.

VOCABULARY REVIEW

Trade advertising	Downplaying
Professional advertising	Puffery
Institutional advertising	Weasel claim
Public-issue advertising	Endorsement claim
Persuasion	Bait and switch
Intensifying	Advertised specials

False price comparisons   Ad substantiation
Corrective advertising   Self-regulation

QUESTIONS FOR REVIEW

1. What is advertising, and what are the two major purposes of all advertising?

2. State three criticisms of advertising as it is used in the marketplace.

3. Name three of the benefits of advertising claimed by the defenders of advertising.

4. List the three features which consumers should look for in advertisements.

5. What are the criteria used by the FTC to determine if an ad is misleading or deceptive?

6. What are three advertising practices which the FTC has ruled as being unfair, deceptive, and misleading?

7. What powers of enforcement does the FTC have to regulate advertising?

8. What is the name of the board which provides a means of self-regulation for advertisers? How does this board operate?

PROBLEM-SOLVING AND DECISION-MAKING PROJECTS

1. In small groups, plan an ad for a product commonly sold in department stores. The ad is to appear in a magazine. Read your ad to the class. Ask the class to prepare a list of questions to ask about the product in order to determine if the product is really as good as the advertisers claim.

2. Identify advertising slogans that use at least five of the techniques described on pages 55-58. State the claim(s) that each of the ads made.

3. There are various types of advertisements. Name the type of advertising which is designed:

(a) to inform consumers of legal services

(b) to reach other manufacturers

(c) to create goodwill for an industry or group of businesses

(d) to promote a beneficial action or to provide useful information

(e) to promote a particular point of view or idea

(f) to build business for a retail store

4. Some brand names are advertised so much that consumers use the brand name instead of the given name of the product. In small groups think of products which have become commonly associated with their brand names rather than their given names. For example: Kleenex.

COMMUNITY AND HOME PROJECTS

1. With the permission of your parents, collect the direct-mail ads received at home during a two-week period. How many ads were received during that period of time? What type of information and what type of appeals were used in the direct-mail ads?

2. With the permission of the teacher, make a collage of every type and medium of advertising you can collect. For example: trade ads, professional ads, public-issue ads, matchbook ads, classified ads, direct-mail ads, and others.

RESOURCE MANAGEMENT

Chapter 5

Nutrition and Food

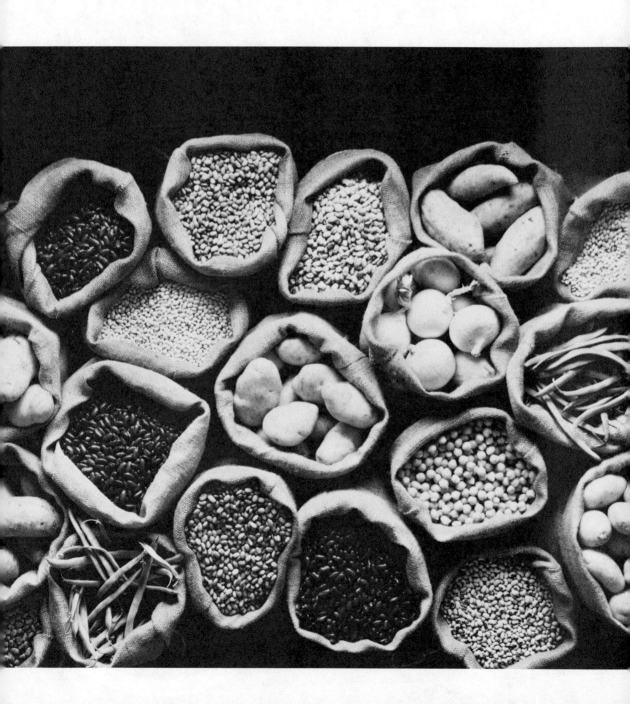

It is often stated that "we are what we eat." If so, how do you rate? The food we choose to eat influences what we are physically, mentally, and emotionally. In this chapter we will discuss the cost of food and the effect of it and nutrition on our health.

HOW AMERICA EATS

American eating habits are changing. More people are eating outside the home, demanding more services from food stores, and seeking convenience in foods purchased for preparation at home. These changes have come about for several reasons. Incomes have risen. The educational level of the population has increased. Over one-half of the households now contain only one or two persons. The proportion of females in the work force has increased significantly.

The way we eat is often a subject of conversation. Most food experts believe that the American diet today is better than ever before and that it is one of the best, if not the best, in the world. In the United States we have eliminated most of the diseases (such as scurvy and rickets) which result from poor nutrition. People are living longer. The quality of our food has improved. On the other hand, the Senate Select Committee on Nutrition and Human Needs took a dim view of the way we eat. While in the past nutrition science was concerned with the topic of nutrition deficiency or malnutrition, today a major problem facing nutritionists and American food consumers is *overconsumption*. According to the Senate committee, "The simple fact is that our diets have changed radically within the last 50 years with great and very harmful effects to our health. . . too much fat, too much sugar or salt can be and are linked directly to heart disease, cancer, obesity, and stroke among other killer diseases. In all, six of the ten leading causes of death in the U.S. have been linked to our diet."

Food at Home

A few years ago, the home was the center for the control of the family diet. Breakfast, lunch, and supper at the table with all family members present was the traditional way of eating. Most Americans ate only at home or carried home-prepared lunches to work or school. Even now, about two-thirds of all food consumed is in the form of meals prepared at home. The situation is changing, however. Today the homemaker no longer directs the family's eating habits. Family members often have different schedules that make a family breakfast or lunch a rare occasion. Someone in the household probably wants to lose or gain weight. Preparing food to please everybody's tastes makes meal planning difficult. More and more meals are purchased and consumed "on the run."

Eating Out

Consumers are spending more of their food dollars for prepared meals and snacks away from home. Eating outside the home may not always save actual eating time, but it does reduce preparation and clean-up time. It also provides for some leisure and recreation. Eating out usually costs more than food prepared and eaten at home. As a matter of fact, eating out accounts for 35 percent of the total expenditures for food. Surveys show that the amount spent on eating away from home is the highest for college graduates, upper-income families, single people, and small families.

Convenience Foods

Another significant change in the way Americans eat involves *convenience* foods such as frozen TV dinners, ready-to-eat puddings, canned and frozen vegetables, and packaged cake mixes. Convenience foods make up nearly half of all foods sold for consumption at home and can be prepared in one-fourth the time required to prepare meals from basic ingredients. But what about the cost of

Meals eaten out can be convenient as well as nutritious.

Source: *Norton Simon Inc.*

convenience? According to an extensive study done by the U.S. Department of Agriculture, about 58 percent of the convenience products cost more per serving (based on retail food prices) than their home-prepared versions, 24 percent cost less, and 18 percent cost about the same. However, when fuel and preparation time were added to food prices, 60 percent were less expensive than their home-prepared versions. Cost comparison of some selected items can be seen in Table 5-1.

Food Costs

Department of Agriculture figures show that the typical American family now spends from 16 to 20 percent of its budget on food. Poorer families spend a greater portion of their incomes on food. At the beginning of this decade, a family of four spent between $175 and $400 per month on food at home — or nearly $300 billion a year.

Table 5-1

Cost Comparison of Selected Convenience
and Prepared-at-Home Foods

Product	Serving Size (Ounces)	Home Prepared (Cents)	Convenience Forms (Cents)
Beef Dinner	11.3	75.8	102.7
Lasagna	9.8	57.7	112.6
Pie	7.4	26.2	46.4
Meat Loaf Dinner	9.1	37.1	91.4
Chicken a la King	5.7	27.8	47.4
Fried Chicken Dinner	9.3	40.8	81.7
Haddock Dinner	11.2	88.0	129.9
Tuna Casserole	7.8	30.3	87.6
Pizza	8.3	37.8	73.2
Asparagus	2.1	34.5	28.9
Carrots	2.8	10.1	11.0
Corn, cut	2.9	16.6	15.8
Green Peas	2.8	41.1	15.7
Orange Juice	4.4	25.1	9.4
Brownies	.7	5.2	3.7

Source: *USDA Convenience Foods and Home-Prepared Foods, Comparative Costs, Yield and Quality*, Agricultural Economics Report 429 (1979).

Table 5-2 shows the weekly cost of food prepared at home. Naturally the cost of food depends upon many factors such as the size, age, sex, and activity level of the family members, the types of foods purchased, the shopping skills of the purchaser, and the amount of money available. This cost has become a source of frustration for many individuals and families. Where does the money go? Farmers receive about $31 of each $100 spent on food products. The marketing system receives the remainder; that is, $69 for each $100 worth

Table 5-2

Weekly Cost of Food at Home
Four Plans
(June, 1981, U. S. Average)

Size and Age Groups	Cost for 1 Week			
	Thrifty Plan	Low-Cost Plan	Moderate-Cost Plan	Liberal Plan
Families	Dollars			
Family of 2:				
20-54 years	$32.90	$42.30	$52.90	$ 63.40
55 years and over	29.60	37.70	46.60	55.50
Family of 4:[1]				
Couple, 20-54 years and children –				
1-2 and 3-5 years old	46.70	59.40	73.90	88.40
6-8 and 9-11 years old	56.30	72.00	90.00	107.60

[1]The costs given are for individuals in 4-person families. For individuals in other size families, the following adjustments are suggested: 1-person – add 20 percent; 2-persons – add 10 percent; 3-persons – add 5 percent; 5 or 6 persons – subtract 5 percent; 7 or more persons – subtract 10 percent.

Source: *Family Economic Review*, (Fall, 1981).

of food purchased. The marketing bill, as presented in Illus. 5-1, is the total annual charge for transporting, processing, and distributing domestic farm foods.

NUTRITION AND HEALTH

There is an important relationship between good food and good health. With approximately $1,200 spent yearly on food for every person in the United States, what kind of nutrition are we getting for our money? The problem is in selecting the right food in the right amounts. There are more than 10,000 products to select from at the supermarket, and often there are conflicting claims about which are

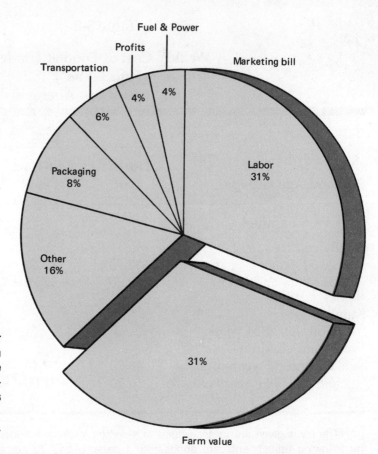

Fuel & Power

Profits

Transportation

Marketing bill

4%

4%

6%

Labor
31%

Packaging
8%

Other
16%

31%

Farm value

Illus. 5-1

Over two-thirds of every dollar spent on food for consumption at home and away from home goes to pay the cost of marketing. Less than one-third goes to the producers of the food.

Source: *Agricultural Outlook,* (Nov. 1981).

good and which are bad for you. Dr. Jean Mayer, former Harvard professor and nutritionist, states the problem succinctly: "If you know something about nutrition and about shopping, you can go into a typical supermarket and come out with an excellent diet. You can also come out with a terrible diet if you don't know any nutrition."

What is nutrition? *Nutrition* is the process by which the body acquires and uses food for growth, maintenance, repair, reproduction, and regulation of body functions. Understanding nutrition means knowing the composition of foods and how to select foods for an adequate diet. There is no such thing as an ideal diet for everyone, but a proper *diet* is one which assures:

1. An adequate intake of all essential nutrients
2. A moderate intake of those foods which can contribute to major health problems
3. A caloric intake equal to energy output

Essential Nutrients

The human body requires nutrients. *Nutrients* do one or more of three jobs: (1) they furnish the body with fuel needed for energy, (2) they provide materials needed for the building or maintenance of body tissue, and (3) they provide substances that regulate body processes. All foods contain nutrients, but each food varies in the kinds and the amounts of nutrients provided. The major categories of nutrients are protein, carbohydrates, fats, vitamins, minerals, and water.

Protein. Protein is the basic matter of cells and the main tissue builder in the body. It is the substance of which muscle, hair, bone, enzymes, hormones, and blood are made. Protein is partially responsible for regulating such things as digestion and growth, it helps form antibodies which fight infection, and it can supply energy (although this is not one of its primary functions). Good sources of protein are: meat, fish, poultry, eggs, milk, cheese, dried peas and beans, nuts, enriched breads, and cereals.

Carbohydrates. Carbohydrates supply energy for body processes, activity, and growth as well as help the body use fats efficiently. Carbohydrates come in three forms: starches, sugars, and fibrous materials called cellulose. Starches and sugars are the major sources of energy for human beings. The fibrous materials furnish the bulk or roughage needed for digestion and elimination. Good sources of carbohydrates are: breads, cereals, rice, pasta, potatoes, sugars, and other sweets.

Fats. Fats are distributed throughout the body and support and protect vital organs and tissues. They provide more than twice as much energy as either carbohydrates or protein. Some fat is needed by everyone. Fats provide Vitamins A, D, E, and K as well as linoleic acid which is essential for proper growth and healthy skin. Fats also add flavor to and improve the texture of prepared foods. Good sources of fats are: butter, margarine, vegetable oils, salad dressings, meat, and dairy fats.

Vitamins. Vitamins help release energy from food, promote normal growth of different kinds of tissues, and are essential to the proper functioning of nerves and muscles. A dozen or more vitamins have been identified. Six are listed here:

—*Vitamin A*

Function: Promotes normal vision in dim light, healthy skin and lining tissues, and resistance to infection.
Good Sources: Liver, eggs, dark green and yellow vegetables, butter, margarine, milk, peaches, and cantaloupe.

—*Vitamin D*

Function: Helps the body build calcium and phosphorus for healthy bones and teeth.
Good Sources: Fish liver oils, fortified milk, and margarine. Formed in the skin when exposed to sunlight.

—*Vitamin C or Ascorbic Acid*

Function: Important for healthy tissues, gums, blood vessels, bones, and teeth. Promotes healing.
Good Sources: Citrus fruits, strawberries, cantaloupe, broccoli, cabbage, tomatoes, green peppers, and potatoes.

—*Thiamine or Vitamin B_1*

Function: Promotes normal appetite and digestion and helps keep the nervous system healthy.
Good Sources: Meat, especially pork and liver, enriched breads and cereals, dried peas, and beans.

—*Riboflavin or Vitamin B_2*

Function: Helps keep eyes, skin, and mouth healthy.
Good Sources: Meat, especially liver, milk and milk products, eggs, green leafy vegetables, enriched breads, and cereals.

—*Niacin*

Function: Helps keep skin, mouth, and nervous system healthy.
Good Sources: Liver, fish, meat, enriched breads and cereals, milk, and peanuts.

Mineral Elements. The body requires many minerals. They strengthen certain body tissues, particularly bones and teeth, and they help with vital body processes. Two important minerals are calcium and iron. Calcium builds bones and teeth; helps nerves, muscles, and heart function properly; and promotes blood clotting. Good sources of calcium are milk and milk products, salmon, sardines, green leafy vegetables. Iron helps build red blood cells. Good sources of iron are meats (especially liver), egg yolk, oysters, green leafy vegetables, dried fruits, enriched breads and cereals.

Water. The most abundant nutrient in the body is water, which is approximately 65 percent of body weight. Water carries other nutrients to the cells and carries waste products from the cells. It regulates body temperature and helps in digestion and the building of tissues. Water is essential for life. A person can live for many days without food but only a few days without water.

Fresh fruit is a good source of nutrients.

Calories

As you probably realize, most of the nutrients provide energy for the functions of the body at work or play. Food energy, kilocalorie, is commonly called calories. *Calories* are the measurement of food energy. Calories come from fats, carbohydrates, and proteins in the foods you eat. Some foods provide many more calories in a given serving than others. Take starch as an example. Through the digestive process, the body changes the starch in food to glucose which is a source of energy. If the body receives more glucose than it can use as energy, the excess is converted into fat. How many calories you need depends on how much energy you use up. Generally older people need fewer calories than younger people, women fewer than men, and bridge players and bookkeepers fewer than tennis players and construction workers. Table 5-3 shows the calories needed for different levels of activity.

Table 5-3

Calories and Activity Level

Activity	Calories Per Hour
Lying down or sleeping	80
Sitting	100
Driving an automobile	120
Standing	140
Domestic work	180
Walking, 2½ mph	210
Bicycling, 5½ mph	210
Gardening	220
Golf; lawn mowing, power mower	250
Bowling	270
Walking, 3¼ mph	300
Swimming, ¼ mph	300
Square dancing, volleyball, roller skating	350
Wood chopping or sawing	400
Tennis	420
Skiing, 10 mph	600
Squash and handball	600
Bicycling, 13 mph	660
Running, 10 mph	900

Physical activity is generally classified as sedentary, light, moderate, vigorous, or strenuous, according to the intensity. The above chart can be used to estimate daily energy output and to determine whether sufficient vigorous and strenuous activity is included.

Source: U. S. Department of Agriculture and U. S. Department of Health and Human Services, Nutrition and Your Health, *Home and Garden Bulletin No. 232 (February, 1980).*

SELECTING FOODS FOR NUTRITION

Some nutrition scientists use two common guides for food selection: (1) the basic food groups and (2) the U.S. Recommended Daily Allowances.

Basic Food Groups

The foods we eat may be divided into five groups: Milk-Cheese, Meat-Poultry-Fish-Beans, Fruit-Vegetable, Bread-Cereal, and Miscellaneous. Each of the first four groups contribute nutrients as well as the calories the body needs. The fifth group, Miscellaneous, provides mainly calories and little in the way of nutrients.

Milk-Cheese Group. Foods from the milk group are relied upon to meet most of the calcium needs. The milk group also provides protein, riboflavin, Vitamin A, and many other nutrients. This group includes milk in any form: whole, skim, lowfat, evaporated, buttermilk, and nonfat dry milk as well as yogurt, ice cream, ice milk, and cheese.

Meat-Poultry-Fish-Bean Group. The meat group and its substitutes are valued for their protein. These foods also contain iron and B-vitamins. Meat substitutes include dried beans, dried peas, lentils, nuts, peanut butter, soybeans, eggs, seeds, and cheese. Since meat, poultry, and fish often are the most expensive foods consumers buy, those who must cut costs will need to select inexpensive meats or meat alternatives.

Vegetable-Fruit Group. Vegetables and fruits are valuable sources of vitamins and minerals. This group is needed to supply the Vitamin C and a large share of the Vitamin A in our diets. Vitamin C should be included in a diet each day. Good sources are dark yellow or green vegetables.

Bread-Cereal Group. Whole-grain enriched bread, cereal products, biscuits, muffins, waffles, pancakes, spaghetti, and rice furnish protein, iron, several of the B-vitamins, and food energy.

Miscellaneous. In this group are foods such as butter, margarine, salad dressings, candy, soft drinks, and alcoholic beverages. The proper quantity of these foods depends upon the number of calories you require. It is best to eat foods in the calorie-plus-nutrient categories for a proper daily diet.

Dietary Guidelines

Good health depends upon many things including heredity, lifestyles, personality traits, environment, and nutrition. The following dietary guidelines suggest good eating habits and offer recommendations for selecting foods that will provide a healthful diet.

—Because no single food provides 100 percent of the essential nutrients, you should eat a variety of foods from each group every day.

—Maintain ideal weight.

—Avoid too much fat, saturated fat, and cholesterol by choosing lean meat, fish, poultry, and dried beans and peas as

Good eating habits include fresh vegetables and meat.
Reprinted from DuPont Magazine

your protein sources, by limiting your intake of butter, cream, shortenings and coconut oil, and by broiling, baking, or boiling rather than frying.

—Eat more complex carbohydrates—or foods with adequate starch and fiber—by substituting starches for fats and sugars, and by selecting more whole-grain breads and cereals, fruits and vegetables, beans, peas, and nuts.

—Avoid excessive sugar by using less white sugar, brown sugar, raw sugar, honey, and syrups, and by eating less candy, soft drinks, ice cream, cakes, and cookies.

—Avoid too much sodium by learning to enjoy the unsalted flavors of foods. Cook with only small amounts of added salt. Add little or no salt to food at the table. Limit your intake of salty foods such as potato chips, pretzels, salted nuts, and popcorn.

—If you drink alcohol, do so in moderation.

Planning Meals with Food Groups

Variety is a key factor in planning meals. To achieve variety, it may be helpful to plan meals on a weekly basis. Weekly planning can save time, money, and energy. More importantly, it helps assure that all the nutrients needed for an adequate diet are included. The consumer does not, however, need to be overly concerned if the most favorable amounts of every essential nutrient are not provided each day. With the exceptions of Vitamins C and B complex, the body can easily adjust to minor dietary changes. The body has the ability to store excess nutrients, then distribute them for use during periods of stress, illness, and poor health. See Table 5-4 for examples of daily nutrient needs.

Planning Meals by Recommended Dietary Allowances

The second guide for selecting foods is the Recommended Dietary Allowances. The *Recommended Dietary Allowances* are the levels or amounts of essential nutrients considered adequate to meet the known nutritional needs of most healthy persons. Amounts are determined by the Committee on Dietary Allowances of the Food and Nutrition Board of the National Academy of Sciences—National Research Council. The Recommended Dietary Allowances are based on the average needs for various age groups and the activity patterns for each age group in our country. Individuals who

Table 5-4

Daily Nutrient Needs

Food Group	Daily Recommendation
Milk and Dairy Products	**2 or more servings.** Examples: 1 cup milk, 1 cup yogurt, 1½ oz. cheese (not cottage).
Meat Category	**2 or more servings.** Examples: 2 oz. cooked lean beef, fish, or poultry, 1 cup dried beans, 4 tablespoons peanut butter. Check for high quality protein.
Vegetables and Fruits	**4 or more servings.** Examples: 1 medium apple, ½ grapefruit, ½ cup vegetables. Be sure to include a dark green or deep yellow vegetable at least every other day as well as Vitamin C and A rich foods.
Grains	**4 or more servings.** Examples: 1 small potato, 1 slice of bread, ½ cup cooked cereal. Check for good sources of iron.
Miscellaneous	In proportion to individual needs to make the diet more palatable and satisfying. Examples: butter, salad dressings.

Table 5-4 shows daily recommended servings for five common food groupings. Since individual needs vary, the number of daily servings should be based on personal factors such as age, sex, and weight.

consume the Recommended Dietary Allowances for all nutrients are unlikely to develop nutritional deficiencies.

Any food for which a nutritional claim is made, or to which a nutrient has been added, under Food and Drug Administration regulations, must have the nutritional contents listed on the label. *Nutrition labels* are divided into two parts. Part 1 tells the size of a serving, the number of servings in the container, the number of calories per serving, and the amounts in grams of protein, carbohydrates, and fats per serving. Part 2 tells the percentage of the *U.S. Recommended Daily Allowance* of protein, five vitamins (Vitamins A and C, thiamine, riboflavin, and niacin), and two minerals (iron and calcium) that each serving of the product contains. Notice that protein is listed twice — once in grams and once as a percentage of the U.S. RDA. The U.S. RDAs used for nutritional labeling are a simplified version of the Recommended Dietary Allowances. See Table 5-5.

Consumers can use the U.S. RDAs and nutritional labeling as guides for selecting foods and evaluating their daily nutrient intake. For example, the label may state that one serving of the food contains 35 percent of the U.S. RDA of Vitamin A and 25 percent of the U.S. RDA of iron. When using nutritional information to select and evaluate the nutritional quality of a diet, consumers may believe that it is necessary to consume 100 percent of each nutrient daily. This is not so. The U.S. RDAs shown on food labels are higher than necessary for most people. The maximums are intended to assure that everyone will receive the necessary amounts of nutrients if the guideline is followed. For most adults, 70 percent, and for small children, 50 percent of the U.S. RDAs should assure good nutrition.

EXERCISE AND ACTIVITY

Along with an adequate diet, good health requires exercise and activity. Exercise and controlled eating habits could significantly reduce this country's main health problem — obesity. *Obesity* is defined as weighing 20 percent or more above the ideal body weight, which is based on age, height, and sex. There is a high relationship between obesity and several major diseases. Also, obesity endangers some bodily functions, particularly resistance to disease and infection.

The major cause of overweight is eating too much—or overconsumption—for the amount of exercise and activity expended. When you eat foods that furnish more calories than you need, the excess energy is stored in the body as fat. Body weight

Table 5-5

U.S. Recommended Daily Allowances

Nutrients	Amounts
Protein[1]	45 or 65 grams[2]
Vitamin A	5,000 International Units
Vitamin C (ascorbic acid)	60 milligrams
Thiamine (Vitamin B_1)	1.5 milligrams
Riboflavin (Vitamin B_2)	1.7 milligrams
Niacin	20 milligrams
Calcium	1.0 gram
Iron	18 milligrams
Vitamin D	400 International Units
Vitamin E	30 International Units
Vitamin B_6	2.0 milligrams
Folic acid (folacin)	0.4 milligram
Vitamin B_{12}	6 micrograms
Phosphorus	1.0 gram
Iodine	150 micrograms
Magnesium	400 milligrams
Zinc	15 milligrams
Copper	2 milligrams
Biotin	0.3 milligram
Pantothenic acid	10 milligrams

[1]The nutrients in bold type must appear on nutrition labels. The other nutrients may appear.

[2]45 grams if protein quality is equal to or greater than milk protein. 65 grams if protein quality is less than milk protein.

Source: *Guidelines to Good Health*, Kraft, Inc. (1979), p. 20, and U.S. Department of Health and Human Services, HEW Publication No. 76-2042 (January, 1976).

Plenty of exercise is an important part of good health.

Source: Gulf and Western Industries, Inc.

stays about the same when food energy (calories consumed) equals the energy needs of the body.

To control your weight, rely on discipline and these elementary principles:

— To maintain weight, calorie intake must be equal to energy output.
— To lose weight, calorie intake must be less than energy output.
— To gain weight, calorie intake must exceed energy output.

New diets are often popular and faddish. Basically, however, dieting is founded on three simple concepts:

— Reduce food intake and become more active. Exercise and activity burn up calories.
— Reduce food intake as you become an adult. Adults require less energy to keep the body functioning.

—Cut down on food but do not cut out any important kinds of food.

When our society was mainly agricultural, strenuous physical labor was an everyday activity. Because many jobs today do not require such bodily effort, most people must deliberately seek ways to work exercise into their schedules. To maintain good health, then, you must not only consume all of the essential nutrients, but also avoid overconsumption and participate in physical activity each day. A proper diet and daily exercise are essential for the best health, for a well-formed physique, a wholesome appearance, and vitality in school, on the job, and in leisure activities.

Caveat Emptor: *Natural, Organic, and Health Foods*

The term *natural* foods refers to the ingredients (no preservatives or artificial additives) and to the fact that the food product has undergone minimal processing. Examples are fresh fruits and vegetables. *Organic* generally refers to the way the food is grown such as without pesticides or chemical fertilizers. *Health* food is a vague term that can include natural, organic, and even processed foods. For example, yogurt is generally recognized as a health food, but it is not natural if it contains sugar instead of unprocessed natural honey. It is not organic if the fruit is chemically fertilized

Most of the claims about these foods are not supported by scientific evidence. Some food faddists claim that natural vitamins are superior to artificial vitamins and that the use of natural fertilizers results in better crops than those treated with manufactured fertilizers. There is no scientific basis for claiming that organic or natural foods are more nutritious than regular foods. Some claims and suggestions that certain health foods or diets prevent or cure disease or provide special health benefits are, for the most part, folklore and sometimes outright lies. Comparative shopping shows that the so-called natural, organic, and health foods are generally 15 to 25 percent more expensive than usual supermarket processed foods. Buyer Beware.

VOCABULARY REVIEW

Convenience foods

Nutrition

Nutrients

Calories

Basic food groups

Recommended Dietary Allowances

U.S. Recommended Daily Allowances

Natural foods

Organic foods

Health foods

QUESTIONS FOR REVIEW

1. In the past what has been the center of control for nutrition and food?

2. What are the trends in food consumption patterns in the United States?

3. How do convenience foods compare in cost to prepared-at-home meals?

4. Approximately what percent of the average family budget goes for food?

5. What are the two common guides for food selection?

6. What are the functions of nutrients in the human body?

7. Name the seven dietary guidelines recommended for good nutrition and health.

8. How can the food consumer determine the amount and type of nutrients in processed food?

9. What is the best way to maintain proper weight?

10. What is the main health problem in the United States?

11. What is the commonsense way for the health-conscious consumer to maintain good health?

PROBLEM-SOLVING AND DECISION-MAKING PROJECTS

1. Using Table 5-2 (the weekly cost of food table), calculate the yearly cost of food for your family on a

a. thrifty plan
b. low-cost plan
c. moderate-cost plan
d. liberal plan

2. Prepare a chart on your diet by listing everything you ate yesterday. Divide foods into the basic food groups. Use Table 5-4, "Daily Nutrient Needs," as your guideline. Did you get the recommended number of servings in each category?

3. Plan a nutritious dinner for a family of four. Pick foods from each of the four primary groups.

COMMUNITY AND HOME PROJECTS

1. Keep a record of everything you eat in one day (breakfast, lunch, dinner, and snacks). Classify your diet according to the five food groups. Are you eating well-balanced meals? Write a report on your findings.

2. With the cooperation and permission of your teacher, survey the food sold in your school's vending machines. Analyze the nutritional value and calorie content of these products. Determine what types of other more nutritious products could be substituted. Survey your classmates to determine their attitudes about substituting nutritious snacks for high-sugar and high-salt snacks. If appropriate, report your findings to school authorities or the school newspaper.

Shopping for Food

Today shopping for food is more complex than in the past because there are so many products for people to buy. There are from 8,000 to 35,000 different items in the larger grocery stores. But smart shopping can help the consumer get food for an excellent diet and help the family save money. In this chapter we will discuss some skills which can reduce food costs and study the protection given the food consumer.

GETTING THE MOST FROM YOUR FOOD DOLLARS

Savings of 10 to 15 percent can be realized if you follow a plan when buying food. If the yearly food budget for a family of four is between $2,000 and $5,000, the annual savings can be $300 to $750. Listed below are some of the shopping practices that will help you save money when you shop for food.

Weekly Meal Plan

The first step in skillful shopping is the planning of a weekly menu. When considering menus, it is necessary to think not only of a nutritious balanced diet, but also of personal and family food preferences, family size and makeup, time available for food preparation, life-style, and the amount of money available. The smart consumer also plans menus around a protein food or the main dish of each meal.

Food Ads

One way to cut food costs is to arrange the weekly menu around supermarket *specials*, or products advertised at a lower or reduced price. For example, if chicken is on a special sale during the week, try to have a couple of chicken main dishes. It pays to check the food ads in the local newspaper. Food ads appear regularly and are a valuable source of price information. Also, look for specials advertised in supermarket circulars. *Loss leaders* are products which sell at or near cost and which most large stores advertise to attract customers. Loss leaders do offer significant savings for the food consumer.

According to the Federal Trade Commission, consumers have the right to be able to buy a product advertised at a "special price." The FTC rule states that specials must be available at the price advertised and must be prominently displayed or immediately produced upon the consumer's request. If the advertised item is not available, the manager should offer a "rain check" entitling the customer to the same item when it is in stock. The rule does not apply when limitations, such as "only five in stock" or "only one to a customer," are stated.

Shopping List

To organize your shopping, you should make a list following these steps:

—Keep the list handy in the kitchen so you can write down items needed as food supplies run low.
—Include the basic supplies, or "staples," that need to be restocked.
—Add weekly advertised specials that fit your menus.
—Include any other ingredients needed for the week's menu recipes.
—Write down items for which you have coupons if the items meet your needs.
—Organize the list according to the major sections in a supermarket to save shopping time.

A shopping list helps you avoid *impulse buying* (the unplanned buying of unneeded items) and extra trips to the supermarket to buy what you may have forgotten before. When shoppers wait until they are in the store to decide what to buy, they are open to the suggestions offered on signs and displays designed to encourage spending. It is important, however, to also be flexible enough to take advantage of unadvertised store specials that will save you money.

Comparative Shopping

Comparative shopping is another way the smart shopper can reduce the cost of food. As discussed in Chapter 3, comparative shopping is a way of finding the best price for the same or similar product. There are several ways to compare food products in order to save money.

Unit Price. The *unit price* of any product is the price you pay for the "standard unit" of the item. The standard units of measurement for products sold in the supermarket are weight, volume, area, and count. For example, items of less than a pound are expressed in weight—as per ounce or per gram, and larger products are expressed as per pound or per kilogram. For most liquids sold in the supermarket, the volume—the pint, quart, or liter—is used. For paper products, area is the appropriate unit—square foot or the meter. Some items (vitamins, aspirin, eggs) are sold by count such as per 100 or per one dozen.

Many supermarkets post unit price labels, shown in Illus. 6-1, under the products. If the unit price is not posted, divide the total cost by the number of standard units (ounces, grams, pounds, pints, quarts, liters, etc.). Unit price makes comparison of products easier and helps the shopper find the best buy—at least as far as cost is concerned. Remember, though, that this is a comparison of price only—not quality.

Illus. 6-1

Two unit price labels

Brands. Grocery stores mainly sell two major types of brands: *name brands* and store brands or *private labels*. In recent years, however, *no-name* food products, called *generic products*, have been introduced. The idea is that prices can be reduced by keeping packaging simple and by cutting advertising costs. Generic labels are generally white with bold black letters and state only the basic (or generic) name of the product such as cut green beans or tomato ketchup. Minor differences between no-name and name-brand products may include such factors as appearance, flavor, tenderness, ripeness,

Name-brand, private, and generic labels

size, and uniformity of the product. Major differences are in price and level and consistency of quality.

Surveys comparing no-name products, private labels, and name brands show that with generic items, the consumer can expect to save an average of 25 percent over name brands and 15 percent over private labels. The Food and Drug Administration product regulations apply to all foods, whether they are name-brand or no-name products. For example, generic mayonnaise must meet the same FDA standards as a name-brand product. The label must give the ingredients and nutritional information. The word "imitation" on labels applies equally to generic products and to name-brand products.

Store Comparisons. Prices at local supermarkets vary, and it pays to compare prices at different stores to find which ones offer the best quality and selection for the least amount of money. Usually large chain stores offer lower prices than small neighborhood stores. If possible, take advantage of low prices at two or more markets. You may need more time to shop, but the money saved makes the extra effort worth it.

Substitutes. Costs of similar foods, or *substitutes*, such as turkey for chicken, pears for peaches, rolls for bread, etc., should be compared. Two eggs supply your daily protein needs at a fraction of the cost of beef. An egg-salad sandwich and a big glass of milk make a good, low-cost lunch. Beans, peas, lentils, and soybeans are good substitutes for meat products. Shifting to cheaper substitutes helps cut food expenditures.

Other Comparisons. Compare the cost of the same food in different forms (canned, frozen, fresh, or dried). Also, as shown in Table 6-1, compare the cost of convenience frozen products with the cost of foods prepared from basic ingredients.

Table 6-1

Cost Comparisons

	Cents per serving
PIZZA	
Frozen	86
Homemade	48
CHICKEN CHOW MEIN	
Frozen	83
Homemade	53
FRIED CHICKEN	
Frozen	80
Homemade	36

It pays to compare costs of different forms of the same foods. This chart shows the kinds of savings which can occur if comparisons are made.

Source: "What's to Eat?" The U. S. Department of Agriculture Yearbook (1979), p. 65.

Quantity Buying

If you have extra storage space available, such as a pantry, space in a closet, or a freezer, you can save considerably by quantity buying. *Quantity buying* is buying a large number of sale items in order to save money on nonperishable items. Suppose, for example, that you buy cans of fruit juice at a sale price of four for $3.96 instead of the regular $1.12 each. You will save $.52 or $.13 a can—or 12 percent per can. Use quantity buying for sale items, and after a few months you should have enough staples and food products to last for quite a while. You should then not have to buy anything that is not on sale except weekly perishables such as milk, bread, fresh vegetables, and fruit. When the price is right, it pays to buy in volume for future use.

Big vs. Small Sizes

Money can also sometimes be saved by buying the largest size. But since the largest size is not always the cheapest, it is necessary to consider unit price. Generally there is a 10 to 15 percent savings between the large and the small sizes of containers. Be sure, however, that you can use all you buy before it spoils if you buy the largest size of a food product.

Coupons

Manufacturer's coupons, store coupons, and refund coupons offer consumers a reduced price for a product. Most coupons appear in newspapers, magazines, store circulars, and on or in packages. With a little organization, it is possible to save regularly on grocery bills by using coupons. Start a simple filing system using a shoe box or envelopes and arrange the coupons either alphabetically or according to the major sections in a supermarket. For extra savings, coupons can be used with an item that is on sale in the store. The price of a product can be reduced by the sale price and again by the amount of savings listed on the coupon.

Buying by Grades

Grading of food is done almost entirely by the Department of Agriculture. Sometimes it is possible to save as much as half the cost of an item by buying according to grade rather than by brand name. *Grade* marks on meat, poultry, eggs, cheese, canned fruits, vegetables, and other foods are indications that the consumer is getting certain product quality. Grade, however, has nothing to do with nutrient value. All grades, whether Grade A or B, "prime," "choice," or "good" have the same food value. The chief difference between grades is the appearance and the uniformity of the pieces. For example, if a can of Grade A (fancy) asparagus spears costs $1.39, the same size can of cut asparagus, Grade B (choice), may cost only $.95. With meat, the higher grades may be juicer and sometimes more tender. Table 6-2 shows the different grades used for the various types of food.

Table 6-2

Summary of Federal Food Grades

Food	Best	Second Best	Third Best	Understanding Food Grades
Beef	Prime	Choice	Good	Prime meat is very tender, very expensive, and usually used in restaurants. Choice meat is the grade you're most likely to find in your food store. It is tender, juicy, and flavorful.
Poultry	A	B	—	Grade A poultry is the meatiest and most attractive. The age of the bird is also an important guide to quality. For barbecuing, frying, or roasting, look for such words as "young," "broiler," "fryer," or "roaster."
Pork	Acceptable	Unacceptable	—	All pork sold in retail stores must have acceptable quality. An unacceptable quality which is soft and watery is graded U. S. Utility.
Fish*	A	B	C	Grade A is the top or best quality. Grade A means that products are uniform in size, practically free of blemishes and defects, in excellent condition, and possess good flavor for the species. Although Grades B and C are as wholesome and nutritious as higher grades, generally they are not sold in the marketplace.
Eggs	AA	A	B	AA and A mean that white and yolk stand high. These eggs are ideal for frying and poaching. Grade B spreads out more, but is good for general cooking and baking.

Table 6-2 (Continued)

Summary of Federal Food Grades

Food	Best	Second Best	Third Best	Understanding Food Grades
Fresh fruits and vegetables**	U. S. Fancy	U. S. No. 1	U. S. No. 2	Fancy is the premium quality. Only a few vegetables are packaged in this grade. U. S. No. 1 is the chief grade for most vegetables and fruit. The grades are usually shown on the packing crate. The chief differences are appearance and color.
Canned fruits and vegetables	A	B	C	Grade A means excellent color and flavor, uniformity of size and shape, tenderness, and few defects. Grade B means good quality and suitable for most purposes. Grade C means a thrifty buy when appearance and texture are not too important.

Source: U. S. Department of Agriculture, Agriculture Marketing Service.

*U. S. Department of Commerce grades.
**Some fruit and vegetable grade designations vary from these.

Coupons are a good way to reduce your grocery cost.

Read the Label — Set a Better Table

Take a close look at the labels on food products you buy, and you will find a good deal of useful information. The Food and Drug Administration requires the following on all labels:

- —Name of the product
- —Net contents or net weight itemized
- —Name and location of the manufacturer, packer, or distributor

Other information on the label is optional or voluntary.

Nutritional labeling is voluntary. It becomes mandatory only when a food processor makes a claim about the food's nutritional value, or when the food is enriched with any essential nutrients. As seen in Chapter 5, these labels can help consumers plan more nutritionally balanced meals.

On most food labels the ingredients must be listed in descending order of weight. In other words the largest amount of an ingredient is listed first; the second largest, second; and so on. If coloring or additives are used, they are listed also. The only foods not required to list all ingredients are "standardized foods." The FDA has set Standards of Identity for certain foods. These standards define the composition of more than 300 foods and specify the ingredients for these products. Standardized foods include most canned fruits and vegetables, milk, cheeses, ice cream, breads, margarine, and food dressings. Illus. 6-2 shows other useful information which appears on most labels.

Brand and Product Name. The *brand name* or trademark serves to distinguish one similar product from another. The brand name allows consumers to exercise their own judgment based upon satisfactory or unsatisfactory past experience. The *product name* makes a difference. For example, beef with gravy must be 50 percent beef, but if the label says gravy with beef, then it is only 35 percent beef. FDA regulation requires that when mixtures include meat, the food item that makes up most of the contents must be named first.

Net Weight. *Net weight* is what the product weighs (including liquid, if any). The *drained weight* is the weight of the product without liquid. The net weight of the contents must be reported on the container—not the *gross weight* which would include the weight of the container.

Ingredient List. Unless the product is a standardized food, the ingredients must be listed in decreasing order of occurrence.

Nutrition Label. *Nutrition information* on a food label must be provided in a standard format: serving size, servings per container, and calories, protein, carbohydrates, and fats in grams for each serving. In addition protein and specified vitamins and minerals are expressed as a percentage of the U.S. RDA.

Universal Product Code (UPC). These vertical black marks tell an *electronic scanner* (computer) at the checkout counter the name, manufacturer, and price of the product. When the cashier pulls the UPC mark over the scanner, the computer's laser beam sees the code and searches its memory to find the price. Then the computer prints the name and price of the item on the receipt tape.

Preparation Instructions and Recipes. Often useful directions, recipes, or suggestions for ways to serve the product are provided on the label.

ON THE LABEL

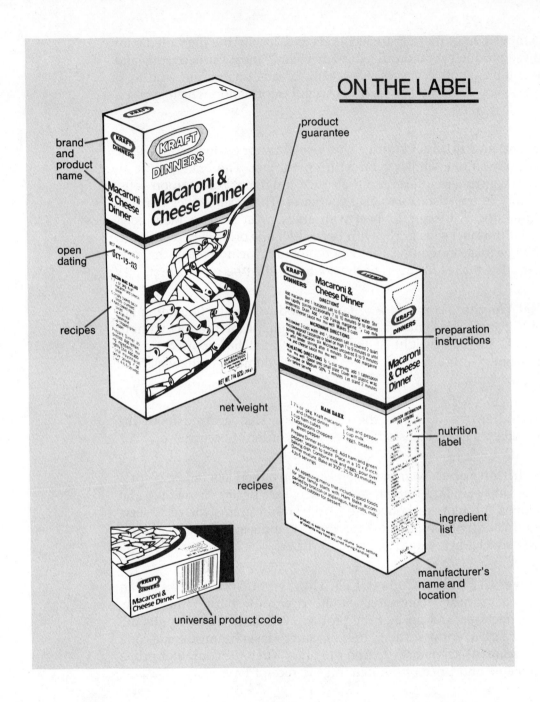

brand and product name

product guarantee

open dating

recipes

net weight

preparation instructions

nutrition label

recipes

ingredient list

manufacturer's name and location

universal product code

Illus. 6-2

Reading the label on a product can tell you what you need to know before you buy.

Source: Learning from Labels, Consumer Affairs Department, Kraft, Inc., (Glenview, Ill., 1981), pp. 6-7.

Manufacturer's Name and Location. This section usually tells the name and location of the manufacturer or distributor.

Open Dating. An *open date* is a calendar date on a food package which indicates the product's freshness. It tells when a product was packaged or processed, when the product should be sold by the store, or when the product should be used by the consumer. When a calendar date is used, it will be explained in terms such as "packaging" date, "sell by" date, or "use before" date.

Product Guarantee. Many companies guarantee complete satisfaction with the product.

Co-ops Cut Costs

Food co-ops represent another way to reduce the food budget by 5 to 35 percent. Cooperatives are not-for-profit organizations owned and operated by co-op members for the common benefit of the members. Food co-ops go back many years; but lately as food costs have risen, there has been a large growth in cooperative buying.

Membership in a food co-op is another way to reduce the cost of food.

Members usually gather once or twice a month and turn in their shopping lists to a coordinator who determines how much of various food items to purchase. Then a food buyer, usually a member, goes to one or more wholesalers (sellers who sell to grocery stores, and not to consumers) to purchase meat, produce, cheese, dairy products, and other items. The prices are usually lower because the purchases are made in large quantities. The members then gather in someone's home or in a community center to divide the items into individual orders.

Instead of taking orders from members, coordinators of larger co-ops make wholesale purchases of items that members usually buy. The food is available for pickup by members twice a month at a central location. If the co-op is large enough, there may be an elected board of directors and volunteer committees that govern store policies. Co-ops may have anywhere from 5 to 500 members. Each co-op operates independently with its members deciding how it will be run, what operating costs will be included in the food prices, and what type of food it will buy.

Caveat Emptor: *The Supermarket Trap*

In our economy food prices have gone up constantly in recent years. For this reason shoppers must be prepared to avoid supermarket traps that encourage impulse buying and increased spending. Stores use four main methods to encourage impulse buying. These are: marketing gimmicks, traffic patterns, shelf positions, and illusions of bargains.

Marketing Gimmicks. Competition between stores is often so keen that managers resort to *marketing gimmicks* to persuade consumers to shop at their particular stores. Gimmicks include contests, sweepstakes, trading stamps, and games. But these promotions merely hinder price comparison, and the store's cost of such gimmicks is added to consumers' food bills.

Traffic Pattern. The floor layout of most supermarkets is planned to meet a shopper's need to find things easily and the store's need to encourage more spending than the shopper intended. Shoppers normally walk around the perimeter of the store. In these areas, grocers display meats, produce, baked goods, dairy products, frozen foods, and other products that are more profitable. According to Jennifer Cross, author of the *Supermarket Trap*, "by design, the store leads people to these profitable items, especially early in the trip while they still have money." The meat department is placed at the back of the store in order to lead you past special displays and end-of-aisle displays. End-of-aisle locations are choice spots for high-profit impulse items such as crackers, cookies, candy, and snack foods. Other impulse items such as cigarettes, candy, magazines, gum, and mints are located near the checkout counter.

Shelf Position. Store managers have found that a shopper is more likely to buy an item if it is positioned between the shopper's waist and neck. For this reason, the more expensive items are often located on the middle shelf at hand or eye level, and the lower priced items are on the bottom or upper shelves. Another practice is to place children's products — toys, candy, cookies, cereals — on the lower levels. This practice gives children more of a chance to see the item.

Illusion of a Bargain. Supermarkets often use psychological pricing. For example, prices generally end in a "9" because "$5.99" seems to the shopper to be much cheaper than "$6.00." Another technique used to increase sales is multiple pricing. Instead of 30¢ each, the sale item calls for 2 for 59¢. A 20¢ item may be on sale at 6 for $1.19. Multiple pricing sells substantially more than does single-item pricing. Often savings is 1¢ per item, but this practice increases the volume by two, four, or six times. Buyer Beware.

PROTECTING THE FOOD CONSUMER

"Filth in food," "Additives," "Pesticides," "Unsanitary Conditions." Such headlines often shock and get the attention of consumers. There are, however, many people who are committed to safeguarding the American food supply. In this section we will look briefly at the responsibilities of the food industry, government agencies, and individuals for protecting the food consumer.

Industry Responsibilities

Only a small percentage of our population produces its own food. Most consumers rely on the food industry—farmers, processors, distributors, and grocers—to supply their food. Safety throughout the food industry is controlled by standards and procedures established by individual companies as well as by the government. This protection is costly, but it is necessary. Quality and safety are accomplished through rigid sanitation policies and procedures, inspection programs, and monitoring operations. Many food manufacturers have built-in controls that are often far more exacting than those imposed by government agencies.

Government Responsibilities

Plants and distribution and storage facilities must meet standards and pass inspections by numerous federal, state, county, and municipal agencies. The three agencies that exercise the greatest control over the food industry are the Food and Drug Administration (all foods other than meat, poultry, and fish), the U. S. Department of Agriculture (meat and poultry), and the Department of Commerce (fish).

Food and Drug Administration. The FDA is responsible for assuring that the food industry meets its obligation to supply the nation with safe, pure, and wholesome food. There are five main laws that give the FDA its authority:

—The Federal Food, Drug, and Cosmetic Act (1938) requires that foods be safe and wholesome, that drugs be safe and effective, and that cosmetics and medical devices be safe.
—The Fair Packaging and Labeling Act (1966) requires that consumers be given adequate information about product ingredients, net weight, and quality.
—The Public Health Service Act (1944) gives the FDA authority over vaccines, serums, and other biological products. It

is also the basis for the FDA's authority over milk and shell-fish sanitation, restaurant operations, interstate travel facilities, poison, and accident prevention.

—The Radiation Control for Health and Safety Act (1968) protects consumers from unnecessary exposure to radiation from X-ray machines and consumer products such as microwave ovens and color television sets.

—The Hazardous Substances Act (1960) and the Child Protection Act (1966) require prominent warning labels on hazardous household chemical products and articles intended for household use.

The FDA has far-reaching control over processed foods. However, the FDA can act only on products sold through interstate commerce (commerce between two or more states). The FDA carries out its duties in three ways:

—By informing and educating regulated groups so that they will obey the law.

—By conducting inspections of food processing plants and warehouses, including laboratory examination of food products sampled from warehouses and stores across the country.

—By taking action in the court if the law is broken.

When the FDA discovers a product that is unsafe or mislabeled, it has four procedures to follow which protect the consumer. They are:

—Under the threat of legal action, ask the manufacturer to remove (recall) the dangerous, contaminated, or mislabeled product from the supermarket.

—Seize the offending product or products.

—Prosecute the person or firm responsible for violating the law.

—Obtain a court order to keep the offending articles from entering into interstate commerce.

U. S. Department of Agriculture. The USDA is responsible for assuring that meat and poultry and products made from them are safe, wholesome, and truthfully packaged. There are three major laws that give the USDA its authority:

—The Meat Inspection Act (1906) requires inspection of meat packaging plants for sanitation and carcass inspection for contamination.

—The Wholesome Meat Act (1967) and the Wholesome Poultry Act (1968) provide that uniform inspection procedures must be adopted for meats shipped within states as well as between states. State inspection services are required to have an inspection program comparable to that of the federal government.

The USDA was created in 1862 by President Lincoln to help farmers improve the size and quality of their crops. Today the USDA has many programs that benefit consumers as well as farmers. The USDA carries out its responsibilities in the following ways:

—By sponsoring research on consumer products.

—By sponsoring educational programs such as the Cooperative Extension Services. (The purpose of the CES is to make research done at state universities available to consumers. This program provides such community programs as 4-H clubs, family counseling centers, and soil-testing services.)

—By enforcing regulations that require quality standards for the meat and poultry eaten by consumers. (In addition the USDA administers the national food stamp program and the federally-subsidized school lunch program.)

There are two types of USDA inspections: mandatory meat and poultry inspection and voluntary grading services and standards.

Meat and Poultry Inspection. In packing and processing plants the USDA (The Food Safety and Quality Service) inspects meat and poultry for sanitation, accurate labeling, and proper use of food additives. The USDA monitors meat and poultry to detect potentially hazardous chemical or pesticide residues. Meat may be inspected anytime during processing, manufacturing, or distribution. Any product that fails to pass inspection must be destroyed or reprocessed to satisfy inspection standards. If products are found to be unsuitable for human food, they are marked "Inspected and Condemned." Otherwise the meat and poultry seals shown in Illustration 6-3 appear on products which have passed USDA inspection standards.

Illus. 6-3

Inspection marks for fresh meat and poultry

Voluntary Grading Services and Grade Standards. The USDA provides a voluntary grading service and develops grade standards for meat, poultry, eggs, dairy products, and fresh or processed fruit and vegetables. The purpose of the grading service is to provide buyers (particularly large volume buyers) with some standards of quality. As mentioned before, consumers can use these grading standards to judge the standard quality for different food products.

Consumer Responsibilities

The final responsibility for safe and wholesome food is with the consumer. The home is one of the major sources of food contamination, spoilage, and misuse. Food problems are sometimes the result of the consumer's failure to follow label directions or warnings. To get maximum protection, the consumer must read labels carefully, follow directions, and know about daily nutritional requirements.

VOCABULARY REVIEW

Specials

Loss leaders

Unit price

Quantity buying

Grade

Food co-op

QUESTIONS FOR REVIEW

1. What is the first step that food consumers should follow in getting the variety of foods needed for adequate nutrition?

2. What is the best source of price information on food items?

3. What can food shoppers do to decrease impulse spending in the supermarket?

4. How can a food shopper easily find the best price among the same or similar products?

5. When nonperishable food items are on sale, how can the consumer lower the cost of buying food?

6. How can a consumer use coupons to get "double" savings on food items?

7. What is a useful source of information about food products?

8. What are some of the techniques used by supermarkets to promote sales and gain customer loyalty?

9. Which government agency has primary responsibility for assuring safe and pure food in the marketplace?

10. Which government agency administers federal inspection of meat and poultry products to assure safety and wholesomeness of these products?

PROBLEM-SOLVING AND DECISION-MAKING PROJECTS

1. Suppose you are asked to buy the soft drinks for an after-the-game party. Which would be the best buy? What other consideration might be given to this buying decision?

Container and Size	Price
a. Six 12-ounce cans	$1.54
b. Six 16-ounce bottles	2.29
c. One 2-liter (67.6 oz.) plastic bottle	1.39

2. Suppose you went to a supermarket for a particular item advertised as being on sale. When you arrived at the store, the advertised product was sold out. Which of the following actions would be the most appropriate to take?
   a. Wait until the product is on sale again.
   b. Ask for a rain check.
   c. Stop shopping at the store.
   d. Request a substitute of similar quality at the same price.

e. Complain to the manager.

f. Purchase the item at the regular price when the store restocks the item.

3. Assume that the class has an opportunity to have a class party. As a group decide the party menu: potato chips, cola, hot dogs, fruit or mixed nuts, etc. As a group, also decide the quantity of each item which will be needed for the party. After deciding on the menu and the quantity of each item, divide the class into small groups of two or three students. The problem for each group is to shop for the party menu. Each group should shop independently and obtain the prices for the same items and quantity. Which group can obtain the party items for the least cost? After the shopping experience, discuss the use of unit price, private labels, generic products, volume buying, specials, and other shopping procedures used in the project.

COMMUNITY AND HOME PROJECTS

1. Survey your local supermarket to determine:
   a. The use of unit price labels.
   b. The use of open dating.
   c. The store's return and refund policy.
   d. The use of games, stamps, or gifts.
   Prepare a report on your findings.

2. Collect advertisements from various supermarkets during one week.
   a. Prepare a weekly dinner meal plan based upon advertised specials. Include in each meal the essential items from the basic food groups.
   b. After preparing seven menus which provide for variety and personal preference, use the food advertisements to prepare a shopping list.
   c. Beside each item on the shopping list record the price of the product. Determine the total cost of the items on the shopping list.

3. In groups consisting of three people, prepare a shopping list that includes common grocery products with the same unit size containers or packages. Determine the cost difference for generic products, private labels, and name brands. Prepare a chart to show the potential savings between the types of brands.

Chapter 7

Transportation — Wheels and Deals

Our nation's transportation system gives us freedom in the choice of a place to live, work, shop, and recreate. A well-developed transportation system increases economic activity, ties the nation together, and serves as a means of distribution for our goods and services. Transportation ranks third after food and shelter in the order of expenditures for the average American.

The automobile dominates the transportation system in the United States. Our way of life centers on the private automobile. Suburbs developed because of the automobile. Working, shopping, and living in the suburbs is impractical without a car. No other form of transportation in the near future is likely to satisfy so fully our need for mobility. The Department of Transportation projects that by the year 2000 the automobile will still account for 78 percent of all domestic transportation.

There are over 100 million cars on America's roads. Approximately 10 million new cars are added each year. In this chapter we will make suggestions about the purchase of used and new cars. In Chapter 8 we will examine the costs of owning and operating a car and discuss automobile insurance.

BUYING A CAR

As a first-time car buyer, you must prepare well for this big expenditure. You must decide which car is best for you, research the types of cars you are interested in, and consider the amount of money you have to spend.

Determine Your Needs

A decision on which kind of car is best for you requires an inventory of your needs, personality, and expectations. Consider

The automobile is easily the most-used form of transportation in America today.

Source: Photo courtesy of — GREATER LOS ANGELES VISITORS AND CONVENTION BUREAU

what you are really buying. Is it transportation, style, status, comfort, reliability, or efficiency? Cars may offer some status, but you must consider how much such things are worth. The status of a "muscle car" will quickly disappear when the gas pump registers $$.$$. A classy sports model may lose some of its class when your friends cannot ride in the back seat and choose to go with someone else because your car is too small. Models loaded with power-operated windows and seats and other conveniences can be troublesome as a car gets older because repairs are expensive.

Shop Before Going to a Car Lot

Generally the first-time buyer has some car model in mind. Much preliminary shopping can be done by reading past issues of car reports which appear in automobile and consumer magazines such as *Car and Driver*, *Auto Mechanics*, *Motor Trend*, *Consumer Reports*, and *Changing Times*. By using information in these publications, it is possible to look up price information as well as a car's repair ratings.

Published price information on new cars and comparing this information to the prices of several dealers can help you negotiate a reasonable price instead of guessing at a price or "knocking a couple hundred dollars off." If you send the make, model, and options of the car you desire to Car/Puter, you will receive a computerized printout listing of dealers' cost, manufacturers' suggested retail list price, and a suggested purchase price. Similar information is available in paperback books such as *Edmund's New Car Prices* and *Kelley Blue Book New Car Price Manual*. Price information on the value of trade-ins is also available.

In the area of used cars, the government can also help. If you are looking for a used car of a particular model, contact the National Highway Traffic Safety Administration (NHTSA) for information on safety defects and any manufacturer recalls. *Edmund's Used Car Prices, Automotive Market Report,* and the *Official Used Car Guide Book* provide retail and wholesale prices for various makes and models of used cars. These sources are usually available at local libraries, banks, and credit unions.

Money Decisions

It is extremely important to know what you can afford before going to the car lot. Set a maximum limit for what you can afford, and be realistic about the amount. Remember that there will be taxes, license fees, insurance fees, and operating expenses. Ask yourself whether you are willing to pay the extra money required to finance the purchase. If so, determine in advance where the money is coming from—credit union, bank, or through dealer financing. Whatever you decide, be sure to determine the difference between paying cash and buying on credit. (See Chapter 15 for determining the cost of credit.)

BUYING A USED CAR

Buying a used car can result in considerable savings, or it can turn into an expensive nightmare. Some people think that buying a used car is like buying "another person's headache." Others think it foolish to pay 40 to 50 percent more for "the smell of a new car."

Optimal Time and Value

Used car buyers are in the majority. Three out of every four cars sold are used cars. The smart buyer can take advantage of a new car's rapid depreciation during the first two or three years of the life of the car. *Depreciation* is a decrease in the value of property caused by time and use. According to the *Official Used Car Guide Book*, a new car loses approximately 50 percent of its value in the first two years. Assuming that the normal life of a car is seven years, after two years a buyer can get five-sevenths (70 percent) of the useful life of the car for approximately one-half (50 percent) of its original value. Therefore, the best time to purchase a used car is when it is two or three years old.

Maintenance costs increase as a car gets older, but increased maintenance costs are not greater than the depreciation—which is the largest cost factor in the first two years. For a young, first-time car buyer, it is advisable to let someone else take the largest share of depreciation costs.

Where to Buy

Once you have narrowed your selection to two or three types of cars and have set your price limit, it is time to start the actual shopping. The common places for a used car purchase are new car dealers, used car dealers, and private sellers.

New Car Dealers. New car dealers who sell used cars tend to charge more than other sellers. New car dealers are more likely to keep for resale the best used cars traded in for new cars. They have service shops to recondition used cars and, with such a shop, the dealer is able to honor any warranty given with a used car. On the other hand, new car dealers often consider used cars merely a nuisance and give priority to new car service. Many times very little repair work is done on used car trade-ins except for cosmetic changes to make the car look good.

Used Car Dealers. Used car dealers may have less extensive service facilities or no facilities at all. They obtain their cars from new car dealers and car auctions which are conducted about once a week in most larger cities. There are three types of used car dealers:

(1) fly-by-night operators who stay in business until forced to close, (2) small owner-operated lots which obtain top quality trade-ins from the used car managers of new car dealerships, and (3) large independent dealers who use extensive newspaper and television advertising to get high volume sales. When shopping for a used car, you should find out how long the dealer has done business in the same location. The longer a dealer has done business in the community, the better are your chances of being treated fairly and of finding out about the experiences of others who have bought cars from the dealer.

Many people buy used cars from used car lots or new car dealers.

Private Sales. You can find good used cars by checking the classified advertisements in the local newspaper. When you follow up on an ad, always ask if the advertiser is a dealer. If so, look elsewhere. This is a roundabout technique designed to get buyers. Private parties sell some perfectly good used cars at fair prices. However, some try to sell cars that reputable dealers will not accept or will accept only at junk prices.

The advantage of a private sale is that the dealer's profit is avoided — but there are disadvantages as well. Generally there will not be any warranty, you must handle the legal matters relating to the sale, and you can spend an enormous amount of time checking out cars in classified ads.

When dealing with private sellers, it is extremely important to check the title to the car before giving a deposit or transferring money to the seller. Check the title to determine whether the party selling the car has clear title, that is, owns the car and is named in the title. A clear title to an automobile may be seen in Illus. 7-1. In one case, a teenager bought a used car from a private party, received a receipt, and was promised the title would be sent in a few weeks.

STATE OF OHIO, COUNTY OF CRITTENDEN

CERTIFICATE OF TITLE No. 130944315
TO A MOTOR VEHICLE

Previous No.

This is to certify that

Roy   Claude   Brown   9-28-81
(Owner's First   Middle   Last Name)   (Date This Title Issued)

114 Roby Drive, Terrace Park, OH 45140
(Owner's Address in Full)

Is the owner of the following described Motor Vehicle:

YEAR 1977   Mfr's Serial No. 177513449
MAKE VW   MODEL 1654
BODY 2DR   Mtr. No.

having acquired title to said Motor Vehicle from:

Previous Owner Luis Moreno
Route 6, Marion, KY 42904
(Address of Previous Owner in Full)

on which Motor Vehicle are the following liens, mortgages or encumbrances:
if none state here None.

FIRST LIEN: Nature of Lien
Held by
Holder's Address in Full
Date of Notation   Clerk's Signature
Above Lien Discharged   Date of Cancellation

          SIGNATURE OF LIENHOLDER   CLERK'S SIGNATURE
By   By   Deputy Clerk

SECOND LIEN: Nature of Lien
Held by
Holder's Address in Full
Date of Notation   Clerk's Signature
Above Lien Discharged   Date of Cancellation

          SIGNATURE OF LIENHOLDER   CLERK'S SIGNATURE
By   By   Deputy Clerk

THIRD LIEN: Nature of Lien
Held by
Holder's Address in Full
Date of Notation   Clerk's Signature
Above Lien Discharged   Date of Cancellation

          SIGNATURE OF LIENHOLDER   CLERK'S SIGNATURE
By   By   Deputy Clerk

If Dealer, Vendor's License No.   Dlrs. Permit No.
Delivered Purchase Price $ Gift   Ohio Sales or Used Tax Paid $
The mileage registered on the odometer of this vehicle at the time the previous title
was assigned was 3,600   miles.

Witness my hand and official seal this 28th day of September , 1981

(SEAL) Robert S. Spears   Clerk of Courts
By C. Hooper   Deputy Clerk

Illus. 7-1

Clear title to a motor vehicle

Later the young car buyer discovered that the seller had never finished paying for the car and that the bank kept the title. You should receive the title at the time you pay for the car.

Car Rental Company Sales. Rental car offices, such as Hertz, Avis, and National also sell used cars. Most are nine- to twelve-months old and have under 25,000 miles. Critics claim that rental cars are risky because they are abused by drivers. Those who favor buying rental cars claim that most of the drivers are business people who do not abuse the cars. In addition rental cars have had more extensive maintenance than the typical family car. These cars usually sell for several hundred dollars less than comparable models at used car dealerships.

Iron Dealers. It is advisable to avoid *iron dealers*. These small operations advertise easy credit terms, no money down, and low prices. The old cars sold in such operations are known as the "sleds" and "dogs" of the used car market and often are just one step from the junk yard. Young people and people with little money who need transportation to get to work sometimes take a chance with such dealers.

Inspecting a Used Car

Staring at an engine or kicking the tires will not tell you what you want to know about the condition of a used car. The best assurance for getting a reliable used car lies in making a selection after some performance checks and tests. The smart used car buyer conducts three types of inspections: on-the-lot, on-the-road, and in-the-garage.

On-the-Lot Tests. Follow these on-the-lot checks to help in your choice.

1. Look for signs of new paint, repainted parts, or new or refinished chrome. Paint overruns on the underside of the hood or trunk lid indicate a recent paint job which could mean that the car was in an accident. Inspect the rest of the car carefully for weld marks or a bent frame.

2. Watch for rust spots. Some small amounts of rust are normal but extensive rust is a serious problem.
3. Check the tail pipe for black, gummy deposits. Such deposits can mean carburetor trouble or worn piston rings.
4. Push down hard on each corner of the car. The car should bounce upward once and level off into position. If a car bounces up and down more than twice, the shock absorbers are badly worn.
5. Inspect the tires for signs of alignment problems. Tires unevenly worn may indicate a need for a front-end alignment. New tires on an older car may be retreads. Retreads may be perfectly fine for your driving conditions, but know what you are buying.
6. Check for dampness or water stains on the carpet and interior. Cars which have been in floods or other natural disasters are often sold in auctions and later wind up in used car lots.
7. Examine the accelerator, brake pedals, and floor mats for evidence of heavy use. New mats and pedals can cover up rust or other damage.
8. Inspect all electrical accessories including external lights, high and low beams, warning flashers, turn signals, brake lights, radio, heater, windshield wipers, dome light, and dash lights.
9. Check the *odometer* (the gauge for measuring the distance traveled). Federal law prohibits rolling back mileage, but there are still dealers who do. The average car is driven 10,000 miles a year. Expect a five-year-old car to have at least 50,000 miles. Be careful of anything less. If the digits are not in alignment, perhaps the odometer has been turned back. Check the odometer behind the dash. Look for signs of chewed-up screw heads. Also look for oil change stickers on the car door which would tell the mileage at the last oil change. It is another warning sign of mileage tampering if all the stickers have been removed. The Odometer Protection Act of 1972 requires that anyone selling a vehicle or transferring ownership must provide the buyer with a signed statement indicating the mileage registered on the odometer at the time of sale. If you are interested in the car, ask to see the *odometer disclosure statement* of the previous owner.

On-The-Road-Tests. The on-the-road test is an opportunity to see the car in operation. Do not hesitate to make on-the-road tests even if a salesperson accompanies you. Allow 30 to 45 minutes for the tests. Do not deal with those who say you cannot take the car out because their insurance will not cover you. Young people should take an adult along.

1. Take the car onto a highway which is not heavily traveled. Accelerate from 15 to 55 miles per hour. If the car moves smoothly without stalling or hesitating, chances are that the engine is in fair condition. Decelerate to about 15 miles per hour, then accelerate rapidly with a strong push to the accelerator. Watch for blue or dark smoke from the tail pipe. This could mean worn piston rings.
2. Check the steering and braking. With manual steering, check the play in the steering wheel while the car is parked. More than ten inches of play in either direction indicates that the front end is improperly aligned. In cars with power steering, make sharp turns left and right. There may be trouble if the steering tightens up or requires unusual effort. Drive straight and slowly, then apply the brakes to determine if the car pulls to one side or the other. Check to see if the brakes are weak or noisy.
3. After driving awhile, park the car for several minutes. Then move it forward a few feet and check the ground under it for oil or water leaks.

In-The-Garage Tests. The final step in the selection process is to have a mechanic check the used car you choose. You can detect a few problems from your on-the-road tests, but a mechanic can do a much better job. You may wish to use a car clinic or diagnostic center. It may be necessary to make arrangements in advance with both the used car dealer and the mechanic. For $25 to $40, a mechanic or diagnostic center will check brakes, wheels, universal joints, cylinders, the transmission, and other parts of the car. Ask for a written estimate for the cost of repairs. Use this estimate of repair costs to get the seller to reduce the price of the car. A tip for the young consumer is to arrange a repair deal with a mechanic you can trust. If the mechanic will check the car out, promise to bring it back for service and repair. Even if such an arrangement cannot be made, the $25 to $40 spent for a mechanic's opinion is worth the money.

You should perform on-the-lot, on-the-road, and in-the-garage tests when you are considering buying a used car.

BUYING A NEW CAR

Everyone wants to get a "good deal" on a new car and there are many ideas about where to shop and how to bargain. In the past new car buyers selected new cars only from car dealers—either large-volume dealers or small dealerships. Today there are other ways to buy new cars. These include auto buying services and auto brokers.

New Car Dealers

Large- or small-volume dealers buy cars from manufacturers. Most dealers finance their car purchases through local lenders or through arrangements with manufacturers. Every new car must have a manufacturer's suggested retail list price displayed on the window. The Automobile Disclosures Act, 1954, makes it illegal for a dealer to offer for sale any new car without this sticker price properly displayed on the car. The sticker price is not the amount you are expected to pay. The *manufacturer's suggested retail list price* is the maximum price which manufacturers believe should be paid for the car.

When buying a car from a dealership, you will most likely talk with a salesperson who is paid by *commission* — or a percentage of the sale price of each car sold. Some car buying authorities suggest that the best bargains can be made at the highly competitive, high-volume dealerships. This assumes that high-volume dealers are more willing to make less profit on each car in an effort to maintain higher sales. Other experts suggest that the small-volume dealer is in a position to make a better offer because of lower operating expenses, less advertising, and fewer salespeople. The buyer must also recognize that a low purchase price is not everything. As important as price is a convenient, respectable dealer with a good service department. Car buyers should always compare prices and services offered at several dealerships.

Auto Buying Services and Auto Brokers

Many individuals and families are eligible to buy new cars for prices that are only $100 to $250 above dealer's cost. *Auto buying services* specialize in fleet or volume sales and sell cars to large companies. Some of these services allow a car buyer to obtain from a company a purchase certificate which entitles a company employee to order any car from the auto buying service. Other company plans limit the choice of cars to certain models and makes. In either case the buyer does not have to go through a salesperson at a dealership.

For persons who are not eligible for a company plan, auto brokers, such as United Auto Brokers, can order most domestic cars for $125 above cost. An *auto broker* specializes in selling new cars directly to consumers at a low cost because dealership showrooms or salespeople are not utilized. These brokers will ship a car to a cooperating dealer who works with them. An additional $75 courtesy delivery charge may be added to the cost if there is no cooperating dealer in your area.

Dealing with Dealers

After you have shopped around, it is time to bargain. It is advisable to keep your mind open so you can walk away from a car if necessary. Dealers believe that once you "fall in love" with a particular model, you will eventually talk yourself into buying it. There are three essentials when it is time to bargain: (1) use competitive market conditions to your advantage, (2) know the dealer's costs and the wholesale value of your trade-in, and (3) be reasonable. A reliable dealer with good service facilities is more important than a savings of $50 from a dealer who is 40 miles from your residence.

Special Ordering. If you have decided your automotive needs in advance of shopping, then you may want to consider *special ordering*. By special ordering you can get a new car with the specific *options* (extra features) you need and you can avoid settling for a "loaded" model already in stock. Many dealers prefer not to special order because the cars in stock yield a quicker profit. In addition it is a standard practice for dealers to overload cars in stock with options. Dealers know that buyers with "new car fever" will buy now rather than wait. Cars loaded with options hurt your pocketbook in three ways: they cost more to begin with, they cost more to maintain, and they often consume extra fuel.

Calculate the Cost. If it is not possible to obtain car price information from any of the sources named earlier in the chapter, then use the following procedure to calculate the cost:

Step 1. Subtract the transportation charge from the bottom line of the sticker price.

Step 2. Take a percentage of this figure. For a subcompact, multiply by 85 percent. For a compact- or intermediate-size car, multiply by 82 percent. For a full-size car, multiply by 80 percent. This figure is the cost to the dealer to within about 1 percent of the actual cost. Remember that you cannot expect to get the car at cost.

Step 3. Add a reasonable profit to the figure obtained in Step 2. Consider it reasonable to add $100 to $300 depending on the size of the car. For subcompact cars, add $100; for compact or intermediate cars, add $200; and for the large, luxury cars, add $300.

Step 4. Add the transportation charges back to the figure derived in Step 3, and you have determined a fair and reasonable price. This may be your offer.

Step 5. If you have a trade-in, subtract the wholesale value from the figure in Step 4. Again, used car price information can be obtained from published sources such as the *Black Book* for used car

It pays to talk to several dealers before buying a new car.

projected values. If this is not possible, take the used car to two different dealers to get an estimate of its value. Add sales tax, license fees, and registration to this final figure. This is the actual cost of the new car.

You can figure out an offer for the car by using these steps. Do the calculations in the privacy of your home, away from the high-pressured atmosphere of the new-car showroom. Then go to the showroom with this information in hand. After discussing the type of car and the options wanted, you might say to the salesperson: "I'm ready to give you an order if the deal is right. Give me your best price with the options included. Talk with your manager and see what you can do." Those are the key words and the salesperson will respond. The salesperson will most likely go out of the room to consult with the sales manager and come back with a "best offer." The salesperson's first offer might be $300 to $500 off the sticker price. This is only a tentative offer to test you. You might counter with an offer close to your cost-plus-profit figure (Step 3). If the counteroffer is still too high, make your cost-plus-profit-plus-trans-portation offer (Step 4), and let the salesperson know that you con-sider this offer fair and reasonable.

Remember the essential steps. You have to be well informed about the dealer's cost and trade-in price of your used car and be willing to walk away. One large-volume buyer advises consumers to consider it a good deal to get 8 percent to 10 percent off the sticker price on a subcompact, 12 percent on an intermediate or compact, and 14 percent on a full-size model.

Caveat Emptor: *Trade-In Confusion*

A trade-in can confuse the pricing of a new car unless the buyer has a clear idea of the value of the trade-in. Some dealers practice a technique called *high-balling*. This approach involves quoting a higher figure than normal for the trade-in. When it is time to close the deal, the sales manager becomes very apologetic and claims that the car is not worth the amount offered. As a result of the so-called mistake, the sales manager offers less for the trade-in than the salesperson offered.

Another variation of this technique, called an *overallowance*, involves quotes on trade-ins which are far above the actual value of the trade-in. This means that the dealer merely asks more for the new car. For example, Dealer A offers $1,100 for your trade-in, and the asking price on the new car is $4,550. Dealer B offers actual wholesale value for the trade-in, $900, and the asking price of the new car is $4,250.

	Dealer A	Dealer B
Sticker Price	$4,850	$4,850
Asking Price	4,550	4,250
Trade-in Quote	1,100	900
	$3,450	$3,350

In this illustration the higher trade-in offer may not necessarily be the best deal for the new car buyer. For this reason, the buyer must know the actual value of the trade-in or ask for a price quote on the new car without a trade-in. Then ask for a price that includes the trade-in. The difference between the two prices is the trade-in value of the used car. Buyer Beware.

VOCABULARY REVIEW

Depreciation

Iron dealers

Odometer

On-the-road tests

In-the-garage tests

Auto brokers

QUESTIONS FOR REVIEW

1. For the average American, where does transportation rank in the order of expenditures?

2. Which method of transportation dominates the U.S. transportation system?

3. When is the best time to purchase a used car to get the maximum value for transportation?

4. What is likely to be the best place to buy a good used car?

5. Name five on-the-lot tests which should be made when you are shopping for a used car.

6. When you are buying a used car, what should you ask and look for to determine the truthfulness of the odometer reading?

7. What is the final step in determining the mechanical condition of a used car?

8. Is the manufacturer's suggested retail list price the amount the buyer is expected to pay for a new car? Explain.

9. What are some sources of information which can help consumers determine price information about new or used cars?

PROBLEM-SOLVING AND DECISION-MAKING PROJECTS

1. Analyze your own transportation needs. Then prepare a chart listing the advantages and disadvantages of owning a car as compared to alternative transportation such as a bicycle, moped, or motorcycle.

2. Assume that you decide to buy a new car. Having determined your needs and financial limits and having shopped at several dealers, you have narrowed your choice to three dealers with

essentially the same car. Dealer A is asking $5,215 for the new car and is offering $1,100 for your trade-in. Dealer B is asking $4,900 for the new car, but is offering only $600 for the trade-in. Dealer C is asking $5,450 and is offering the top price on your trade-in, $1,200.

a. Which dealer is giving the best price considering the trade-in?

b. What is the best way to avoid trade-in confusion?

COMMUNITY AND HOME PROJECTS

1. Describe in detail the type of used car that meets your needs. Then visit several used car dealers in your community. Use the "on-the-lot" check list on pages 117-118 to evaluate the used cars. Prepare a report on your findings.

2. Interview someone you know who has bought a car within the past year. Find out about the type of car purchased, how the deal was made, the warranty, the comparative shopping process, and after-purchase satisfaction/dissatisfaction. Report to the class on the useful information discovered in this interview.

Chapter 8

Transportation — The Cost of Auto Ownership

Getting a car is an exciting experience for most teenagers. For a young person with a first-time driver's license and money saved from a job, car ownership is often given top priority. But the purchase is only the beginning. The expenses associated with operating a car are three times the cost of buying.

COSTS

Many first-time car owners think of costs in terms of gasoline, oil, tires, and tolls. A careful examination shows that some costs occur whether or not the vehicle is driven and that others are directly related to the amount of travel. The first group is known as *fixed costs* or ownership costs. The latter group is known as *variable costs* or operating costs.

Fixed Costs

Below is an explanation of the factors that you should consider when computing the fixed cost of operating an automobile.

Depreciation. As stated in Chapter 7, a decrease in the value of property (a car, for example) caused by time and use is known as *depreciation*. Though not a visible out-of-pocket expense, such as gasoline, depreciation is the single largest expense for new car owners. Assume that a new car is purchased for $6,200. If resold one year later, the car owner would be offered approximately $4,300. The decrease in value is depreciation. Depending on the make and model, cars depreciate at different rates. Generally cars depreciate 25 to 30 percent during the first year, 18 to 20 percent the second year,

14 to 15 percent the third, 10 to 11 percent the fourth, 9 to 10 percent the fifth year, 6 to 8 percent the sixth year, and 2 to 6 percent the seventh year.

Insurance. Another cost of owning a car is insurance. Much more will be said about auto insurance on pages 138-143. Insurance is ordinarily a fixed cost because the cost remains the same whether the car is driven 3,000 or 30,000 miles a year.

Finance Charge. Buying a car with cash is the cheapest way to buy a car. If the car is financed (paid for over a period of time), the finance charge should be considered a cost of purchasing. The finance charge is a fixed expense because it remains the same, whether the car is driven or parked in a garage most of the time.

Taxes, License, Registration Fees. Usually when a car is purchased, there is a big gap between the sticker or window price and the final cost. A sizable portion of this gap will come from sales taxes, license and registration fees, and perhaps a city sticker fee for the community in which you live. Title registration fees and sales taxes occur only at the time a car is purchased, but license and sticker fees occur annually.

Other Costs. Other charges associated with the ownership of a car are sometimes overlooked. They include dealer preparation and transportation charges for a new car, garage and parking fees, and occasional traffic tickets and parking fines.

Variable Costs

Variable costs are determined by the number of miles driven each year. The rapid increase in gasoline prices makes variable costs the major expense of operating a car. Variable costs are based to a large degree on your driving habits, the type of driving you do, such as in the city or country, the type of climate where you live, and the size of your car.

Gas and Oil. The best way to find the per-mile cost of gasoline is to develop your own figures. The following is an example of how to learn your car's mileage and cost per gallon of gasoline.

The purchase of gasoline is the major variable cost of owning an automobile.

Source: Ashland Oil, Inc.

Tank filled . . . . Odometer reading: 11,400
Bought gas   12 gallons . . . . cost $18.00 11,604
Bought gas   13.6 gallons. . . . . cost $20.80 11,842
Bought gas   10.3 gallons. . . . . cost $15.45 . . . . <u>12,027</u>

    Total   35.9 gallons. . . . . cost $54.25
    Ending Odometer Reading   12,027
    Starting Odometer Reading . . . . <u>−11,400</u>
    Miles driven   627
    Miles per gallon 627 ÷ 35.9 = 17.5 miles per gallon.
    Cost of gas per mile $54.25 ÷ 627 = 8.7 cents per mile.

The cost of oil, which will vary from car to car, may be added into the cost of gasoline. Table 8-1 can be used to estimate the annual cost of gasoline depending upon the miles per gallon of your car.

Table 8-1

Fuel Costs, in Dollars, Per 15,000 Miles

Estimated Miles Per Gallon	Cost of Gas Per Gallon				
	$2.00	**$1.80**	**$1.60**	**$1.40**	**$1.20**
50	$ 600	$ 540	$ 480	$ 420	$ 360
48	624	564	500	434	375
46	652	588	522	456	392
44	680	615	546	478	410
42	716	642	572	500	428
40	752	675	600	526	450
38	788	711	632	552	474
36	832	750	666	584	500
34	884	795	706	618	530
32	936	843	750	656	562
30	1000	900	800	700	600
28	1072	963	858	750	642
26	1152	1038	808	808	692
24	1252	1125	876	876	750
22	1364	1227	954	954	818
20	1500	1350	1050	1050	900
18	1668	1500	1166	1166	1000
16	1876	1689	1312	1312	1126
14	2144	1929	1500	1500	1286
12	2500	2250	1750	1750	1500
10	3000	2700	2100	2100	1800
8	3752	3375	2626	2626	2250

Source: U. S. Department of Energy, 1980 Gas Mileage Guide (2nd ed., 1980).

Maintenance. Tune-ups, parts, and repairs are typical maintenance costs. The newer the car, the less these expenses will be. Even a car under warranty requires checkups and service. The best way to know accurately the cost of maintenance is to keep a record of all maintenance expenses.

Tires. Another variable expense is tire wear. If the car is driven with reasonable care and the wheels are properly aligned, the wear can be kept to a minimum. However, over or underinflation of the tires, sharp cornering, rapid acceleration, and quick stops all contribute to tire wear. In addition high-speed driving generates heat which also increases tire wear.

Figuring the Cost

Only simple automobile expense records are needed to figure the actual costs of owning and operating a car. If records of the total miles driven during the year and of fixed and variable operating expenses are kept, then a cost calculation is easy. The fixed costs plus variable costs divided by the number of miles driven equals the cost per mile for the operation of an automobile. For example, one car owner kept a record of operating expenses. At the end of the year, fixed expenses were $771, variable expenses were $2,480, and the car had been driven 12,000 miles.

Fixed Expenses . . . . $ 771
Variable Expenses . . . .   + 2,480
Total Cost . . . . $3,251 ÷ 12,000 miles = 27¢ per mile

There might be a more deliberate effort by drivers to reduce the cost of owning an automobile if more car owners knew the actual costs of operating one.

Reducing Operating Costs

The high price of gasoline requires every car owner to seek ways to get maximum fuel efficiency. Below are some factors which affect fuel efficiency or gas mileage and ultimately affect the total cost of operating a car.

Size of Car. Cars are classified as subcompact, compact, mid-size, and large according to interior size and weight. The weight of a car contributes to its cost of operation. Gasoline mileage is reduced by 1 to 2 percent for every 100 pounds of added weight. The size, weight, and horsepower of the engine will increase the purchase price, insurance rates, the rate of depreciation, gasoline consumption, maintenance costs, and in some states even the license fees.

Options. According to the U. S. Department of Energy, an air conditioner decreases gas mileage by 9 to 20 percent with stop-and-go driving. An automatic transmission can reduce fuel economy by as much as 15 percent. Power equipment adds weight to the car and increases the amount of fuel required. Such extra features can also add 20 to 25 percent to the cost of a car.

Driving Habits. High-speed driving increases gasoline consumption. Fast acceleration and hard braking use about 15 percent more gas than gradual accelerating and braking.

Maintenance. Proper car care, including regular tune-ups and properly inflated tires, improves gas mileage and minimizes repair costs. Many communities offer auto repair courses for the non-mechanic. A little knowledge about the mechanical features of your automobile can go a long way in saving you money on auto repair.

Auto repair expenses can be lessened through proper maintenance.

Length of Ownership. Some people trade cars every two years in the belief that older cars cost more to maintain. Studies show, however, that the per-mile cost to own and operate a car begins to decrease after the first year and continues to decline with each additional year. These studies show that the longer an owner keeps a car, the lower will be the overall lifetime cost of operation, assuming that the car is driven and maintained properly. To keep and repair a car is cheaper than to trade it in for a new one and begin to lose 25 percent of its value in depreciation during the first year of ownership.

AUTOMOBILE REPAIRS

Automobile service and repair have long been the consumer's primary problem. Annually, over $50 billion is spent on auto repairs. The U. S. Department of Transportation estimates that 50¢ out of every dollar spent on auto repairs is wasted. Below are some things to look for in repair garages and service rip-offs.

Auto Repair Garages

Auto repair garages may be classified as follows: (1) new-car dealerships with attached service and parts departments; (2) large independent general repair garages with six to twelve service stalls and hoists; (3) garages franchised by national companies which advertise about transmissions, brakes, and mufflers; (4) small one- or two-person garages located in low-rent areas where the owner/mechanic often crawls out from under a car to greet you; (5) gas stations with one or two service stalls; (6) automotive diagnostic centers which electronically test a car and provide a report on any faults the car may have.

If you use the services of a repair garage, remember these suggestions:

1. When you take the car in for repairs, avoid peak periods, such as mornings, when the service writer is rushed.
2. Describe the symptoms and when they appear. Be specific in your description. Unless you are certain of the problem, do not tell what you think is wrong. Otherwise, the garage may repair what you think is wrong just to satisfy you, and the repair may or may not be needed. Expect the mechanic or service writer to provide the diagnosis.
3. Request a written estimate of repair costs.
4. Request that your approval be given before work is done which exceeds the estimate or was not included in the estimate.
5. Request that old parts be returned to you. Some states and local ordinances require that old parts be given to you. This

procedure allows you to examine them and determine if they were replaced.

6. Pick the car up before service personnel leave for the day. Then you can ask about the repairs made and, if something is wrong, someone will be there to listen to your concerns.

7. If possible, deal with a reliable garage which has professionally qualified mechanics. Two independent organizations, the symbols of which appear in Illus. 8-1, have

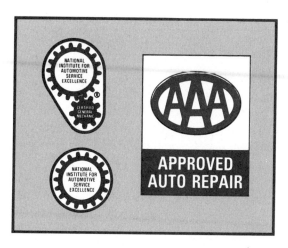

Illus. 8-1

Choosing a reliable repair garage is often a risky task. You can be better assured of good service if you will choose a garage which displays one or both of the symbols shown here.

Source: National Institute for Automotive Service Excellence and American Automobile Association.

set up programs which can be of assistance in making this determination.

— The National Institute for Automotive Service Excellence (NIASE) is a nonprofit organization that tests and certifies auto mechanics. To be certified, the mechanic must have at least two years work experience and pass an examination on parts, repairs, and diagnostics. In order to remain certified, the mechanic must take requalification tests every five years.

— The American Automobile Association, the nation's largest drivers' association (over 22 million members in the United States and Canada), through its Approved Auto Repair Services program, identifies reliable garages which have proven they can provide consistent, high-quality workmanship and will guarantee their work. To quality, a garage must offer specific services, have certain types of equipment and NIASE-certified mechanics to support these services, offer a written cost estimate which cannot be exceeded by more than 10% without authorization, make replaced parts available for inspection, and guarantee its service work for 90 days or 4,000 miles, whichever occurs first, under normal operating conditions. Additionally, the garage must agree to cooperate fully with AAA as a third party arbitrator, in the investigation and resolution of any dispute involving the repair facility and an AAA member.

Caveat Emptor: *Auto Service and Repair Problems*

Some repair and service problems result from outright deception, but most result from unnecessary repairs and the incompetence of some mechanics. Below are some illustrations of deception, unnecessary repairs, and incompetent repairpersons.

Rip-Offs: Fill It Up. You drive into a gas station and tell the attendant to fill it up. The pump which was used to fill your car reads $23.80, but the attendant records $25.50 from another pump on your credit card charge slip. Stay at your car; watch the pump and the amount of gasoline being put in the tank.

Rip-Offs: Short Sticking. "Shall I check your oil?" The attendant lifts the hood, disappears from your line of sight, and comes up with a dipstick showing that "you need a quart of oil." Actually the attendant did not push the dipstick all the way down when checking the oil.

Rip-Offs: Pouring the Oil. When you need oil, you may not get it. The attendant may go into the station office, come back with a can showing the spout in place and appear to pour the oil into the engine; however, the can is empty.

Rip-Offs: Shock Treatment. You take your car in for lubrication and, while the car is on the rack, the mechanic shows you that your shock absorber is leaking oil. The attendant squirted oil on the shock while your back was turned to make you think that the seal was broken.

Rip-Offs: Unnecessary Repairs. Investigators for the Department of Transportation took five cars, each with one defective spark plug, to different repair shops. The investigators stated that the car was losing power and using too much gasoline. The actual required cost of replacing the defective spark plug averaged $13.63 per car or $68.17 on all five cars.

Mechanics, however, added an additional $426.91 of unnecessary repairs or an average of $85.38 per car. These repairs, shown in Illus. 8-2, included complete tune-ups, new ignition wiring, overhauled carburetor, and new gas filters.

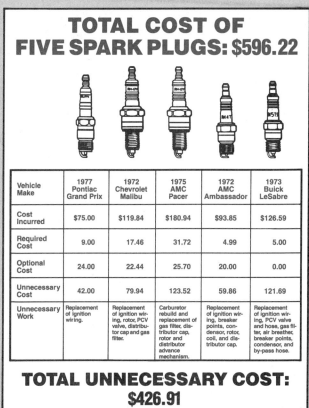

TOTAL COST OF FIVE SPARK PLUGS: $596.22

Vehicle Make	1977 Pontiac Grand Prix	1972 Chevrolet Malibu	1975 AMC Pacer	1972 AMC Ambassador	1973 Buick LeSabre
Cost Incurred	$75.00	$119.84	$180.94	$93.85	$126.59
Required Cost	9.00	17.46	31.72	4.99	5.00
Optional Cost	24.00	22.44	25.70	20.00	0.00
Unnecessary Cost	42.00	79.94	123.52	59.86	121.69
Unnecessary Work	Replacement of ignition wiring.	Replacement of ignition wiring, rotor, PCV valve, distributor cap and gas filter.	Carburetor rebuild and replacement of gas filter, distributor cap, rotor and distributor advance mechanism.	Replacement of ignition wiring, breaker points, condensor, rotor, coil, and distributor cap.	Replacement of ignition wiring, PCV valve and hose, gas filter, air breather, breaker points, condensor, and by-pass hose.

TOTAL UNNECESSARY COST: $426.91

Illus. 8-2

Cost of unnecessary repairs

Source: U. S. Department of Transportation (May 7, 1979).

In another example, you get into your car, turn the ignition, and your usually dependable automobile refuses to start. It is towed to the garage, and you sign a repair order authorizing work to begin. Before the day is out, your phone rings and you are told that the car's fuel and ignition systems have been checked and that new plugs and points have been installed. The car is running but the mechanic believes that one of the pistons is bad. You give permission to pull the head. In reality the problem was a cracked distributor cap, which could have been replaced relatively inexpensively.

Rip-Offs: Incompetence. Your alternator light stays on, and a local service station replaces your alternator. When you drive away, the red light is still on. The mechanic failed to check and recheck the work or to road test the car. The problem was merely a disconnected light wire.

Poorly trained and unqualified mechanics are a large part of the auto service problem. Automobile mechanics are not tested or licensed in this country and do not serve an apprenticeship (a training period) as they do in many other countries. Buyer Beware.

AUTOMOBILE INSURANCE

Not every state requires auto insurance, but all states do require drivers to prove financial responsibility at the time of an accident. *Financial responsibility* laws require drivers to pay (either through insurance or through personal savings) for damage to other persons or to the property of other persons up to the minimum amounts prescribed by law; these laws do not require drivers to protect themselves from financial losses. In states that do not have mandatory insurance, drivers must post a bond or put up thousands of dollars as proof of financial responsibility. Failure to show financial responsibility at the time of an accident may result in a suspended or taken away driver's license.

Most people, however, use auto insurance as their proof of financial responsibility. Six basic types of auto insurance coverage will be described in this section.

Bodily Injury Liability

This coverage will pay for the personal injuries you cause others when you are held responsible for an accident. *Bodily injury liability* coverage is protection against claims or lawsuits which are brought against you by pedestrians, riders in your car, and persons in other cars. If you are found liable (responsible) for an accident, your insurance company will pay for your legal defense and for damages up to the amount stated in the policy.

Bodily injury liability coverage is typically purchased in amounts ranging from $10,000 to $300,000. The amount purchased is usually expressed as two-figure maximums, such as 50/100. The first amount ($50,000) is the maximum that the insurance company will pay for a claim made by one person. The second amount ($100,000) is the maximum the insurance company will pay for all claims from one accident. If claims for injury are in excess of these maximum amounts, the driver at fault is financially responsible for the difference.

Property Damage Liability

Coverage for *property damage liability* will pay for the damage done to another person's property up to the amount stated in the policy. For example, the property may be another person's car, a light post, a building, or a fence. Both property damage and bodily injury liability coverage apply when your car is driven by members of your immediate family and others to whom you give permission. Property damage insurance is usually sold in amounts ranging from $5,000 to $25,000. When property damage liability and bodily injury coverage are purchased, the policy protection may be expressed in three figures: 100/300/25. In this case the insurance company will pay bodily injury claims up to $100,000 for one person, $300,000 for one accident, and $25,000 for property damage.

Medical Payments

Coverage for *medical payments* will pay for the medical costs resulting from an auto accident whether or not you are at fault. Coverage applies to you and the members of your family who are riding in your car or in the car of another person. Medical payment coverage also applies to you if you are driving another car with the permission of the owner. This coverage is designed to cover medical expenses — usually hospital and surgical costs and x-rays — incurred during the year following the accident.

Collision

Coverage for *collision* will pay for the damage to your car if it hits another vehicle, is hit while stationary or moving, or turns over. Older cars which have depreciated to a low price value generally do not need collision insurance. Collision insurance is expensive coverage. If your car is not too valuable, collision may not be worth the cost.

Insurance is a fixed cost of owning an automobile.

Collision coverage is typically sold with a $100 to $250 *deductible clause*. If damage occurs, the deductible is the amount you absorb. The company pays for any amount of damage in excess of the deductible. One way to decrease the cost of collision insurance is to increase the deductible. The higher the deductible, the less the cost of the insurance; the lower the deductible, the greater the cost.

Comprehensive Physical Damage

Coverage for *comprehensive physical damage* pays for damages which result from a fire, falling object, theft, windstorm, flood, earthquake, mischief, flying object, and vandalism. Comprehensive physical damage coverage is usually sold with a deductible.

Uninsured Motorist Protection

Coverage for *uninsured motorist protection* pays for your personal expenses in an accident with a hit-and-run driver or a person at fault but without bodily injury insurance coverage. The cost of uninsured motorist insurance is low, but often it is difficult to collect when claims are made against your insurance company. Uninsured motorist insurance usually applies only to bodily injury claims. For this kind of coverage, it is especially important to keep track of evidence to show that someone else caused the accident.

No-Fault (First-Party) Auto Insurance

For many years, insurance experts and auto insurance consumers have recognized problems with the traditional system of automobile insurance. Under this system auto accident victims have relied upon liability insurance (bodily injury and property damage) for the recovery of losses caused by another driver. The fault system which requires you to sue for losses frequently results in lengthy court proceedings. In addition many accident victims receive very little compensation for losses after lawyer fees have been paid. According to investigations conducted in 1978, the current "fault system" wastes money, with 44¢ of every premium going to pay legal fees rather than to help accident victims. A study done by the Department of Transportation points out that the average waiting period for a court case to be heard is 16 months, and that 45 percent of badly injured accident victims in this study received no money from automobile insurance companies.

In order to correct problems associated with liability insurance, no-fault insurance laws have been passed in more than 24 states. This is also called "first-party" coverage. In states with no-fault coverage, a police officer will still issue a ticket to the party at fault in an accident. However, accident victims do not have to prove in court who was at fault in order to collect for their injuries and financial losses. No-fault insurance allows financial losses, such as medical and hospital bills and loss of income, to be paid by the insured's own company, regardless of who is at fault. With no-fault coverage, claims are paid more quickly—usually within 30 days. Medical bills are paid in full and a substantial part of an injured person's loss of wages is paid automatically.

No-fault laws vary from state to state, but most states continue to allow lawsuits under conditions of severe negligence and large financial losses, as in cases of death, serious and permanent disfigurement or serious impairment of a bodily function. In some of the states that have adopted no-fault laws, the cost of insurance has been reduced.

BUYING AUTO INSURANCE

The cost of auto insurance is affected by many factors. Such factors may include where you live, how old you are, your sex, whether you are married, how much you use the car, what kind of driving record you have, and what kind of car you drive. Some companies give discounts for certain types of cars. Some cars cost less to insure because experience has shown that they are damaged less or are less expensive to fix after being in an accident.

Reducing the Cost

The amount which you pay for auto insurance is called the *premium*. Below are some steps you can take to reduce the cost of auto insurance premiums.

1. Do everything to avoid an accident. Drivers with safe-driving records are given the preferred or best rates.
2. Pay premiums in full when you are billed every year or six months. It costs more to pay for insurance through monthly installments.
3. Use a large deductible for collision and comprehensive physical damage coverage. The larger the deductible, the lower the premium.
4. Ask for a discount. Discounts are sometimes given for some of the following reasons: a grade average of B or better (good student discount), completion of an accredited

driver-training course, passive restraint systems (automatic seat belts), anti-theft devices, and nonsmoker and/or nondrinker.

5. As stated earlier, some companies give discounts for some types of cars based on expected repair costs. Check with your insurance agent to find out whether the company charges extra or gives a discount for the car you want to buy.

6. Discounts are given by most companies when more than one car is insured with the same company. For the young driver, the best way to get insurance is through a multi-car family policy. Multi-car family coverage can reduce the cost of a second car by as much as 10 percent.

Selecting the Company

Auto insurance rates differ from company to company so it is essential to shop around and compare rates. One study found that for a St. Louis couple with an 18-year-old son and one car, premiums ranged from $405 to $2,086. Of course, it is not possible to contact every auto insurance company, but it is essential to compare a few companies. The cost of your insurance will depend greatly on your choice.

The auto insurance buyer can learn about insurance companies by looking up the financial strength and stability of the companies in *Best's Insurance Reports*, an annual publication which is available in most public libraries. Best's reports management and investment practices and offers information on the claims-paying record of companies.

It is also recommended that the insurance consumer obtain information from the State Commissioner of Insurance. The insurance industry in each state is regulated by a Department of Insurance which approves rates charged for various types of policies and often publishes valuable information on rates and policies.

VOCABULARY REVIEW

Fixed costs	Variable costs
Depreciation	Financial responsibility law

Bodily injury liability
insurance

Property damage liability insurance

Collision insurance

Deductible clause

No-fault insurance

Premium

QUESTIONS FOR REVIEW

1. Approximately how much does a new car depreciate by the end of two years?

2. Name five ways a consumer can reduce the cost of owning and operating a car.

3. What is considered the primary problem related to owning a car?

4. What are some ways to reduce the problems related to auto repair?

5. What are two types of certification for auto mechanics and garage repair facilities?

6. What is the meaning of insurance coverage when stated as 100/300/25?

7. Who is covered by medical payments insurance?

8. What is the major difference between a fault and a no-fault auto insurance system?

PROBLEM-SOLVING AND DECISION-MAKING PROJECTS

1. Tomoko Akita lives at home and drives daily to the local community college. She kept the following record of gas purchases and mileage driven for a two-week period. (a) Determine the miles per gallon for her car and (b) determine the cost per mile for this two-week period.

Tank filled . . . . odometer reading: 36,042
Bought gas . . . . . . 18 gallons . . . . cost $32.40 36,438
Bought gas . . . . . . 14 gallons . . . . cost $25.62 36,739

Total: 32 gallons . . . . . . cost $58.02.

2. Paul Green kept a record of all auto expenses for one full year. Paul owns an older model, standard-size car and drives approximately 40 miles each day to and from work. He drove approximately 9,600 miles to and from work and approximately 5,400 miles for personal/family driving. He summarized his owning and operating costs as follows:

Fixed-owning cost . . . . $ 771
Variable-operating cost $2,480

Using these summary figures, determine the cost per mile for the 15,000 miles driven during the year. Paul is contemplating ways to cut down on the cost of operating the car. Make three suggestions on ways to cut the operating cost of the family auto. The family car is four years old. Would you recommend the purchase of a new, but smaller size car as a way to reduce costs? Explain.

3. What kinds of insurance coverage would be needed for each situation below?
   a. As required by the financial responsibility laws of his state, Martin Jacobs had 10/20/10 liability insurance coverage on his car. During a rainstorm one evening, Martin ran into the rear end of a car owned by Jill McAlpin. The accident was clearly Martin's fault. As a result of this accident, Martin was in the hospital for two days. Jill was treated at the hospital and released. Both cars were badly damaged. What type of insurance coverage protection would Martin need? Describe the coverage Martin would need to cover all the expenses which would result from the accident.
   b. Manuel Ramos parked his car at the airport while he returned home during a school vacation. When he came back, he discovered that his hubcaps and tape deck had been stolen. In addition a window was broken. What type of insurance coverage would Manuel need to replace his losses from theft?

COMMUNITY AND HOME PROJECTS

1. Keep a record of gasoline purchases and mileage driven for a two-week period. Use a chart similar to the information on page 130. Remember that you must obtain the odometer reading when the tank is full. Calculate the number of miles per gallon for your own car or the family car and the cost per mile for gasoline.

2. With the cooperation of your teacher, survey your community to determine the number and location of auto repair garages which have certified mechanics or AAA approved facilities and procedures. Write a report on your findings.

3. With the permission of your parents, determine the type of auto insurance coverage on the family car, the cost of insurance, and the amount of deductibles. Write a report on your findings.

Chapter 9

Housing

Apt. for Rent. Two bedroom, fully carpeted, close to public transportation. $1,050 per month, plus utilities. No pets, laundry facilities available, references required.

A misprint? No. As expensive as this apartment may appear, it could be typical of apartment rental ads appearing in local newspapers well before the end of this century. In fact the rental price of $1,050 assumes only a yearly inflation rate of 6 percent. With rising prices and energy costs, finding shelter at a reasonable price has become a serious problem for many consumers. In this chapter we will examine different types of shelter, discuss the advantages and disadvantages of renting and buying shelter, and present some of the legal and financial aspects of renting and owning a place to live.

HOUSING DECISIONS

Eventually you will be faced with the need to provide yourself with a roof over your head. Deciding on a place to live can be an exciting yet sometimes perplexing experience. When choosing a place to live, you must consider your life-stage, your preferences, the location desired, and the amount of money you have available for shelter.

Stage in Life

Your stage in life (see page 220 for further discussion) plays a large part in your housing needs. Single persons, the elderly, young married couples, and childless couples obviously have housing needs that are different from the needs of families with children. A family's need for housing is not the same when children are small as it is when the children are grown.

Families with children have housing needs different from those of people in other stages of life.

Source: Abbott Laboratories.

Preferences

When deciding about housing, think about what kind of life you now live and intend to live in the future. Then relate your preferences to your housing needs. People like different housing styles. Some need space for hobbies, games, and indoor recreation. Some like to entertain friends at home. Others prefer a quiet, peaceful home life free from noise and visitors. Preferences may also include having a pet or having use of a swimming pool. These are all important considerations for people when they choose a place to live.

Location

Many experts believe that location should be a top priority when you define your housing needs. You must ask yourself whether you want to be close to work or school, near friends and family, what kind of community you want to live in, and what kind of social and recreational opportunities you want. Some people want to be close to a place of worship, theaters, a library, or a shopping center.

Location will determine your transportation needs. Therefore, the type of transportation available (railroads, buses, taxis, subways, expressways) is a serious part of selecting shelter. Transportation is closely related to housing costs since approximately half of this expense is incurred in getting to and from work or shopping.

Price

How much can you afford to pay for housing? Most likely this factor will determine whether you rent or buy. Housing represents the major item in almost everybody's budget. Costs for housing include not only rent, but also related expenses such as furniture, utilities, and insurance. Your monthly housing cost generally will take one fourth to one third of your monthly take-home pay. Obviously the amount of money you spend on meeting housing costs will affect how much or how little you have left for food, clothes, school, recreation, and savings.

HOUSING ALTERNATIVES

Once consumers weigh their needs, it is time to look at housing alternatives. In the housing market, there are many alternatives from which consumers may choose.

Stay with Parents

One alternative for a young person is to stay at home with parents while going to college and even after starting to work. Because of the rising costs of education and housing, staying at home is becoming acceptable for more young people. Usually it is good to work out with parents agreements about sharing expenses and household responsibilities.

Single Room

The single room, sometimes called a sleeping room, is often in a home or hotel. Some rooms may have kitchen and laundry facilities. Rent is paid weekly or monthly, and the room usually comes furnished.

Dormitory

For many young people, the first place away from home will be a college or university dormitory. Most dormitories are double occupancy sleeping rooms with a study area and closets. Eating facilities may or may not be available. The cost of a dormitory is based on a semester or school term, but it is generally less expensive than other private types of housing.

Apartments

The apartment is the most popular type of housing for young singles, unmarried adults, recently married or childless adults, and elderly persons. Apartments come in a great many styles and sizes. The studio, also called an *efficiency,* is the least expensive type of apartment. It is usually one main room which serves as a kitchen, living room, and bedroom. Larger apartments and luxury apartments cost more because of the increased size of the unit.

Apartments usually require the least amount of responsibility because someone else takes care of the heating, yardwork, and repairs. Some or all of the utilities are included in the monthly rent payment. Apartments are ordinarily in multiple-unit dwellings where the number of units may range from 2 to 200 or more. Most apartments are unfurnished, but some are available with furniture. They seldom have any private yard space, but other conveniences such as parking space and coin-operated washing machines are generally provided.

Condominiums

A condominium may be an apartment in a multiple-unit building, or a semi-detached living unit with common areas. *Condominium* means individual ownership of one unit or space intended for living and joint ownership with the other unit owners of the facilities and common areas (yards, pool facilities, patios, hallways, etc.). All of the unit owners make up the owners' association which is responsible for management of the building, grounds, and common areas. The purchase of a condominium means that the buyer automatically shares in the administration of the building and property. The condominium owner pays a monthly fee to cover the costs of operating and maintaining all of the common elements.

A condominium is an apartment that is owned—not rented.

Townhouses

The distinction between a townhouse, sometimes called a row-house, and a condominium is not clear. *Townhouses* are really houses put side by side with no yard space between them. This arrangement saves on land usage and reduces the cost of the dwelling. Some townhouses are built in a row, but today many are built as fourplexes (four units) and sixplexes (six units). Some townhouses can be purchased in the conventional manner; that is, you buy the unit, the land upon which it stands, a patch of lawn in front, and a patio in the rear. Other townhouses are being sold as condominiums. Under such an arrangement, you own only the interior space while the grounds belong jointly to you and your neighbors. The condominium townhouse is managed and maintained through a homeowners' association.

Cooperatives

A *cooperative* is similar to any other multiple-unit apartment, but legally it is different from other forms of ownership. A cooperative requires the purchase of stock in the corporation or company that owns the multi-unit building. (See Chapter 14 on Saving and

Investing, page 254). The corporation owns the apartment, but because buyers own the corporation, they are entitled to live in the apartments. The building is owned by all the residents and is operated by an elected board of directors.

Instead of paying rent, the members pay a monthly fee based on their share of the cost of maintenance, property taxes, and mortgage on the building. The board of directors of the corporation sets the policies of the cooperative. Members of a cooperative select who is allowed to buy into the property. If members of the coop fail to make their monthly payments, those payments are assessed to the other members. Cooperatives are usually more common in large metropolitan areas than in suburban or rural areas.

Mobile Homes

A *mobile home* is a vehicular, portable structure built on a chassis and designed to be used without a permanent foundation as a year-round dwelling. In other words, a mobile home is a roof with wheels. According to the Bureau of the Census, mobile homes have grown in popularity in recent years and now account for more than half of all new housing sold in the United States to people with annual incomes of $15,000 or less.

Today nearly 10 million people live in mobile homes. More than half of the buyers of mobile homes are young couples. Mobile homes are about the only new housing which can be purchased for under $25,000. The price includes wall-to-wall carpeting, draperies, furniture, and kitchen appliances. In most cases the purchaser of a mobile home does not buy land but rents a space in a mobile home park. Mobile home parks in some areas have become like resorts with pools and recreational facilities.

Detached House

The *detached house*, commonly called the *single-family home*, is the American dream. According to the U.S. Census Bureau, 62.9 percent of families in the United States live in houses they own. Most of these houses are traditional single-family dwellings set off on a plot of land. Houses are often given style names such as colonial, ranch, Tudor, and Williamsburg, but basically houses are either single story, split level, or two story. Homes are also classified as existing or new. New homes usually have many of the most recent features and designs. The Department of Commerce reports that the average typical new home at the beginning of this decade cost $77,500.

Public Housing

Housing which is built with federal, state, or local money is called *public housing*. Public-housing apartments and single-family dwellings are rented to families or persons who have low incomes. Rent is usually set according to the amount of income the renter earns.

RENTING YOUR SHELTER

If you are like most people, the first place of your own will be an apartment. Approximately two out of every five families rent the places they live in. Not everyone wants to or can afford to own a home.

Some of the advantages to renting are:

—You know exactly how much you must spend each month.
—You are not tied down to one spot.
—Maintenance is not your responsibility.
—There is little or no risk involved.
—You can get to know the community well enough to know if you want to remain there.

Perhaps the main advantage to renting is that over the short run, renting usually costs less than buying. Renters have an opportunity to save the difference between the cost of renting and the cost of owning when the monthly cost of renting is less than the cost of owning a home. If renters can save this difference, then they can build up capital and reduce the investment advantage of buying.

Sharing

Probably one of the initial housing decisions you will make is whether or not to share an apartment with a friend. This is a way to

People who are on their own for the first time usually live in an apartment.

cut the cost of renting in half. Sharing can be to your advantage if the proper procedures are followed. If not, it can end a friendship in a hurry.

Remember the following when you are ready to consider a roommate:

—Discuss living habits such as hours for listening to music or watching TV, responsibilities for washing dishes, making beds, etc.

—Discuss independence versus companionship. Some people want a roommate only to cut costs and wish to live independently of the roommate. Others want a roommate for friendship and companionship.

—Determine the means of dividing the rent, utility bills, food costs, and furniture expenses. Decide in advance who will contribute furniture and what has to be bought. Put your agreement in writing.

—Agree in advance and in writing about how the security deposit will be paid. (See page 159 for explanation of a security deposit.)

—Agree in advance about your plans for how many and how often guests may stay overnight.

—Agree in advance about how moving out will be determined. Each roommate should agree on giving an appropriate notice and agree on the means of settling the cost of any damage done to the house or apartment.

—Look together for the apartment. In this way the roommates can mutually determine if the rental is in a convenient location, has sufficient space, and is a satisfactory choice.

Shopping for Shelter

Finding a suitable place to rent can be a tedious and time-consuming activity. Regardless of what type of rental housing you are seeking, you will need to shop around. Don't rent in haste or try to rent the first vacancy you see. Look at models of the type of unit you want, and ask to see the exact unit you might occupy. Below are some suggestions for finding a place of your own.

Friends. Ask your friends if they know of any available places to rent. If they are currently renting, they can easily inform you of the problems of renting or of the procedures to follow. Friends are often a good source of information.

Newspapers. Newspaper classified apartment listings will give you an idea of the rents being charged for various types and sizes of apartments in various locations. An example of such a listing is shown in Illus. 9-1.

Real Estate Agencies. Owners often list available rental units with a local real estate broker. By calling brokers, you can get some leads on available units. Avoid apartment finders. Apartment finding businesses are often operated by persons who do not have a real estate broker's license. They sometimes charge for lists that can be obtained from the daily newspaper.

Apartment Management. If you know of an apartment in a building where you think you might like to live, go there and talk with the management. Be sure to ask these questions:

—What is the amount of rent, when is it due, and to whom is it paid?

—Who pays utilities (gas, water, heat, and electricity)?

—Are additional charges likely to occur?

—Is a regular janitor on duty? If so, what are the janitor's duties?

—Who should the tenant contact for maintenance and repair? (Get in writing an address and telephone number where the owner can be contacted while you are living in this property.)

—Is a 24-hour phone number designated to reach the apartment house management in case of an emergency?

HYDE PARK/Oakley — Edwards Rd. 1 bdrm, free heat. 984-1279

HYDE PARK/OAKLEY — Efficiency. Equipt., carpet, heat, air, parking. $175. 321-6845

HYDE PARK — Oakley. Carpeted, equipt, 1 bdrm, adults. $225. 931-3446

HYDE PARK/PAXTON — 1 bedroom, equipt, heat, garage, adults. $240. 561-6789

HYDE PARK — Spacious 1 bdrm, equipt, heat, air, garage, security locked bldg, no pets, mature adults. $350. 321-9012

●HYDE PARK — 1 bdrm., 2½ rms. ●Small kitchenette. $220. 871-0123

HYDE PARK — 1 bdrm. or studio, utilities included, $200-$225. mo. 281-6607 or 541-5322

HYDE PARK
★ 1 bdrms, equipt kitchen.
★ Wall-to-wall carpeting.
★ Spacious closets.
From $235-$245   791-0055

KENWOOD — Deluxe 1 bdrm, carpeted, equipt, laundry on floors, nr. shopping & I-71. Adult, 984-6619

LEBANON — Bellflower Apts. Furnished 1 bedroom & unfurnished 1 bedroom, Flexible lease 1-932-6395

LEBANON — Elegant 1 bdrm apt in restored 1840 brick building. 22'x17' carpeted bdrm, high ceilings, hardwood floors, 1st floor, $285 mo. All utilities pd except heat. 1-932-6794

LIBERTY HILL — Spacious 1 bdrm, equipt kitchen, fireplace, carpet. Dep. 381-5498 day, 241-5771 eve.

MADISONVILLE S — 1 bdrm, equipt, garage. Pay all utilities, dep required. $200. 871-9179

MADISONVILLE — Efficiency. 1 & 2 bdrm. Carpet, air, equipt, heat furnished. 272-5601

MARIEMONT — Efficiency, equipt, all utilities. $120. 271-9990

MARIEMONT NR — 1 bdrm, equipt kitchen, carpet, 271-7200

MASON - 1 bdrm, adults, equipt kitchen, heat/water furnished. $215 mo. 398-1076

MILFORD AREA — On Rt. 28, newly completed 1 bdrm, full carpeting, modern kitchen, resident mgr, $210. 575-7272

Illus. 9-1

Newspaper advertisements for apartments

Inspecting the Apartment

Inspect the apartment thoroughly. Look inside closets, look under the sink, inspect basement areas, flush the toilet, and test the shower. Is the cabinet space sufficient, and is the refrigerator large enough? Is the number of electrical outlets sufficient to avoid over-loading? Will the size and shape of the rooms accommodate your furniture? Are locks and security systems adequate? Are storage facilities, laundry facilities, and parking areas available?

As you inspect the apartment, make a written list of damages previously done to the dwelling unit. Ask the owner to repair them prior to your signing a rental agreement or to list them on the lease agreement if you plan to rent in spite of them. A written list of damages will assist you in settling claims for any damage done to the apartment at the time you want to have your security deposit refunded.

When you are really interested in an apartment, try to speak with other tenants in the building. Ask them such questions as:

—Is routine maintenance adequate and prompt?
—Are complaints responded to quickly and is the owner accessible?
—Is the building unusually noisy?
—Have rent increases been excessive?
—Does the building have a high turnover of tenants?

Reading the Lease

When you find an apartment, you probably will be asked to sign a *lease* or a rental agreement. The rental agreement is a contract that spells out your rights and responsibilities and those of the owner. Be certain you read all of the clauses. Even more important, be sure you understand them. The following is an interpretation of some standard lease clauses.

Term of Lease. *This clause sets the length of your lease.* It protects you from rent increases during the length of the lease and from eviction without proper cause. Most leases are for 12 months. For a shorter period, informal written agreements are sometimes used which allow month-to-month rental. Shorter leases allow owners more opportunity to change rent prices.

Rent. *You agree to pay this amount on time.* In exchange for the prompt payment of the rent, you are given possession of the dwelling. If you fail to meet the payment as stated in the rental agreement, the owner may terminate the rental agreement or evict you. In some states when the rent is not paid, eviction is possible only after a written notice of nonpayment and notice of intention to end the lease or rental agreement is given to the tenant by the owner.

Security Deposit. *The owner keeps this amount of money in the event you damage the apartment.* The security deposit will be required in addition to the first month's rent. Before you sign the lease, determine if this deposit covers the last month's rent, or if it is to be used strictly for any damages done to the apartment. Also find out when it will be returned. The money should be kept only if you leave the apartment in worse condition than you found it. The owner should keep only enough to put the apartment in the same condition as when you moved in.

Condition of Premises. *You agree that the premises are fine as they are.* This means that you accept the property as it is, and that unless the owner has agreed in writing to make some changes, you cannot force the owner to make any desired changes. Do not rely on any oral promises about changes or repairs. Remember that a verbal agreement is not legal unless the agreement is also written on the lease.

Repair. *You agree not to damage the property of the owner.* If damage does occur, you can be charged for it. The amount can legally be taken from the security or damage deposit.

Limitation of Liability. *You agree that the owner is not liable if you are injured or if your property is damaged.* This clause attempts to relieve the owner of responsibility for damages or injuries to persons or property, even if the damages are due to the owner's neglect. Most state laws declare that such clauses which attempt to limit liability from negligence are void and unenforceable.

Use; Sublet Assignment. *You agree that no pets or other persons will live with you.* This clause establishes the appropriate use of the apartment. It prohibits all animals; it prevents you from operating a business out of the apartment, and it prohibits you from collecting rent from someone who uses your apartment while you are away. This clause also prohibits you from having other persons live with you unless they are a party to the contract. The restriction does not mean you cannot have overnight guests, but it does mean that you do not have control over who lives in your apartment. This clause also states clearly that any additions, improvements, or alterations you make to the apartment become the property of the owner.

Right to Relet. *You agree to pay the full term of the lease even if you leave.* If you leave before the lease expires, the owner will use the security deposit to cover the loss in rent. You are responsible for paying the rent for the rest of the lease period if the security deposit does not cover it. This clause, however, is difficult to enforce except for the amount of the security deposit.

Holding Over. *You agree to double your rent if you stay beyond the end of the lease.* Most owners expect 30 to 60 days' notice when tenants plan to leave, and most issue new leases at least 30 days prior to the renewal of the lease. The owner is permitted one of three alternatives if you stay beyond the lease expiration: (1) automatic lease renewal at double the previous rental rate, (2) month-to-month tenancy at double the rental rate, (3) a per-day rate which should be specified.

Access. *You give the owner permission to enter your apartment.* The owner has the right to enter your apartment unannounced and uninvited. In practice this should be restricted to normal business hours, and some notice should be given the tenant unless there is an emergency.

Compliance. *You agree to obey the law regulating animals, sanitation, and noise.* You should know the local ordinances regarding such matters as sanitation, noise, and animals. You should also know what the housing codes require of the owner. Local ordinances usually set standards of quality for housing in the community. The tenant should know the city ordinances regarding such matters as safe and sufficient heating, garbage bins, lighting in public halls, sanitation standards, and working bathrooms and kitchen facilities.

Default. *You agree that if you miss your rent payments the owner has a right to your personal property.* In most states it is illegal to throw out or lock out a tenant from the apartment except by court order. Possessions cannot be taken without a similar court order. It is important to know your local ordinances and state laws because the matter of default varies from area to area.

Confession. *You agree that you are guilty.* Any lawyer may appear in court without your knowledge or presence and say that you have broken some clause of the lease. Confession of judgment clauses have been ruled illegal in some states, but not in all. You do have the right to appeal although almost all leases claim you do not have such a right.

Payment of Costs. *You agree to pay the owner's fees for an attorney.* You pledge to pay the owner's legal costs in seizing your property or evicting you.

Plurals; Successors. *If you have a roommate, both of you share responsibility.* Any lease signed by more than one tenant creates a situation in which each person is responsible for all terms in the lease. It pays to pick your roommates carefully.

Consumer Redress — Tenant Rights

There are no national laws regarding the rights of renters or tenants except for civil rights laws. Each state has its own laws on housing. Some progress for tenants has been made since 1972 when the National Conference of Commissioners on Uniform State Laws introduced the Uniform Residential Landlord and Tenant Code. This is a model code which establishes obligations and rights for both tenants and owners. Nearly half of the states have adopted landlord-tenant laws that are similar to the Uniform Residential Landlord and Tenant Code. Among its provisions are:

—Security deposits must be returned within 14 days after the tenant moves. Any deduction from the security deposit must be listed in writing.
—When an owner fails to live up to the terms of the rental agreement, the tenant can recover actual damages. Some states and large cities provide for a mechanism, usually a lower court, through which disputes can be resolved.
—When the cost of repairs is less than a specified amount, usually $100 or one-half the monthly rent, whichever is greater, the tenant may make repairs and deduct the repair

expense from the rent. This procedure, called "repair and deduct," is subject to state and local regulations. You should give reasonable notice to the owner and an opportunity for the owner to complete the repairs before you exercise "repair and deduct." The "repair and deduct" procedure is an excellent remedy for tenants if the legal restrictions are followed.

—An owner cannot raise the rent, decrease services, or evict a tenant for filing a lawsuit or complaint with a government agency or participating in a tenant's group.

The basic right of all tenants is a concept called an *implied warranty of habitability*. This warranty means that when owners rent property, they are saying that the dwelling is suitable for human habitation. Thirty states have adopted the warranty of habitability into their housing laws. These laws require that the owner's right to receive rent is related to an obligation to provide a rental dwelling that is habitable. If it is not habitable, in many cases the tenant can pay rent to the clerk of courts rather than to the owner. Habitability standards are usually established through local housing codes. A housing code is a certified list of building regulations pertaining to safe and healthy living standards that all rental dwellings are required to meet. Tenants should check with the local authorities at city hall, the municipal building, or courthouse to determine if a habitability law exists.

THE ADVANTAGES OF HOME OWNERSHIP

You are likely to have to decide between renting or buying at some time in your future. For most people, home ownership is the largest and most important purchase made in a lifetime. Below is a look at the major advantages of home ownership.

Gives a Feeling of Security and Independence

Most Americans choose to buy homes for such noneconomic reasons as the desire to have pets or the space to plant a garden or the freedom to make home improvements. Owning a home often gives people a feeling of independence and family security.

Helps Build Equity

Home ownership usually costs more than renting; but, in the long run, buying a home builds up equity. *Equity* is the difference between what your home is worth and what you owe on the home. When a home is paid in full, the homeowner has a 100 percent equity in the property. Monthly home payments decrease the debt and increase the amount of equity in the property.

Many homeowners take pride in doing their own home improvements.

Source: Courtesy of Evans Products Company—Portland, Oregon.

Serves as a Good Investment

Home ownership has been a particularly good investment in recent years. Throughout the last decade, many Americans found that a house was their best investment. Because of the increase in property values, many people have been able to experience a large *capital gain* (increase in the value of property) when selling their homes. Owning a home or other shelter is a good investment because homes usually increase in value. The amount of increase in the value of property is known as *appreciation*.

Offers Tax Benefits

When you buy a house or other shelter, you may benefit by being able to deduct certain costs of ownership when you file your income tax return. Mortgage interest and property taxes can reduce the amount of income taxes a homeowner pays because such amounts are deductible items on federal and state tax returns. The effect of such benefits is to lower the cost of home ownership. Renters do not have similar benefits.

Another tax benefit from home ownership occurs when the house is sold. Profit on the sale of a house is not taxed at all if it is reinvested in another home within 24 months. Even if the gain is not reinvested, it is usually regarded as a capital gain and only 40 percent of the amount is taxed.

THE COST OF OWNING YOUR HOME

With the average sale price for new homes over $75,000, the homeowner is becoming an "endangered species." By the mid-1980s the average price of a new home in the United States will probably exceed $85,000 and before the turn of the century it could easily break $100,000. As a result, only one in four American families can afford an average house at today's housing costs.

Since 1970, house prices have consistently outpaced consumer incomes. For this reason, nearly two thirds of the families buying homes have two incomes. Six out of ten first-time buyers are families in which both husband and wife hold jobs.

Because of the high cost of new homes, first-time home buyers often face a variety of options. These options may include:

- —Buying a condominium as a first home.
- —Commuting longer distances in order to buy cheaper housing.
- —Living in smaller and older homes that may need repairs.
- —Borrowing money from parents.
- —Buying a manufactured home, generally called a mobile home or prefabricated home.
- —Accepting a more moderate life-style in order to pay for the shelter.

Determine How Much to Spend

A rule of thumb used in past years to determine how much money an individual or family could spend on housing was that the home buyer should look for shelter selling within 2½ times the buyer's annual income. For other expenses, such as taxes, insurance, and house maintenance, nearly two fifths of all of today's home buyers spend more than 25 percent of their incomes. One third of all home buyers spend more than 33⅓ percent of their incomes for these expenditures.

The Mortgage

A *mortgage* is a loan on which both principal (the amount loaned) and interest are paid back over a fixed number of years, usually 20 to 30 years. A mortgage contract is signed between a lender and a borrower for the purpose of buying property. Usually the amount of the monthly mortgage payment is based upon the amount of the loan, the interest rate, and the length of the loan. Some lenders may include the cost of taxes and insurance in a mortgage payment. Many home buyers never realize that at the end of the 25 or 30 years a mortgaged home can cost two or three times as much as the purchase price of the home. The alternative — saving until one can pay cash for a house — would prevent most Americans from ever being able to buy a home.

Down Payment

You will usually need to make a *down payment* (pay part of the purchase price) when you buy shelter. A down payment can range from nothing to 5, 10, 20, or 30 percent or more of the purchase price of a home. The higher your original down payment, the lower your monthly mortgage expenses will be. For example, a $75,000 house with a 25-year mortgage at 14 percent interest and a $7,500 down payment (10 percent) results in $812.70 as a monthly mortgage payment. With a $15,000 down payment (20 percent), there is a $722.40 monthly mortgage payment. These examples exclude taxes and insurance.

Closing Costs

In addition to the down payment and the monthly mortgage payments, the home buyer should have enough cash available for the closing costs which occur at the time the sale is completed. *Closing costs* are the charges and fees associated with the transfer of ownership of a home to a new buyer. These costs are incurred by the buyer for the work involved in preparing and processing all of the documents needed to complete the purchase of the home.

So that the buyer can anticipate these closing expenses, Congress passed the Real Estate Settlement Procedures Act of 1974, thereby regulating closing and settlement procedures. The buyer should receive a home buyer's guide to settlement costs and a good faith estimate or disclosure statement prior to closing. Under the provisions of the act, the borrower has the right to review the settlement statement at least one business day before closing.

HOMEOWNERS AND RENTERS INSURANCE

It is essential to get protection for your property with homeowners or renters insurance. Below and in Illus. 9-2 are some kinds of protection you can get in a typical homeowners or renters insurance package.

For homeowners only:

- —Damage to your home from fire and lightning, theft, windstorm, hail, explosion, riot, vandalism, smoke, broken glass, crashing airplanes, motor vehicles, building collapse, excessive electrical current, frozen pipes, falling objects, roof cave-in caused by ice and snow, and some types of water damage.

For both homeowners and renters:

- —Damage to your personal possessions caused by any of the perils or risks listed above.
- —Lawsuits by persons injured on your property (you will be defended even if you are not at fault).
- —Temporary additional living expenses when you cannot live in your home or apartment because of damage.

Some coverages provided by homeowners insurance

❶Fire   ❸Water damage   ❺Additional living expenses   ❼Property-damage liability (if owner negligent)
❷Theft   ❹Storm damage   ❻Bodily-injury liability   ❽No-fault medical payments

Illus. 9-2

Some kinds of insurance protection

—Medical payments for people who receive minor injuries at your home.

You should examine the policy carefully to determine the specific coverages shown in Illus. 9-3. The homeowner or renter should not rely totally on the name of the policy. An "all-risk" (comprehensive) policy sounds like it would provide protection against every possible risk, but it doesn't. All-risk policies usually provide protection against most possible risks. It is important to know what your insurance covers. Even a comprehensive policy does not cover floods or earthquakes.

Basic (HO-1)	Broad (HO-2)	Comprehensive (HO-5)	Perils against which properties are insured
■	■	■	1. fire or lightning
■	■	■	2. loss of property removed from premises endangered by fire or other perils
■	■	■	3. windstorm or hail
■	■	■	4. explosion
■	■	■	5. riot or civil commotion
■	■	■	6. aircraft
■	■	■	7. vehicles
■	■	■	8. smoke
■	■	■	9. vandalism and malicious mischief
■	■	■	10. theft
■	■	■	11. breakage of glass constituting a part of the building (not included in HO-4)
	■	■	12. falling objects
	■	■	13. weight of ice, snow, sleet
	■	■	14. collapse of building(s) or any part thereof
	■	■	15. sudden and accidental tearing asunder, cracking, burning, or bulging of a steam or hot water heating system or of appliances for heating water
	■	■	16. accidental discharge, leakage or overflow of water or steam from within a plumbing, heating or air-conditioning system or domestic appliance
	■	■	17. freezing of plumbing, heating and air-conditioning systems and domestic appliances
	■	■	18. sudden and accidental injury from artificially generated currents to electrical appliances, devices, fixtures and wiring (TV and radio tubes not included)
		■	All perils except flood, earthquake, war, nuclear accident and others specified in your policy. Check your policy for a complete listing of perils excluded.

Illus. 9-3

Kinds of coverage offered by different insurance policies

Source: Insurance Information Institute, "Insurance for the Home," 1979.

Caveat Emptor: *Mechanic's Lien*

You've closed the deal, signed the papers, bought a lawn mower, and moved into your new home. Two months later you receive a notice that a mechanic's lien was filed against the home because the builder did not pay all the construction bills. A *mechanic's lien* is a claim made against a homeowner for unpaid services, labor, or materials put into a home. Its purpose is to give security to those who perform or furnish material in the improvement of real estate. Your property could be sold to satisfy the lien. In this case the consumer's best protection against a mechanic's lien would be title insurance. Quite simply, with title insurance the home buyer is protected from claims made on the property. The *title insurance* will cover financial losses that the homeowner may incur as the result of a mechanic's lien or other claims on the property.

In real estate a *title* refers to the instrument or document by which a right of ownership is established (title documents), or it may refer to the ownership interest a person has in the property. Since other people and institutions can sometimes gain an interest or a right to the property, buyers should have a title search. A *title search* is an examination of public records to discover liens and court decisions against a particular piece of property. The title company searches the public records and makes property inspections to uncover anything that might affect the title. A *clear title* is one which has no liens or other claims against it. Buyer Beware.

VOCABULARY REVIEW

Efficiency apartment	Sublet
Condominium	Implied warranty of habitability
Cooperative	Mortgage
Lease	Closing costs
Security deposit	Mechanic's lien

QUESTIONS FOR REVIEW

1. What are four considerations in choosing a place to live?
2. What housing alternatives are available to most young consumers?

3. When sharing an apartment with another person, what are some steps you should take to assure a satisfactory arrangement?

4. Name three advantages of renting and three for owning a house or other form of shelter.

5. What are two provisions of the Uniform Residential Landlord and Tenant Code?

6. When buying a house or other shelter, how can the buyer be protected against any claims or liens on the property?

7. What are some perils or risks that both homeowners and renters need to insure themselves against?

PROBLEM-SOLVING AND DECISION-MAKING PROJECTS

1. Connie Gordon and Teresa Mendez wish to share an apartment after they graduate from high school. Connie expects to make $3.50 an hour at her 40 hour a week job, and Teresa has been offered a job as a beginning typist at $150 a week. Determine approximately how much they can spend for a two-bedroom apartment. Make a list of other matters they should discuss before sharing an apartment.

2. Arlene and Jim Dorsey want to buy a new house. A commonly used rule-of-thumb suggests that a home buyer should look for shelter selling within 2½ times a family's annual income. Their combined salary is $32,000, and they have nearly $10,000 saved for a down payment.
   a. Determine the approximate amount they can afford to spend on a house.
   b. Since they wish to finance the house, do they have sufficient money to pay a mortgage which requires a 20 percent down payment?
   c. What type of housing would you recommend in your area with the amount of income they have?

3. You plan to buy a home. Carefully analyze your needs and list the things you want in a home. Consider type of neighborhood, arrangement of lot and plan of the house, and construction features.

COMMUNITY AND HOME PROJECTS

1. Using the classified advertisements of your local newspaper, determine the current average monthly rental cost of a studio apartment, a one-bedroom, and a two-bedroom apartment in your area. Prepare a report about your findings.

2. With the permission and cooperation of your parents, determine the percentage of the family income which goes to pay the mortgage or rent, property taxes, insurance, and utilities. Prepare a report showing your calculations.

3. Interview three loan officers of local banks or savings and loan associations to determine:
   a. The current state of the real estate market
   b. The current interest rate on conventional loans
   c. Ways a buyer can finance a home with a small down payment
   Report your findings to the class if possible.

4. Interview at least two real estate agents to determine
   a. The commission policies of the firm for which the agent works
   b. The total range of services which the agent is prepared to offer you
   c. The listing options available — exclusive, multiple, or open listing
   Write a report on your findings.

5. As a committee of students and with the cooperation of your teacher, determine the local and state tenant ordinance for your area. Research whether your state tenancy laws provide the warranty of habitability. Find out the proper procedures for eviction notices and the housing codes (not building codes) for your area. If a tenant has a problem with inadequate heat or water, what means of redress are available? Find out which court in your area handles tenant/owner cases. Prepare a report entitled "What Every Tenant Should Know."

Chapter 10

Clothing

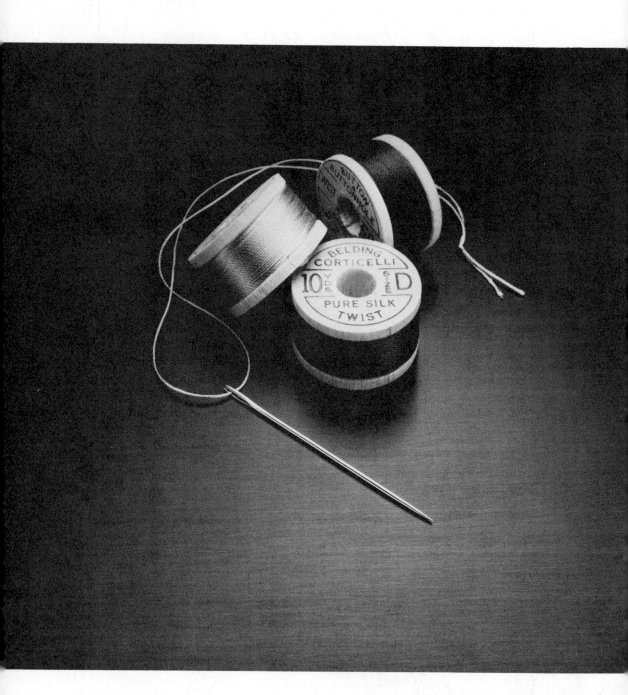

We usually take for granted that clothes are a necessity. Actually clothing serves three functions. It protects us from the weather, it helps us conform to laws governing standards of modesty, it makes us "look good" to ourselves and to others. The first two functions of clothing may need no explanation, but not everyone realizes the importance of clothing for the purpose of presenting ourselves. According to John T. Molloy, author of *Dress for Success*, it is possible through skillful dressing to evoke a favorable response to yourself in any particular situation. From his research, he concludes that "people who look successful and well educated receive preferential treatment in almost all of their social and business encounters." In one test Molloy explained to passers-by at a bus stop that he had lost his wallet and needed money to get home. He collected $7.23 when casually dressed, but $26.00 when he wore a tie. This shows that the way we dress does have an impact on the people we meet and does greatly affect how people treat us.

In this chapter we will present some steps for developing a well-balanced wardrobe, look at fibers, fabrics, and finishes, and discuss the laws that aid consumers.

FASHION AND FADS

The way people dress reflects current trends, membership in a particular social group, level of status in society, and/or local weather conditions. *Fashion* is the prevailing manner of dress accepted by the majority of a group at any given time. Acceptance by others is the key to fashion.

One aspect of modern-day fashion is the rapid change in style. *Style* is the special quality of a garment, such as the length of a skirt or the width of a lapel on a jacket, which makes it different from similar garments. Fads are a common occurrence in modern fashion, too. *Fads* are trends which last for a brief period of time. Some popular fads were unisex pendants for men, graffiti-print T-shirts, flares and bell-bottoms, maxi-coats, mini-dresses, Nehru jackets, and fake-fur jackets. Both style changes and fads are used by the fashion industry to stimulate new sales. Smart buyers should build up resistance to fads and the annual style changes planned by the fashion industry and clothing designers.

Many people allow current styles to determine how they will dress.

Source: The May Department Stores Company

CHOOSING YOUR CLOTHES

The clothes you select reflect who you are and represent the image you will present to the world. You should purchase clothes that suit you best, that are in harmony with the way you live, and that make you feel comfortable and confident.

Your clothing needs depend on your life-style. If your activities include a part-time job, you will need clothes suitable for the job. The type of your social activities will dictate your need for formal clothes. Naturally the extent of your wardrobe will depend on how much money you have. However, careful thought and smart buying will help you stretch your clothing dollars. A few rules of wardrobe planning and clothes shopping are discussed below.

Inventory Your Clothing

The first step in choosing your clothes after you determine your clothing requirements is to inventory your existing clothing. You may want to make a chart, such as the one shown in Illus. 10-1. This

Clothes You Have on Date of Inventory	Description of Usable Clothing (Including Colors)	Clean, Alterations, Other	Description of Additional Clothing Items Needed	Approximate Cost
Clothes for Everyday Use — List items				
Clothes for Casual Use — List items				
Clothes for Formal Use — List items				
Clothes for Outerwear — List items				
Other Essentials — List items				

Illus. 10-1

Wardrobe inventory chart

will help you discover which items you are lacking. As you list your clothes, be sure to note the colors that appear most often.

A balanced wardrobe might include five types of clothing:

Clothing for Everyday Use. These are the clothes you wear to school, to work, to shop, and for most everyday activities. This category will probably dominate your wardrobe. Work clothes will vary with the kind of work environment (office, factory, hospital, etc.).

Clothes for Casual Use. Casual clothes are worn for out-of-door activities, sports, and leisure use. They will usually fall into seasonal groups such as summer wear and winter casuals.

Clothes for Formal Use. Formal clothes are for special occasions such as job interviews or eating out at a nice restaurant, or when custom suggests more formality, such as going to a synagogue, church, wedding, or funeral.

Outerwear. Your need for outer wear will be determined by the weather conditions in the region where you live. Included in this group may be raincoats, jackets, hats, sweaters, and gloves.

Other Essentials. This category includes underwear, shoes, and clothing accessories (belts, scarves, jewelry, ties, etc.).

Make a Wardrobe Plan

The second step in choosing your clothes is to make a wardrobe plan that will fill in the gaps you may find in your inventory. A *wardrobe plan* helps you avoid buying on impulse, helps you coordinate colors, and helps you stretch your clothing allowance. Use the following three rules when making a wardrobe plan.

Select Clothes That Have Multiple Uses. Try to plan your wardrobe to include items that can be worn for different occasions such as dates and work. Some articles of clothing can be "dressed up" for formal use by adding a tie, jewelry, or other accessories.

Keep Your Colors in Mind. Stick to your color preferences and to the colors that already dominate your wardrobe. It is easier to build a balanced wardrobe around one or two colors than around many different colors. One helpful practice is to keep swatches (small pieces) of material from your clothes and carry them with you when you go shopping for accessories and for additional shirts, blouses, sweaters, shoes, ties, or jewelry.

Avoid Faddish, Trendy Clothes. You can stretch your clothing budget by selecting traditional or classic styles which can be worn many times and for more than one year.

Shop Carefully

The third step in choosing your clothes is to actually shop for what you will need to achieve a *balanced wardrobe*. Shopping for clothes is fun for some but an unpleasant task for others. The wardrobe plan allows you to put some order into clothes shopping and to avoid haphazard buying which results in not having anything appropriate to wear. Keep in mind these simple suggestions when you shop for clothes.

Take Your Time. Remember that you are choosing the image you will present to the world. Take time to review your wardrobe plan and note the items that are missing. Take time to shop for quality and to compare prices. Take time to try on the clothes and get the proper fit and feel of the item you wish to purchase. In order to avoid buying an item of clothing on impulse, it is advisable not to shop when especially eager for something. Know ahead of time what you want, and know your correct sizes. This practice saves time which could be wasted by looking in the wrong racks.

Look for Signs of Quality. Good quality clothing can be worn many times and will last several years. Some "signs of quality" to look for are smooth linings; neat, secure stitching of buttonholes and firmly attached buttons; straight, smooth, and flat zippers; wide, finished seams and hems; neat, close stitching and fabric cut straight along the grain. Poor quality clothing usually has seams with fewer stitches per inch, while better quality garments will have tighter

Clothes of good quality last several years and are the best buy in the long run.

stitching. Watch for mismatched plaid fabric, and flaws in material such as snags and pulled or loose thread or holes. Look for proper reinforcements, such as double stitching and tacks at points of stress (for example, the zipper closure or the pockets of jackets and pants). Know the characteristics of fabric, and select quality material. Judging quality is not always easy, and it may be necessary to use brands and trademarks as indicators of quality.

Read the Permanent Care Label. The most important source of information about clothing is the label. Specifically, a permanently-sewn care label should tell:

—The generic name of the fibers, such as cotton, wool, acetate
—The trademark
—The percent of weight of each fiber in the fabric; for instance, 65 percent polyester, 35 percent cotton
—The country from which an imported fiber comes
—How to care for the garment; that is, methods of washing and drying, appropriate use of bleach, dry cleaning instructions, and warnings about procedures that might cause damage

Seek Ways to Cut Costs

The final step in successful wardrobe planning and clothes shopping is to seek ways to cut costs and still dress well.

Buy Clothes During the Off-Season. Savings of 20 to 50 percent are possible for buying in the off-season. *Off-season* sales are usually near the end of one season and before the beginning of another. At this time, stores clear seasonal inventories or holiday items. Effective off-season buying requires that the consumer buy traditional or classic styles—not last year's fads. A seasonal clothes calendar such as the one shown in Illus. 10-2 can be used to keep track of the right time to buy off-season.

Shop at Economical Clothing Stores. It pays to learn the location of factory and independent outlet stores, sample shops, clothing exchanges, resale shops, and high-fashion discount outlets. These *clothing outlet stores* sell overruns, extras, and end-of-season leftovers of stores and manufacturers at 20 to 50 percent below customary prices. If you live near a large metropolitan area, there are "seconds" shops were clothes are offered at a substantial savings.

Buy Certain Items in Large Quantity. It pays to buy such items as socks, underwear, panty hose, and similar items in quantity and in the same color. For example, you might buy three pairs of socks of the same type and color. When one sock is lost, you can match the sock that is left with the others on hand. Buying in quantity is often cheaper than buying one at a time.

Store Sales. Most clothing and department stores conduct annual and semiannual sales designed to clear merchandise or to promote new fashions. To be sure you are saving, find out the nonsale price of the item and compare it with the sale price. Also, buy only items which are within your wardrobe plan. Do not buy a bargain just because it is a bargain. You do not have a bargain if clothes fail to coordinate with your existing wardrobe or if you have to buy other articles to go with the purchase.

Illus. 10-2

Clothing sales calendar

JANUARY	FEBRUARY	MARCH
Costume and fine jewelry, women's dresses, furs, handbags, men's hats, women's and men's shoes, girls' and boys' shoes, infants' clothing, lingerie, sportswear, toiletries, men's shirts	Millinery, men's shirts, sportswear	Hosiery, girls' and boys' shoes
APRIL	**MAY**	**JUNE**
Women's and children's coats, women's dresses, housecoats, millinery, men's and boys' suits	Handbags, housecoats, infants' clothing, lingerie, sportswear	Women's dresses, housecoats, piece goods (fabric)
JULY	**AUGUST**	**SEPTEMBER**
Bathing suits, children's clothing, handbags, men's hats, children's hats, infants' clothing, lingerie, millinery, men's shirts, sportswear, toiletries, girls' and boys' shoes, women's and men's shoes	Back-to-school clothes, bathing suits, women's and children's coats, furs	Children's clothing, piece goods
OCTOBER	**NOVEMBER**	**DECEMBER**
Back-to-school clothes, hosiery, housecoats	Children's clothing, women's and children's coats, women's dresses, housecoats, men's and boys' suits, piece goods, women's and men's shoes	Children's clothing, women's and children's coats, children's hats, men's and boys' suits, women's and men's shoes

Adapted from Sylvia Porter's New Money Book for the 80's.

FIBERS, FABRICS, AND FINISHES

Clothing dollars often are wasted because consumers know little about the clothes they wear. Smart buying is easier when consumers understand that fiber, fabrics, and finishes determine the durability, cost, upkeep, and appearance of their clothes.

Fibers

Fibers are the "building blocks" of clothing. Basically there are three types of fibers: natural fibers, synthetic fibers, and blends or combinations. *Natural fibers* are those which nature provides: cotton, wool, silk, and linen. Other natural sources include hair and hide: mohair, cashmere, fur, leather, and so forth. *Synthetic fibers* are constructed from such raw materials as petroleum, air, water, coal, and wood pulp. These synthetic fibers can be manufactured to give special qualities and characteristics in fabrics.

The Federal Trade Commission, under the Textile Fiber Products Identification Act, has assigned 19 general names to the various synthetic fibers. The most common synthetics used in wearing apparel are rayon, acetate, nylon, acrylic, polyester, modacrylic, olefin, and spandex.

Blends are the combination of natural and synthetic fibers. To form a blend, two or more fibers are combined into a single yarn which has the appearance and performance of both fibers. Each of the fibers has different uses, characteristics, and care requirements as shown in Table 10-1.

Fabrics

Before fibers are useful as cloth, they must be spun or formed into yarn. As yarn, they are ready to become fabrics. *Fabric* construction is either woven, knitted, or nonwoven. *Woven* fabrics are made by interlacing a series of yarns at right angles on a loom. The three methods of weaving—or different ways of arranging and intermeshing the yarns—are called plain, twill, and satin. These are shown in Illus. 10-3, p. 187. *Knitted* fabrics are made by pulling one loop of yarn through another loop. *Nonwoven* fabric is made by bonding fibers together through chemistry, heat, or mechanical means or through some combination of these methods. For example, under pressure of heat and moisture, chemicals are applied which

Table 10-1

Uses, Characteristics, and Care of Common Fibers

Fibers	Uses	Major Characteristic	Care
Cotton	Used alone or in blends in apparel, carpets and rugs, home furnishings, household textiles, and industrial products; accounts for about 30 percent of all fibers used in textiles.	Strong, soft, natural fiber, versatile, cool, absorbent, easy to care for. Wrinkles easily but can be treated for wrinkle resistance, color fastness, and shrinkage control.	Cotton can be machine washed and tumble dried, dry cleaned, and bleached with chlorine or peroxide bleaches, but excessive or prolonged use of bleach may weaken the fabric; cotton may be ironed, but "easy-care" finishes may not require it. A safe ironing temperature is 400° F.
Wool	Used in woven, knit, or felt fabrics; woolen fabrics are made from wool yarns containing both long and short fibers; commonly used in apparel, blankets, and carpets.	Natural fiber made from the hair of sheep and lambs. Excellent warmth and wear, resistant to wrinkle, colorfast, absorbent, pills easily, poor resistance to moths.	Wool can be laundered, but only with extreme care using cool water, mild detergent, and gentle action. Never rub. Felting occurs when wool is subjected to heat, moisture, and mechanical action. Laundered garments should be dried on a flat surface or spread over two or three lines to distribute weight. Wool products should be handled carefully when they are damp or wet. Dry clean. Press with a cool iron and steam.
Linen	Used in many handmade fabric products such as apparel, handkerchiefs, home furnishings, table linens, towels; may be used as sheer or coarse weight and texture; used alone and in blends.	Fiber from the flax plant. Cool, absorbent, colorfast, durable, resistant to heat. Wrinkles easily.	Linen can be machine washed and tumble dried. Dry clean. Bleach (although bleaching tends to weaken linen fibers). A safe ironing temperature is 400° F.

Table 10-1 (Continued)

Uses, Characteristics, and Care of Common Fibers

Fibers	Uses	Major Characteristic	Care
Silk	Used alone or in blends; used in beautiful, luxurious garments and home furnishings.	Natural fiber obtained from the cocoon of the silkworm. Strong, colorfast, absorbent, wrinkle resistant, not durable, weakens in heat and perspiration. Yellows by age and sunlight.	Silk can be hand laundered; however, certain dyes "bleed" color when washed. Dry clean. A safe ironing temperature is 250-275° F. White silk can be bleached with hydrogen peroxide or sodium perborate bleaches, but chlorine bleaches should not be used.
Polyester	Used in durable-press apparel, curtains, draperies, thread, carpeting, furniture, rope, and tie cord.	Wrinkle resistance in laundering, wearing, and packing; quick drying, easily washed, strong, abrasion resistant, resistant to stretching and shrinking. Blends well with cotton and rayon for durable-press garments. Polyester is not absorbent; it pills, and stains are difficult to remove.	Polyester can be machine washed and tumble dried. Articles containing fiberfill may also be machine washed and dried, depending on the cover fabric. Bleach with chlorine bleaches. A safe ironing temperature is 300-350° F. Dry clean.
Triacetate	Used for dresses, foundation garments, lingerie, draperies, upholstery, blouses, and fabrics such as satin, jersey, taffeta, lace, brocade, and crepe.	Silklike, colorfast, shrink resistant, high lustre, soft and crisp, luxurious feel and appearance. Does not keep a crease, wrinkles easily, and does not wash well.	Triacetate can be machine washed and tumble dried. Iron, if necessary, with a hot iron. A safe ironing temperature is 450° F.

Table 10-1 (Continued)

Uses, Characteristics, and Care of Common Fibers

Fibers	Uses	Major Characteristic	Care
Nylon	Used in lingerie, hosiery, ski pants and jackets, golf shirts and swim wear, upholstery, carpets, sheer curtains, tire cord, rope, tents.	Strongest of all synthetic fibers. Lightweight, strong, durable, colorfast, abrasion resistant, dries quickly; pills, wrinkles, and is easily damaged by sunlight.	Nylon can be machine washed and tumble dried at low temperatures. Nylon absorbs other colors during washing. Bleach with chlorine bleach. Iron. A safe ironing temperature is 300-375° F (depending on type.)
Acrylic	Used for sweaters, skirts, dresses, suits, blankets, socks, carpeting, draperies, upholstery fabrics, fleece, and furlike fabrics.	Soft, warm and lightweight, shape retentive, quick drying, fluffy, furlike appearance, resistant to shrinkage and wrinkling. Pills, not absorbent, and holds static.	Acrylic can be machine washed and tumble dried at low temperatures. Dry clean. A safe ironing temperature is 300-325° F. Bleached with either chlorine or peroxide bleaches.
Modacrylic	Used for fake fur coats, deep pile coats, trims and linings, fleece fabrics, rugs, carpets, hair pieces, wigs, stuffed toys, draperies, knitwear, and blankets.	Soft, resilient, quick drying, resembles fur in appearance and warmth. Pills, not durable, and loses shape easily. Self-extinguishing fibers.	Modacrylics can be machine washed in warm water and tumble dried at low temperatures. Remove article from machine as soon as tumble cycle stops. Iron if necessary. A safe ironing temperature is 220-250° F. Dry clean. The fur cleaning process is recommended for deep-pile fabrics.

Table 10-1 (Continued)

Uses, Characteristics, and Care of Common Fibers

Fibers	Uses	Major Characteristic	Care
Spandex	Used in bras, bathing suits, ski pants, surgical and support hose, lace, and other items where stretch is desired.	Lightweight, highly elastic, strong, durable, abrasion resistant, soft and smooth, resistant to damage from body oils and perspiration. Yellows when old and is sensitive to high temperatures.	Spandex can be machine washed and tumble dried at low temperatures. Bleach, except with chlorine bleaches. Iron if necessary. Safe ironing temperature is below 300° F; iron quickly and do not leave the iron in the same position too long. Dry clean.
Rayon	Used for dresses, suits, blouses, coats, lingerie, slacks, ties, lining fabrics, draperies, curtains, upholstery fabrics, tire cord.	Versatile, economic, soft, pliable, comfortable to wear, highly absorbent, colorfast. Wrinkles easily, does not hold shape well and is not strong.	Rayon can be washed by hand with lukewarm water, unless manufacturers specify otherwise. Squeeze gently; do not wring or twist. Machine wash and tumble dry. Bleach with chlorine bleach, unless resin finished. Some resin finishes used on rayon discolor in the presence of chlorine bleach. Iron with a moderate iron temperature. Safe ironing temperature is 300-350° F. Rayon will scorch, but not melt if the iron is too hot. Dry clean.

Table 10-1 (Continued)

Uses, Characteristics, and Care of Common Fibers

Fibers	Uses	Major Characteristic	Care
Olefin	Used in carpeting, knitwear, sportswear, pile fabrics, upholstery, blankets, and thermal insulation.	Lightweight, strong, non-absorbent, bulky, abrasion resistant, quick drying, stain resistant. Sensitive to heat; difficult to dye. Made from petroleum products.	Olefins can be machine washed in lukewarm water. Tumble dry at low temperatures EXCEPT when the fiber is used as the batting or filler in quilted pads and other items and is not treated with a wash resistant antioxidant by the manufacturer. In these forms, the heat from the dryer builds up in the fiber filling and cannot escape. Under these conditions, the temperature may reach the kindling point of the fiber, resulting in fire. Bleached at low water temperatures (below 150° F). Dry clean. Articles made of 100 percent olefin cannot be ironed, but blends may be ironed at low temperatures (250° F or lower).

Adapted from The National Bureau of Standards, Fibers and Fabrics, NBS Consumer Information Series #1 (1970); and Man-Made Fiber Producers Association, Guide to Man-Made Fibers (1971).

cause the fibers to interlock and form a usable, solid fabric. These construction processes result in a vast array of textures, designs, weights, and types of fabrics from which the consumer may select.

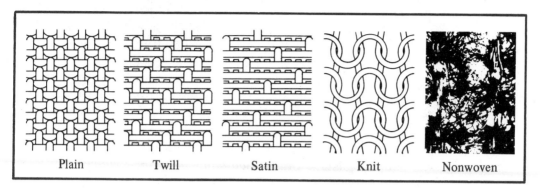

| Plain | Twill | Satin | Knit | Nonwoven |

Illus. 10-3

Fabric Construction

Source: Textiles from Start to Finish, American Textile Manufacturers Institute, (Washington, D.C.), p. 7.

Finishes

Different *finishes* are applied to fabrics to improve their appearance or performance. The finishes often add desirable features such as water repellency, and shrinkage and wrinkle resistance. Some of the different finishes are discussed below.

—*Antistatic.* This finish prevents or reduces electrical charges that cause clinging in nylon and polyester.

—*Brushed.* A brushed finish appears on woven or knitted fabric which has been brushed to give a napped or fleecelike appearance. Napped and brushed finishes raise the fibers giving a soft, fuzzy surface.

—*Durable Press.* A treatment which eliminates the need for ironing and makes a garment nearly wrinkle-proof. Durable press is often called permanent press.

—*Embossed.* This finish gives fabric a raised design on the surface.

—*Flame Resistant.* Flame resistant is a chemical finish which reduces the risk of flammability but does not make a fabric fireproof. Flame resistant fabric will burn, but it is able to resist flames better than ordinary fabrics.

—*Mercerized.* This gives cotton a silklike lustrous finish. This finish makes fabric stronger, more absorbent.

—*Preshrunk*. Clothes have been shrunk before sale in order to avoid further shrinkage when they are washed. Preshrunk clothes shrink up to 3 percent. Other no-shrink finishes, such as Sanforized, are trademarks which guarantee shrinkage of less than 1 percent in length or width.

—*Pebble*. Pebble is a rough surface texture of fabric giving a pebblelike appearance as in pebble crepe.

—*Sanitized*. Sanitized is a chemical finish which protects the fabric from deterioration and odor caused by bacteria, mildew, and mold.

—*Silicone*. This is a general term for certain chemical compounds used to give fabrics a water repellent, spot, and stain resistant finish. See stain resistant, waterproof, and water repellent.

—*Soil Release*. This is a chemical treatment applied to a fabric which makes soil and most stains wash out or wipe off easily.

—*Stain Resistant*. Stain resistant is a chemical finish which makes it easier to lift off or sponge away spills of food, water, and other substances.

—*Waterproof*. This is a water shedding finish. The pores of a fabric are filled so water cannot pass through. Such garments are often hot and uncomfortable.

—*Water Repellent*. This is a chemical finish that causes the fabrics to shed water in normal wear, but does not make them completely waterproof. The finish lets the air flow so the garments are more comfortable.

There are numerous other finishes which alter the appearance of the garment, make soil and stains wash out easier, and increase comfort. Some finishes are known better by trade names like Scotchgard and Sanforized. The many combinations of fabrics, fibers, and finishes on the market make it essential to read the label before purchasing clothes.

CONSUMER PROTECTION

Clothing technology has created a complex and sometimes confusing clothing marketplace. There are over 600 clothes manufacturers. These companies offer over 700 registered trade- or brand-name fabrics and many finishes. Over the years Congress has passed legislation to (1) protect consumers against mislabeled garments, (2) limit the number of hazardous, flammable fabrics on the market, and (3) provide instruction for the care and maintenance of clothes. Consumers should use this legislation to guide them in both the selection and care of clothing.

Textile Identification

Because of the enormous number of textile fibers, fabrics, brands, and manufacturers, labeling laws requiring truth-in-fabric identification were passed to prevent deceptive sales promotion and misleading identification of clothing. Each of the three textile identification laws is enforced by the Federal Trade Commission.

Wool Products Labeling Act (1940). Wool can be combined with other fibers in the formation of fabrics. A practice of reusing wool in new garments led to the passage of the Wool Products Labeling Act. This act is based on the principle that consumers should know if a garment is made of new, used, or reprocessed wool. The law requires that labels specify the type of wool used in a product.

—*Virgin wool* means that the fiber (from the fleece of a sheep or lamb or the hair of the Angora or Cashmere goat) has never been used to make any other product.
—*Recycled wool* means that the fiber has been reclaimed from other wool products.

Fur Products Labeling Act (1951). Would you buy a Hudson seal coat, Mendoza beaver, mountain sable, or a rabbit fur coat? These are some deceptive names, created by manufacturers, for rabbit fur. The Fur Products Labeling Act was created in the belief that consumers have the right to be informed of the true name of the animal fur used in coats and fabrics. Consumers will now find fur products labeled with:

—The type of animal fur
—The country of origin
—Whether the fur is dyed or colored
—Whether the fur is made from scraps of fur

Textile Fiber Product Identification Act (1958). This law requires that most textile products show the following information on the label or tag:

—The generic name of the fibers in the order of predominance by weight. This law defined the 17 machine-made fibers and required that manufacturers use the English generic (general) name, such as cotton, rayon, silk, linen, or nylon
—The percentage of the fibers used unless the fibers are less than 5 percent of the total (for example, 35 percent cotton and 65 percent polyester)
—The name of the manufacturer
—The name of the country from which textile fiber products are imported

Consumers can use Federal Trade Commission regulations to help them select and care for clothing.

Flammable Fabrics

"Several pots were heating on the gas range. Susan reached over a lighted burner to stir something in a pot on a back burner. Her long-sleeved robe ignited and the flames began to travel up her arm. Fortunately she dropped to the floor immediately and rolled to smother the flames. She suffered burns on her arm and part of her face." This case is just one of the thousands which occur annually from flammable fabrics. Because of injuries and deaths resulting from flammable fabrics and other products, two laws were passed to provide consumers a greater assurance of safety. These acts came about because consumers have a basic right to product safety.

Consumer Product Safety Act (1972). This law created the United States Consumer Product Safety Commission and gave it jurisdiction over product safety. CPSC has responsibility to establish flammability standards and carry out the enforcement of the Flammable Fabrics Act.

Flammable Fabrics Act (1953), Amended 1967. The Flammable Fabrics Act and its amendment enable the Consumer Product Safety Commission to set flammability standards for wearing apparel, carpets, rugs, mattresses, and children's sleepwear.

Flammability standards apply to clothing and sleepwear. Flammability laws for clothing textiles, which include all wearing apparel except interlining fabrics and certain hats, gloves, and footwear, prohibit the sale of extremely flammable apparel, such as rayon sweaters, from all interstate commerce. The flammability standard for nightgowns, pajamas, and other types of sleepwear, excluding underwear and diapers, requires that the garment will not catch fire when exposed to a small fire or match. The flame retardant finish must last for 50 washings and dryings. All sleepwear must be labeled with proper care instructions to protect them from agents or treatments known to cause deterioration of the flame retardant finish. If the consumer does not follow the correct procedures for laundering, the flame resistance of the fabric will be lost after a number of washes.

Care Labeling

One of the most useful aids for the consumer is the FTC Trade Regulation Rule on *care labeling*. This ruling is based on the principle that the consumer has the right to full information about how to properly care for and maintain products.

The FTC requires that clothing labels or tags give the consumer information about caring for a product. The rule applies to all articles of clothing except those sold for $3 or less. Care labeling is important because the cost of caring for a garment can double the lifetime cost of a product. Labels must give specific "regular" care and maintenance information, that is, instructions for washing, drying, ironing, bleaching, or dry cleaning a particular item. The ruling requires warnings to the consumer about any washing procedures which might harm or diminish the use or enjoyment of the product, such as using chlorine bleach or petroleum solvents. When a garment can be washed or dry cleaned, both statements must appear on the label as alternative care instructions.

Caveat Emptor: *Damaged Clothing*

Suppose you take a two-piece suit or dress to the cleaners. When you get it back, the skirt does not match the jacket in color or the slacks do not match the jacket in color. Who is at fault? When damage results during dry cleaning, consumers usually blame the dry cleaning establishment because it was the last place to handle the garment. However, the fault may lie with the manufacturer, the retailer, the dry cleaner, or you.

If there is no care label as required by government regulation, and the damage results from lack of information, it is the manufacturer who is at fault. When the information is available to you, but you have failed to follow it carefully, then you are at fault. If the dry cleaner failed to follow label instructions, or did not exercise reasonable care, the dry cleaner is at fault.

How can the consumer know who is at fault? The International Fabricare Institute, a trade association and cleaning research facility for dry cleaners, provides a means for consumers to determine "fault" when garments are damaged in cleaning. For a small fee, technicians will examine damaged garments, report on the cause of the damage, and determine responsibility for the damage. The IFI accepts only garments submitted by professional dry cleaners or launderers who are IFI members, the Better Business Bureau, stores, or a government consumer affairs office. IFI will not accept garments sent by consumers or nonmember dry cleaners.

You should look for the IFI membership symbol at the dry cleaner in order to be assured of this service. In the event that the cleaner is at fault, the consumer is entitled to recover the value of the remaining life expectancy of the garment. According to the "National Fair Claims Guide for Consumer Textile Products" issued by the IFI, the consumer can expect suits to last two to four years, dresses one to five years, coats four years, and dress shirts two years. The worth of a garment is based on the unused portion of the garment's life expectancy at the time it is lost or ruined. It is up to the consumer to negotiate an adjustment with the cleaner.

With an IFI report, the responsible party will usually provide a replacement garment or monetary reimbursement. In the case of the two-piece suit or dress, it is the manufacturer's fault because different bolts of material with different dye lots were used on each piece of the garment. This resulted in a lack of uniformity in the colorfastness of the material. Buyer Beware.

VOCABULARY REVIEW

Fashion

Fads

Natural fibers

Synthetic fibers

Blends

Fabrics

Finishes

Flame resistant

Water repellent

Waterproof

QUESTIONS FOR REVIEW

1. What effect does the "way you dress" have on others?

2. How do fads and annual style changes affect the consumer?

3. What are three guidelines you should follow in choosing your clothes?

4. When planning a balanced wardrobe, what are the five categories of clothes which should be included?

5. What are some signs of quality in clothing construction?

6. What useful information must appear on the care label?

7. What determines the durability, cost, upkeep, and appearance of clothes?

PROBLEM-SOLVING AND DECISION-MAKING PROJECTS

1. Discuss the topic "Fashion is Never Static." In class determine what the current fashions are among your peer group. Report your findings to the class.

2. Discuss in a group what basic clothes are essential for each of the following groups:
   a. high school student
   b. college student
   c. first-time employee
   d. businesswoman
   e. businessman
   f. construction worker
   g. homemaker
   h. retired person
   Report your findings to the class.

3. Work up a wardrobe plan for typical male and female students in your school. Plan a wardrobe that would take most students through the things they do and the places they go.

4. Look through several fashion magazines for the past few years. Pick out and describe items that you could still wear today and the items that are too old to wear today. Try to identify features that make items of apparel long-lasting (that is, are likely to stay "in" for years of wear).

COMMUNITY AND HOME PROJECTS

1. Select an item of apparel (suit, shirt, T-shirt, blouse, or skirt) and shop for the item in three different stores (a department store, a specialty store, and a discount store). Can the same item be found in each store? If so, what is the price range? If not, can you find an item similar in style, color, and quality at lower cost? Of what

fabric is the apparel item made? Rate the appearance, signs of quality, and price of the garments in each store. What information is available on the permanent care label and the fabric identification label? What are the differences among the stores, that is, store personnel, displays, and services such as alterations and return policy? Where would you buy the item if you needed or wanted it? Why?

2. With the assistance of the teacher, construct a bulletin board collage of current men's and women's fashions. Use the same categories as in Problem-Solving question No. 2 and include in each category examples of recent styles, fads, and classics.

3. Survey your community for economical sources of clothing. Include factory outlets, seconds shops, discount clothing stores. List your findings.

Chapter 11

Human Services

What do these activities have in common? A visit to the dentist. A bus ride downtown. Lunch at a new restaurant. The pick up of laundry and dry cleaning on the way home. Each activity involves the use of a human service. According to the Bureau of Labor Statistics, approximately 40 percent of all consumer expenditures is for services such as medical care, transportation, household, and miscellaneous services. In this chapter we will examine the importance of services in our society, discuss the problems associated with buying services, suggest some general procedures for dealing with public and private services, and offer some specific suggestions for choosing medical, legal, and funeral services.

IMPORTANCE OF SERVICES

What do you think of when you hear the term "goods and services"? Almost immediately many people think of cars, televisions, and clothes. But more and more, services are just as important as goods — perhaps even more important. The useful work performed by others, known as *human services*, contributes to the welfare of all consumers. Some services we all take for granted. Examples are public transportation, medical care, radio-television, government, and education to name just a few. The Census of Services Industries reports that there are 1.8 million service establishments in the United States. Service industries are the fastest growing source of jobs in this country.

PRIVATE SERVICES AND PUBLIC SERVICES

Private services are those that are provided by privately owned businesses. They include such services as personal care and grooming, food preparation, household services, sporting events, automobile repair and maintenance. Individuals select these services on a *fee-for-service* basis; that is, after the service is performed you pay a fee. For instance, when you go to a dentist, you will pay immediately after the service or when you are billed. However, if a consumer has dental insurance, the insurance company may pay all or part of the fee.

The services provided by governmental agencies are known as *public services*. The role of government as a provider of human services has greatly increased in the past 50 years. Most of the public services are provided without a direct payment. However, government services are not free. The services of government are paid indirectly through federal, state, and local taxes. Public services include education, park and recreation programs, public health clinics and centers, public day-care centers, family counseling, museums, libraries, postal delivery, law enforcement, courts, and consumer protection. For some public services, the recipient of the

Public services, such as this museum, are indirectly supported through taxes.

service pays a small fee, but usually the fee is not sufficient to cover the cost of the service. Such services are *subsidized* (supported by the government). College education, college dormitory housing, public transportation, public housing, Medicare, and Medicaid are examples of services subsidized by government.

In addition to public and private services, there are public utilities. A *public utility* is a business that performs an essential service to the public but is privately owned. Public utilities include telephone, electric, gas, water, and garbage disposal services. Public utilities often have a monopoly on a particular service area.

A *monopoly* occurs when only one company provides a service. Monopolies are allowed because certain services are provided more efficiently and at a lower cost by one company than by several competing companies. Public utility services are regulated by governmental agencies called regulatory commissions. In most states utility commissions regulate electricity, gas, transportation, communications, and other basic utilities. When public services cross state boundaries, federal commissions regulate public utility companies.

PROBLEMS WITH BUYING SERVICES

You will remember that the process of buying goods includes getting information, evaluating the information, comparing alternatives, considering the consequences, and making a decision. If something goes wrong, the consumer has a product warranty or can seek a remedy from the merchant or manufacturer. However, buying services is much different from buying goods. Consider the following examples which illustrate the problem of buying services.

In one large metropolitan area, two good nursing homes are located within five miles of each other. One charges $1,100 less per year than the other, yet the less costly maintains a nursing staff-to-patient ratio 60 percent higher than its higher priced competitor. Of two pharmacies in the same area, one charges $1.25 for filling a prescription of 30 capsules of a common antibiotic; the other charges $7.40 for the same prescription.

When consumers buy human services, they are often unaware of price differences and are unable to judge quality differences. Some of the reasons that service buying is more complicated than product buying are discussed below.

Price Information

Price is a central factor in the decision to buy. Usually when consumers buy products, they have some price information, and competition exists among sellers. And with some services, such as nonemergency home repairs, consumers can ask for bids from several service persons or contractors. However, when people buy services, such as medical or legal, it is not possible to get bids, and price information is often either missing or there are limitations on the information. For example, few professionals advertise, even though it is no longer prohibited, because it is still considered to be in poor taste. Consumers should try to obtain information about fee schedules and extra charges by calling several of the professionals whose prices they wish to know. Occasionally some professionals will advertise, and this can provide valuable price information.

Quality or Performance Information

Performance information is generally available and sometimes required on products. For instance, Environmental Protection Agency mileage estimates per gallon must be posted on new cars, and energy efficiency labels must be provided with certain appliances. But when one buys a service, information about performance standards is seldom, if ever, to be found. Usually information comes only from the experiences of friends and other users of the services.

Some service facilities and institutions, such as hospitals, day-care centers, and nursing homes are inspected and are required to meet minimum standards, but information about compliance with these standards is not made public. Performance standards for most professional services are evidenced through college degrees, certificates, and licenses.

Consumers should try to obtain information about the nature of the service, its value or benefit to the consumer, and the consequences of its use. For example, when you select a college, it is important that you gather as much information as possible about that college. You should not rely solely on catalogs for information. It is important to also talk to students currently enrolled, graduates, and other persons such as counselors or people who are knowledgeable about the reputation and programs of the school. An essential part of the information needed when purchasing services is information about alternative choices. A person choosing a college should consider such alternatives as community colleges, private colleges, or state-supported universities.

Decision Making

The decision-making process in buying services is much different from that in buying products. Some services are a necessity; therefore, the consumer has little or no choice in the matter. Education, required to a certain age in all states, is an illustration of this.

In other cases the provider of the service tells the consumer whether the service is needed or not. We go to a doctor who diagnoses and then treats us for an illness or to a lawyer who advises us to seek legal help and then takes the case to court. When we use public services, we usually have few or no alternatives because the governmental agency or regulated business often has a monopoly on the service. This is particularly the case with welfare and public health agencies, educational institutions, and public utilities.

Redress Procedures

Consumers of products usually have some type of warranty or guarantee. Consumers can take products back for repair or replacement if there is a problem. However, when there is a problem or a complaint about a service, consumers must actively seek redress or reform. Redress procedures usually involve professional review boards and self-regulation. Currently, though, redress remedies are difficult to pursue. Resolving a complaint or a problem may require taking the matter to a licensing board or a commission for the professional service. For example, a patient may have to take a problem with a doctor to a medical society or a professional standards review committee. A client with a complaint against a lawyer would have to go before the professional review committee of the bar association. The legal system may have to be used in some instances for such matters as pursuing medical malpractice claims or applying pressure to reform public services.

When consumers are angry because of rising utility costs, there is usually no remedy except to pay the higher rates. Challenging a public utility in a rate proceeding is a complex process requiring the help of lawyers, expert witnesses, and the efforts of consumer groups opposed to rate increases. Federal and state public service commissions are supposed to protect the interests of consumers. They attempt to act in the public interest and ensure that utilities can make only enough profit to maintain their services. In establishing the rates for public utility services, the commission must consider the needs of both the utility company and consumers.

Consumer as a Producer

The consumer is not a factor in the production of goods. However, in obtaining human services, the consumer of the service is often responsible for the end result. For example, in education student-consumers are responsible for their own learning. The teacher's contribution is important, but it is the student who must do the learning. The purchase of a service requires the consumer (user) to be an effective producer; that is, to learn well.

HEALTH-CARE SERVICES

"Health," Ralph Waldo Emerson said, "is the first wealth." Unfortunately, according to the Bureau of Labor Statistics, the cost of health care has increased more in the last 15 years than any other major consumer product or service. Medical care expenses take 3 to 10 percent of the average consumer's income, and for older consumers, the range can easily be much larger. In the following section we examine three facets of health care—self-help, the choice of a doctor, and alternative health-care services.

Self-Help Health Care

Some critics charge that there is an overdependence on doctors for health care, but these critics do not suggest giving up on your doctor or the current health-care system. On the contrary, they believe that the key to preventing illness and preserving health lies with the individual. Individuals must be responsible for their own health-care decisions and actions. The concept of *self-help* stems from an awareness of the role life-styles play in maintaining good health.

The self-help prescription for good health is the Seven Golden Rules of Health.

—Get seven to eight hours sleep each night
—Eat breakfast every day
—Stay slender
—Seldom snack between meals
—Stay active through planned exercise (sports, walking, or vigorous work)
—Use alcohol moderately
—Never smoke

Research by the University of California, Los Angeles School of Public Health shows that people who practice all seven rules are generally in better health than those who practice only five or six rules; and, in turn, these people are in better health than those who practice only three or four rules. If you want to help yourself maintain good health, it will pay you to take a look at your daily living habits. The best treatment for poor health is prevention. Good health means good habits and a wholesome life-style.

Choosing a Doctor

Choosing a doctor is probably one of the most important decisions consumers have to make, but they often spend more time and effort shopping for a car than for a doctor. Below are some suggestions for selecting a doctor.

Choose a Doctor Before You Are Sick. The best way to choose a doctor is before an illness occurs. When you are well, you have both the time and the proper frame of mind to evaluate the doctor objectively.

When choosing a doctor for the first time, you should look for a *primary care physician.* This doctor is a generalist who can take care of 85 percent of your health problems and refer you to a specialist if

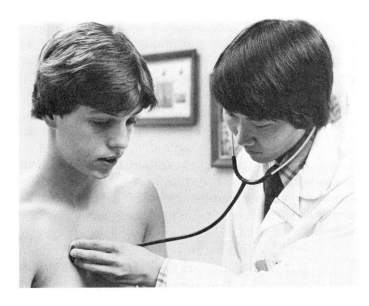

When choosing a doctor, you should look for one who is concerned with your overall health.

Source: Dennis Ferree photo

necessary. You can select from doctors called general practitioners (G.P.), internists, or family physicians (F.P.).

Many patients use internists for primary medical care. An *internist* is a physician with training in all areas of medicine except surgery (operations), obstetrics (childbirth) and pediatrics (children).

A *family practitioner* is a medical specialist who provides medical care for all members of a family, regardless of age, sex, or the nature of their illness. Family practice is unique in that it is concerned with the family as a unit and with the interactions of family members as the interactions may affect health. Family practitioners are generally trained in internal medicine, pediatrics, orthopedics, obstetrics, minor surgery, gynecology, psychiatry, sexual and family counseling.

Choose from More Than One Candidate. Make a list of recommended doctors. You can get a recommendation from family members, friends, the local medical society, or by calling the nearest accredited hospital or teaching hospital. Once you get a list of recommended doctors, you can check their qualifications.

Check the Doctors' Credentials. There are at least four credentials which are important: the M.D. degree, a state license to practice medicine, hospital appointments, and board certification. The M.D. degree and state license are the minimum requirements to practice medicine in any state. Of more value are hospital appointments and specialty training. Hospital appointments indicate that a doctor is on the staff of a particular hospital and can admit patients to that hospital. Try to choose a doctor who holds at least one appointment to a medical-school-affiliated hospital. These hospitals have training programs for medical students, resident doctors, and other medical personnel such as nurses, and technicians. They also help assure that the latest medical practices are observed.

Today, many doctors specialize in a certain field of medicine. According to the American Medical Association, 48.5 percent of the total number of doctors are certified by at least one of the 22 medical specialty boards. These boards are responsible for establishing training requirements and for administering specialty certification examinations. To be a *specialist*, a doctor can be either board certified or board eligible. *Board certified* means that the doctor has fulfilled the training requirements and has passed the examination given by the specialty board. *Board eligible* means that the doctor has taken the training but has not taken the examination. The best way to learn about doctors is to look them up in *The Medical Directory* and *The Directory of Medical Specialists*. These books are available in many public libraries and from local medical societies.

Call the Doctors. Call the doctors on your recommended list. Explain to the receptionist that you are looking for a personal or family doctor. Find out if the doctor is taking new patients. Also get information about office hours, customary fees, appointment procedures, use of medical assistants, office location, and whether the doctor practices in a group or alone. Whether the doctor is in a group practice or not can be an important consideration. If your doctor is out of town, others in the group usually "cover" your doctor's practice. This assures you of round-the-clock doctor's care when needed.

Visit the Doctor. From your list of doctors, select the one who appears most suitable, and call to make an appointment for a checkup. The way the checkup is handled will tell you much about the doctor. During this initial visit, the physician should be thorough and try to learn some things about you as an individual, your family, and your work. You should expect and receive full, unrushed attention, and you should leave the office feeling that your questions were answered. Try to assess the doctor's attitude toward preventing illness. You want a doctor who is interested in your overall health — not just any illness you may have. You will need to judge whether or not the doctor is a person who shows compassion toward the patient. Only you can determine whether it is easy to talk to the doctor about your medical concerns and questions.

Alternative Health-Care Services

Greater numbers of individuals are using some alternatives to traditional forms of medical care. Since you are going to spend a lot of money on health care in your lifetime, you should know the types of health-care alternatives which are available to you. Some of these are discussed below.

Hospital Outpatient Departments. An alternative source of primary care for many people is the hospital outpatient department

(OPD). The procedures at outpatient departments vary with the size and type of hospital, but most of them offer excellent medical care.

Doctors who work in outpatient departments see many patients and many different diseases. This exposure makes them well prepared to recognize and treat a variety of illnesses. Laboratory and x-ray services are available on the spot. Doctors of almost every medical and surgical specialty are available for consultation. The price charged for outpatient services is usually comparable to what you would pay for a visit to a doctor's office.

Neighborhood Health Centers. These centers are funded by the federal government and were originally set up for low-income families, but most of them will accept members of the general public. Patients may have to come from a certain geographic area. Payment is usually on a sliding scale and is based on the level of income of the patient. The quality of care in neighborhood health centers has been judged to be as good as that in the best hospital outpatient departments. Where they exist, neighborhood health centers offer comprehensive primary care.

Public Health Services. Many county-run public health departments offer a wide range of family and individual health services. These services usually include child-care clinics, immunization clinics, alcoholic treatment, mental health care, family planning, venereal disease treatment, vision, hearing, and blood pressure screening. Most of these health services are either free or are offered at a small fee to patients.

Health Maintenance Organizations. Prepaid group health care and health maintenance plans, often referred to as HMOs (Health Maintenance Organizations), are oriented toward preventing illness. By 1978, there were 8.8 million members in HMOs. Members pay a yearly fixed fee which remains the same regardless of the patient's illness or the amount of use. This fee is in contrast to the traditional fee-for-service system. In the traditional system a person is charged for each visit to the doctor. In an HMO plan, a member who becomes seriously ill and requires extensive care costing thousands of dollars still pays the same yearly fee as a member who does not use the service very much.

The Health Maintenance Organization Act of 1973 requires that all employers who are subject to minimum wage laws and who have

25 employees or more offer the employees a choice between a traditional medical plan and an HMO. Most HMOs offer members the services of a group of doctors working together at the plan's facilities and at hospitals chosen by the HMO.

LEGAL SERVICES

Like doctors, lawyers have become increasingly specialized in their practices. But even so, it is advisable to have a family lawyer to handle such general matters as a contract, a will, or perhaps a lawsuit stemming from an automobile accident. Below are some suggestions for finding a personal attorney.

Compile a List of Recommended Attorneys

There are numerous ways to get names of recommended lawyers. You can ask someone who is connected with the case or problem. For example, if you have a financial problem, you can ask a banker, an accountant, or someone who handles business affairs at your place of employment. If you have a domestic problem such as divorce, adoption, or guardianship, consult with a psychologist, a member of the clergy, or a social worker.

Another way to get names of lawyers can be through a friend who has had a similar legal problem. The best recommendations generally come from someone who has had a problem like yours resolved satisfactorily.

Since lawyers are no longer prohibited from advertising, it is also possible to get names and fee information from advertisements. In addition, most state, city, and county bar associations have a lawyer referral service. A *referral service* has a list of attorneys, and the service will give you the names of those who may be willing to handle your case. Most services refer the callers to lawyers in the order in which they appear on a list; attention to individual problems is not given at this time.

Call the Attorneys

The next step in selecting an attorney is to call each one on your list. Explain that you are seeking a lawyer to handle routine legal matters. Ask if the attorney will agree to a free initial consultation.

Do not ask for specific legal advice in this call. Merely obtain information such as office hours, billing practices, and fees. Every case is different and, therefore, lawyers may not be able to quote a specific sum, but they can give you an estimate.

You should understand that attorneys use three different ways of billing for their services. The *flat rate* is used for simple matters such as a will, divorce, or purchase or sale of property. *Billing by the hour* is used when the amount of time involved in your case cannot be estimated. In such cases lawyers will charge a fixed dollar amount for each hour they work on your behalf. The hourly rate can range from $15 per hour to over $100 per hour depending on the lawyer, the complexity of the case, and the need for a secretary and a legal assistant. A *contingency fee,* usually 25 to 40 percent of the amount awarded by the court, is paid only if the lawyer wins the case.

It is good to have a family lawyer to handle general matters.

Consult with the Attorneys

Consult with two or three of the attorneys whom you judge to be most suitable. During the initial consultation find out if the attorney handles the matters of interest to you. Find out if the attorney specializes in any particular area of the law. Try to determine if the attorney has kept up with the changes in law. During the initial consultation you can see office procedures and the way the attorney deals with clients.

Decide on an Attorney

Once you reach a decision on a particular attorney, it is advisable to ask the attorney to give you an estimate in writing of how much the handling of your case will cost, the method of billing, and how much time it will take to handle the case. This estimate serves as your contract and should help you evaluate the lawyer's performance. Expect the following basic considerations from any competent lawyer.

—To be kept informed at all times about your case
—To have legal points, questions, and both sides of issues explained in understandable terms
—To be consulted and involved in all important decisions
—To have your case and affairs kept confidential
—To be given an itemized bill at the end of the case

Alternative Legal Services

In some communities there are legal clinics. These are low-cost clinics which assist consumers with the relatively simple matters, such as wills and uncontested divorces. Legal clinics charge less by working with a large number of clients, by using legal assistants, and by using simplified forms. They are often located near where people live and are sometimes in storefronts. They often have bilingual staffs and even maintain evening and weekend hours.

Other alternative legal services available to consumers are *Legal Aid* and *Legal Services* offices. These are privately and federally financed offices which give free legal services to persons who cannot afford a lawyer. In order to use either Legal Aid or Legal Services, one must have a very low income.

A relatively new legal concept is group *prepaid legal services.* Group prepaid legal programs are employee plans which provide members with consultation, advice, and other legal services. Prepaid legal services can be either an open panel plan, where members choose any lawyer, or a closed panel plan, where services are provided by a certain law firm or staff. These legal services are provided for a set fee paid by each member of the group. Like medical insurance, employees pay a small amount regularly so that they have legal protection if and when needed. Most prepaid legal service programs practice preventive law; that is, prepaid programs encourage consumers to seek legal advice early so that potential legal problems can be resolved early.

FUNERAL SERVICES

In 1980, according to the National Funeral Directors Association, a complete funeral, without cemetery expenses, cost between $1,000 and $2,000. With cemetery expenses, the cost can easily reach $3,000 or more. Unfortunately costly mistakes occur when a funeral is arranged at the last minute by someone who is grief stricken and who knows little about funeral services. For this reason, we will look at the traditional funeral and alternatives to the traditional funeral, and we will discuss the information consumers need to know when making decisions about a funeral.

The Traditional Funeral Service

The traditional funeral in our modern society has value for the living as well as for the dead. The funeral has several important functions: to honor the deceased by offering people a chance to pay their last respects; to provide an acceptable, hygienic way of disposing of the body; and to satisfy family feelings and beliefs.

Most people in modern society accept the purpose and value of the funeral, but too often it is purchased under a great deal of stress by persons who are confused and heartbroken. After a six-year study of the funeral industry, the Federal Trade Commission concluded that "the emotional trauma of bereavement (grief), the lack of information, and time pressures place the consumer at an enormous disadvantage in making funeral arrangements." The FTC investigation, completed in 1978, identified the following unethical practices:

—Grossly inflated prices, massive overcharges, and purchases of unnecessary products and services
—Claims that a casket is required by law for all funerals, even for cremations
—Claims that embalming is required by law

—Claims that embalming is a vital health measure

—Claims that burial vaults or grave liners are required by law

—Claims that "sealed caskets" preserve the body for long periods

The Association of Funeral Directors disputes these findings and attributes unethical practices to a few unscrupulous funeral directors.

One important function of the funeral is to satisfy family feelings and beliefs.

Caveat Emptor
Funerals: The Consumer's Last Rights

Because consumers who have to make funeral arrangements are often handicapped by their grief, they are less likely to exercise their rights than consumers in other situations. Consumers should expect the following practices and standards of conduct.

—The funeral director should explain that embalming is not required by law and will not be performed without permission. Although embalming is customary for traditional funerals when the body is viewed, it is required in most states only if the body is to be transported to another state or if the cause of death was a communicable disease.

—The funeral director should provide you with a list of casket prices from the least to the most expensive. The funeral director should explain that most states require only a "suitable container" which is firm enough for a burial, combustible if for a cremation, and that a casket is not required for a cremation.

—The funeral director should provide, in advance, item-by-item prices for the principal services of a funeral. Do not accept an all-inclusive package price. The funeral director should give you options and prices concerning not only the caskets, but also the use of the hearse and limousine, and any other services. You should be charged only for those items you use. According to the FTC, the worst problem faced by consumers in buying funeral services is the lack of price information. Price advertising is considered unethical by the National Funeral Directors Association, and many funeral homes refuse to give price information over the telephone. In practice funeral service prices vary greatly from one funeral home to another and from one part of the country to another.

Consumers need to have a clear idea of what to expect when arranging for a funeral. There is no better protection for the consumer than knowledge! Buyer Beware.

Alternatives to Conventional Funerals and Burials

The conventional American funeral, with an open coffin for the viewing of the body, requires a number of services provided by a funeral home. These services can be expensive. However, there are respectable low-cost alternatives to the conventional funeral. These include cremation, direct burial, and membership in a memorial society or preneed plan.

Cremation. The process of reducing a corpse to ashes is known as *cremation*. It is an alternative to earth burial. A cemetery plot, the opening and closing of a grave, and grave markers are not needed if ashes are scattered on sea or land or are given to survivors. The number of cremations in the United States increases each year, and probably will continue to increase, as burial space becomes less available and more expensive.

Direct Burial. As the name suggests, the body is disposed of simply and immediately, either by burial in a grave or by cremation. This procedure eliminates most of the expenses of the conventional funeral and burial. The statistics show that the price for direct disposition ranges from $300 to $550. Family and friends usually hold a memorial service in a church, synagogue, or home. This provides the opportunity for the expression of grief in the same manner as conventional funerals where the body is present.

Memorial Societies. Another way to reduce the cost of funerals is to make the arrangements ahead of time. Anyone may join a memorial society for a one-time fee of usually less than $20. Currently there are about 150 memorial societies in the United States. Memorial societies are nonprofit consumer organizations which stress simplicity, dignity, and economy in death as well as the right of individuals to plan the disposition of their own bodies. A memorial society will prepare a simple funeral for its members for about one-third the cost of the average funeral. The members run the society and contract with a funeral director to bury its members at a modest price.

Preneed Plans. This alternative involves buying a funeral beforehand and usually paying for it on an installment plan. A *preneed funeral plan* ensures that the funeral and burial will be paid for without a financial burden on the survivors. An advantage of preneed plans, as with the memorial societies, is that individuals make their own funeral arrangements in a calm, objective manner. One disadvantage is that buyers cannot be sure that the amount contracted and paid for will be enough at the time of death to cover the services chosen. The contract holds, but pressure is sometimes put on the relatives to change to more expensive arrangements.

Probably the best way to avoid the high cost of funerals is to plan in advance. To do this, you must know the alternatives before you make your decision. You should state your own wishes to your family and friends or put your instructions in writing. If you think you may be responsible for making funeral arrangements for a friend or relative, discuss their wishes in an open and frank manner. By making predeath arrangements, consumers can take the time to plan and prepare the kind of funeral the family will approve of and can afford.

VOCABULARY REVIEW

Human services	Primary care physician
Fee-for-service	Internist
Public utilities	Lawyer referral service
Self-help health care	Prepaid legal services

QUESTIONS FOR REVIEW

1. Approximately what amount of the average consumer's expenses are expenditures for services?

2. What is the difference between public services and private services? Cite examples of each category.

3. How is the process of buying services different from buying goods or products?

4. What are the Seven Golden Rules for good health?

5. How can a consumer find out information about a doctor's qualifications?

6. How are HMOs different from traditional doctor's health-care services?

7. What are the main reasons that most individuals need to have a personal or family lawyer?

8. What are the three methods of billing used by attorneys?

9. When using an attorney, what essential information and procedures should you expect?

10. What are four ways a person can reduce the cost of traditional funerals?

PROBLEM-SOLVING AND DECISION-MAKING PROJECTS

1. A friend asks you to suggest ways to locate a doctor. You know that your doctor no longer accepts new patients. Make a list of suggestions for locating a competent personal physician.

2. Assume that you have been asked to go to a funeral home with a friend who has lost a relative. This is your first experience in making funeral arrangements. Make a list of practices or standards of conduct which you should expect from a funeral director.

3. Assume that your public library has recently voted to shorten its evening hours. The school library is also closed at night. You and some friends believe that one of the libraries should be open during the evening for research and access to reference books and periodicals. What action would be most appropriate in dealing with this public service problem?

COMMUNITY AND HOME PROJECTS

1. Select a public service in your community and investigate it by visiting the agency and by answering the following questions: (a) What are the services provided by the agency? (b) Who are the primary users of the agency? (c) How is the agency financed? (d) What do the people in the agency think they need to do to improve their service? (e) Are there alternatives to the use of this service? (f) Who is on the governing board of the agency? (g) How does a consumer or user of the service express dissatisfaction or a complaint about the service?

2. In small groups, survey your community to determine the types of alternative health-care services available. Determine the prices,

eligibility requirements, and location of each type of service. Report your findings to the class. If possible, compile your report into a health-care directory.

MONEY MANAGEMENT

Chapter 12

Earning and Managing Income

Would you invest money in a firm which does not have an accounting system? Financial success for such a firm is highly unlikely. Now, what do you think is the chance for financial success for the average family or individual who does not have an accounting system? Managing income and budgeting are topics everyone talks about but few do anything about. In this chapter we will examine financial planning, earning income, and establishing an accounting system for an individual or family.

FINANCIAL PLANNING AND ACCOUNTING

Financial planning requires a careful assessment of an individual's or a family's financial status. It requires you to determine priorities and to channel your activities and resources toward attaining what is important to you. Your values control the choices that you make regarding the use of your income, and these choices in turn determine the life-style you achieve. These decisions should be made carefully rather than haphazardly. The point is that financial planning helps maintain a proper balance between long-term goals and short-term goals, and between spending and saving.

Personal or *family accounting* is merely business financial planning applied to a person or a family. Successful firms establish financial goals, design plans to achieve the goals, establish accounting systems for controlling income and spending, and implement the plans. A family or individual should do the same. Unfortunately many people fail to establish financial goals. As a result they fumble along from payday to payday or month to month in debt or near debt. Over 400,000 families each year declare personal bankruptcy.

Setting Goals

A financial plan begins by establishing goals. These may be short-, intermediate-, or long-range goals. For the individual or family, a financial plan consists of four steps: (1) establishing the goal, (2) expressing the goal in a specific dollar amount, (3) setting a date by which each goal can be reasonably achieved, and (4) dividing the dollar amount of the goal into small manageable weekly, monthly, or yearly amounts. For example, if you want to save $2,000 by the time you graduate in a year and a half, divide $2,000 by 78 weeks. Your goal could be accomplished by saving $25 a week. Goals are more easily fulfilled when broken down into small amounts. In the process of carrying out the financial plan, you will quickly discover that it is often necessary to compromise short-term goals in order to accomplish long-term goals. This may mean some sacrifices in immediate wants or desires.

Life Cycle

Financial responsibilities and resources will change during your life. Each stage in life has its own unique requirements and expectations. Obviously not everyone's life follows exactly the same pattern, but most do seem to have a predictable pattern called the *life cycle*. Table 12-1 shows the financial tasks associated with each stage in the life cycle. The differences between teenage spending patterns and adult spending patterns, as shown in Illus. 12-1 and Illus. 12-2, exemplify the changes in life cycle financial tasks. But even though the financial tasks are different, the practice of financial planning, earning and maximizing income, and budgeting are as applicable to teenagers as to adults.

Early involvement in family financial affairs is often recommended by financial counselors. Certainly teenagers should assume some personal and family financial responsibilities. Being accountable for your allowance or part-time income is good preparation for handling financial affairs later on.

Table 12-1

Financial Planning Throughout the Life Cycle

Age Group	Unique Financial Tasks
13-17	Develop plans for eventual independence Evaluate future financial needs and resources Explore career options Develop an understanding of the financial system Develop record-keeping systems
18-24	Establish household Train for career Attain financial independence Purchase risk coverage Establish financial identity Establish a savings program Make a spending plan Develop effective financial record-keeping system Develop an effective financial planning system
25-34	Provide for child-bearing and rearing costs Provide for expanding housing needs Expand career goals Manage increased need for credit Provide for training-education funds Purchase additional protection coverages Draw wills Maximize financial management skill of all members of household
35-44	Upgrade career training Continue to build education fund Maximize head-of-household protection Provide greater income for expanding needs Establish and work toward retirement goals

(Continued)

Table 12-1 (Continued)

Financial Planning Throughout the Life Cycle

Age Group	Unique Financial Tasks
45-54	Provide higher education/training for children Maximize investments Evaluate and update retirement plans Communicate with family members about estate plans Assess and explore estate plan
55-64	Consolidate financial assets Provide for additional future security Re-evaluate method of intended property transfer Investigate part-time income or volunteer work for retirement Assess housing location and expense for retirement Meet responsibilities for aging parents or other dependents
65 & over	Re-evaluate and adjust living conditions and spending as they relate to health and income Evaluate and adjust programs for increasing risks Secure reliable assistance in managing personal and economic affairs Finalize plan for sharing estate Finalize letter of last instructions

Source: A Date with Your Future, *American Council on Life Insurance,* p. 7.

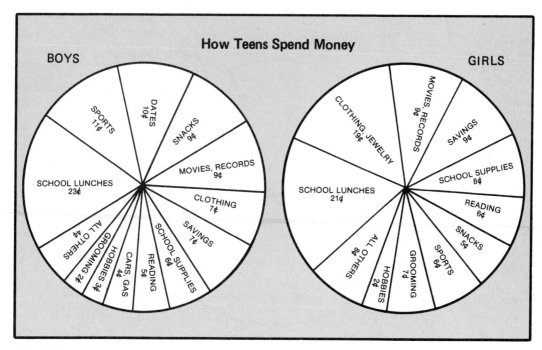

How Teens Spend Money

BOYS

- SPORTS 11¢
- DATES 10¢
- SNACKS 9¢
- MOVIES, RECORDS 9¢
- CLOTHING 7¢
- SAVINGS 7¢
- SCHOOL SUPPLIES 6¢
- READING 5¢
- CARS, GAS 4¢
- HOBBIES 3¢
- GROOMING 2¢
- ALL OTHERS 4¢
- SCHOOL LUNCHES 23¢

GIRLS

- CLOTHING, JEWELRY 19¢
- MOVIES, RECORDS 9¢
- SAVINGS 9¢
- SCHOOL SUPPLIES 8¢
- READING 6¢
- SNACKS 5¢
- SPORTS 6¢
- GROOMING 7¢
- HOBBIES 2¢
- ALL OTHERS 8¢
- SCHOOL LUNCHES 21¢

Illus. 12-1

As an individual moves from one life cycle stage to the next, the financial tasks and responsibilities change. Most teenagers' money can be spent as the teenagers please.

Copyright © 1978 CURRENT CONSUMER. Reprinted by permission.

EARNING INCOME

Consumers' standards of living greatly depend on the amount of income they earn. *Income* is the money received (or the financial reward) from investments or from one's activities at work or in business. These activities are usually the labor services needed to produce products or to provide human services. A labor service is commonly called an *occupation,* that is, the employment, job, trade, or profession by which one earns a living. Other sources of income are wages, rent, interest, and profit.

Income from Labor

Most Americans depend on their labor for their primary income. Approximately nine out of ten American workers earn income in the

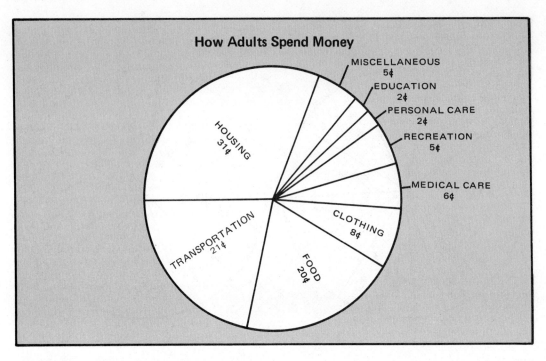

How Adults Spend Money

MISCELLANEOUS 5¢
EDUCATION 2¢
PERSONAL CARE 2¢
RECREATION 5¢
MEDICAL CARE 6¢
CLOTHING 8¢
FOOD 20¢
TRANSPORTATION 21¢
HOUSING 31¢

Illus. 12-2

The expense categories for adults of housing, food, and transportation require approximately 60 to 80 percent of the ordinary family's income.

Figures from U. S. Department of Labor, Bureau of Labor Statistics.

form of wages or salary. A *wage* is an hourly or daily rate of pay while a *salary* is a weekly, monthly, or yearly rate. Most clerical workers and people who do physical labor are wage earners, and professional and technical workers are salary earners. About 10 percent of all workers are in business for themselves and earn *self-employment income* instead of wages or salaries. These include such people as physicians, shopkeepers, writers, photographers, and farmers.

Wages and salary are only one type of financial reward for work. Paid vacations, life and health insurance, free uniforms, retirement plans, stock options, and discounts on company products are also part of total earning. These other benefits are called *fringe benefits*. Fringe benefits are like a hidden paycheck within a paycheck. About 15 percent of total employee compensation consists of fringe benefits.

You may have wondered why a boxer like Muhammad Ali gets $5 million for an evening while the President of the United States earns $200,000 a year, or why a professional athlete earns far more than a professional accountant or teacher. Income from labor reflects social values, the monetary worth of your labor, and the demand for labor in relation to the number of people able to do the job.

The primary source of individual income in the United States is one's own labor.

Source: U. S. Department of Agriculture

Occupation. A major factor affecting the level of a worker's earnings is occupation. Managers and administrators, professionals and technical workers, craftworkers, and transport equipment operators generally earn more than the average for all occupations. In contrast clerical and service workers, farm workers, factory workers, and nonfarm laborers earn less than the average income.

Sex and Age. Men usually earn more than women at every age, but there are exceptions and this is changing. Women's earnings are highest from ages 25 to 34. Men's earnings are highest between ages 35 and 44. Several factors contribute to the differences. Women work fewer hours on the average than men. Women's earnings are frequently diminished by the interruption of their careers by family responsibilities. Another factor, particularly in the past, is the tendency of women to be grouped in relatively low-paying professions. Over the last decade, however, women have progressed into the higher paying brackets of managerial, administrative, professional, and technical occupations.

Race. Blacks and Hispanics generally earn less than Whites. But here, too, are exceptions and this also is changing. The earnings gap between Blacks and Whites has narrowed somewhat and can be attributed, in part, to the greater opportunity for employment, training, and promotion among minority groups. A large part of the earnings disparity occurs because of the concentration of Blacks and Hispanics in low-paying occupational groups.

Union Status. About 20 million full-time workers, or 29 percent of the total, are covered by union contracts. The average weekly earnings of this group averages about 34 percent higher than that of other workers. Differences exist within industries, but union earnings generally exceed nonunion pay by 15 to 40 percent.

Education. Education makes a difference in occupational choice, weekly earnings, and lifetime income. According to the most recent available data, people who have postsecondary education can expect to earn more than $760,000 in their lifetime. This is nearly 2¾ times the $280,000 likely to be earned by workers who had fewer than eight years of schooling, nearly 2 times the amount earned by workers who had one to three years of high school, and more than 1½ times as much as high school graduates. In order to maximize income, it pays to acquire additional education and training.

Employers are seeking people who have higher levels of education because many jobs are more complex and technical and require greater skill. Employment growth and income increases will be faster in those occupations requiring special education and training. Employers increasingly demand better trained workers to operate complicated machinery.

Minimum Wage Rates

A number of laws protect American workers. Probably the best known is the "minimum wage law," established by the Fair Labor Standards Act and administered by the U.S. Department of Labor. The federal law sets a uniform minimum wage scale for almost all workers. The law also requires overtime work to be paid at 1½ times the regular rate for all hours worked over 40 hours in one work week. Under certain circumstances, learners, apprentices, and handicapped workers may be paid less than the minimum wage. Currently the minimum wage is $3.35 (1982).

The Fair Labor Standards Act provides that you are entitled to minimum wage (1) if you work directly or indirectly in interstate commerce; (2) if you work for an employer who produces goods for interstate commerce; (3) if you are employed by an enterprise or business that has two or more workers who are engaged in interstate commerce; and (4) if the enterprise that employs you does an annual business of $250,000 or more.

The minimum wage affects about 5 million workers at the bottom of the wage scale. Those most likely to be affected by minimum wage are nonunion, young, or minority workers. In addition restaurant waiters and dishwashers, porters and hotel maids, messengers, store trainees, and unskilled laborers and many others are affected by minimum wage standards.

The minimum wage law sets a uniform wage scale for about five million Americans.

Income from Capital

You may have wondered what makes some people rich. Wealthy people usually own *capital,* such as buildings, equipment, stocks, and land, which is essential for the production of goods and services. The majority of the households in the United States, however, are not owners of capital. It is estimated that 98 percent of these households depend solely upon their labor for their daily, weekly, or monthly income. When most people want or need to increase their incomes, they often attempt to do so by working second jobs or overtime—but this is still income from labor. It is usually only a temporary increase in income because it lasts only as long as the person can tolerate the extra work or the loss of time away from a family or friends.

Converting Labor Income into Capital

When individuals are totally dependent on their labor income and they spend all their income on consumer items, nothing will be left with which to acquire capital. This is the unfortunate dilemma of most American workers. Currently American workers are saving on the average of only 5 percent of their incomes.

The expression, "the rich get richer," is true because the rich have the two factors for earning income—their labor and their capital. The real key to financial independence is converting the income from labor into the capital which will earn additional income. Individuals or households who are dependent on labor as the sole source of income may obtain capital through reduced consumption; that is, by saving and investing the income from labor into capital ownership.

Median Income

Median income is the midpoint in the distribution of earnings from all sources; that is, the income of half of the population falls below the figure and half falls above the figure. At the beginning of this decade Americans were earning more money than ever before, but their personal standards of living were not improving. Median income rose from $9,900 to $18,800 from 1970 to 1980, but the purchasing power was no better. When prices rise as rapidly as incomes, there is no change in standard of living. Consumers can buy no more goods and services with their increased incomes than they could before. In recent years many American families have seen their standards of living decline as wages fail to keep ahead of rising prices.

Reading Your Paycheck

Income from employment is your first step toward financial security. Obviously your pay, wage or salary, is one of the first considerations. Young workers are often shocked by the difference between *gross pay* — or the total pay — and take-home pay. *Take-home pay* (or *net pay*) is the amount left over after federal and state taxes and other deductions have been taken out of the check. After deductions your take-home pay is likely to be about 20 to 30 percent less than your gross pay. Illus. 12-3 corresponds with the parts of a paycheck discussed below.

1. *Paycheck*. Your paycheck usually will come in two parts—the paycheck which you will cash or deposit and the paycheck stub which is your record of earnings.
2. *Paycheck Stub*. The stub lists your gross pay, your deductions, and your net pay. It is important to check the stub carefully for errors and to keep the stub for tax records.
3. *Pay Period*. The stub will identify the ending of the pay period, which is usually one week, two weeks, or a month.
4. *Employee Information*. This section will give your name and may also give a social security number. (Check shown in Illus. 12-3 does not give a social security number.)
5. *Pay Rate*. This is your hourly pay or salary.
6. *Hours*. This number will be the number of hours which you worked. It may be expressed as the number of regular hours and also the number of overtime hours. It is wise to keep your own record of the number of hours you work in order to verify the hours on the stub.
7. *Gross Earnings*. This is the number of hours worked multiplied by the hourly pay rate.
8. *Deductions*. There may be several categories of deductions. Some are required by law, namely, Federal Insurance

Contributions Act (FICA) tax for social security, federal income tax, and state and local income taxes. In addition there may be other deductions for insurance, union dues, and the like.

9. *Net Earnings.* This is your take-home pay, or the difference between gross pay and the deductions.

10. *Year-to-Date Totals.* Many paycheck stubs show year-to-date totals. These are the amounts which have been earned and deducted for the year from January to the current date.

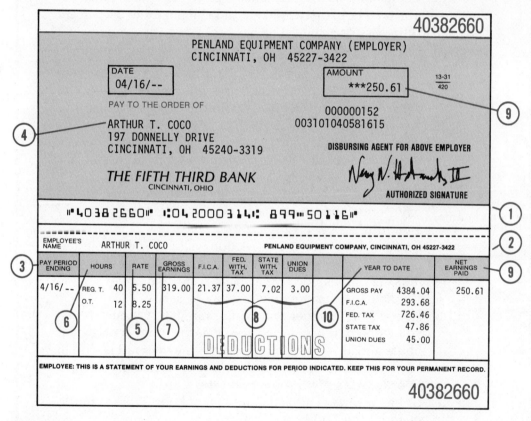

Illus. 12-3

An employee receives a paycheck with an attached record of earnings and deductions.

MANAGING INCOME: BUDGETING

With the high cost of necessities in the 1980s, consumers are having less personal income available for nonessential spending. This means that when the bills for food, housing, heating, and gasoline are paid, the amount left for entertainment, education, services, and consumer products will be less. As one financial advisor puts it—budgets are back in style. A *budget* is a saving and spending plan designed to keep control on your spending and to achieve individual or family financial goals. Quite simply, budgeting is planning the use of your income. An example of a budget is shown in Illus. 12-4.

It Pays To Budget

Budgeting is the final phase in family accounting. Below are a few of the benefits to be gained from budgeting.

1. Budgets provide an understanding of the individual or family financial condition.
2. Budgets encourage a sensible use of income.
3. Budgets require examination of goals, values, and priorities.
4. Budgets help individuals and families to get maximum value from expenditures.
5. Budgets encourage awareness of alternatives.
6. Budgets help to modify or to reduce spending and, therefore, help individuals or families to live with current income.
7. Budgets help the family or individual to adjust to irregular or unusual expenditures or to changes in income.
8. Budget records can be helpful for income tax purposes.

The Budget Process

Developing a well-conceived budget requires three steps: (1) assessment of spending, (2) adjustment in spending, and (3) achievement of control over spending and saving.

Assessment. The first step in budgeting is assessing your income and noting where it goes. This requires a simple record keeping routine. Keeping track of your income and expenditures does not

Item	Jan.	Feb.	Dec.	Total
Total Money Income	$2,083			
Savings for:				
Future Purchases	45			
Emergency fund	50			
Additional income	50			
Major fixed expenses:				
Taxes:				
Federal	189			
State	47			
Property	78			
F.I.C.A.	119			
Rent or mortgage payment	350			
Insurance				
Medical (including prepaid care)	34			
Life	25			
Property	16			
Auto	34			
Debt payments				
Auto	126			
Other	0			
Flexible expenses:				
Food and beverage (including eating out)	414			
Utilities	114			
Furnishings and equipment	80			
Clothing	107			
Personal care	39			
Auto upkeep	50			
Fares, tolls	4			
Medical care	0			
Recreation and education	50			
Gifts and contributions	42			
Total	$2,063			

Illus. 12-4

A budget such as this one can help you control your spending and achieve your financial goals; $20 is not accounted for.

Adapted from A Guide to Budgeting for the Young Couple, *Consumer and Food Economics Institute, Science and Education Administration, U.S. Department of Agriculture.*

have to consume a lot of time, and it does not have to be, nor should it be, complicated. It is also not necessary to keep records of every dollar spent for months or years. During the first phase of budgeting, a reliable record of your expenditures can be kept for one or two typical months out of the year. Your checkbook, cancelled checks, and deposits serve as an excellent record of income and expenditures. A small card can be carried in your pocket or purse to record daily cash outlays. The more you use your checking account, the better your record of expenditures.

After keeping a record of expenditures for one month, identify savings and the expense items which should be included in your budget. These expense items are likely to include: rent or mortgage

Budgets encourage a sensible use of income.

payments, utilities, food, household maintenance, house furnishings, clothing, transportation, medical and dental care, education and reading, recreation and entertainment, gifts and contributions, personal items, and miscellaneous items. Your record of spending should be divided into two general categories: fixed and variable expenses.

Fixed expenses include such items as rent, mortgage payments, insurance premiums, and installment loan payments. These are recurring expenses which you are absolutely committed to. *Variable expenses* are such items as food, clothing, transportation, recreation and entertainment, medical care, and utilities which may vary from week to week or month to month. Variable expenses can be adjusted to some degree. Remember that a budget is built around your lifestyle and must not be so rigid that it cannot be changed.

Recreation is a variable expense which can change from week to week.

Source: The Roaring Tiger roller coaster. Circus World. Orlando, Florida

Another phase of assessment involves identifying the expenditures which cause cash shortages. Cash shortages, sometimes called *cash-flow problems,* occur because of large, irregular expenses such as insurance, auto repairs, and clothing. By carefully identifying and anticipating large items, you can provide a way to have the money to meet these bills at the time they come due. After you account for your daily and monthly expenses, determine your large, irregular expenditures. Divide these by 12 in order to estimate an amount which should be set aside monthly in savings for these costs. Setting aside money for large, irregular expenditures in a separate *cash-flow account* helps you manage your finances.

Adjustment. The second step in budgeting involves making adjustments, particularly if the individual or family is overspending. Once you determine your spending patterns, you should make some comparisons with average spending patterns. Of course, there is no "average family," but a comparison of your expenditures with some standards, as shown in Table 12-2 can alert you to areas for possible adjustment. You may find that your family is spending more than

Table 12-2

Summary of Annual Budgets for a Four-Person Family at Three Levels of Living, Urban United States, Autumn, 1981

	Budget Level		
	Lower	Intermediate	Higher
Total Budget	$15,323	$25,407	$38,060
Total family consumption	12,069	18,240	25,008
Food	4,545	5,843	7,366
Housing	2,817	5,546	8,423
Transportation	1,311	2,372	3,075
Clothing	937	1,333	1,947
Personal care	379	508	719
Medical care	1,436	1,443	1,505
Other family consumption	644	1,196	1,972
Other items	621	1,021	1,718
Social security & disability	1,036	1,703	1,993
Personal income taxes	1,596	4,443	9,340

Note: Because of rounding, sums of individual items may not equal totals.

Source: Bureau of Labor Statistics, U. S. Department of Labor, April 16, 1982.

average on certain items. When adjustments are being considered, all members of the family who can understand the purpose of budgeting should be involved. Family involvement encourages participation and agreement in identifying areas for reduction or adjustment.

It is extremely important to be reasonable when making adjustments. The purpose of a budget is to gain control over your income and spending. The adjustment step in the budget process gives you

It is important to involve all family members in budget planning.

an opportunity to concentrate on ways to get more value out of your spending. Budgeting requires considering alternatives and making choices. You may have to reduce your lunch expenditures by bringing lunches from home, writing a friend instead of phoning long distance, or spending less on clothing in order to own a car.

Budgets need to be evaluated periodically to see if adjustments should be made. Many circumstances can and should change the budget. Inflation, changes in salary, and life cycle stages are factors which cause changes in the budget categories and amounts.

Achievement. The last step in the budgeting process is to achieve financial control of your income and spending. Control is gained only after actual spending records are assessed and adjustments are made. Below is what a successful budget can do for you.

1. You know how much money is coming in during the next few weeks or months.
2. You know how much has to be set aside for large expenditures and for savings in the weeks or months ahead.
3. You know how much is available for day-to-day expenses, both fixed and variable.
4. You know how much is available, if any, for luxuries, recreation, and entertainment.
5. You avoid financial stress when emergencies occur.
6. You enjoy achieving your financial goals and plans.

VOCABULARY REVIEW

Family accounting   Median income

Financial planning   Take-home pay

Life cycle   Deductions

Fringe benefits   Budget

QUESTIONS FOR REVIEW

1. How is an individual or family similar to a company or firm?
2. What are the financial responsibilities associated with your current stage in the life cycle?
3. Name the factors that may affect the amount of income you earn.
4. How can income earners acquire capital?
5. What is the key to financial independence?
6. What is the budgeting process?
7. How should an individual or a family designate money for large annual expenditures?
8. What are the two general categories for recording spending in a budget?
9. What are some of your alternatives when a budget is not working?

PROBLEM-SOLVING AND DECISION-MAKING PROJECTS

1. Yi and Tien Chan kept the following record of expenditures for one month: food, $348; housing, $384; transportation, $131; and clothing, $101. They have a take-home salary of $1,551 per month.
   a. What percent of their take-home salary goes to the big four—food, shelter, transportation, and clothing?
   b. Given these monthly expenditures, what is the annual total (multiply by 12) for food, housing, and transportation?
   c. The Chans take home $18,612 annual gross salary. After food, shelter, and transportation expenses, what amount remains for all other expense categories?

2. In a small group, discuss 10 expenditures that are fixed and 10 expenditures that are variable for teenagers. Make a list of your findings.

3. Assume that you are working, single, and sharing an apartment with a roommate. You know you will have a large $240 semiannual payment for auto insurance, and you will need approximately $280 for a round-trip ticket for a vacation you are planning. You also estimate that you will need at least another $400 for vacation expenses. It is six months before your vacation and your next auto insurance payment. (a) What can you do to have the amount for the insurance and the vacation? (b) What amount would it be necessary to save each month?

4. Assume that an individual earns $18,000 gross salary and desires to save 10 percent of this amount. How much will the person have to save each month in order to accomplish the savings goal?

COMMUNITY AND HOME PROJECTS

1. Keep a record of your monthly income from part-time work, an allowance, gifts, and so forth, and keep a record of your expenditures. Classify your expenditures according to the categories shown in Illus. 12-1 (for a girl or for a boy). After one month divide the amounts spent by your total monthly income. How does your spending compare to average teenage spending?

2. Ask your parents to discuss common mistakes made in managing their money. Outline the consequences of these mistakes and ways to correct them.

3. Develop a budget to take you through one week of living as a high school student. Remember that the first step in budgeting requires taking an assessment of how much income you have and where it goes. Knowing where your money goes is essential to managing your financial affairs wisely, especially if spending is to reflect your short-range and long-range goals. After one week compare your estimated expenditures with your actual expenditures. Did you find that your actual spending exceeded your estimate and your income?

Chapter 13

Banking and Checking Services

Commercial banks serve most people as multipurpose financial centers. Typically, banks offer checking accounts, savings accounts, loan services, trust and investment services, financial counseling, safe deposit boxes, travelers checks, money orders, savings bonds, student loans, and 24-hour tellers. In this chapter we will discuss the traditional banking service which most consumers use—checking—and some electronic (computerized) banking services.

CHECKING ACCOUNTS

The check is the most widely used means of transferring money. Nearly 90 percent of all monetary transactions, such as buying goods and paying rent, are made with checks. *Checks* are orders written by a depositor directing a bank to pay out money. Checks are safe, convenient, and provide a proof of payment and a record for tax and budget purposes.

Most young people open their first checking accounts shortly after they go to work after high school or when they go to college. When a person opens a checking account, the bank and the customer establish a contractual agreement which allows the customer to deposit money in the bank and to write checks on the account. The bank agrees to maintain the account, provide records, and honor checks when they are presented to the bank for collection. When a customer writes a check, it is a demand on the customer's deposits. It is for this reason that checks are called *demand deposits*.

The following is an explanation of the different types of checking accounts available.

Cost-Per-Check Accounts

Cost-per-check accounts, sometimes called *special accounts*, are considered thrift accounts or minimum use accounts. Generally one

The check is the most widely used means of transferring money.

has to maintain a minimum balance and pay a fee for each check. The per-check fee may range from $.20 to $.25 per check. Some banks may also charge a maintenance fee that ranges from $.50 to $1.50 per month even if there is no activity in the account.

Minimum Balance Accounts

Minimum balance accounts require the customer to maintain a certain balance, often $100, but sometimes as much as $300 or more. The minimum balance may be a low balance or an average balance. With a *low balance account*, the customer is charged a service fee even if the account falls below the minimum only one day in a month. An *average balance account* can drop to zero as long as the customer deposits enough money during the month to bring the account up to the minimum required. If a depositor's account balance dips below the minimum, the depositor will pay a service charge. Some banks advertise minimum balance accounts as "free checking accounts." They may be low-cost accounts, but they are not free.

Free Checking Accounts

Some banks provide totally free checking, that is, there are no minimum balance requirements or service charges. Such accounts are the best type for checking account customers. Free checking is provided by some banks on the basis that checking account customers will also use the bank's other services such as savings accounts or safe deposit boxes.

NOW (Negotiable Order of Withdrawal) Accounts

One of the newest types of checking services which appears to be gaining acceptance is an interest-bearing account known as the *NOW account*. NOW accounts earn interest at the rate of 5¼ percent. The drawback to NOW accounts is the $200 to $5,000 minimum balance requirement. If the account balance falls below the required balance, the bank charges a monthly service fee or check handling fee.

WRITING AND USING CHECKS

As stated earlier, money transactions take place with checks. When checks are properly written and endorsed as shown in Illus. 13-1 and Illus. 13-2, they provide proof of payment and are an excellent record of expenditures.

Procedures for Writing a Check

Follow these procedures when writing a check.

1. Record the *payee* (the person to whom the check is written), the purpose, and the amount of the check in the register before writing the check. A *check register* is a separate form on which a checking account holder keeps a record of deposits and checks written. Record the number of the check properly.
2. Date the check. Checks are proof of payment.

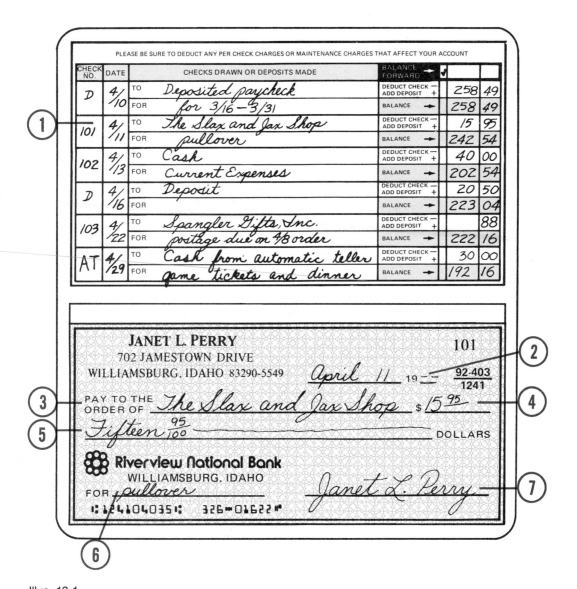

PLEASE BE SURE TO DEDUCT ANY PER CHECK CHARGES OR MAINTENANCE CHARGES THAT AFFECT YOUR ACCOUNT

CHECK NO.	DATE	CHECKS DRAWN OR DEPOSITS MADE	BALANCE FORWARD	✓		
D	4/10	TO Deposited paycheck	DEDUCT CHECK – ADD DEPOSIT +		258	49
		FOR for 3/16 – 3/31	BALANCE →		258	49
101	4/11	TO The Slax and Jax Shop	DEDUCT CHECK – ADD DEPOSIT +		15	95
		FOR pullover	BALANCE →		242	54
102	4/13	TO Cash	DEDUCT CHECK – ADD DEPOSIT +		40	00
		FOR Current Expenses	BALANCE →		202	54
D	4/16	TO Deposit	DEDUCT CHECK – ADD DEPOSIT +		20	50
		FOR	BALANCE →		223	04
103	4/22	TO Spangler Gifts, Inc.	DEDUCT CHECK – ADD DEPOSIT +			88
		FOR postage due on 4/8 order	BALANCE →		222	16
AT	4/29	TO Cash from automatic teller	DEDUCT CHECK – ADD DEPOSIT +		30	00
		FOR game tickets and dinner	BALANCE →		192	16

JANET L. PERRY
702 JAMESTOWN DRIVE
WILLIAMSBURG, IDAHO 83290-5549

101

April 11 19 __ 92-403 / 1241

PAY TO THE ORDER OF The Slax and Jax Shop $ 15 95

Fifteen 95/100 _____ DOLLARS

Riverview National Bank
WILLIAMSBURG, IDAHO

FOR pullover

Janet L. Perry

⑆1241040351⑆ 326⑈01622⑉

Illus. 13-1

Check and check register

3. Designate the payee. Always use ink—never pencil or erasable ink.
4. Write the amount of the check in numbers next to the dollar sign.

5. Spell out the amount of the check on the middle line and draw a line to fill in the space to the word "Dollars." For example,

One Hundred Twenty-Five $\frac{50}{100}$ _____.

If the check is for less than one dollar, write "Only Seventy-Five Cents" and cross out the word "Dollars."
6. Write the purpose for which each check is written on the line labeled "For" at the bottom of the check.
7. Sign your name as the *drawer* — the person who wrote and signed the check.

Endorsements

An *endorsement* is a signature and a message to the bank to cash, deposit, or transfer one's right to the check to someone else. There are three common endorsements: blank, restrictive, and full.

A *blank endorsement* is your signature only. A check with a blank endorsement is like cash. Anyone who has possession of the check can present it for payment at the bank. For this reason, you should not endorse a check "in blank" unless you are at the bank.

A *restrictive endorsement* is your signature and a message which limits the use of the check. A restrictive endorsement usually reads "For Deposit Only." This type of endorsement allows you to send the check by mail to the bank for deposit without fear of loss. If the check is lost or stolen, it cannot be cashed.

A *special (full) endorsement* is your signature and a message which directs the transfer of the check to someone else whom you designate. A special endorsement is written: "Pay to the order of . . . ." and then your signature. This endorsement transfers the right of payment to the new payee.

Endorsements are made on the back of the check exactly as your name appears on the face of the check. Even if your name is misspelled, sign it as it is written on the face, and then add the correct spelling.

Outstanding Checks

When a check is received, it should be deposited immediately. This should be done out of courtesy to the *drawer*. A check held for

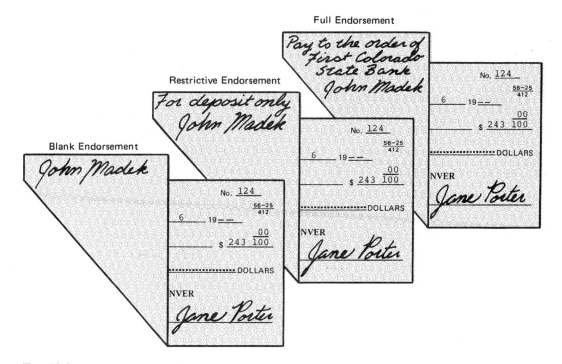

Illus. 13-2

Three types of endorsements

too long makes accurate record keeping more difficult for the person who wrote the check. Checks which have not been presented to a drawer's bank for payment are called *outstanding checks*. Technically checks are valid for six years; but in actual practice, banks often hold up payment on checks which are three to six months old until they are confirmed by the drawer.

Stop Payment Orders

A person may wish to *stop payment* on a check by instructing a bank not to pay a certain check. For instance, if a check is lost or stolen, a stop payment should be requested. A stop payment on the check can be made by telephoning the bank's bookkeeping department. Usually the bank will ask for the date, payee, amount, and number of the check. Banks may charge as much as $15 for a stop payment request. Notification should also be made to the person or company legally holding the check on which you have stopped payment.

Overdrawn Checking Accounts

When people open a checking account, they agree to have sufficient funds on deposit to cover any checks which they write. The bank is not obligated to honor the check if it is written for more money than the amount on deposit. The bank can charge a penalty for each check not covered by sufficient funds. Banks have established "no-bounce" plans. In one plan the bank will deposit money in your account if your balance goes below zero. In that case you should understand that you are being loaned money. Usually the bank will deposit a minimum of $100 even if your account becomes overdrawn by only one cent. It should be remembered that loans are in increments of $100 and that a fee of $1\frac{1}{4}$ to $1\frac{1}{2}$ percent per month is charged to the account holder. Nevertheless, the fee of $1.25 to $1.50 on $100 per month is frequently less than the amount charged for a check that bounces. Another plan allows automatic transfer from regular savings accounts to checking accounts. A transfer fee such as $1 per transfer will be charged for this service. Such "no-bounce" accounts must be applied for at the time of opening the account.

COMPARING YOUR RECORD WITH THE BANK'S RECORD

Bank customers receive monthly statements (see Illus. 13-3) which reflect all checking account transactions: deposits, checks cleared, service charges, and the ending balance of the account at the close of the statement period. Several days elapse from the date the *bank statement* is prepared to the time the statement is received by the customer. During this time, additional checks may be written and deposits made which are recorded in the check register. Also, if someone is holding a check, the bank will not have subtracted that amount from the account. Each of these reasons will cause the customer's check register and the bank statement to differ. The process

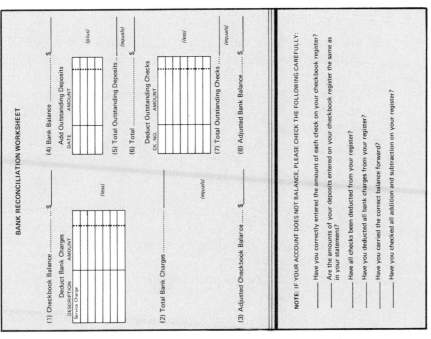

Illus. 13-3

Bank statement and reconciliation worksheet

of finding the correct balance is called *reconciliation*. In order to reconcile a bank statement, follow this procedure.

To the bank statement balance:

1. Add any deposits not shown on the bank statement which you show deposited and recorded in your check register.
2. List all checks which you have written but which have not cleared through the bank (*outstanding checks*). Subtract the total amount of these checks from the bank statement balance.
3. Determine the new bank statement balance.

To your check register balance:

1. Add any deposits and credits (such as interest earned on a NOW account) not recorded in your check register.
2. Subtract any service charges, stop payment fees, or charges for insufficient funds.
3. Determine the new check register balance.

The adjusted balances should agree after this procedure is completed. The adjusted balances should represent the correct amount of money which remains in the checking account. Each month when the check register and the bank statement are in balance, make a notation or underscore the balance. If the check register and the bank statement do not agree, take the following steps.

1. Check your arithmetic in the check register. Make sure that balances were carried forward correctly to the next page of the register. Look for transpositions (where two numbers are reversed).
2. Most bank statements are computerized and are highly accurate, but you should still check the accuracy of the addition of deposits and subtraction of checks written.
3. Find out which checks are still missing. Arrange the checks by number to determine precisely which checks are outstanding. (Some banks keep your checks instead of returning them to you. The practice is called *check truncation*. What you get is a monthly statement listing the number and the amount of each check that has been cashed.)
4. Compare the amount of each canceled check with the amount recorded in the check register and the amount recorded on the bank statement.

If there is still no agreement in the balances after double checking for arithmetic errors, accounting for all outstanding checks, and making certain that the correct amounts were recorded in the register and the bank statement, report the matter to the bank within ten days of receiving the statement. Personnel in bank bookkeeping departments work with customers to determine if there has been an error or mistake by the bank and will help customers correct the reason for differences. Some banks charge a fee for assistance with reconciliation.

COMPUTERIZED BANKING

The computer is bringing many changes to the banking industry and to bank customers. As a result, new words are creeping into our vocabulary—"automatic tellers," "debit cards," and "paperless banking." Computerized banking makes possible some alternatives to traditional checking accounts. These include bill-paying services, telephone transfers, automated teller machines, and point-of-sale transfers. All of these new services stem from the development of electronic fund transfers, or EFT. Through *electronic fund transfers*, dollars can flow from buyer to seller or from employer to employees without the use of cash or a check. The system is paperless.

Automatic Bill Paying

Banks provide prearranged bill-paying services or telephone transfers of money. Arrangements can be made to pay fixed or regular bills such as mortgage payments and insurance premiums. The transfer of money by telephone allows the customer to keep money in checking or savings until just before payment must be made. Quite naturally, there are fees and charges associated with these new services.

Automated Teller Machines (ATMs)

No longer do customers have to rush to the bank before it closes. Automated tellers allow customers easy access to their accounts during banking or nonbanking hours. By using a special EFT card and punching in a personal identification code, a customer can deposit or withdraw money and even obtain a loan at the site of an

Computerized banking allows customers access to their accounts at any hour.

Source: AmSouth Bancorporation, 1977 Annual Report

automated teller. Automated tellers are placed in convenient locations such as airports, shopping malls, and on street corners.

Point-of-Sale Transfers

Point-of-sale transfers let you pay for retail purchases with a debit card. The cashier imprints a receipt using the customer's debit card and asks the customer to sign the receipt. A *debit card* is similar to a credit card but with one big difference — it doesn't give you the opportunity to buy something today and pay for it at a later date. In one automated system a customer simply passes a debit card through a reader and punches a code into a point-of-sale (computer) terminal that also functions as a cash register. The customer's checking account is drawn down, or debited, by the amount of the purchase. The bank's computer automatically transfers the amount of the purchase from the customer's account into the store's account.

Caveat Emptor: *Electronic Fund Transfers*

Electronic banking is here and is most likely the banking of the future. But what if your EFT card is lost, stolen, or used without permission? And what type of bookkeeping does EFT require?

In 1979 Congress passed the Electronic Fund Transfer Act which provides some protection for consumers. The law provides that:

—Banks must offer you a record or receipt for all transactions made on computers. Statements must show the amount and the date of the transfer, the names of any retailers involved, the location or identification of the terminal, and fees and telephone numbers for inquiries and error notices.

—If there is a bank error, the bank must investigate and get back to you within ten business days after your first report of the problem. If the bank takes longer, it must return the money to your account until the error is found. The bank must notify you in writing if it wasn't in error. You have a right to request copies of the bank's investigation documents and to make your own investigation.

—If you lose or misplace your EFT card, you must notify the bank immediately. The most you will have to pay if you notify the bank within two business days is $50. You can be liable or responsible for up to $500 if you wait beyond two business days, and you are liable for all unauthorized withdrawals if you wait more than 60 days after getting your monthly statement.

Follow these simple rules of bookkeeping when using electronic banking.

1. Always keep a record of your transaction. Check for the date, amount, location, and type of transaction to verify the bank's monthly statement.
2. If a mistake is made at the time of the transaction, call your bank for direct customer service. If you cannot get service at the time, contact the bank as soon as possible.
3. Enter your debit transactions in your check register just as you would a check or deposit transaction. This practice

allows you to maintain an accurate running total of how much money you have.

4. When you receive the bank statement, reconcile your check register with the statement, and include all debit transactions just as you would other transactions.

An EFT card is no use to a thief or anyone else without your access code or personal identification number (PIN). The computer terminal will not operate without your code. Choose a code that you do not have to write down; for example, the name or initials of your parents or a relative's date of birth. Your best protection is to keep your code to yourself. Buyer Beware.

VOCABULARY REVIEW

Check	Endorsement
Payee	Reconciliation
Check register	Debit card
Drawer	

QUESTIONS FOR REVIEW

1. What are the services which most commercial banks provide consumers?

2. What is the technical name for checks?

3. Why do most people use checks?

4. What are four types of checking accounts?

5. What are the three commonly used check endorsements? When is each type used?

6. When a check is lost or stolen, what should a person do?

7. What new banking services are available to consumers as a result of computerized banking?

8. What is the maximum amount an EFT card owner would have to pay if the owner fails to notify the bank of the loss of a card?

PROBLEM-SOLVING AND DECISION-MAKING PROJECTS

1. Karl Klemecki opened a checking account after graduation from high school. He is charged $.15 per check for each check written. During the first month, his check register showed a balance that was $1.50 more than the bank statement. Karl had written 10 checks, each of which had been returned. What is the likely cause for the difference between the bank statement balance and the check register balance?

2. In June, Sue Ellen Brown received a bank statement that showed a balance of $568.00. The service charge was $1.00. Sue Ellen found that the following checks were outstanding: No. 431, $5.80; No. 436, $15.60; No. 437, $9.55. Her check register balance at the end of June was $538.05. Reconcile the bank balance.

3. An EFT card carries advantages but also poses risks for the person who uses this card. What are sensible rules, appropriate to any life-style, for managing the use of EFT cards safely?

COMMUNITY AND HOME PROJECTS

1. Use a local telephone directory to determine the number of banks in your community. Each student should select one bank and investigate the services of that bank. Determine the following information.
   a. types of checking accounts offered and service charges
   b. minimum balance required for a checking account (if any)

2. Find out what type of checking account your family uses. Assist your parents with reconciling a bank statement.

3. Locate an automated teller in your community. Write a brief report on the steps a customer would take to use the automated teller for the following transactions:
   a. pay a utility bill of $50
   b. deposit cash of $20
   c. withdraw cash of $50
   d. transfer $75 from checking to a savings account

Chapter 14

Saving and Investing

Most people work for their money. Some people let their money work for them. An interesting idea? *Saving* is putting aside money for future use. Money set aside can be put to work to earn even more money. The process of putting money to work is called *investing*. In this chapter we will discuss some saving and investing options for small investors.

WHY PEOPLE SAVE

Nearly everyone has some amount of savings. One person may be saving for a summer vacation, another for a stereo or sports equipment, and another may be "just saving." Saving for future purposes, either long range or immediate, is the primary reason for saving. This is a sound habit which should be established.

Most people have sufficient common sense to save for emergencies. Unknown events cause problems for many families and individuals. Loss of income from an accident, illness, or unemployment happens quite often. Financial advisors recommend a savings of three to six months' salary to cover sickness or unemployment.

Some people save to earn income. When money is set aside (saved) and used by someone else, it earns interest; in other words, money makes money.

WHERE PEOPLE USUALLY SAVE

People usually save through commercial banks, savings and loan associations, and credit unions. Savings in these institutions are safe, secure, and offer a relatively fixed rate of return on money.

Commercial Banks

By far the most common financial institution in the United States is the commercial bank. Commercial banks offer a wide variety of services which make the bank the center of an individual's or family's financial affairs. As mentioned in Chapter 13, some of the services offered by commercial banks are checking accounts, savings accounts, credit cards, loans, financial counseling, safe-deposit boxes, travelers checks, money orders and transfers, trust and investment services.

Savings Banks

Savings banks operate much like commercial banks in that they offer such services as savings accounts, check cashing, safe-deposit boxes, and savings-bank life insurance. They also specialize in real estate loans. Savings banks are commonly found in the northeastern part of the United States.

Savings and Loan Associations

Savings and loan associations, as the name implies, specialize in handling savings and in lending money. Savings and loan associations are sometimes called *thrift institutions*. Generally they lend money for home purchases and home construction. Until 1980 a major difference between a savings and loan association and a commercial bank was that the savings and loan did not offer checking services. Now, however, some savings and loan associations do provide checking accounts.

Credit Unions

Credit unions are not-for-profit savings and lending financial institutions. Are they different from banks and savings and loan associations? Actually the major difference is in who can belong to a credit union. Membership in a credit union is made up of individuals who have something in common such as a professional organization, church, or place of employment. Loans are made to its members from the savings of other members.

HOW TO SELECT A SAVINGS ACCOUNT

What should you look for when selecting a savings account? Below are some points which will help you in selecting a place for savings.

Interest

When money is put to work, expect it to work as hard as possible. *Interest* is the return savers get for letting someone else use their money, and it is the most important factor in determining the amount of money a savings account will earn.

A factor that influences how much money a savings account earns is *compounded* interest. As soon as interest is added to the account, the interest will also earn interest. *Compounding* is the process of earning interest on interest. Interest can be compounded annually, semiannually, quarterly, monthly, or daily. If all other things are equal, daily compounding results in the highest earnings as shown below with $1,000 at 6 percent.

Method of Compounding Interest	Interest Earned
Annually (12 months)	$60.00
Semiannually (6 months)	60.90
Quarterly (3 months)	61.36
Monthly	61.68
Daily	61.83

Liquidity

The liquidity of a savings account will also influence how much the account earns. Liquidity means the ease and speed with which savings can be converted to cash. The longer the savers are willing to tie up their money, the higher the interest rate.

Regular accounts are the most flexible or liquid; that is, deposits and withdrawals can be made at any time. Regular savings accounts allow you to deposit small amounts of money and to withdraw your savings whenever you want to. The law allows the bank to require from a customer up to 60 days' notice before a withdrawal, but this technicality is seldom enforced. To open a regular account, you fill

Interest is one of the most important factors in choosing a place to save.

out a signature card, make a deposit to your account, and receive a savings account passbook. A *passbook* shows your deposits, withdrawals, interest earned, and the balance of your account.

Special savings accounts, often called time deposits, specify a fixed amount of money that must be deposited and a period of time during which the saver promises not to withdraw money from the account. The savings placed in these special accounts may be recorded on forms called *certificates of deposit,* or they may be recorded in passbooks similar to those provided for regular accounts. These passbook accounts are known by various names such as bonus savings accounts or golden passbooks. A bank or other financial institution usually pays a higher interest rate for money left on deposit for a certain period of time. This period varies from three months to six years or more. Often there is a penalty, such as a reduction in the interest earned, for withdrawing money from savings before the stated time.

Safety of Principal

What would happen to savers' money if a bank or other financial institution closed? Occasionally these institutions do go out of business or have losses, so the safety of deposits is an important consideration. The majority of savers rely on the insurance systems which cover deposits in financial institutions. Not all banks, savings and loan associations, or credit unions are required to have insurance protection; therefore, it is important to know what to look for.

Most commercial banks are insured by the Federal Deposit Insurance Corporation. The FDIC symbol will be prominently displayed by banks which are under its protection. The FDIC insures accounts up to $100,000, but coverage is limited to $100,000 for each depositor in all types of accounts. For example, if a customer has a checking account of $1,500 and a savings account of $3,000, the customer will have total insurance coverage of $4,500.

Many savings and loan association accounts are insured by the Federal Savings and Loan Insurance Corporation. The insurance coverage — $100,000 on savings accounts — is comparable to FDIC coverage. Like commercial banks, all savings and loan associations are not required to have depositors' insurance. In 1970 the National Credit Union Administration (NCUA) was created to provide up to $100,000 insurance protection for each account in all federally chartered unions. Depositors should look for these insurance symbols.

Besides insurance coverage, these agencies also conduct periodic inspections in order to expose unsound or risky practices which could endanger an institution's financial stability. Financial institutions which do not adhere to sound, stable practices can lose insurance coverage. The symbols for FDIC, FSLIC, and NCUA are shown in Illus. 14-1.

Illus. 14-1

Symbols of insurance systems for financial institutions

Other Considerations

There are some other factors which must be considered when you select a savings institution.

Free Gifts. Savers are often enticed into making deposits by offers of thermos bottles, stuffed toys, plants, wigs, or television sets. Remember that the interest rate is far more important than a plant or a thermos bottle.

Base your choice of savings institution on interest and convenience – not on free gifts.

Grace Days. Some financial institutions allow grace days when computing interest. The term *grace days* refers to the method of figuring interest on your account. Some financial institutions calculate interest from the first of the month, even if the deposit is not made until the tenth of the month. Others may pay interest until the end of the month even if money is withdrawn a few days before the end of the month. The wise saver looks for regular accounts that pay interest from the day-of-deposit to the day-of-withdrawal (DD/DW).

Convenience. Many savers consider convenience an important feature. Some savers keep their savings in a financial institution because of the location or free services such as checking accounts, safe deposit boxes, and travelers checks. The smart saver considers how much convenience is costing, since with more convenience you may earn a lower rate of interest on savings.

Minimum Balance and Excess Withdrawals. Watch for banks or other financial institutions requiring a minimum balance. A *minimum balance* is an amount which must be kept on deposit in order to earn interest. Some financial institutions charge penalty fees for excessive withdrawals over a period of time. Put your money in financial institutions which do not require minimum balances or charge penalties for excessive withdrawals.

BONDS AND STOCKS AS INVESTMENTS

Savings accounts are popular ways to invest money, but there are other ways to invest such as buying bonds and stock. Over 25 million individual Americans own shares of stock in American businesses. Millions of others buy municipal or corporate bonds.

Bonds

A *bond* is a printed promise to pay a definite amount of money, with interest, at a specified future time. When you buy a bond, you lend money to either a corporation or the government. Actually a bond is a long-term loan. You get three things when you buy a bond: (1) an obligation by the bond issuer to pay back the entire amount—or the face value; (2) a maturity date; (3) an interest rate. For example, if you buy a $1,000 Ford $8\frac{1}{8}$90 bond from Ford Motor Company (the issuer), you will be paid an annual interest rate of $8\frac{1}{8}$ percent, or $81.25 per $1,000, until 1990. At the date of maturity (1990), Ford will pay back the $1,000, or face value, of the bond.

There are two ways of collecting the interest on bonds. Some bonds have *coupons* which must be clipped from the bond and taken to a designated bank or other location for payment. Other bonds are *registered* in your name, and interest payment checks are sent directly to you in the mail.

Bonds are issued by municipalities and corporations. *Municipal bonds* are issued by states, cities, counties, school districts, and other governmental bodies to raise money for schools, hospitals, streets, and so forth. A municipal bond is shown in Illus. 14-2. *Corporate bonds* are issued by private companies to raise money for plant expansion or other company operations.

Illus. 14-2

Municipal bond

Stocks

Investors earn money from shares of stock through dividends or capital gains. *Dividends* are earned when a company makes a profit and distributes the profit to its shareholders. Generally dividends are issued four times a year. It is also possible to make money on common stock through a *capital gain,* or an increase in the market value of a share of stock. A capital gain occurs when you sell stock for more than you paid.

When you buy *common stock* — which represents a share of the ownership in a company — you are entitled to vote on company issues. Common stock is presented in Illus. 14-3. *Preferred stock* has preference over common stock in the payment of dividends. The dividends paid preferred stockholders are usually limited to a certain rate, such as 10 percent. Preferred stockholders are paid first if profits are available for distribution, but they do not vote on company-related issues.

To buy and sell stock, the investor must open an account with a *broker,* that is, a salesperson who specializes in buying and selling stocks and bonds. Only brokers can trade stock, but the investor instructs the broker when to buy or sell. Investors pay a *commission,* a fee paid a broker for services in buying and selling securities such

Illus. 14-3

Common stock

as stock. Commission rates vary according to the brokerage house and the size of the trade.

Many investors buy a hundred shares which is called a *round lot*. A purchase of less than 100 is called an *odd lot*. Small investors pay higher broker commissions if they buy or sell odd lots.

Stocks are traded in national and regional stock exchanges. The biggest of these is the New York Stock Exchange where over 84 percent of all listed securities are bought and sold. The American

The New York Stock Exchange is the largest stock exchange in the United States.

Source: Edward C. Topple, N.Y.S.E. Photographer

Stock Exchange is the other national exchange. The over-the-counter market is also a national network of dealers and brokers who trade among themselves by telephone, telegraph, or teletype.

Caveat Emptor: *Investment Schemes*

"Worried About Inflation? Diamonds Will Protect You." "Need Extra Money? Earn $350 weekly part-time—$750 weekly full time...$45,000 potential...operate out of your home...your investment totally secured with vending machines." "Make quick money—join a pyramid club. For only $1,000 you can earn $16,000." These investment scams and many more like them are found many times in the marketplace. Unfortunately they are hard to stamp out. Most operate on the principle that greed will overcome common sense.

After the stock market crash of 1929, Congress established the U. S. Securities and Exchange Commission, a federal agency whose purpose is to correct the unsound stock selling practices and schemes which occurred prior to the crash. The commission has two basic responsibilities:

—To see that companies which offer *securities* (stocks, bonds, and the like) for sale in "interstate commerce" file with the commission and make available to investors complete and accurate information.

—To protect investors against misrepresentation and fraud in the issuance and sale of securities.

The SEC requires issuers of new securities to publicly disclose in a *prospectus* (a printed statement) all relevant facts needed to evaluate carefully a stock issue, a land development venture, and other investments. The SEC requires disclosure of facts which are essential for informed analysis, but it cannot bar the sale of securities or other investments which have little or no value.

Defrauded investors generally must use the courts to recover money. The investor's best protection is the following SEC advice:

—Don't deal with strange security firms or salespersons. Consult your banker or other experienced person you know or trust.
—Be sure you understand the risk of loss.
—Tell the salesperson to put all the information in writing or to mail you a prospectus.
—Give at least as much consideration to investing as you would to buying other valuable products or property.
—Don't speculate or play the market.
—Don't listen to high pressure sales talk.
—Beware of tips, rumors, and promises of spectacular profits.

You must protect yourself when investing. Buyer Beware.

OTHER INVESTMENT OPTIONS

The small investor, who has limited knowledge about financial investments and/or is too busy to study the stock or bond market and handle a variety of investments, has some options which should be investigated. Below we will discuss U. S. savings bonds, U. S. government securities, money market funds, mutual funds, investment clubs, and employee stock purchase plans.

U. S. Savings Bonds

U. S. savings bonds were established nearly forty years ago and ever since have provided a means for millions of Americans to save regularly. The popularity and success of the bonds appear to result from the payroll savings plan, whereby individuals can buy a bond each month through a payroll deduction.

U. S. savings bonds are backed by the power of the government to tax and the country's faith in the government to pay its debts. Although sometimes criticized for being low, the rate of interest on

U. S. savings bonds is guaranteed. It may be increased in the future, but it cannot be decreased. Bonds can be cashed in after six months. They are considered a secure form of savings because if they are lost, stolen, or destroyed, they will be replaced upon receipt of a valid claim.

U. S. Government Securities

When the United States government needs money, it sells U. S. government securities known as bills, notes, and bonds. This is the government's way of borrowing money. U. S. securities are as safe as any insured savings account since they are backed by the government. Interest on U. S. government securities is free of state income taxes. The most common U. S. security, the U. S. Treasury bill, is sold for a minimum purchase price of $10,000. It can be purchased through a local bank for a small service fee or directly from a Federal Reserve Bank.

Certificates of Deposit

Commercial banks and savings and loan associations, in order to remain competitive in the market for money, offer certificates of deposit. The interest rates for six-month certificates are tied to the weekly U. S. Treasury bill interest rate. The federal government has imposed stringent penalty regulations for early withdrawal from a certificate of deposit. A depositer can lose three months' interest on certificates of less than one year, and six months' interest on longer certificates, whether earned or not.

Money Market Funds

Money market funds provide high rates of interest, liquidity, and safety of principal for savers. Money market funds invest in short-term securities such as corporate notes, U. S. Treasury notes, and certificates of deposit. Money market funds usually require a minimum deposit such as $1,000 to $2,500. Thereafter, it may be possible to make deposits of as little as $100. Some money market funds allow checks to be written on the account. Money market funds are not insured but are considered safe. Interest rates on money market funds vary from day to day.

Mutual Funds

Small investors seldom have enough money to diversify and enough knowledge to make a sound stock or bond investment decision. For such investors, a mutual fund is a means of pooling funds with thousands of other people in order to acquire a wide variety of stocks, bonds, and other types of investments. When investors buy a share in a mutual fund, they are buying shares in a mutual fund company which will then purchase the different stocks, bonds, and other investments.

Investment Clubs

One way for the small investor to learn about investing and also to begin making regular investments is to join an investment club. The number of investment clubs varies from year to year. In recent years the number has ranged from 12,000 to 50,000 clubs, with each club having between 10 and 15 members. Often the members know each other socially, or belong to the same firm or organization. Every month, the club meets to make decisions about buying or selling stocks.

Members are expected to make stock investigations. The members pick stocks, pool their money, and share in the expenses, losses, or gains in proportion to the amount each member has invested in the club. According to the National Association of Investment Clubs, the average club has earned 10 percent annually.

Employee Stock Purchase Plans

Many companies offer attractive stock purchase plans to their employees. These plans provide a way to save and invest regularly through payroll deductions. Some companies will match all or part of the employee contributions, others will put the contributions into a fund with professional management, and others may use the funds to purchase the company stock. People who have employee stock purchase plans should take advantage of this convenient means of investing.

HOW TO INVEST WISELY

Achievement of certain investment goals can be reasonably assured when the following three principles are applied. Generally the higher a rate of return from an investment, the greater are your chances of experiencing a loss from the investment.

Establish an Investment Goal

Establish an investment goal which is suitable to you. Most investments earn income in two ways: dividends, interest, or rent, and/or growth (an increase) in the value of the stock, real estate, and the like. Your investment goal, either income or growth, will depend largely on your stage in the life cycle. A young person or young family will usually seek an increase in the value of the investment. An older person not able to wait for growth because of advanced age may set income as the investment goal.

Seek Diversification in Investments

One requirement for successful investing is finding a mixture of investments suitable for your goal. The concept of *diversification* can best be summed up with the expression, "Don't put all your eggs in one basket." For example, an investor can diversify by investing in stocks, savings accounts, bonds, and real estate. In addition there may be diversification within a type of investment such as investing in the stock of at least three different companies. This procedure prevents the investor from committing all funds to one stock. By diversifying, the investor stands a much better chance of earning money and avoiding losses.

Revise Investments when Conditions Change

It is necessary for investments to be revised or adjusted when economic conditions or personal circumstances change. No one type of investment works best all the time. Changing conditions in the economy, in the marketplace, or in interest rates may require the investor to shift from bonds to common stocks, or from common stock to money market funds.

Caveat Emptor: *Personal Financial Planners*

Financial planning consultants all claim to have some expertise in helping people map out their financial goals and develop a strategy for accomplishing these goals. Some operate from door-to-door, and others represent the biggest banks and brokerage houses in the country.

Financial consultants are individuals with differing backgrounds and varying degrees of competence in money management. There are no standards for financial planners. Anyone can enter the field. Some financial planning consultants are insurance brokers, securities dealers, mutual fund salespeople, accountants, lawyers, and bankers. A few are people who are selling fraudulent schemes or investments which pay them a commission, but offer the investor very little value.

At this time financial planners do not have to register with the Securities and Exchange Commission or file any kind of financial-disclosure information. Some earn their incomes from a flat-fee ranging from $40 for a simple computer printout to $2,500 or more for an elaborate financial plan. Most financial planners earn commissions from the sale of stocks or bonds, mutual funds, life insurance, real estate, and so forth.

Sometimes there may be a lack of objectivity and a conflict of interest. Abuses can occur when financial planners have a direct interest in the sale of stocks, bonds, insurance, tax shelters, and various other financial products which are a part of their advice and plan. This is not to say that financial planners are modern day financial quacks. Far from it. Many do provide valuable, expert services. But until professional standards are achieved, look for evidence of professional credentials. Ask for the following: a full disclosure of costs, how the planner is to be paid, and an explanation of the nature of the financial plan. Buyer Beware.

SAVING AND INVESTING = ECONOMIC GROWTH

Saving results from spending less on consumer goods. When individuals save, they reduce present consumption for larger future consumption. Obviously when individuals and families save, they benefit by building up wealth, or capital, as economists call it. By building up some surplus money or capital, consumers can often achieve a comfortable standard of living. In addition to the personal benefits, there are social and economic benefits to the nation as a result of saving and investing. Economists consider saving to be critically important for a nation's economic growth and standard of living. When individuals save, the money generally goes into financial institutions. These financial institutions channel the money into business ventures, buildings, inventories, industrial expansion, new enterprises, new tools, replacement of old equipment with new equipment, development of new technology, and so forth. This is called *capital formation*. Investment money, then, must be available in order for economic growth to continue. In short, savings flow into investments. Investments achieve economic growth. Saving and investing help to build and maintain a strong economy.

VOCABULARY REVIEW

Saving	Common stock
Investing	Odd lot
Municipal bonds	Mutual fund
Corporate bonds	

QUESTIONS FOR REVIEW

1. What are three reasons for saving?

2. What is a credit union, and how can a person belong to a credit union?

3. What are three main features an investor should look for when opening a savings account?

4. What are the different ways in which interest can be compounded, and when all other factors are the same, which method results in the highest yield for consumers?

5. What are the ways an investor can earn income from investing?

6. What are three basic principles of investing which help to reduce the risks of investing?

7. Name at least five ways for small investors to invest other than in savings accounts.

PROBLEM-SOLVING AND DECISION-MAKING PROJECTS

1. Assume that you have $1,000 to put into a savings account. After investigating a commercial bank, a savings and loan association, and a credit union, you have the following information.

Commercial Bank	Savings and Loan Association	Credit Union
5.25% interest (Annual effective rate 5.39%)	5.5% interest (Annual effective rate 5.61%)	6% interest
Compounded daily	Compounded quarterly	Compounded annually
DD/DW	DD/DW	DD/DW
FDIC insured	FSLIC insured	NCUA insured

Which account would earn the highest rate of return on the $1,000 in one year? Which is more important, the interest rate or the method of compounding interest?

2. If you've ever saved money for a specific goal, can you describe how it made you feel? Assume that you have a goal to have $2,000 saved in three years. How much would you have to save each month to accomplish the goal? Devise a simple plan to help you accomplish this goal.

3. From the financial section of the daily newspaper or the *Wall Street Journal*, obtain the names and high-low and closing prices of two of each of the following types of investments:

a. Stock traded on the New York Stock Exchange
b. Stock traded on the over-the-counter market
c. Mutual funds
d. Municipal or corporate bonds

COMMUNITY AND HOME PROJECTS

1. Visit one of your community's financial institutions and get some descriptive literature from them and make a report to your class on the different kinds of savings plans offered. Find out what rules affect each of the plans and what interest rates are for each plan.

2. The National Association of Investment Clubs can be of great assistance to persons who want to form an investment club. Write the NAIC or contact a local stockbroker and make a report on the specific aids available for persons interested in forming an investment club.

   National Association of Investment Clubs
   115 E. 11 Mile Road
   Royal Oak, Michigan 48067

3. Information about a company is contained in an annual report. Even if you are not a shareholder, you may request an annual report from a company. Obtain the annual report of a company listed on the New York Stock Exchange and find an account of the earnings, the company's view on its prospects for the future, and any discussion of its research, new products, and relationships with any subsidiaries (a company wholly owned and controlled by another).

Chapter 15

Consumer Credit (Part 1)

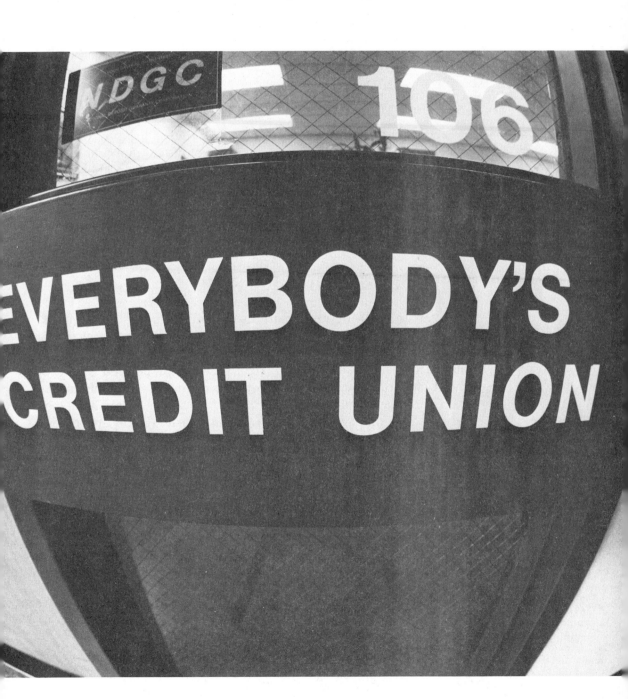

"Buy now, pay later," appears to be the philosophy of many Americans. Credit usage has been a way of life for most consumers in the past few decades. Actually the term "credit" is another way of saying "debt" or "money owed." In this chapter we will discuss some of the reasons for using credit, present the types and sources of credit, and examine some of the laws which give consumers rights and responsibilities when using credit.

CREDIT — TOOL OR TRAP

Credit allows the immediate use of products or services in exchange for a promise to pay in the future. In other words the use of credit creates a debt — but people generally find the term "credit" more acceptable than the term "debt." Credit can be used wisely, or it can be badly abused. Used properly, it can be a valuable tool in money management. Used improperly, it can be a trap that may result in a credit habit and even financial disaster. Below are some of the reasons people use credit.

1. *Allows Consumers Immediate Use of Products.* A young person who has little money may want to set up an apartment which requires cash outlay for furnishings of various kinds. With credit, the furniture can be paid for while the person is using it.

2. *Is Convenient and Safe.* Credit allows consumers to travel or shop without carrying large amounts of cash. If a person does not have cash on hand but needs gasoline, a credit card can be used. In addition credit gives the consumer the

ability to purchase goods that are on sale at a time when cash is not available for the purchase.

3. *Can Help in Emergencies.* When consumers experience medical expenses, or loss of a job, credit can be used to pay living expenses during the emergency.

4. *Promotes Efficient Record Keeping and Budgeting.* Monthly statements from credit card companies can easily be used to keep track of expenditures. Complaints and returns are often easier to handle since credit card receipts are your record of purchase.

5. *Establishes Proof of Financial Responsibility.* Getting credit can be difficult at first; but once a credit record is established, it is evidence of your ability to handle credit wisely.

When used wisely, credit is a valuable tool in money management.

Source: Wickes Companies, Inc.

Americans use credit to borrow money from a bank or other financial institution, or to obtain the use of merchandise from a retailer before paying for it. The use of credit has become associated with the good life—a means by which wage-earners can acquire goods and services that they might otherwise not be able to afford. Americans are heavy credit users, and almost everyone arranges to use some sort of credit in a lifetime. Since credit is so popular among Americans, is there anything wrong with using credit? Below are some of the problems of using credit.

1. *Credit is rented money.* You spend more money when you use credit than when you use cash. Later we will look at the cost of credit and ways to reduce the cost of using credit.
2. *Credit ties up future income.* When credit purchases are made, you are actually spending future income or earnings. Too much future income tied up in making credit payments can be a burden. Use only as much credit as you can repay comfortably.
3. *Credit makes it easy to overspend.* Avoid credit buying just because it is easy to say, "Charge it." Statistics show that consumers with credit cards spend 20 percent more in a store than customers without credit. Be sure each credit purchase is something you really want or need. Try to use credit only for purchases that will have some value after you finish paying for them.

TYPES OF CREDIT

Consumers get either cash or goods and services in exchange for a promise to pay when they use credit. Basically, two major types of credit are available to consumers: loan credit and sales credit.

Loan Credit

Loan credit is credit used to borrow money. Loan credit is available to consumers from banks and other financial institutions. Loans to meet personal and family needs for relatively small amounts are called *personal* or *consumer loans.* For example, a person may borrow money to pay for a new motorcycle. Personal loans can be repaid in *installments* (small amounts paid over a period of time) or in a single large payment. A personal loan agreement is shown on page 305.

More will be said about installment loans later in this chapter and in Chapter 16.

Sales Credit

Sales credit is used to acquire goods and services and pay for them at a later time. Sometimes called *retail credit*, it is made available by retail stores, oil companies, furniture stores, banks, and the like. There are three types of sales credit: regular charge accounts, revolving charge accounts, and installment credit.

Regular Charge Accounts. The seller agrees to let you purchase what you want during the "open" period and expects full payment at the end of the period. The open period is usually one month. There are no finance charges for the services received during the month; but if the amount due is not paid within the specified period of time, finance charges may be added to the next monthly statement in some cases.

Revolving Charge Accounts. Most credit cards issued by oil companies, banks, and department stores use the revolving charge account, which allows customers to pay the whole bill every month and avoid any finance charge. Consumers who cannot pay the entire amount due are required to pay a minimum payment and the balance over a period of time. Revolving charge accounts are sometimes called *open-ended credit*. Finance charges of 12 to 21 percent are assessed on the unpaid amount. Monthly payments will vary depending on the balance due at the end of a billing period. The finance charges (the cost of credit) will be stated as both a monthly rate such as 1½ percent per month, and as an annual percentage rate (APR) such as 18 percent annually.

A revolving charge account is opened by filling out an application and signing a credit agreement. The credit agreement covers all future purchases and establishes the *credit limit* or the maximum amount which can be bought on credit. Credit agreements should be read carefully and understood since the provisions of credit agreement establish a legal obligation which can be enforced in a court of law.

As Illus. 15-1 shows, the finance charge on revolving charge accounts can vary even when the APR is the same and the payments

PREVIOUS BALANCE METHOD:

Previous Balance on December 1, 1983	$100.00
Payment on December 10, 1983	10.00
New Charges on Account	0.00
FINANCE CHARGE	1.00
Computed as 1% per month on the	
Previous Balance which is an	
ANNUAL PERCENTAGE RATE OF 12%	
New Balance January 1, 1984	91.00

Finance Charge is computed as 1% of previous balance before deducting payments or credits. $100 × 1% = $1

AVERAGE DAILY BALANCE METHOD:

Previous Balance on December 1, 1983	$100.00
Payment on December 10, 1983	10.00
New Charges on Account	0.00
FINANCE CHARGE	.96
Computed as 1% per month on the	
average daily balance which is an	
ANNUAL PERCENTAGE RATE of 12%	
New Balance January 1, 1984	90.96

Finance Charge is figured as 1% of the average daily balance. The average daily balance of $96.13 is computed thus:

December 1–December 10 daily balance of $100	$10 × 100 = \$1,000$
December 10–December 21 daily balance of $90	$21 × 90 = \underline{1,890}$
	$2,890

$$\frac{\$2,890}{31} = \$96.13 \times 1\% = \$.96$$

ADJUSTED BALANCE METHOD:

Previous Balance on December 1, 1983	$100.00
Payment on December 10, 1983	10.00
New Charges on Account	0.00
FINANCE CHARGE	.90
Computed as 1% per month of	
adjusted balance which is an	
ANNUAL PERCENTAGE RATE OF 12%	
New Balance January 1, 1984	90.90

Finance Charge is figured as 1% of adjusted balance after payments and credits are deducted. $90 × 1% = $.90

Illus. 15-1

Different methods of determining finance charges on revolving charge accounts are the same. The best method for customers, the adjusted balance, is the least used. The most commonly used method is the average daily balance. The credit agreement and the billing statement will tell which method is used.

Installment Credit. *Installment credit*, in which a debt is repaid in a series of payments, is used primarily for larger, more expensive purchases. It is usually necessary to make a down payment and sign a separate contract for each purchase. Monthly payments are made in fixed, small installments over a period of time ranging from 6 to 48 months. Finance charges of 12 to more than 24 percent are added to the cash price. Two out of every three buyers of new cars finance part of the purchase price with an installment contract. An installment contract is shown in Illus. 15-2.

INSTALLMENT CONTRACT AND SECURITY AGREEMENT

Sergio Sound Systems, Inc.
The South Mall • Amarillo, TX 79199

I (we) the undersigned buyer(s) buy from, and grant a security interest, to SERGIO SOUND SYSTEMS, INC. in this property:

Quantity	Description	Amount	
1	Model XV-466	400	00
	Turntable		
Description of Trade-in:			
	Sales Tax	16	00
	Total	416	00

Buyer's Name Maria Benitez
Buyer's Address 805 Elberon Ave.
City Amarillo State TX Zip 79199

1	Cash Price		$ 400.00
2	Less: Down Payment	$ 40.00	
3	Trade-in	$ —	
4	Total Down		$ 40.00
5	Unpaid Balance of Cash Price		$ 360.00
6	Other charges: Sales Tax		$ 16.00
7	AMOUNT FINANCED		$ 376.00
8	FINANCE CHARGE		$ 37.68
9	Total of Payments		$ 413.68
10	Deferred Payment Price (1 + 6 + 8)		$ 453.68
11	ANNUAL PERCENTAGE RATE		18.5 %

Insurance Agreement

Credit life insurance is available at a cost of $3.00 for the term of the credit. The purchase of insurance is voluntary and not required for credit.

I want insurance.

Signed: — Date: —

I do not want insurance.

Signed: Maria Benitez Date: 1/15/--

Signed: Date:

The Buyer(s) agrees to pay to SERGIO SOUND SYSTEMS, INC. at their store the "Total of Payments" shown above in 12 monthly installments of 34.47 and a final installment of 34.51. The first installment is due February 15, 19-- and all other payments are due on the same day of the month until paid in full. The finance charge applies from 1/15/--.

Signed: Maria Benitez Date: 1/15/--

Notice to Buyer: You should get a copy of this contract when you sign. You can pay in advance the unpaid balance of this contract and get a partial refund of the finance charge based on the "Actuarial Method."

Illus. 15-2

Installment contract and security agreement

THE COST OF CREDIT

The Consumer Credit Protection Act, commonly known as the Truth in Lending Act, requires that creditors tell consumers exactly the cost of buying on credit. The purpose of the law is to assure full disclosure of all credit costs in terms so that consumers can compare costs. It does not set interest rates or other credit charges. Disclosure of costs must be made in writing before credit is extended.

The *finance charge* is the total dollar amount it costs to use credit. The finance charges include *interest* (the cost of using someone else's money) and sometimes other costs. For example, it could cost $70 in interest, as well as a credit investigation fee of $10, to borrow $1,000 for a year. The dollar amount of the finance charge would be $80.

The *annual percentage rate* (APR) is the percentage cost of credit on a yearly basis. The borrower does not have to know how to compute the APR but should know that the APR is the key to comparing credit costs. Assume again that you wish to borrow $1,000 with a dollar finance charge of $80. It might appear that the $80 represents 8 percent of $1,000. Actually if you could keep the full $1,000 for the whole year and pay it all back at one time, the APR would be 8 percent. But with installment contracts, you do not have the full $1,000 for the entire year. If the $1,000 is repaid in 12 equal payments of $90 each, the balance of the debt decreases each month. At the end of six months, only $500 remains of the amount originally borrowed. In fact, you have less and less of the $1,000 each month. By the last month, all but $90 of the original loan has been repaid. In this example the $80 finance charge on $1,000 amounts to 14.5 percent for the year.

Credit insurance is another cost of credit. It is sold to persons borrowing money or purchasing goods or services on an installment contract. The purchase of insurance is voluntary and not required for credit. There are two types of credit insurance: credit life and credit disability. With *credit life* insurance, the debtor's life is insured for the amount of the unpaid loan. If the debtor dies, the proceeds of the policy go to the *creditor* (the one to whom money is owed) to pay off the loan obligation. *Credit disability* (accident and health) insurance provides that the insurance company will make installment payments on money owed while a debtor is disabled. Disability is defined in the policy; plans differ according to the number of days the debtor must be disabled before benefits will begin to be paid. Credit disability insurance rates are nearly always higher than the rates for credit life insurance.

Caveat Emptor: *Credit Insurance*

The cost of credit insurance is usually expressed as a certain number of cents per $100 of debt. If credit life insurance in your state costs 75¢ per $100 of debt, then the cost of $3,000 of credit insurance for a three-year loan would be 75¢ × 30 × 3 years or $67.50. Credit insurance often appears inexpensive, but it actually is three to four times higher than other types of life insurance.

Credit insurance is sold by finance companies, car dealers, banks, and other lenders who act as agents for companies that sell credit insurance. Credit insurance can be valuable in some circumstances but not in others. Credit life insurance should be considered when:

1. the amount of the loan contract is large such as a home mortgage
2. the contract is spread over a long period of time such as a home mortgage
3. the person is 50 years old or older, and the person has an inadequate existing insurance plan
4. the person has a health problem that makes conventional life insurance or health insurance too costly or impossible to obtain

Credit life insurance does not make economic sense when:

1. the installment contract is for a relatively small amount such as a car loan, appliance, or furniture loan
2. the installment contract is for a relatively short period of time, particularly less than 48 months
3. it is for young people who are very likely to pay off their installment contracts
4. it is for people who have adequate existing life insurance coverage

Critics often claim that lenders influence consumers into taking credit insurance. One Federal Reserve Bank study found that among people who had purchased credit insurance, 36 to 45 percent thought that it was either required or strongly recommended by banks, retailers, and finance companies. The Federal Trade Commission found that of a group of consumers who had actually bought credit insurance, 45 percent did not understand that they did not have to buy it. Although state laws and the federal Truth in Lending Act require that the purchase of credit insurance be voluntary, consumers often think that it must be purchased in order to qualify for the loan. Buyer Beware.

SOURCES OF CONSUMER CREDIT

As stated earlier, consumers can get cash credit or sales credit from a number of different sources: banks, finance companies, retail stores, travel and entertainment companies, and oil companies. Following is a closer look at some of the common credit-granting institutions.

Commercial Banks

Commercial banks offer consumers loans that can be repaid in one lump sum or in regular monthly installments. Banks typically make installment loans on automobile and other larger consumer good items. Some banks also offer credit cards which can be used to buy goods and services at stores which participate in the credit card plans.

Credit Unions

Credit unions (cooperative associations which accept savings deposits and make small loans to their members) are the fastest growing financial institutions in the United States. These cooperative associations are organized by persons who have a common occupation, association membership, or residence. Nationwide there are over 22,000 federally and state chartered credit unions with 36 million members. Credit unions have low operating costs

Commercial banks are only one of the many kinds of credit-granting institutions.

(they are owned and operated by the members themselves), free office space, and minimal clerical and management expenses. As a result, they can lend money to members at rates slightly less than commercial banks and less than other financial institutions. Credit unions, generally the cheapest source of credit, can make installment loans, personal loans, home improvement loans, and even home mortgage loans.

Finance Companies

Finance companies, sometimes called consumer finance companies or personal finance companies, often appeal to people with emergency needs or to people who have been turned down by other lending agencies. *Finance companies* specialize in loans with either single or installment repayments. Finance company interest rates are higher — sometimes two to three times higher — than those of commercial banks or credit unions. This is because these companies lend to individuals who would not be considered credit worthy by commercial banks. Finance companies spend a great deal of money trying to collect from people who are unable or unwilling to pay. They often experience losses from uncollectible loans.

Finance companies usually limit loans to between $500 and $2,500. The interest rates and the loan limits are set by state law. On a 12-month, $1,000 loan at a finance company, the annual percentage rate can be as high as 35 percent, but the rates range between 26 and 30 percent in most states.

Savings and Loan Associations

Savings and loan associations specialize in home mortgage and home improvement loans. They also are authorized to make educational loans and personal loans. The interest rates are comparable to those of commercial banks. Some savings and loan associations also issue VISA and MasterCard credit cards to customers.

Pawn Shops and Loan Sharks

When individuals or families are not able to get loans from financial institutions such as banks or small finance companies, they sometimes turn to pawn shops and loan sharks. This form of borrowing money can be very expensive and should be avoided.

For a cash loan, pawnbrokers accept collateral (something of value) such as jewelry, art objects, watches, and clothing. The pawnbroker usually lends only about 40 percent of the resale value of the

Borrowing money from a pawn shop is an unsound financial decision.

article at a high interest rate of 36 to 50 percent. The pawnbroker keeps the collateral for the period of the loan and returns it when the loan has been repaid. Problems occur when people do not save the money to repay the loan, and they lose their collateral which was worth more than the loan.

Desperate or ignorant borrowers may turn to loan sharks. These are illegal credit lenders who charge very high rates for money; for example, $50 now in exchange for $75 on payday. Usually loans are cash loans for one week or one month. Rates are not quoted because they range from 100 to 500 percent. Collection practices often involve threats of harm and violence, even though federal law forbids the use of violence, threats, or other criminal methods to collect a debt. Loan sharks should be avoided regardless of how bad your financial circumstances might be.

HOW CREDIT IS GRANTED

Credit is granted to consumers on the basis of their ability to earn a regular income, their past record of paying bills on time, and other evidence of financial responsibility. The applicant will be asked to complete a credit application form which will ask for the following type of information: length of residence, evidence of home and car ownership, a checking account or savings account, the kind of job held and income earned, how much money was borrowed in the past, the source of borrowing, whether the loan was repaid or not, and other current loans or types of charge accounts. From the information provided, a loan officer tries to determine the applicant's credit worthiness. *Credit worthiness* is a person's ability to repay debts, and it is determined either by judgment or by a scoring system.

Judgment of Creditor

If credit is based on judgment, the creditor will consider the "three C's" of credit: capacity, character, and collateral.

Capacity: Do you have the capacity to repay the loan? Creditors ask for employment information such as your occupation, how long you have worked, how much you earn. They also want to know about your expenses such as rent, mortgage, car payments, and the like.

Character: Will you repay the debt? Have you been responsible about meeting financial obligations? How often and how much have you used credit? Have you paid bills on time? Paying on time is a sign of good character. Creditors also look for other signs of stability such as how long you have lived at your present address or whether you own a home or rent.

Collateral: Is the creditor protected from loss if you fail to pay? What sources do you have for repaying debt other than wages or a salary? Creditors want to know if you have a savings account or other assets (car, home, etc.) to offer as security for a loan.

Credit-Scoring Systems

Because of laws which prohibit discrimination, large credit lending institutions have developed credit application scoring systems. These replace the human judgment factor and reduce the possibility of discrimination in rating someone for credit. Credit-scoring systems work on the principle that credit worthiness is based on a combination of characteristics which can be scored or given points. Such a scoring system is shown in Illus. 15-3. If applicants obtain a certain score, they get credit; if not, they are usually denied credit.

EQUAL CREDIT OPPORTUNITY ACT

Consumers have rights which they should know when they apply for credit. The Equal Credit Opportunity Act makes it illegal for lenders to grant credit on any characteristics other than those which reflect credit worthiness. Credit can be denied only because of an applicant's financial status, credit history, or other money-related reasons. The law specifically says that creditors cannot:

—deny credit on the basis of sex, marital status, race, color, religion, national origin, or age (if old enough to enter into a binding contract)

—deny credit because an applicant receives any income from a public program

Hypothetical Credit-Scoring Table

1.

Fill out your credit profile by answering the nine questions below in Table 1. Circle the one response that applies to you, and then find your total score by adding up the points you got for each response. The points are found in the lower right-hand corner of each box. (For example: if you are under 25 years old, you get 12 points.) Once you've totaled your score, look at Table 2 to find out how good a credit "bet" you may be.

	under 25	25-29	30-34	35-39	40-44	45-49	50 or over
age?	12	5	0	1	18	22	31
time at address?	less than 1 yr. — 9	1-2 yrs. — 0	2-3 yrs. — 5	3-5 yrs. — 0	5-9 yrs. — 5	10 yrs. or more — 21	
age of auto?	none — 0	0-1 yr. — 12	2 yrs. — 16	3-4 yrs. — 13	5-7 yrs. — 3	8 yrs. or more — 0	
monthly auto payment?	none — 18	less than $125 — 18	$126-$150 — 6	$151-$199 — 1	$200 or more — 0		
housing cost?	less than $274 — 0	$275-$399 — 10	$400 or more — 12	owns clear — 12	lives with relatives — 24		
checking and savings accounts?	both — 15	checking only — 2	savings only — 2	neither — 0			
finance company reference?	yes — 0	no — 15					
major credit cards?	none — 0	1 — 5	2 or more — 15				
ratio of debt to income?	no debts — 41	1%-5% — 16	6%-15% — 20	16% or over — 0			

2.

A lender using this scoring table selects a cutoff point from a table like this, which gauges how likely applicants are to repay loans.

Total Score	Probability of Repayment
90	89 in 100
95	91 in 100
100	92 in 100
105	93 in 100
110	94 in 100
115	95 in 100
120	95.5 in 100
125	96 in 100
130	96.25 in 100

Source: Federal Reserve Board. Developed by Fair, Isaac, and Co., Inc. Modified to update.

Illus. 15-3

A credit-scoring system such as this one can help a lender determine whether the applicant is a good risk.

—ask questions concerning birth control practices, plans for children, or assume that a female applicant is likely to become pregnant and have an interruption of income

—ask about an applicant's marital status unless a spouse will be contractually liable for the loan, a spouse's income is counted on to repay a loan, and a spouse plans to use the loan

—refuse to consider part-time income of a working spouse, alimony, child support, or social security payments

—cancel a divorced or widowed person's credit when a marriage ends unless the income has dropped so much that the person may not be able to pay

The act does not entitle you to credit whenever you want it. You must still pass the creditor's tests which indicate your financial ability and willingness to repay the debt.

FIRST-TIME CREDIT

Credit is one of those things that is easy to get if you have had it before. But what about getting credit the first time? Below are some suggestions for establishing a credit reputation.

—Open a retail account at a store where your parents have an account. Some stores offer special teenage accounts with low credit limits.

—Establish a checking and savings account at the local bank. The way in which you manage your accounts can be a good indication of your financial responsibility. A savings account can be used to secure a first loan.

—Get a parent to *cosign* a small loan. By cosigning, your parent promises to pay if you do not. When you repay on time, your credit record has been established. The next time the store or financial institution may be willing to give you credit without a cosigner.

—Join a credit union. If your parents belong to a credit union, find out if they automatically grant membership to children of members. Many do. Credit unions are a good source for small loans.

—Be responsible in your work. Creditors generally ask for length of employment at a job and for personal references. Job related references can be important to the loan officer who has to judge your character.

CREDIT REPORTING AGENCIES

A credit record can be as important as a school academic record. Credit history is big business. There are about 2,500 credit bureaus, called credit reporting agencies, in the United States. These agencies process from 125 to 150 million credit reports each year. Credit bureaus collect information from merchants with whom consumers have credit, from public records, and from other sources of information. Credit reporting agencies exchange information among themselves and between regional bureaus. For this reason, a credit record will follow a consumer who moves from one state to another. Reporting agencies for a fee provide retailers, financial institutions, and government agencies with credit information on a person. Credit record information also is used by employers and insurance companies when considering an applicant for a job or for insurance.

Credit bureau reports are subject to errors which can unfairly deny credit to an applicant. Because of abuses and mistakes in credit reporting, the Fair Credit Reporting Act was passed to give consumers protection against inaccurate or obsolete information in credit files. Among other things, the act requires that:

—Within 30 days after consumers apply for credit they must be told whether their application has been approved. If denied, the consumer can request the reason for the denial and the name and address of the credit bureau that issued the report. Consumers who have been refused credit are entitled to a free copy of their report.

—Consumers have the right to know the substance and nature of the information contained in their credit files. Credit bureaus are not required to show you your records but may merely read to you information in the file. A small fee may be charged for the service.

—The credit bureau must reinvestigate information which consumers consider inaccurate. If data cannot be verified, it must be removed from the file. Consumers also have the right to insert a 100 word statement of their viewpoint about any unresolved disputes. Any revision must be sent to all creditors who received a report in the previous six months.

—Credit bureaus are required to remove most kinds of negative entries from the files after 7 years. The exception to this rule is bankruptcy which may be identified for 14 years.

YOUR RIGHTS AS A CREDIT CARD HOLDER

Credit cards—cards which identify the holder and give the holder the privilege of obtaining goods and services on credit—are now issued by numerous companies. Examples of these companies are local department stores, national retail chains, car rental companies, travel and entertainment companies, airlines, telephone companies, oil companies, hotel/motel chains, and commercial banks. These can be divided into three categories: (1) single-purpose cards; (2) multipurpose travel, food, and entertainment cards; and (3) all-purpose bank credit cards.

Single-purpose cards include those from oil companies such as Exxon, and those from department stores such as Sears or Montgomery Ward. There is no fee for the card, and the card allows the owner to make purchases or obtain services by presenting the card at the store, station, or company which issued the card. The card owner is billed once a month. If the bill is paid promptly, there is no finance charge. If not paid, a finance charge, usually 1 to 1½ percent per month, is charged on the unpaid balance.

Multipurpose travel and entertainment cards include American Express, Diners Club, and Carte Blanche. There is an annual membership fee. Card holders are billed every 30 to 60 days and are expected to pay promptly. If the bill is delinquent for 60 to 90 days, a finance charge may be added.

All-purpose bank cards include VISA and MasterCard. Some financial institutions charge a yearly fee for use of the card. Like single-purpose cards, a finance charge is levied on unpaid balances. Rates vary from state to state but are typically 18 percent yearly (1½ percent per month). See Illus. 15-4 for a credit card billing statement.

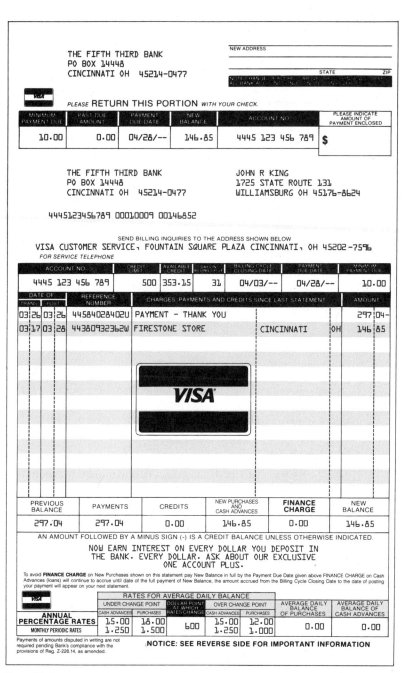

Illus. 15-4

Credit card billing statement

DEBIT CARDS

Debit cards look like credit cards and act like credit cards but with one major difference — these cards do not give you credit. When a salesperson imprints a receipt with your debit card and asks you to sign the receipt, you are spending your money and not the bank's. When the receipt is returned to your bank, your checking account is drawn down or debited. In effect you are paying by check. If you have a bank credit card, you are also entitled to hold a debit card issued by VISA or MasterCard.

People prefer credit cards because they can purchase an item now and pay later. Debit cards should be more widespread now that credit card issuers are charging annual fees for the use of credit cards. However, debit cards do not always come free either; banks sometimes levy an annual fee or a charge for each debit card transaction.

Credit Card Liability

The Truth in Lending Act also protects consumers against unauthorized use of credit cards. You do not have to pay for *any* unauthorized charges made *after* you notify the card company of loss or theft of your card. The maximum amount you have to pay is $50 — even if someone runs up several hundred dollars worth of charges before you report a card missing. As soon as you realize your card is stolen or lost, however, you should notify the issuer.

Billing Errors

The Fair Credit Billing Act requires prompt correction of credit card billing errors, sets up a procedure for correction of errors, and prevents damage to a credit rating while errors are in dispute. If there is a credit card billing mistake, the consumer should follow these steps.

—Notify the creditor in writing within 60 days after the bill was mailed. The notification must be in writing to the creditor on a separate piece of paper. Do not make a note on the bill. The notice should include your name, number of the account, a description of the suspected error, and the amount of the error.

—The creditor must reply within 30 days and resolve the matter within two billing periods, or within 90 days. The error must be corrected, or the creditor must explain why the bill is correct. During this period, it is not necessary to pay the amount in question; however, any other part of the bill not in question must be paid.

—Once a possible error has been reported to a creditor, the creditor cannot give out information to other creditors or credit bureaus or threaten to damage a consumer's credit rating. Until the letter is answered, the creditor cannot take any action to collect the disputed amount.

Cash Discounts

Retailers can give a discount on cash purchases. Retailers who give cash discounts often post a sign explaining the discount. Many merchants prefer to receive cash rather than to experience the delays

Some creditors will give a discount to customers who use cash instead of credit.

and expenses associated with credit card collections. Companies and banks that issue credit cards charge retailers 2 to 8 percent of the purchase price for collection and processing payments. The discount to cash customers is based on the assumption that the goods are marked up to cover the credit handling expenses. The cash discount passes a part of the retailer's savings back to the cash customer.

Defective Products

Consumers can withhold payment of a bill on defective merchandise purchased with a credit card. The consumer must try to resolve the problem directly with the seller and does not have to pay until the matter is resolved. In the case of credit cards not issued by the store, such as bank cards, two limitations apply to this right:

1. The original amount of the purchase must exceed $50.
2. The sale must take place in the consumer's state or within 100 miles of the consumer's current address.

VOCABULARY REVIEW

Finance charge	Revolving charge account
Loan credit	Installment credit
Sales credit	Credit worthiness
Regular charge account	Creditor

QUESTIONS FOR REVIEW

1. Why do so many consumers use credit?
2. What are five common institutions that provide consumer credit?
3. What are the "three C's" of credit?
4. What does the Equal Credit Opportunity Act say that creditors cannot do?
5. How can a teenager establish a credit reputation?
6. What are your rights under the Fair Credit Reporting Act?
7. What are the three types of credit cards? Cite examples of each.

8. When a credit card is lost or stolen, what is the card owner's financial liability?

PROBLEM-SOLVING AND DECISION-MAKING PROJECTS

1. Use the credit-scoring table on page 287 to determine how likely you are to repay a loan in the eyes of a lender. What information on this scoring table would make you a "high risk" borrower in the eyes of the lender? What information would make you a "good risk"? In your opinion what groups of people would have trouble getting credit after completing the credit-scoring table?

2. Assume that a friend, age 20, is buying a new car on a 36-month installment contract for $4,200. The friend has to decide whether to take insurance on the contract at a cost of $81. The friend asks you for advice. Explain what credit insurance is and whether you would recommend that the person should take this coverage.

3. A good friend of yours, Cinci Stowell, wants to borrow money from you. She is twenty-one, single, and fancy free. Cinci works as a typist at a local government agency. She is borrowing the money for a $150 emergency repair to her automobile. She has never borrowed money before or even charged anything. Therefore, she has no established credit rating. You have over $1,000 in your savings account, so lending the money would be no problem.
   a. What questions would you ask Cinci before lending the money?
   b. Would you lend Cinci the money and under what circumstances?
   c. If you do make the loan, how would you react if it was not repaid as promised? What do you do about the loan then?
   d. Would your decision differ if you worked as a loan manager at a bank? a credit union? a finance company? Explain.

COMMUNITY AND HOME PROJECTS

1. With the permission of your parents, do an inventory of your family's use of credit. How many credit cards do your parents

carry and use regularly? Discuss with your parents their attitudes toward using credit.

2. Investigate how and why a married woman should establish credit and a financial history in her own name. How does the Equal Credit Opportunity Act make it possible to do this?

Chapter 16

Consumer Credit (Part 2)

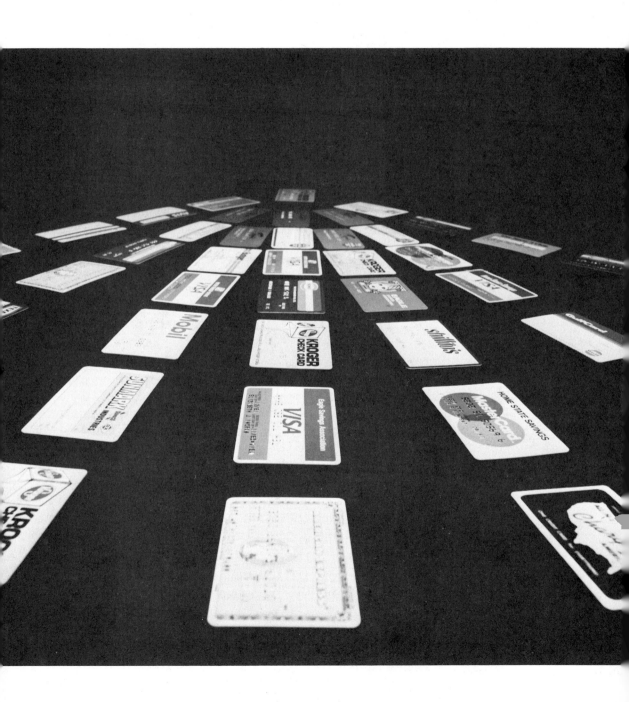

When you make purchases with credit, you are actually spending future income or earnings. This can lead to financial problems. The use of credit commits a portion of your future income to paying off the debt. Meeting credit payments can mean less money for the regular expenses that have to be taken care of each month.

Credit makes it easy to spend when you would not spend if cash were required. Statistics show that consumers with credit cards spend 20 percent more in a store than customers without credit cards.

As discussed in Chapter 15, credit can be a useful tool until it is misused. Then it can create serious financial problems for a family or individual. In this chapter we will discuss consumers in trouble with debt, debt collection practices, garnishment, bankruptcy, guidelines for using credit wisely, and tips on reducing the cost of installment loans.

CONSUMERS IN TROUBLE WITH DEBT

Can a person get too much of a good thing? In the case of credit the answer is definitely *yes*. Too much debt is a very serious problem for at least one out of every twenty Americans. Excessive debt can undermine the debtor's job, marriage, and even health. (A *debtor* is one who buys or borrows and promises to pay later.) Many consumers suffer from the stress and strain of debt problems.

One convenient yardstick for measuring your ability to handle debt is as follows: no matter what your income, 10 percent of take-home pay, excluding a home mortgage, is comfortable, 15 percent is manageable, and 20 percent or more is a dangerous credit overload. Some other indications of credit overload are when an individual or family

—is forced to miss some installment payments in order to pay rent or the monthly mortgage payments

—has to seek a new loan before an old one is repaid

—can pay only the minimum amount due on credit card accounts but continues to use the cards

—has taken out loans to combine debts or has asked for extensions on existing loans

—has begun to receive repeated overdue notices from creditors

—has little or no savings, or has drawn on savings to pay regular bills that once were paid out of monthly income

—has telephone calls or letters from creditors demanding payment of overdue bills

What can be done when a person is in financial trouble? Where can a person get help? Below are some suggestions.

Agreement with Creditors

Creditors are usually very understanding if the slow or overdue payments are the result of job loss, serious illness, or other unforeseen events. If you find yourself in trouble, you should explain the reasons for the payment delays. It is often possible to work with the creditors to pay them back in smaller amounts over an extended period of time. Most creditors would rather extend the payment period or take partial payments than pursue bankruptcy proceedings or expensive collection procedures.

Credit Counseling Services

It is best to seek professional help when debts are really out of control. There are nonprofit agencies in most communities which provide debt counseling services. The National Foundation for Consumer Credit certifies counseling agencies in more than one hundred communities around the country. When a credit counseling agency is certified by the NFCC, it is allowed to use the symbol CCCS (Consumer Credit Counseling Service). These offices offer services ranging from free budget and financial counseling for anyone wanting assistance to debt management and repayment guidance for those whose debt problems have reached the dangerous level.

Some consumers who are in trouble with credit stop using credit altogether.

Debt Consolidation

Debt consolidation is an attempt to combine many payments into one smaller payment stretched over a longer period of time. Instead of making payments to six or eight creditors, for example, it is possible to borrow money to pay off all the debts and owe only one creditor. To qualify as a solution to the problems of a financially troubled consumer, the consolidation loan should have an interest rate lower than the rate being paid on the other loans. For instance, if a person were paying 18 to 24 percent on charge accounts but could pay off the accounts with a credit union loan at 12 to 15 percent, the consolidation loan could have merit. But consolidation loans often result in greater debt over a longer period of time — not less debt. All too often debtors can obtain consolidation loans only from finance companies which charge high rates.

DEBT COLLECTION PRACTICES

Creditors often employ professional collection agencies to collect overdue accounts and repossess articles on which money is due. The collection agencies and some lawyers specialize in collecting bad debts for fees which range from one third of the amount collected on large debts to one half of the amount collected on small debts. The collection process has included everything from collection letters, late-night telephone calls and abusive language to threats of having consumers fired from their jobs because of nonpayment of debt. In order to stop these practices, Congress passed the Fair Debt Collection Practices Act which declares that the following collection actions are illegal:

—threatening violence, using obscene language, publishing shame lists of debtors, and making harrassing phone calls at night
—calling a debtor at work or contacting a debtor's employer
—claiming that the collector is from a state or federal agency or is a government official
—revealing the existence of a bad debt to third parties such as neighbors or employers
—using false or deceptive means to obtain information about a debtor

If the debtor requests, debt collectors must have the creditor verify a debt. If a request is made within 30 days after the debtor is contacted, the collection agency must wait for verification before continuing with collection activities. Debtors also have the right to notify a collection agency in writing that they do not wish to hear from the agency again, except for legal notices and notices of possible further action.

Debt collection agencies or collectors who violate the law are liable for actual damages plus civil damages up to $1,000. The law applies only to debt collection agencies—not to banks and other financial institutions or stores.

GARNISHMENT

Creditors can use a legal procedure, known as *garnishment*, to withhold a part of a debtor's earnings for the payment of a debt. The Truth in Lending Act limits the amount of an employee's disposable earnings (take-home pay) which may be subject to garnishment in a week. Weekly garnishment cannot be in excess of 25 percent of the disposable weekly earnings, or the amount by which disposable earnings for a week exceeds 30 times the federal minimum hourly wage, whichever amount is less. The law also prohibits an employer from firing an employee because of garnishment of wages for indebtedness.

BANKRUPTCY

Straight *bankruptcy*, also called *liquidation bankruptcy*, requires debtors to sell most of their assets at public sale through a trustee in return for a discharge from most, if not all, of their outstanding debts. The money from the sale is apportioned among the creditors. The concept behind bankruptcy is to wipe out debts and give the debtor a new start. Following are some important considerations about liquidation bankruptcy.

1. A person who has previously declared bankruptcy may not file for bankruptcy again for six years.
2. Not all obligations are discharged with bankruptcy. There are some debts which bankruptcy will not wipe out; for example, taxes, criminal or traffic violation fines, child support, alimony, and debts which are secured by collateral.
3. Not everything is liquidated. The Federal Bankruptcy Act establishes a list of federal exemptions which protects the debtor from losing everything; for example, $7,500 in property (usually a home), $1,200 of a motor vehicle, and $200 for every item of household goods, furnishing, and clothing.

A debtor should consult with a lawyer who will process the petition and provide the debtor with legal advice. Low-income debtors are eligible for free legal advice from community legal services and the Legal Aid Society.

WAGE EARNER PLAN—CHAPTER XIII

Chapter XIII of the Federal Bankruptcy Act is an alternative to declaring bankruptcy. Chapter XIII allows the debtor, creditors, and a judge, acting together, to set a monthly amount for the debtor to pay over an extended repayment period. The debts are not wiped out, but the court takes a portion of each paycheck and distributes it to the creditors. Chapter XIII does not require the debtor to give up assets such as personal property and real estate.

In order to qualify for the Wage Earner Plan, debtors must earn more than 50 percent of their income from wages or commissions. The court will administer the debt reduction plan, protect the debtors from lawsuits and harassment by creditors, and stop service charges, interest, and other charges on debt. Under the Wage Earner Plan debtors keep 75 percent of their salary. The plan must have the approval of 50 percent of the creditors and the debt must be eliminated in three years. The advantage of the Wage Earner Plan is that debtors avoid being listed in credit bureau files as bankrupt. The disadvantage is that the agony of the debt is prolonged over three additional years.

GUIDELINES FOR USING CREDIT WISELY

Credit can be an important tool in money management if it is used wisely. Some suggestions from financial advisors and credit counselors about the proper use of credit are discussed below.

Buy on Credit Only Those Things Which Appreciate in Value

This is probably the most conservative position regarding the use of credit. The principle behind this recommendation is to avoid paying finance charges for something that depreciates (decreases) in value. When you buy an item on credit that decreases in value, such as a car, you are losing twice. You are losing on the declining value of the item and losing by having paid more than the cash price. But when you buy an item that appreciates or increases in value, the amount of the finance charge will be recovered through the increase in value. This rule is most applicable to products that can be bought and resold later at a higher price, such as real estate and antiques. Most consumer goods, once used, depreciate considerably and have relatively little resale value.

Limit Installment Debt, 15 to 20 Percent of Take-Home Pay

Fifteen to twenty percent of take-home pay is the manageable amount of monthly installment payments a family or individual can afford. Any amount above 20 percent will reduce an individual's ability to pay for food, shelter, transportation, clothing, and other essentials. Probably an even more realistic guideline is one recommended by Sylvia Porter, a columnist and authority on money matters. Her recommendation: Do not owe more than one third of your *discretionary income* for the year. This is the income you have left after you pay for the basic needs of food, clothing, and shelter. This approach assumes that the individual or family has figured out the actual yearly expenses for the essentials.

Purchase Durable Products Which Will Outlast the Payment Period

If credit is going to be used for items that do not appreciate, it is wise to restrict it to durable products such as household appliances or cars. One common source of financial frustration is trying to finish installment payments on a product that no longer works or is out of style. This rule would eliminate such expenditures as expensive "fly-now, pay-later" vacation trips which could become extremely difficult to repay during the next year or more. It applies also to the length of loans on used-car purchases. Certainly it would be difficult to make payments on a car for two years if the car has not been running for the last six or eight months.

Recognize the Cost of Using Credit

Using an oil company credit card, bank card, or a department store charge account is a form of borrowing, and a finance charge will be added each month unless the entire balance due is paid by a certain date. The monthly statement will tell you how much time you have to pay the bill before a finance charge is added to the cost of the purchases. If you go beyond the due date, you will pay a finance charge. By paying the entire balance owed before the due date, it is possible to use credit cards for convenience without paying the cost of a finance charge. When using installment credit, reduce the cost of credit with a large down payment, a relatively short payment period, and the lowest possible annual percentage rate offered.

If you are thinking of borrowing money or opening a charge account, always remember that your first step should be to figure out how much it will cost you and whether you can afford it. Then you should shop around for the best terms.

INSTALLMENT LOANS

When you borrow money, you may repay the loan in several part payments instead of one large payment. A loan that is repaid in part payments is called an installment loan. Below are some ways to reduce the cost of installment loans. (An example of an installment loan may be seen in Illus. 16-1.)

INSTALLMENT LOAN CONTRACT

PURPOSE ___Personal use___

THE FIFTH THIRD BANK   No. __1531__

$__2,305.00__   CINCINNATI, OHIO   January 5 19__

___24__ months after date, for value received, the undersigned promise(s) to pay to the order of The Fifth Third Bank (hereinafter called the "Bank"), the sum of __Two Thousand Three Hundred Five__ _____ Dollars, in __23__ consecutive monthly installments of $__96.00__ each, commencing __Feb. 5__ 19__, and on even date of each succeeding month, and a final installment of $__97.00__ on __Jan. 5__ 19__ with interest from maturity at maximum legal rate in State of execution, until paid.

Upon failure to pay any installment as herein agreed, or in the event of the death, insolvency, bankruptcy, or failure in business of any of the undersigned, all unpaid installments under this Note shall, at the option of Bank, become immediately due and payable, without demand or notice (after calculation of the Prepayment Rebate as per Item 7, below). Further, if any monthly installment stipulated herein is not paid on or before ten days after the due date thereof, in addition to all other rights and remedies of Bank given by law or the terms of this Note, the undersigned promise(s) to pay to Bank a sum calculated at the rate of 5¢ for each dollar of such defaulted installment; but in no event shall the delinquent charge of any such defaulted installment exceed $3.00. Acceptance of such delinquent charge by Bank shall not constitute a waiver of any default or any rights of Bank hereunder.

(ADDITIONAL TRUTH IN LENDING ACT DISCLOSURES)

1. Proceeds of Loan $__2,000.00__

2. Other Charges:

   †a. Credit Life Insurance $__--__
   ††b. Credit Accident & Health Ins. $__--__
   c. Official Fees $__--__
   d. Other_____ $__--__

   Total Other Charges $__--__

3. Amount Financed (1 + 2) $__2,000.00__

4. FINANCE CHARGE* $__305.00__

5. Total of Payments (3 + 4) $__2,305.00__

6. ANNUAL PERCENTAGE RATE   __14.6__ %

*FINANCE CHARGE includes interest and group credit life insurance premiums paid by Bank for its benefit if purpose of loan is for **Home Improvement** or unsecured personal use.

OPTIONAL INSURANCE

Borrower authorizes Bank to obtain for Borrower only the following insurance coverages to remain in effect during the entire term of this loan.

†2a. **Credit Life Insurance on the life of Borrower provided by** _____

in accordance with the separate Application, Notice, Certificate and Policy being issued herewith.

††2b. **Credit Accident and Health Insurance for Borrower provided by** _____

in accordance with the separate Application, Notice, Certificate and Policy being issued herewith.

NOTICE TO BORROWER: You are not required to obtain Credit Life and/or Credit Accident and Health Insurance, and such is not a factor in Bank's extension of this credit. ACKNOWLEDGING the foregoing, Borrower requests and authorizes Bank to obtain each insurance coverage set forth above.

Borrower's Signature ▶→ _____
                                              Date

7. **PREPAYMENT REBATE:** Borrower may prepay the obligation under this Note in full at any time prior to maturity and receive a refund credit computed in accordance with the Rule of 78's. Such rebate will be computed after first deducting from the Finance Charge an acquisition charge in the amount of $10.00.

8. **AGREEMENT NOT TO ENCUMBER OR TRANSFER PROPERTY:** As an inducement to the making of this loan, Borrower will execute an agreement whereunder Borrower agrees to pay all taxes and assessments levied against the real property located at _____, and agrees not to transfer or assign any interest of Borrower therein, and agrees to not permit any lien or other encumbrance to be placed against said real estate, without the consent in writing of Bank. Said agreement further provides that, upon breach of any of these covenants, the payments due under this Note may be accelerated, whereby the entire remaining unpaid balance of the principal, and interest earned to the time of acceleration (after calculation of Prepayment Rebate), would be immediately due and payable.

9. **SECURITY INTEREST:** As collateral security for the payment of this and any and every liability and liabilities of the undersigned to Bank, however created, direct or contingent, due or to become due, now existing, and whether the same may have been or shall be participated in, in whole or part by others by trust agreement or otherwise, or in any manner acquired by or accruing to Bank, whether by agreement with the undersigned or by endorsement to Bank by anyone whomsoever, the undersigned do hereby assign to and pledge with said Bank the following property, to wit _____

in which property Bank has been granted a security interest by ☐ Security Agreement ☐ Pledge Agreement (check one if applicable), executed by the undersigned on even date herewith, default under the terms of which could result in default under this Note.

The others of the undersigned jointly and severally agree to make each of the said installments promptly if the said Borrower should default in making the same. The undersigned hereby severally waive presentment, demand for payment, protest, notice of protest and notice of nonpayment of this Note.

BORROWER ACKNOWLEDGES RECEIPT OF A COMPLETED COPY OF THIS NOTE AND THE ABOVE INFORMATION AT THE TIME OF SIGNING

ADDRESSES (GIVE COMPLETE ADDRESS)
305 Branch Hill Rd., Loveland, OH

1915 Oak St., Amelia, OH

237 Park Ave., Cincinnati, OH

SIGNATURES (WRITE IN FULL AND IN INK)

Michael Emerick
                              BORROWER
Nick Gregory
                              CO-MAKER
Sally Bester
                              CO-MAKER

Illus. 16-1

Installment loan

Make a Large Down Payment

The larger the down payment, the less the borrower has to borrow. Money is saved by paying a larger part in cash and by financing a smaller portion. For example, assume that you want to purchase a $3,500 used car. Table 16-1 shows the amount which can be saved with a larger down payment.

Table 16-1

Size of Down Payment
Terms: Two-Year — 14% Car Loan

Car Price	$3,500	$3,500
Down Payment	500	1,500
Amount Financed	3,000	2,000
Total Finance Charge	457	305
Amount Saved	$152	

Have a Short Payment Period

Some consumers have the idea that paying for a product or service over a longer period of time does not cost more. Actually the longer the payment period and the smaller the payments, the greater the cost of financing the item. The amount which can be saved by larger payments for a shorter payment period is presented in Table 16-2.

Compare Interest Rates

The interest rates of loans can vary dramatically from lender to lender, so it is wise to shop for interest just as you would shop for the best product. Table 16-3 shows the amount which could be saved by comparing interest rates and financing a car at the lowest interest rate.

Table 16-2

Payment Period
Terms: 14% — $3,000 Car Loan

	Two Year 24 Months	Four Year 48 Months
Car Price	$3,500.00	$3,500.00
Down Payment	500.00	500.00
Amount Financed	3,000.00	3,000.00
Monthly Payment	144.04	81.98
Total Finance Charge	457.00	935.00
Amount Saved	$478.00	

Table 16-3

Compare Interest Rates
Terms: $5,000 — 20% down, 48 months

	Credit Union	Bank	Dealer	Finance Co.
Car Price	$5,000.00	$5,000.00	$5,000.00	$5,000.00
Down Payment	1,000.00	1,000.00	1,000.00	1,000.00
Amount Financed	4,000.00	4,000.00	4,000.00	4,000.00
Interest Rate	12%	14%	15%	18%
Monthly Payment	105.00	109.00	111.00	117.50
Total Finance Charge	1,056.00	1,247.00	1,344.00	1,640.00
Amount Saved (by using a credit union instead of a dealer)		$288		

ADD-ON AND DISCOUNT INTEREST

Consumers should know that there are two other ways of stating interest rates. An *add-on rate* means the finance charge is added to the amount borrowed. For example, with an add-on loan, the borrower of $1,000 would have to pay back the amount borrowed plus a finance charge. When the finance charge is $80, the borrower would be required to pay back $1,080. In reality the borrower is using less than $1,000 since a portion of the loan ($90) is repaid each month. A *discount rate* means that the finance charge is subtracted from the amount borrowed. The borrower gets a check for the amount borrowed minus the finance charge but pays back the full amount. For example, on a discount loan of $1,000 with an $80 finance charge, the borrower would get $920 but would have to pay back $1,000 in monthly installments of $83.33. This method always carries a higher annual percentage rate than any other method because from the beginning borrowers have less than they actually borrowed.

Both the add-on and discount methods of quoting finance charges understate the actual annual percentage rate. When borrowing money or buying something on credit, you should know which method is quoted. Again, the annual percentage rate reflects the actual finance charge, and it is the only rate which is useful for a meaningful comparison of credit rates.

Caveat Emptor: *Reading the Fine Print of a Credit Agreement*

You may not be aware of it, but when you use credit, you could be signing away your rights should a dispute arise between you and your creditor. Installment contracts and credit card agreements are often written in legalese (legal jargon) rather than in understandable English. So, before you sign any agreements, understand what you are agreeing to. Below are some English translations of common clauses used in credit agreements.

Security Interest

THE SELLER RESERVES A PURCHASE MONEY SECURITY INTEREST IN THE GOODS UNTIL THE TOTAL OF PAYMENTS IS PAID IN FULL.

The creditor (the seller) keeps the title (ownership) of the merchandise until you (the purchaser) complete all of the payments. In effect the creditor still owns the product, but you get to use it and be responsible for it. If you stop paying, the creditor can repossess it, that is, take it back.

Deficiency Clause

IN THE EVENT OF REPOSSESSION OF SAID PROPERTY THE SELLER SHALL HAVE THE RIGHT TO APPLY THE PROCEEDS OF DISPOSITION TO THE REASONABLE EXPENSES OF RETAKING, HOLDING, PREPARING FOR SALE, SELLING AND THE LIKE, REASONABLE ATTORNEY'S FEES, LEGAL EXPENSES INCURRED, AND SATISFACTION OF THE INDEBTEDNESS. ANY SURPLUS SHALL BE PAID TO THE BUYER OR AS OTHERWISE REQUIRED BY LAW. THE BUYER SHALL BE LIABLE FOR ANY DEFICIENCY.

The merchant not only can repossess and resell the goods, but also can force you to pay the difference between the resale price and the sum still owed on the installment contract.

Default Payment Clause

PURCHASER AGREES TO PAY A DELIQUENCY CHARGE OF 5 PERCENT OF THE AMOUNT OF ANY INSTALLMENT OR FIVE DOLLARS ($5.00) WHICHEVER IS LESS, WHEN ANY SUCH INSTALLMENT IS IN DEFAULT FOR TEN DAYS OR MORE.

There is a penalty in the event of late payment. With many installment contracts you may receive a payment book. Usually the late payment penalty is built into the payment schedule. For example, it is likely to read: Due date pay $76.25. After this date pay $81.25.

Credit Insurance

ALTHOUGH NEITHER CREDIT LIFE INSURANCE NOR CREDIT LIABILITY INSURANCE IS REQUIRED BY THE SELLER, SUCH INSURANCE HAS BEEN OFFERED TO ME AND I VOLUNTARILY ELECT TO TAKE SUCH COVERAGE CHECKED BELOW.

This is credit insurance which pays off the debt if you become disabled or die. Credit insurance adds to the cost of the loan and often is not necessary. Creditors cannot legally make you buy the insurance to get a loan.

Acceleration Clause

IN THE EVENT PURCHASER DEFAULTS ON ANY PAYMENT DUE ON THIS CONTRACT, OR COMMITS A BREACH OF ANY TERMS OR CONDITIONS OF THIS CONTRACT, OR ANY INSOLVENCY OR BANKRUPTCY PROCEEDINGS ARE INSTITUTED BY OR AGAINST THE PURCHASER, THE FULL AMOUNT OF THE UNPAID BALANCE OR THE TOTAL OF PAYMENTS AT THE ELECTION OF THE HOLDER, SHALL BECOME DUE AND PAYABLE.

All payments are due at once if you miss a payment or if bankruptcy is declared. Creditors do not apply this clause rigidly. Most will not demand full payment when you miss a single installment, particularly if you notify them of your reason for missing it.

Confession of Judgment

THE UNDERSIGNED HEREBY IRREVOCABLY AUTHORIZES ANY ATTORNEY OR ATTORNEYS TO APPEAR FOR ANY ONE OR MORE OF THE UNDERSIGNED AFTER DEFAULT OF THIS NOTE AND CONFESS JUDGMENT AGAINST US, IN FAVOR OF THE HOLDER OF THIS NOTE FOR SUCH AMOUNT AS MAY THEN APPEAR UNPAID THEREON, AND TO RELEASE ALL ERRORS WHICH MAY INTERVENE IN ANY SUCH PROCEEDINGS, TO SAVE APPEAL FROM ANY SUCH JUDGMENT, AND TO CONSENT TO THE IMMEDIATE ISSUANCE OF EXECUTION THEREON.

You plead guilty before the fact. If you do not pay as agreed, creditors can take legal action against you, sometimes even when the creditors have not lived up to their end of the agreement. Confession of judgment clauses have been outlawed in some states; in others they are ignored because many judges and the legal profession consider them unconstitutional.

Wage Assignment

> AS SECURITY FOR THE ABOVE DESCRIBED DEBT, WHICH IS THE TIME BALANCE DUE ON A RETAIL INSTALLMENT CONTRACT, I HEREBY SELL, ASSIGN, TRANSFER AND SET OVER TO YOU, YOUR SUCCESSOR AND ASSIGNS 15% OF MY GROSS SALARY, WAGES, COMMISSIONS, AND OTHER COMPENSATION FOR SERVICES HERETOFORE EARNED...UNTIL ALL OBLIGATIONS SECURED HEREBY AND DESCRIBED HEREIN SHALL HAVE BEEN PAID AND DISCHARGED.

The creditor is allowed to make your employer deduct payments from your paycheck if you do not pay on time. This clause is not a "garnishment." The wage assignment is a way for creditors to by-pass the requirements of garnishment laws.

Rule of 78's

> IF THIS CONTRACT IS PREPAID IN FULL ONE MONTH OR MORE PRIOR TO THE FINAL DUE DATE, A REFUND WILL BE MADE OF THE UNEARNED PORTION OF THE FINANCE CHARGE AND THEN AP-PLYING THE DIRECT RATIO REFUND METHOD KNOWN AS THE RULE OF THE 78's.

Part of your finance charge will be returned if you pay off the loan in advance. The rebate of interest will be figured on the basis of the Rule of 78's. This means that if you pay off a 12-month loan at the end of six months, you will get 27 percent of the interest back (not 50 percent). This rule works in the following way: in the first month of a 12-month loan, you pay off $12/78$ of the interest; in the second, $11/78$ of the interest; and in the third, $10/78$ of the interest, and so on until the last payment when you pay $1/78$ of the interest. If you pay off a 12-month loan in the sixth month, you have paid $12/78$, $11/78$, $10/78$, $9/78$, $8/78$, and $7/78$ which equals 57 when you add the numerators together. Subtract 57 from 78. Then you have $21/78$, or about 27 percent, of the initial interest left to pay. This is the amount of interest which you would get back if you paid off the loan before it matures.

Mutual Assent

> PURCHASER HAS READ AND UNDERSTANDS ALL THE CON-TRACTUAL TERMS ON THE REVERSE SIDE HEREOF AND

ACKNOWLEDGES THAT SUCH TERMS ARE PART OF THIS RETAIL INSTALLMENT CONTRACT.

Once you sign your name, there is nothing you can do to change it. You are fully obligated to all the terms and conditions. Read the contract *before* you sign it, even if it's necessary to take the contract home and read it at your leisure.

Disclaimer

THIS CONTRACT CONTAINS THE ENTIRE AGREEMENT BETWEEN THE PARTIES AND NO WARRANTIES OR REPRESENTATIONS, EXPRESSED OR IMPLIED, AND NO STATEMENT, PROMISES, OR INDUCEMENTS MADE BY ANY PARTY HERETO OR ANY PARTY WHATSOEVER WHICH IS NOT CONTAINED IN THIS WRITTEN CONTRACT, SHALL BE VALID OR BINDING, UNLESS ENDORSED IN WRITING.

All claims should be in writing. Any claims made orally will not hold up in court. This is a *disclaimer* (a denial) of any claims, promises, or statements of guarantee which the salesperson may have made.

Holder-in-Due-Course

ANY HOLDER OF THIS CONSUMER CREDIT CONTRACT IS SUBJECT TO ALL CLAIMS AND DEFENSES WHICH THE DEBTOR COULD ASSERT AGAINST THE SELLER OF GOODS OR SERVICES OBTAINED PURSUANT HERETO OR WITH THE PROCEEDS THEREOF. RECOVERY HEREUNDER BY THE DEBTOR SHALL NOT EXCEED AMOUNTS PAID BY THE DEBTOR HEREUNDER.

Contracts can be sold to third parties—usually finance companies. In the past the third party had no responsibility for making good on the purchase if anything went wrong. This clause means that you have the right to raise against the third party (the holder-in-due-course) any legal claims you may have for defective merchandise. In practice it means that if you buy defective merchandise on an installment contract, you can withhold payment until the matter is settled. If the financial institution sues for payment, you can assert a valid claim (defective merchandise) against the seller as a defense. Buyer Beware.

VOCABULARY REVIEW

Debt consolidation   Bankruptcy

Garnishment   Discretionary income

Wage Earner Plan   Discount rate

QUESTIONS FOR REVIEW

1. What are some indicators or clues that an individual or family has a credit overload?

2. What can a person in trouble do to get help with debt?

3. When can a consolidation loan qualify as a solution to financial problems of a debtor?

4. What types of debt collection practices are illegal?

5. Assuming that the minimum wage is $3.35, what amount of money could be garnished from a worker's paycheck if a judge consents to a garnishment?

6. Name four guidelines for using credit wisely.

PROBLEM-SOLVING AND DECISION-MAKING PROJECTS

1. Examine each of the clauses on pages 309-312. What specific changes or revisions, if any, would you want to make in each clause before agreeing to it?

2. Assume that you wish to buy a $3,500 car with a 14 percent interest loan at a credit union. Use the table on page 314 to answer the following questions.
   a. How much could be saved by financing the car at the least cost instead of the most expensive?
   b. If you have a $1,000 down payment and $800 a month take-home pay, which length of loan would be the least costly way to finance the car?
   c. How much could be saved by financing the car with a $1,000 down payment over two years instead of four years?

14 Percent APR Car Loan			
	500 Down 3,000 Financed	1,000 Down 2,500 Financed	1,500 Down 2,000 Financed
Two-Year Loan			
Monthly payments	$144	$120	$ 96
Total finance charge	457	381	305
Three-Year Loan			
Monthly payments	103	85	68
Total finance charge	708	576	461
Four-Year Loan			
Monthly payments	82	68	55
Total finance charge	936	780	640

COMMUNITY AND HOME PROJECTS

1. Visit a local commercial bank, credit union, and finance company to get information on current rates charged for a consumer loan of $1,000 for 12 months. Obtain contract forms and bring them to class for comparison. Determine which institution is the best source for a loan, and discuss why there is a difference in their lending rates. Circle any terms or phrases you do not understand. Discuss in class the agreements, terms, and probable reasons for various provisions in credit agreements.

2. Collect credit card applications and other credit information from local specialty stores, department stores, banks, and credit unions. Compare the finance charges and methods of computing finance charges for the different types of credit cards and charge accounts.

Chapter 17

Taxes and Social Security

—Taxes are what we pay for civilized society.

Oliver Wendell Holmes, Jr.

—In this world nothing is certain but death and taxes.

Benjamin Franklin

—The income tax has made more liars out of the American people than golf has.

Will Rogers

A *tax* is a compulsory contribution of money to local, state, and federal governments. The taxes we pay are necessary to furnish the funds for services we expect from these governments. In any community individuals must provide some portion of their private income for public services such as highways, park facilities, school systems, and the like. The Tax Foundation estimates that typical workers pay approximately one third of their earnings into local, state, and federal taxes. In this chapter we will present some uses and classifications of taxes, discuss common tax forms and filing procedures, and examine the programs associated with social security.

THE PRICE TAG ON GOVERNMENT

The Constitution of the United States originally prohibited direct taxes. A *direct tax* is one that must be paid by the individual on whom it is levied. Direct taxes cannot be shifted or passed along to customers. For its first 100 years, the United States relied upon taxes on certain goods manufactured at home and brought in from other countries. Then as our country changed from a rural-agricultural society to an industrial society, and as the role of the federal government grew, it became necessary to increase the income of the federal government. The 16th Amendment, adopted in 1913, gave Congress the power to pass tax laws. We now have taxes on income, sales, and property.

The Tax Foundation Incorporated, a private organization, calculates an annual Tax Freedom Day. This is the day each year when the average American will stop working to pay for government services. As shown in Table 17-1, the cost of government as measured by the number of working days has increased considerably between 1930 and 1980. The Tax Foundation estimates typical workers pay approximately a third of their earnings into local, state, and federal taxes.

Table 17-1

Tax Freedom Days

1930	February 14
1940	March 9
1950	April 4
1960	April 18
1970	April 28
1977	May 3
1978	May 3
1979	May 4
1980	May 4
1981	May 8
1982	May 5[a]

[a]Forecast

Source: Tax Foundation Incorporated

United States Individual Income Tax

The *income tax* on an individual's earnings from wages, salary, tips, interest, rents, dividends, and capital gains is the largest revenue-producing tax for the federal government. Approximately 45 percent of the federal government's total income comes from the individual income tax. It is usually the largest amount withheld from workers' paychecks. Each year on or before April 15, American citizens determine their tax liability and voluntarily pay any amount due or request a refund if they have overpaid. Following are some of the characteristics of our income tax system.

Ability to Pay. The federal income tax is based on one's *ability to pay.* Basically this means that the individual income tax rate takes a proportionately higher share of the income of those with higher earnings. (The more you earn, the more you pay.) This concept is called *progressive taxation.* That is, the tax rate increases from 14 percent for the lowest level of income to 50 percent for any amount of income that falls within the highest level.

Voluntary Compliance. Another characteristic of the federal personal income tax is *voluntary compliance.* The Internal Revenue Service (IRS) relies on you to know your tax responsibilities and to meet them faithfully.

Pay-As-You-Earn. Federal and most state income taxes are imposed on a *pay-as-you-earn* basis. As you receive income subject to a tax, you pay the tax. This system helps prevent individuals from owing large amounts of taxes at the end of the year. It is the responsibility of your employer to withhold tax from your paycheck and deposit it with the IRS. The amount of income tax withheld from your paycheck during the year will be summarized and reported to you on a W-2 form (see page 323) provided by your employer.

Self-Assessment. *Self-assessment* means that you prepare your return each year, determine your tax liability, and pay any tax due or request a refund if you have overpaid taxes during the year. The IRS estimates that 97 percent or more of taxable wages is properly reported. Unfortunately about 40 percent of income that is not in the form of wages, such as rents or tips, goes unreported.

Tax on Sales

Sales taxes, those extra pennies or dollars added to each purchase, are the main source of revenue for most state governments. State governments raise about 60 percent of their revenues from taxes on sales. Local governments raise about a third of their revenues from sales tax, and the federal government raises only about 4 percent of its income from this tax. There are two types of sales taxes: general sales taxes and excise taxes.

General Sales Tax. The *general sales tax* is a percentage of the retail price of any items sold. For instance, a 5 percent tax means the consumer pays five cents on every dollar spent on consumer items. Some states exempt from sales tax essential products such as food and medicine.

Although sales taxes are productive in raising revenues, they are criticized for being regressive. *Regressive tax* means that individuals

Law enforcement is just one of the public services funded by our taxes.

Source: Jefferson-Pilot Corporation, Greensboro, NC

or families with low incomes pay a greater percentage of their incomes in taxes than families with higher incomes. This is because low-income people usually spend most of their incomes on consumer goods. For example, assume that a low-income family makes $8,000 which is spent on general consumer items taxed at 5 percent, or approximately $400. Assume that another family earns $20,000 and spends $15,000 on consumer items and saves $5,000; this family pays $750 in sales taxes. The low-income family paid 5 percent of its total income in sales taxes, but the higher income family paid only 3¾ percent of its total income in sales taxes.

Excise Tax. An *excise tax* is a sales tax on a specific product. Excise taxes are created for two reasons: (1) to raise a substantial amount of revenue, and (2) to discourage consumption of certain types of products such as liquor, tobacco, and gasoline. Excise taxes are levied by all levels of government—federal, state, and local. The rates will vary from state to state and from community to community.

Tax on Property

The *property tax* is based on the value of residential property (such as private homes), on commercial property (such as shopping centers or office buildings), and on industrial property (such as factories). For tax purposes, the value of the property is seldom the current market value. Instead, property value is assessed, or determined, by the local government. The amount of tax is obtained by multiplying the value of the property, called the *assessed value*, by the tax rate. The assessed value of property is usually about one third of a property's market value. That is, a property may have a market value of $60,000, but the property probably would have an assessed value of approximately $20,000. Owners of property with an assessed value of $20,000 in a community with a .0450 tax rate would pay $900 in property tax ($20,000 × .0450). The tax rate is set by the local government, and it usually changes every year. The property tax is the mainstay of local governments, accounting for 85 percent of their revenues. Illus. 17-1 shows how these taxes vary from state to state. Everyone pays property taxes—even renters. Renters pay the tax indirectly when they pay the rent.

YOUR FIRST JOB—FORMS AND FILING

When you get your first job, you will begin to pay for some of the citizenship benefits you currently enjoy, and you will assume greater citizenship responsibilities. You will need to be acquainted with a few tax forms and filing procedures.

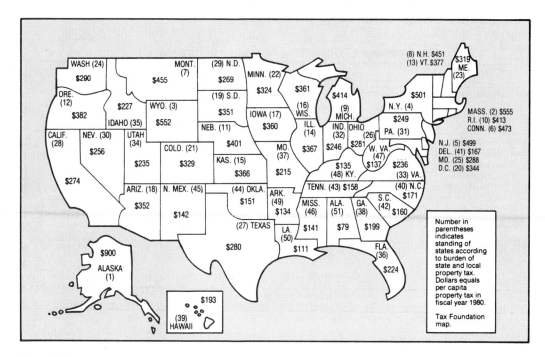

Illus. 17-1

State and local property taxes

Source: Monthly Tax Features, *Tax Foundation, Incorporated (January, 1982),* p. 1.

Form W-4

As a new employee, you will be asked to fill out a *W-4 form* — Employee's Withholding Allowance Certificate (see Illus. 17-2). The information you put on this form determines the amount of money that your employer will deduct from your paycheck for income taxes. The IRS provides tables for the employer to determine how much tax to withhold each pay period. The amount your employer will withhold depends on your income level, your marital status, and the number of allowances that you claim on the W-4 form. You should consider three things when you fill out the W-4 form.

1. Each allowance that you claim reduces the amount of tax that will be withheld from your paycheck. Generally you will claim only one allowance for yourself. More than one allowance may be claimed for blindness, age (over 65), a

1 Type or print your full name

	2 Your social security number

Home address (number and street or rural route)

City or town, State, and ZIP code

3 Marital Status

☐ Single ☐ Married
☐ Married, but withhold at higher Single rate

Note: If married, but legally separated, or spouse is a nonresident alien, check the Single box.

4 Total number of allowances you are claiming (from line F of the worksheet on page 2) . . . .

5 Additional amount, if any, you want deducted from each pay . . . . $

6 I claim exemption from withholding because (see instructions and check boxes below that apply):

  a ☐ Last year I did not owe any Federal income tax and had a right to a full refund of **ALL** income tax withheld, **AND**

  b ☐ This year I do not expect to owe any Federal income tax and expect to have a right to a full refund of **ALL** income tax withheld. If both a and b apply, enter "EXEMPT" here . . . . ▶

  c If you entered "EXEMPT" on line 6b, are you a full-time student? . . . . ☐ Yes ☐ No

Under the penalties of perjury, I certify that I am entitled to the number of withholding allowances claimed on this certificate, or if claiming exemption from withholding, that I am entitled to claim the exempt status.

Employee's signature ▶   Date ▶   , 19

7 Employer's name and address (including ZIP code) (FOR EMPLOYER'S USE ONLY)

8 Office code

9 Employer identification number

------------------------------------ Detach along this line ------------------------------------

Illus. 17-2

W-4 form

spouse, and other *dependents* such as children or other persons whom you support. Some people claim fewer allowances on the W-4 form than they are entitled to in order to have more tax withheld from their pay. In this way they will receive a large refund from the IRS when they file an income tax return. This may seem like a good way to save money to some taxpayers, but actually the taxpayer is losing money. The IRS does not pay any interest on funds withheld. It would be wiser to put the money where it will earn interest such as in a bank, credit union, or savings and loan association.

2. If you work but still depend on a parent or parents for one half or more of your support, your parents may claim one allowance for you, and you may also claim one allowance for yourself.

3. It is not necessary for your employer to withhold any tax from your income if you did not have any income tax liability last year and if you do not expect to have any tax liability this year. This procedure is especially useful to

students who have part-time or summer jobs and do not earn enough money to pay any income tax. By writing "exempt" on the W-4 form, you will not have to file an income tax return just to get a refund. Naturally, if your status changes and you become liable for tax, it is necessary to file a new W-4 with your employer.

Form W-2

After you have been employed, your employer must send you a W-2 *form*, which is a wage and tax statement. A W-2 form is shown in Illus. 17-3. Every employer you work for during the year must send you the W-2 form for the period that you worked. This form provides you with a record of wages earned as well as federal, state, and other taxes withheld during the year. It is necessary to submit a copy of the W-2 form with your tax return. If you have had more than one employer, you will need to combine the wages, salary, or tips earned and the amount of tax withheld and submit the W-2 forms from each employer to the IRS.

1 Control number		For Official Use Only	
	22222		
2 Employer's name, address, and ZIP code		3 Employer's identification number	4 Employer's State number
		5 Stat. employee / Deceased / Pension plan / Legal rep. / 942 emp. / Sub-total / Correction / Void	
		6 *	7 Advance EIC payment
8 Employee's social security number / 9 Federal income tax withheld		10 Wages, tips, other compensation	11 FICA tax withheld
12 Employee's name, address, and ZIP code		13 FICA wages	14 FICA tips
		16 Employer's use	
		17 State income tax / 18 State wages, tips, etc. / 19 Name of State	
15 Employee's address and ZIP code		20 Local income tax / 21 Local wages, tips, etc. / 22 Name of locality	

Form **W-2 Wage and Tax Statement 19--**   Copy A For Social Security Administration
* See Instructions for Forms W-2 and W-2P   Department of the Treasury Internal Revenue Service

Do NOT Cut or Separate Forms on This Page

Illus. 17-3

W-2 form

1040A or 1040 Individual Income Tax Return

Taxpayers have two forms to choose from when they prepare their income tax returns. The *1040A form* is the simpler form and should be used when income is primarily from wages, salaries, or tips, the taxpayer did not earn more than $400 in dividends or interest, and taxable income is less than $50,000. The *1040 form,* the longer form, is used by taxpayers who own a home and have income and expenses that cannot be reported on the 1040A form. Most young people use the 1040A until they are married, have children, homes, or other conditions which may warrant using the longer income tax return.

Either the 1040 or 1040A is used to determine your tax liability, tax due, or tax refund. A *tax liability* is the amount that you owe on the income you have received during the year. A *tax due* is an additional amount you owe on your tax liability. That is, an extra amount is due because not enough tax was withheld from your wages. This tax due must be paid when you file your income tax return. A *tax refund* is the amount withheld from your wages or salary in excess of your tax liability. If you are entitled to a refund, you should file a 1040A or a 1040 form. If you do not file, a return will not be issued.

Most students have to file an income tax return if any of the following conditions apply.

—You earned more than minimum gross income based upon your filing status. For example (1981): single, $3,300; married, filing jointly, $5,400; married, filing separate return, $1,000.
—You received tips from which social security was not withheld, even if your gross income was less than $3,300.
—You were in business for yourself and had net earnings of $400 or more from that business. This is called self-employment income.
—You can be claimed as a dependent on your parents' return, and you had income of $1,000 or more.

Tax Tables

You will have to use the tax tables to determine your tax liability. These tables, one page of which is shown in Illus. 17-4, tell you the amount of tax you owe on the amount of income you earned. To find

19-- Tax Table
Based on Taxable Income
For persons with taxable incomes of less than $50,000.

Example: Mr. and Mrs. Brown are filing a joint return. Their taxable income on line 34 is $23,270. First, they find the $23,250-23,300 income line. Next, they find the column for married filing jointly and read down the column. The amount shown where the income line and filing status column meet is $4,082. This is the tax amount they must write on line 35 of their return.

At least	But less than	Single	Married filing jointly *	Married filing separately	Head of a household
			Your tax is—		
23,200	23,250	5,208	4,069	6,438	4,805
23,250	23,300	5,224	(4,082)	6,462	4,820
23,300	23,350	5,241	4,096	6,486	4,836

If line 34 (taxable income) is— At least	But less than	Single	Married filing jointly *	Married filing separately	Head of a household
			Your tax is—		
0	1,700	0	0	0	0
1,700	1,725	0	0	a2	0
1,725	1,750	0	0	5	0
1,750	1,775	0	0	9	0
1,775	1,800	0	0	12	0
1,800	1,825	0	0	16	0
1,825	1,850	0	0	19	0
1,850	1,875	0	0	22	0
1,875	1,900	0	0	26	0
1,900	1,925	0	0	29	0
1,925	1,950	0	0	33	0
1,950	1,975	0	0	36	0
1,975	2,000	0	0	40	0
2,000					
2,000	2,025	0	0	43	0
2,025	2,050	0	0	47	0
2,050	2,075	0	0	50	0
2,075	2,100	0	0	54	0
2,100	2,125	0	0	57	0
2,125	2,150	0	0	60	0
2,150	2,175	0	0	64	0
2,175	2,200	0	0	67	0
2,200	2,225	0	0	71	0
2,225	2,250	0	0	74	0
2,250	2,275	0	0	78	0
2,275	2,300	0	0	81	0
2,300	2,325	b2	0	85	b2
2,325	2,350	5	0	88	5
2,350	2,375	9	0	92	9
2,375	2,400	12	0	95	12
2,400	2,425	16	0	99	16
2,425	2,450	19	0	102	19
2,450	2,475	22	0	105	22
2,475	2,500	26	0	109	26
2,500	2,525	29	0	112	29
2,525	2,550	33	0	116	33
2,550	2,575	36	0	119	36
2,575	2,600	40	0	123	40
2,600	2,625	43	0	126	43
2,625	2,650	47	0	130	47
2,650	2,675	50	0	133	50
2,675	2,700	54	0	137	54
2,700	2,725	57	0	140	57
2,725	2,750	60	0	143	60
2,750	2,775	64	0	147	64
2,775	2,800	67	0	151	67
2,800	2,825	71	0	155	71
2,825	2,850	74	0	159	74
2,850	2,875	78	0	163	78
2,875	2,900	81	0	167	81
2,900	2,925	85	0	171	85
2,925	2,950	88	0	175	88
2,950	2,975	92	0	179	92
2,975	3,000	95	0	183	95

If line 34 (taxable income) is— At least	But less than	Single	Married filing jointly *	Married filing separately	Head of a household
			Your tax is—		
3,000					
3,000	3,050	100	0	189	100
3,050	3,100	107	0	197	107
3,100	3,150	114	0	204	114
3,150	3,200	121	0	212	121
3,200	3,250	128	0	220	128
3,250	3,300	135	0	228	135
3,300	3,350	142	0	236	142
3,350	3,400	149	0	244	149
3,400	3,450	156	c3	252	156
3,450	3,500	164	10	260	162
3,500	3,550	172	17	268	169
3,550	3,600	180	24	276	176
3,600	3,650	188	31	283	183
3,650	3,700	196	38	291	190
3,700	3,750	203	45	299	197
3,750	3,800	211	52	307	204
3,800	3,850	219	59	316	211
3,850	3,900	227	66	324	218
3,900	3,950	235	73	333	225
3,950	4,000	243	79	342	232
4,000					
4,000	4,050	251	86	351	238
4,050	4,100	259	93	360	245
4,100	4,150	267	100	369	252
4,150	4,200	275	107	378	259
4,200	4,250	282	114	387	266
4,250	4,300	290	121	395	273
4,300	4,350	298	128	404	280
4,350	4,400	306	135	413	287
4,400	4,450	315	142	422	294
4,450	4,500	323	149	431	302
4,500	4,550	332	156	440	310
4,550	4,600	341	162	449	318
4,600	4,650	350	169	458	326
4,650	4,700	359	176	467	334
4,700	4,750	368	183	475	342
4,750	4,800	377	190	484	350
4,800	4,850	386	197	493	357
4,850	4,900	395	204	502	365
4,900	4,950	403	211	511	373
4,950	5,000	412	218	520	381
5,000					
5,000	5,050	421	225	529	389
5,050	5,100	430	232	538	397
5,100	5,150	439	238	547	405
5,150	5,200	448	245	555	413
5,200	5,250	457	252	564	421
5,250	5,300	466	259	573	429
5,300	5,350	474	266	582	436
5,350	5,400	483	273	591	444
5,400	5,450	492	280	600	452
5,450	5,500	501	287	609	460

If line 34 (taxable income) is— At least	But less than	Single	Married filing jointly *	Married filing separately	Head of a household
			Your tax is—		
5,500	5,550	510	294	618	468
5,550	5,600	519	302	627	476
5,600	5,650	528	310	635	484
5,650	5,700	537	318	644	492
5,700	5,750	546	326	653	500
5,750	5,800	554	334	662	508
5,800	5,850	563	342	671	515
5,850	5,900	572	350	680	523
5,900	5,950	581	357	689	531
5,950	6,000	590	365	698	539
6,000					
6,000	6,050	599	373	709	547
6,050	6,100	608	381	719	555
6,100	6,150	617	389	730	563
6,150	6,200	626	397	740	571
6,200	6,250	634	405	750	579
6,250	6,300	643	413	761	587
6,300	6,350	652	421	771	594
6,350	6,400	661	429	781	602
6,400	6,450	670	436	792	610
6,450	6,500	679	444	802	618
6,500	6,550	688	452	812	627
6,550	6,600	697	460	823	635
6,600	6,650	707	468	833	644
6,650	6,700	716	476	844	653
6,700	6,750	726	484	854	662
6,750	6,800	735	492	864	671
6,800	6,850	744	500	875	680
6,850	6,900	754	508	885	689
6,900	6,950	763	515	895	698
6,950	7,000	772	523	906	707
7,000					
7,000	7,050	782	531	916	715
7,050	7,100	791	539	927	724
7,100	7,150	801	547	937	733
7,150	7,200	810	555	947	742
7,200	7,250	819	563	958	751
7,250	7,300	829	571	968	760
7,300	7,350	838	579	978	769
7,350	7,400	848	587	989	778
7,400	7,450	857	594	999	787
7,450	7,500	866	602	1,009	795
7,500	7,550	876	610	1,020	804
7,550	7,600	885	618	1,030	813
7,600	7,650	894	627	1,041	822
7,650	7,700	904	635	1,051	831
7,700	7,750	913	644	1,061	840
7,750	7,800	923	653	1,072	849
7,800	7,850	932	662	1,082	858
7,850	7,900	941	671	1,092	867
7,900	7,950	951	680	1,103	875
7,950	8,000	960	689	1,113	884

*This column must also be used by a qualifying widow(er).

Continued on next page

a If your taxable income is exactly $1,700, your tax is zero.
b If your taxable income is exactly $2,300, your tax is zero.
c If your taxable income is exactly $3,400, your tax is zero.

Illus. 17-4

1040A tax table

your tax, use the appropriate table for your filing status. There are tables for persons who are single, married and filing jointly, and married and filing separately. After you locate the appropriate table, read down the income column until you find your income level (called *adjusted gross income*), then read across to the column headed by the number of withholding allowances you claim. The amount shown is your tax.

Caveat Emptor: *Tax Help – Help!*

At the beginning of the 1980s, over a third of the 90 million taxpayers sought help from the IRS, and millions of others paid from ten dollars to thousands of dollars for tax help. There are four major sources of tax help: the IRS, mass-market tax preparation services, CPA tax specialists, and tax lawyers.

IRS. The Internal Revenue Service has a toll-free telephone answering service and nearly 1,000 tax assistance centers located throughout the United States. Under certain conditions the IRS will figure your tax on either Form 1040 or Form 1040A. Of course, you must provide complete information and appropriate schedules. The IRS has been found to dispense misleading or incorrect advice in its publications, answer questions incorrectly, make mathematical errors, and even give taxpayers wrong forms. Nevertheless, taxpayers are responsible for any mistakes made by agency employees. Claiming that you were misinformed will not help if a tax audit is made on your return (a *tax audit* is an examination of your tax return by the IRS).

Mass-Market Tax Preparation. Some tax preparation services will prepare your 1040A forms for $10 to $25. Since you have to find and provide all the essential records — which is most of the work — this fee hardly represents a bargain. Enormous effort has been made to simplify the forms so you could probably fill them out yourself and save the money. If you feel that preparation service is necessary, however, you should talk personally with the person who works on the return to find out something about the preparer's background. Watch out for tax consultants who cannot answer your questions. Some mass-market preparation services hire persons who are given only a quick course in tax preparation.

Certified Public Accountants. For complicated tax work, a certified public accountant who specializes in taxes is the best source of tax help. Beware, however, of accountants who promise spectacular tax savings. Again, it is important to know something about the background and responsibility of your tax accountant.

Tax Lawyer. If you are notified that the Fraud Section of the IRS is investigating your return, it may be necessary to seek the help of a tax lawyer. Tax lawyers specialize in cases that challenge the tax rulings of the IRS.

Remember, whether you prepare your tax forms yourself or hire someone else to prepare them, you and you alone are responsible for the statements on the return. Buyer Beware.

When preparing their returns, many people seek assistance from tax professionals.

Source: 3M Company

SOCIAL SECURITY

Social security is a national insurance program that provides income for individuals or families who are faced with retirement, disability, death, unemployment, or health needs. Probably no other government program affects the American public as greatly as does social security. Every month nearly 34 million Americans (one out of every seven) receive social security checks. Nine out of every ten working Americans pay social security taxes in order to provide those checks.

Retirement Insurance

Retirement benefits are probably the best known feature of social security. Social security provides full retirement income to individuals who reach the age of 65 and reduced income to those who reach the age of 62. The benefits of workers who retire at 62 are 20 percent less than those of workers who retire at 65.

Disability Insurance

Social security provides income to individuals who become disabled and cannot work. If you are eligible, monthly benefits will be paid to you, your spouse, and your children if they are under 18. Disability income benefits are paid after a five-month waiting period, and after it is determined that your physical or mental disability is severe enough to prevent you from working for one year.

Survivor's Insurance

The Social Security Administration is now paying *benefits*, or money for monthly living expenses, to 8,000,000 survivors of deceased workers who were eligible for social security. These benefits go to children and in some cases to the widow or widower. The benefits are based on the average annual earnings of the deceased wage earner and increase automatically as the cost of living rises. Monthly benefits are received by surviving children until they reach the age of 18. The surviving spouse caring for a child receives benefits until the child is 16 unless the child is disabled. In addition

Social security provides income to individuals who become disabled and cannot work.

Source: Aetna Life and Casualty Co.

to the monthly benefits the family immediately receives $255, at the time of a worker's death, as a burial benefit payable toward funeral expenses.

Unemployment Insurance

The Social Security Act of 1935 requires each state to establish laws which provide for an unemployment insurance program. Today each state determines who is eligible for benefits, how much they receive, and for how long. Nearly 97 percent of all jobs are now covered by unemployment insurance protection.

Unemployment insurance pays benefits to qualified workers who are unemployed and looking for work. In order to be eligible for this insurance, workers must have earned a certain amount of wages or have been unemployed for a certain length of time in a recent one-year period (that is, four consecutive calendar quarters), and they must have worked for an employer covered by the unemployment insurance program. Benefits are often paid entirely by taxes paid by employers. In a few states, however, employees also contribute. Usually the unemployed person who collects benefits must be able to work, be available for work, and be actively seeking work. Each state differs in the amount of unemployment benefits and the way the amount is calculated, but the aim is to pay unemployed persons about 50 percent of what they earned when employed. Most states pay benefits for a maximum of 26 weeks. Unemployed persons can be disqualified from receiving benefits if they voluntarily leave work without good reason, are fired for misconduct, or refuse suitable work without good cause.

Health Insurance

Social security provides a two-part health insurance program called *Medicare* for persons over 65. Medicare consists of hospital insurance and medical insurance. The hospital insurance helps pay the cost of inpatient hospital care and certain kinds of follow-up care. The medical insurance helps pay the costs of doctors' services, outpatient hospital service, and certain other medical items.

SOCIAL SECURITY: HOW IT WORKS

Most employed people have social security taxes, called *FICA* (Federal Insurance Contributions Act) taxes, deducted from their paychecks. Employers also contribute to the program by matching the amounts paid by employees. A percentage of the employee's wages is paid into the social security trust fund which entitles the employee to social security benefits. No other sources of funding are used.

Table 17-2 shows the tax rates and wage base on which employers and employees pay the tax. The transfer of funds from "earners" to "nonearners" (the beneficiaries) is conducted on a "pay-as-you-earn" basis. In other words the taxes collected are immediately transferred to the beneficiaries. People working today pay for those now receiving benefits. When the people now working begin to collect benefits, it is assumed that the next generation will pay the bill.

Table 17-2

Social Security Tax Rates

Year	Tax Rate[1]	Wage Base[2]
1981	6.65	29,700
1982	6.70	32,400
1983	6.70	—
1984	6.70	—
1985	7.05	—
1986	7.15	—
1987	7.15	—

[1]Both the employee and the employer pay this rate.
[2]Automatic cost of living adjustments are made in the wage base for each year.

In 1977 Congress passed the Social Security Amendments in order to control the social security system's rising costs. The amendments sharply increased the amount of FICA taxes that workers and employers contribute as well as the amount of a worker's salary that is subject to the tax. Illus. 17-5 shows how the social security taxes paid by an employee have grown from 1937 to 1985.

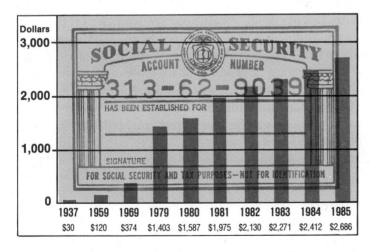

	1937	1959	1969	1979	1980	1981	1982	1983	1984	1985
	$30	$120	$374	$1,403	$1,587	$1,975	$2,130	$2,271	$2,412	$2,686

Illus. 17-5

Social security maximum tax paid by employees 1937 to 1985

Source: Gene Langley in The Christian Science Monitor © 1979 TCSPS.

Social Security Number/Card

When you start your first part-time or summer job, you will need a social security number. You may already have one. If not, you should apply for one at a social security office. Internal Revenue office, or post office. A social security card has a nine-digit account number which is yours for life. There is no other number exactly like yours, even if someone else has a name exactly the same as yours. The social security number serves two specific purposes:

1. It is used by the Social Security Administration throughout your working life to keep a record of all your earnings on which you pay the FICA taxes. As stated earlier, FICA tax entitles you or your survivors to retirement income, Medicare, disability benefits, or death and survivor's benefits.
2. The IRS uses the social security number as a taxpayer identification number. You will find that your social security number will appear on your bank accounts, tax returns, other documents you must file with the IRS, and sometimes on your payroll checks.

Eligibility

In order to be eligible for full social security benefits, you must work and pay into the system for ten years. When you work and pay into the system, you earn work credits which entitle you or your survivors to social security benefits. Social security credit is measured in "quarters of coverage." Each year you can earn four quarters of coverage toward social security benefits. A worker gets one quarter of coverage for each $340 of earnings received as of 1982, and the amount needed to earn a credit will increase automatically in future years as average wages increase. If you stop working under social security before earning enough credit to be eligible, you cannot get full benefits; however, the credit you earn will stay on your record, and you can add to it when you return to work under social security. The latter rule applies primarily to retirement benefits.

Self-Employment

Self-employed persons must report earnings of $400 or more and pay a self-employment contribution of 9.35 through 1984. This tax is paid at the time federal income taxes are paid. Like other workers, the self-employed normally need ten years of coverage to be eligible for retirement benefits. Benefits for the self-employed and their families are figured in the same way as benefits for other workers.

Social Security is Not Enough

Living too long is a risk which everyone faces — that is, living too long to support oneself. Social security never was intended to provide sole support in retirement. It was designed only to provide a supplement to savings and other assets. Even though social security benefits will automatically increase as the cost of living rises, most people will receive far less income than they enjoyed in their working years. Thus, it is wise to recognize that social security should be only a part of your financial planning for retirement. Annuities and Individual Retirement Accounts are also programs for retirement income.

Annuities. An annuity is an investment plan that provides income upon retirement. Annuities are usually purchased through insurance companies and offer two advantages: forced savings and tax deferral. The forced savings is similar to cash-value insurance (see Chapter 18, pages 348-349). With an annuity, taxes are delayed until the monthly principal and interest is paid in retirement years when the tax bracket is lower. The disadvantage of annuities is that they offer lower yields than many other forms of investment, and their returns offer little protection against inflation.

Individual Retirement Accounts. Until recently, only a few people without pension plans could participate in Individual Retirement Accounts (IRA's). An IRA is a tax-sheltered retirement plan that allows you to set aside up to $2,000 a year from your wages or salary. Now, IRA's are available to anyone who wants to accumulate assets for retirement.

Banks, savings and loan associations, credit unions, brokerage houses, mutual funds and other financial institutions offer alternative types of IRA accounts. Consumers need to compare rates, terms, returns, and fees. Money can be withdrawn from an IRA, but you will pay a tax penalty and possibly an interest penalty. Unless you become disabled, the earliest age at which you can withdraw from an IRA without a penalty is 59½. IRA's provide a flexible way of saving for retirement as well as a savings on taxes.

VOCABULARY REVIEW

Tax

Income tax

Progressive taxation

General sales tax

Regressive tax

Excise tax

Property tax

Tax liability

Tax audit

QUESTIONS FOR REVIEW

1. Why are taxes necessary in a community of people?

2. What are the three levels of government which have the power to tax?

3. What are the three major sources of revenue for the operation of government in the United States?

4. Name the primary source of revenue for each level of government.

5. Name the four characteristics of the United States Individual Income Tax.

6. When you first get a job, which federal tax form will you be asked to complete and submit to your employer? Why?

7. When you first file a federal income tax return, which form will you most likely use, and which federal tax form must be submitted to the IRS to document the amount of your wages or salary?

8. Name and explain the five types of insurance coverage that people are entitled to under the Social Security Act.

PROBLEM-SOLVING AND DECISION-MAKING PROJECTS

1. Compute the tax for the following situations:
   a. Assume that you anticipate buying a used car in the near

future and that you wish to pay for it with cash. The used car you plan to purchase costs $2,545, and there is a sales tax in your state of 5 percent. What amount of sales tax will be added to the purchase price of the used car?

b. A house and a piece of property have a market value of $75,000 and an assessed value of $25,000 (33⅓ percent of the market value). If the local property tax rate is .0600, what amount of property tax would the homeowner pay?

c. Bob Russell earns $1,200 per month. What amount of FICA tax will be withheld from his paycheck each month?

2. Assume that after you graduate from high school, you work in the summer for the community park district from which you receive a W-2 form. You report income of $2,625 and federal tax withheld of $105. Also assume that you work part-time for the local community college which you are attending and that you received a W-2 form reporting $1,750 earned and $73 withheld. In addition to this income, you earn $60 in interest on a savings account. Use the tax table on page 325 to determine (a) your tax liability and (b) whether you owe additional tax or get a refund.

COMMUNITY AND HOME PROJECTS

1. Compile a list of all the taxes and the tax rates in your state and community. To get started, obtain the current tax rate for state income tax, local property tax, state or local sales tax, and federal, state and local excise tax on gasoline, cigarettes, and other products.

2. With your parents' permission, obtain the following information from them: tax form used (1040 or 1040A) by your parents, whether your family itemizes deductions, their tax bracket, and the amount of property tax paid on the home, if owned.

3. More and more workers are wondering if social security benefits will still be around years from now — when they want to retire. Investigate some of the problems with social security. Are there any ways to improve the social security system so that workers who retire in the future will be guaranteed benefits? Write a report about your findings.

Chapter 18

Life and Health Insurance

Can you imagine being the head of a family—two children, a pet, a mortgage? Probably not. If you could, you might be more interested in the subject of life and health insurance. But what about life insurance for teenagers? Do your parents have life and health insurance for you? If they don't, should they? If they do, are they wasting their money? In this chapter we will answer these and other questions about life and health insurance.

LIFE INSURANCE

Two thirds of the people in the United States have some type of life insurance coverage. They feel that they need the financial security it provides. Currently over three trillion dollars worth of life insurance is in force on American families.

What's It For?

Life insurance is a nice way of saying death insurance. The primary purpose of insurance is to replace a loss of income for those who depend on you financially—such as children, a spouse, or parents. If no one depends on you financially, then you probably don't need life insurance. Life insurance can be used for other purposes, too, such as savings or investing. But the *first rule* in insurance buying is to seek protection from monetary loss. All other considerations should be secondary to the need for protection.

How Does It Work?

Insurance is based upon two simple ideas—risk sharing and statistical probability. Every person faces financial risks which can

Life insurance is a good way to protect your dependents financially if something happens to you.

result from accidents, fires, death, or other unforeseeable events. One way of dealing with risk is to assume or accept the consequences of the loss. Another way is to share or combine your risk with the risks of others.

Insurance companies combine your risk with those of others. By sharing the risk in this manner, everyone can have financial security for a low cost. In exchange for a *premium* (the amount paid for insurance), the company promises to pay you or your *beneficiary* (a person you designate) an amount of money agreed upon in the policy. The amount agreed upon is called the *face value* of the policy. If you do not have a loss, the company does not pay.

Insurance companies use *statistical probability* to predict the likelihood of an event occurring. Since a company is dealing with large numbers, it is possible to predict what will happen with great accuracy. Based upon *mortality rates* (see Table 18-1) for a large number of people, insurance companies can predict that at age 18 only 1.28 deaths per 1,000 will occur. With this information the insurance company calculates the amount of money necessary to cover losses. Each of the 1,000 in the group can be provided insurance for a low cost. For example, if an insurance company knows that approximately two 18-year-olds will die out of 1,000, they can estimate that if the company collects $5 from each person in the group (1,000 × $5 = $5,000), the company can insure 1,000

18-year-olds for $2,000 each. When the two unlucky ones die, the families will receive $2,000 each for burial expenses. The company will pay out only $4,000 and retain the remainder ($1,000) for company operations.

Table 18-1

Mortality Rates

Age	Deaths per 1,000	Expectation of Life (Years)	Age	Deaths per 1,000	Expectation of Life (Years)
0	20.02	70.75	26	1.43	47.44
1	1.25	71.19	27	1.42	46.51
2	.86	70.28	28	1.44	45.58
3	.69	69.34	29	1.49	44.64
4	.57	68.39	30	1.55	43.71
5	.51	67.43	31	1.63	42.77
6	.46	66.46	32	1.72	41.84
7	.43	65.49	33	1.83	40.92
8	.39	64.52	34	1.95	39.99
9	.34	63.54	35	2.09	39.07
10	.31	62.57	36	2.25	38.15
11	.30	61.58	37	2.44	37.23
12	.32	60.60	38	2.66	36.32
13	.46	59.62	39	2.90	35.42
14	.63	58.65	40	3.14	34.52
15	.82	57.69	41	3.41	33.63
16	1.01	56.73	42	3.70	32.74
17	1.17	55.79	43	4.04	31.86
18	1.28	54.86	44	4.43	30.99
19	1.34	53.93	45	4.84	30.12
20	1.40	53.00	46	5.28	29.27
21	1.47	52.07	47	5.74	28.42
22	1.52	51.15	48	6.24	27.58
23	1.53	50.22	49	6.78	26.75
24	1.51	49.30	50	7.38	25.93
25	1.47	48.37	51	8.04	25.12

(Continued)

Table 18-1 (Continued)
Mortality Rates

Age	Deaths per 1,000	Expectation of Life (Years)	Age	Deaths per 1,000	Expectation of Life (Years)
52	8.76	24.32	67	29.18	13.76
53	9.57	23.53	68	31.52	13.16
54	10.43	22.75	69	34.00	12.57
55	11.36	21.99	70	36.61	12.00
56	12.36	21.23	71	39.43	11.43
57	13.41	20.49	72	42.66	10.88
58	14.52	19.76	73	46.44	10.34
59	15.70	19.05	74	50.75	9.82
60	16.95	18.34	75	55.52	9.32
61	18.29	17.65	76	60.60	8.84
62	19.74	16.97	77	65.96	8.38
63	21.33	16.30	78	71.53	7.93
64	23.06	15.65	79	77.41	7.51
65	24.95	15.00	80	83.94	7.10
66	26.99	14.38			

Source: American Council of Life Insurance, 1980 Life Insurance Fact Book.

Who Needs It?

The answer to this crucial question may make the difference between wasting family financial resources and getting maximum family financial protection. When we started this discussion of life insurance, we asked whether your parents have life insurance for you. If they don't, should they? If they do, are they wasting their money?

In many families there will be a husband, a wife, and children. Each faces the risk of early death. Insurance companies often sell policies designed to include a small amount for the burial of children and a wife, and a larger amount for the father assuming that the father is the breadwinner. One such policy covers $2,000 for each child, $5,000 for the mother, and $15,000 for the father. The *policyholder* (the person who buys an insurance policy) could very likely be grossly underinsured with this coverage. That is, a $15,000 policy would be entirely insufficient for the living expenses and needs of the surviving family if the father should die. The *second rule* in life insurance is to assume your small risks (the children and wife in the case above) and insure against your large losses. This rule means that you should identify the largest risks that you and your family face and purchase insurance according to the potential loss of particular family members.

Breadwinner First. A breadwinner or provider should have top priority for insurance protection. When one member of the family is the only provider, that person's death, not the death of the spouse or children, would cause financial trouble. The major problem in insurance is to buy enough to replace the long-term income that *dependents* (a spouse, children, and other family members) will lose by the provider's death. After the breadwinner has sufficient protection, insurance can be purchased for other family members.

In the past men, rather than women, bought life insurance because the breadwinner was usually the husband. Today with the

Only after the major breadwinner is adequately insured should other family members be insured.

growing number of working women who head the family, women must consider their own need for life insurance. If the woman dies, her children will not only have to replace her income, but will also have to find funds to pay for the household services she performs. Therefore, she needs life insurance based on both the services and income provided.

Children or Teenagers. Many parents buy insurance for their children, but the money is most likely misspent. The important consideration is the cost of the child's policy when weighed against the possible need of additional insurance for the parent. Insurance salespeople use several arguments to encourage the purchase of a family policy that may include coverage for the children or an individual policy for a child or teenager. One such argument is that the cost for a young person's insurance is small and that the coverage would cover most funeral expenses. But it should be remembered that the degree of risk of a child's or teenager's death is very small (see again Table 18-1).

Money spent for insurance for a child or teenager is a diversion of premiums that could be applied to more life insurance for the breadwinner. The best protection for a child or teenager is to make sure the breadwinner is adequately insured.

Singles and Young Adults. Life insurance is best purchased for the protection of dependents. The fewer dependents you have, the less insurance you need. If you are a high school student, or soon to be a college student, you probably do not need life insurance — but you do need to know what life insurance is about. You may be approached to buy life insurance sooner than you think.

Caveat Emptor: *Policies Too Good To Be True*

Consumers are often faced with insurance programs and policies which sound good but may turn out to be worthless or of doubtful value. Much confusion results from the many policies that are available. Misunderstanding also results from the legal and technical jargon used in policies. Often the consumer takes little time to compare insurance plans and therefore frequently buys not enough or too much or the wrong type of insurance. Choosing a good agent is one of the most important steps you can take in building your insurance program. Agents who belong to a local Life Underwriters Association are often among the more experienced agents in your community. Those who are Chartered Life Underwriters, and use the designation C. L. U. after their names, have passed a series of college-level examinations on insurance and related subjects.

Campus Life Policies. Some companies specialize in selling life insurance to college students. Consumers Union studied campus life policies and found companies lending the student money (a loan that must be paid back with interest) to pay the first year's premium. Consumers Union concluded that most policies aimed at the college market should be cautiously considered for these reasons:

1. College students generally don't need life insurance.
2. The amount of protection, the face amount, is too small for future needs.
3. The most commonly sold policies are the wrong type.
4. The policies contain clauses and provisions that should be avoided.
5. The premiums on campus life policies are more expensive when compared to similar policies sold generally.

Debit or Burial Policies. Debit or industrial insurance is sold door-to-door to persons who have little education and low incomes. The premiums for debit or industrial insurance, usually not more than a few dollars, are collected weekly or monthly by smooth-talking, aggressive salespeople. Unfortunately these policies often offer limited protection—$50 to $500 in coverage. In some areas they are called *burial policies.* Often agents overload policyholders with multiple policies or with policies for a child's education. Unsophisticated consumers seldom realize that the policies don't pay back as much as is invested. They pay small premiums on a large number of policies, when they could pay the same or a smaller amount for a single policy which provides much more protection. One typical family was spending $126 a year for what added up to $3,000 worth of coverage on the father, the mother, each of their children, and a grandmother. If they had shopped carefully, they could have bought $3,000 worth of insurance for about $27.

Mail-Order Insurance. You may receive attractive offers for insurance through the mail or even in newspapers, magazines, or on TV. The premiums are low, but a close examination of the fine print usually will reveal at least one provision that makes the policy worthless. In addition the company will not likely be licensed to do business in your state. Even if you have a claim, you may have to hire an attorney in another state and sue in order to collect. The cost of such legal action and the difficulty involved are likely to prevent you from pressing such claims. Buyer Beware.

How Much?

The next important question is how much insurance coverage the breadwinner should have. You should determine the amount of money which the surviving members of your family will need. Blindly accepting a policy designed for your budget is a poor arrangement. Only through careful planning and a study of your family's situation can family insurance needs be determined. Every family must set its goals and analyze its own insurance needs. A young, growing family should purchase enough insurance to provide sufficient living expenses until the children reach the age of eighteen. A surviving spouse should be provided a comfortable living through later years. For a surviving child, a policy might provide a fund for a college education. The purchase of life insurance is not a once-in-a-lifetime matter. As your life and goals change, so do your insurance needs. The *third rule* in buying life insurance is to always consider the long-term income that dependents will lose by your death. There are two ways to calculate how much coverage a breadwinner needs: by calculating the family's future expenses and assets and by using a general guide based upon family income.

Future Expenses and Assets. As accurately as possible, the family should calculate realistic amounts for the following future financial needs:

—Final expenses (funeral, hospital expenses)
—Children's education
—Home mortgage (payments on the home)
—Family living expenses
—Widow's or widower's income and retirement supplement

The surviving family is likely to have *assets,* such as savings, and social security benefits that will help. Again, as accurately as possible, the family should calculate realistic amounts from the following sources of income and assets.

—Savings account/emergency funds
—Securities and other investments
—Social security
—Other income

An inventory of the family's future expenses and assets is one way to determine the amount of insurance that is necessary for the family's financial security. If the gap between future family expenses and family assets is large, which it usually is, the gap should be closed with insurance. Unfortunately most families are underinsured.

General Guidelines. Consumers can also follow another general guideline which will be helpful in making a quick estimate of how much protection they will require. The general rule in the insurance industry is that coverage should be between four and eight times the family's current salary. For a family with a $20,000 income, the rule would suggest $80,000 to $160,000 in insurance coverage.

More recently the Citibank of New York developed a simple procedure for determining how much is needed to replace one's income. See Table 18-2. An ideal goal would be to provide a sum of money that's large enough to permit the family to continue its current standard of living. Accomplishing this goal does not require

Table 18-2

The Multiples-of-Salary Chart
(for net income replacement*)

Your Present Gross Earnings	Present Age of Spouse							
	25 Years		35 Years		45 Years		55 Years	
	75%	60%	75%	60%	75%	60%	75%	60%
$ 7,500	4.0	3.0	5.5	4.0	7.5	5.5	6.5	4.5
9,000	4.0	3.0	5.5	4.0	7.5	5.5	6.5	4.5
15,000	4.5	3.0	6.5	4.5	8.0	6.0	7.0	5.5
23,500	6.5	4.5	8.0	5.5	8.5	6.5	7.5	5.5
30,000	7.5	5.0	8.0	6.0	8.5	6.5	7.0	5.5
40,000	7.5	5.0	8.0	6.0	8.0	6.0	7.0	5.5
65,000	7.5	5.5	7.5	6.0	7.5	6.0	6.5	5.0

*Net income replacement means replacing your income after taxes—not gross income. Net take-home pay (after income taxes and Social Security) is what sets a family's current standard of living. This table tells the approximate amount of income which would be needed to replace current earnings. Social Security benefits, other assets, and insurance will be used to replace a person's income.

To use the chart, multiply the factor under the *income-replacement goal,* either 60 percent or 75 percent, by your present gross (total) earnings. Use as an illustration a family with $23,500 income, a surviving spouse at age 35, and an income-replacement goal of 60 percent. The guide estimates income replacement of $105,000 (23,000 × 4.5). This general guideline is limited because of the many factors that will affect the family's need for insurance. However, there is merit in using this quick, simple method if it helps you judge the adequacy of your family's current insurance coverage.

Source: Citibank, New York.

100 percent of current net (take-home) pay. Seventy-five percent income replacement is ideal, but at least 60 percent would be needed to avoid a serious lowering of the family's living standards.

Which Type?

Once the family's insurance objectives, priorities, and needs are determined, you can ask which type of insurance is best. Essentially all life insurance can be classified as either pure protection (called term insurance) or protection plus savings (called cash-value insurance).

Pure Protection: Term Insurance. Term insurance protects you for a *term* — a time period — usually five years or ten years. If the *insured* (one who carries insurance) dies during the term, the beneficiary receives the face value of the policy. If the insured does not die during the term, the policy expires or must be renewed for another term. The premium is based on the age of the insured. Term insurance is generally the cheapest insurance available until a person reaches approximately age 50. This is because death becomes more likely as people grow older. With term insurance, it's possible to buy large amounts of coverage at low cost. Term insurance provides considerable flexibility because it can be increased or decreased at the end of each term. There are three common types of term insurance.

Group Life Insurance. Group insurance, usually attained through employment, provides insurance for a large number of persons under a single policy without the need for medical examinations. Nearly 40 percent of all insurance in force in the country is group life insurance. Part or sometimes all of the premium is paid by the company as an employee fringe benefit. A disadvantage of group insurance is that it generally ends when an employee is no longer employed by a company.

Renewable-Convertible Term. These policies cover you for the period of time identified (one year, five years, ten years) and can be renewed without a medical examination. Usually the policy specifies an age, such as 65, beyond which renewals are not possible. At each renewal the premium increases because of the higher risk. A renewable term policy allows the policyholder to change the amount of coverage at the end of each term. The convertible feature of the policy allows the policyholder to change to a whole life policy without a medical examination. A guaranteed renewable and convertible term insurance policy provides the consumer with flexibility and maximum insurance protection at a low cost.

Decreasing Term. Often called *mortgage insurance,* a decreasing term policy has a constant premium, but the benefits decrease during the term of the policy, usually over 20 to 30 years. Decreasing term is often used to cover the unpaid debt on a home. As the debt decreases, the amount of insurance coverage also decreases, but the premium remains the same. If the insured dies, the mortgage is paid off, and the family has a mortgage-free home.

Protection Plus Savings: Cash-Value Insurance. The other major type of life insurance is called cash-value insurance. Cash-value insurance offers *protection plus savings.* As you pay the premiums, the policy builds up cash value, much like a savings account. The advantage of cash-value insurance is in what the insurance industry calls the "living benefits." That is, over the years the cash accumulates and becomes available. The savings becomes the *cash surrender value* — the amount the policyholder may collect in cash if the policy is discontinued or is paid up at a certain age.

Cash-value insurance is sometimes called *permanent insurance* because the premiums and the coverage stay fixed from the time the insurance is obtained until death of the policyholder or surrender of the policy. For this reason, insurance agents often recommend that cash-value policies be purchased at a young age to fix the premium rate. When the insured is young, the premium is higher than is warranted by the mortality rate, but when the insured is older, the premium stays the same in spite of the higher death risk. There are three traditional types of protection plus savings policies.

Whole Life. Whole life (also called straight life or ordinary life) is the most widely sold cash-value policy. It pays the beneficiaries the face value of the policy as long as the premiums are paid. The name implies paying the premium your whole life. An attractive feature of whole life, straight life, or ordinary life policies is forced savings—or cash value build-up. Whole life policies are the lowest cost cash-value policies.

Limited Payment. Limited payment insurance has a shorter number of payments and higher premiums. With higher premiums the policy can be paid up to its cash value in fewer years. The end of the premium period may be after 20 years, 30 years, or at a specific age, usually 60 or 65. The desirable feature is that the higher premiums can be limited to a definite period of time, such as during the years of high earnings. However, the premium rate is likely to be so high as to reduce the amount of protection the insurance consumer can buy for a family.

Endowment Policy. An endowment policy is protection plus savings, but the emphasis is on the savings. The cash value build-up accumulates rapidly for a short period of time. If the insured dies before the maturity of the policy, such as before the age of 60 or 65, the face value is paid to the beneficiary. If the insured is living at maturity, the insured can receive the face value. The endowment policy is designed for those who need family insurance protection and also a definite sum of money at a future date. The rapid accumulation of funds can be used for college education, retirement, or as income to support dependents. Premiums on endowment policies are very high.

Which is Best?

Table 18-3 shows the comparative premium rates for each of the major types of insurance. However, to answer the question "Which

Table 18-3

Sample Annual Premium Rates (per $1,000)

Age	Renewable Term	Straight Life	Limited Payment (Paid up at 65)	20-Year Endowment
25	3.23	14.40	16.21	43.52
30	3.60	17.01	19.57	43.83
35	4.57	20.45	24.26	44.92
40	6.45	25.01	30.82	46.98
45	9.72	30.99	41.03	50.18
50	15.30	38.91	56.99	54.85
55	21.93	49.18	85.87	61.27

Multiply the amount in each column by the per $1,000 amount of coverage.

is best?" you should review the characteristics of each type of insurance and then consider the advantages and disadvantages of each.

Advantages. The major advantage of term insurance is that it offers the insurance consumer more coverage for the money. This follows the first rule of buying insurance — which is to buy protection. Another advantage is flexibility. Term insurance provides a means of changing the amount of coverage as the policyholder's needs change. For example, at age 25, the consumer may need a small $5,000 policy; at 35, the same consumer may suddenly need $80,000 or more; and at 50, this consumer may need $20,000 coverage. Term insurance provides maximum protection at a low cost and with flexibility.

The most attractive feature of cash-value policies is the forced savings feature; that is, the cash-value buildup. If you select a strong company, your cash-value buildup represents a secure but conservative investment. The Bureau of Consumer Protection, in a 1979 staff report to the Federal Trade Commission, stated that insurance companies give a low rate of return on cash-value policies. After a person has paid premiums for 20 years, the cash value has earned a rate of return of 2 to 3 percent. The cash-value buildup has always been appealing to consumers because the policy owner may (1) borrow against the cash value of the policy at relatively low rates of interest, (2) take the cash value if the policy is canceled or surrendered, or (3) use the cash value for retirement when the insured reaches age 60 or 65. In addition many people prefer whole life policies because *level* (or the same) premiums are paid for as long as the policy is in existence.

Disadvantages. A disadvantage of term insurance appears to be the increase in the premium as the policy is renewed at older ages. Because of the greater risk of death at 50 years than at 25 years, an insurance company increases the premium. The premiums for term insurance at 50 or over become very high.

A disadvantage to cash-value insurance is in the savings feature. The savings feature causes higher premiums which, unfortunately, causes the insured to purchase less protection than the family needs. Also, by borrowing against the cash value of the policy, a policyholder defeats the actual intent of the policy — that is, financial protection for the family. The loan will be subtracted from the face value of the policy if all or part of the loan has not been repaid at the time of death. You might say that instead of borrowing from yourself, you have borrowed from the family.

Buy Term and Save the Difference. Now back to the question — which type is best? One answer often advocated by insurance experts is to buy term insurance and save the difference between the cost of a term policy and the cost of a cash-value policy. The consumer gets protection and savings, but instead of the insurance company saving the money, the insured saves the money.

Suppose, for instance, that a 35-year-old man buys a $25,000 whole life policy; his annual premium is $511.25. When he retires at 65, he will have $12,613 in cash value, according to the cash-value table in the policy. But if he buys a $25,000 decreasing term to age 65 from the same company, the annual premium is $140.75 or $370.50 less. If he *invests the difference* or *saves the difference*, $370.00 yearly, in a regular savings account at 5 percent, he will accumulate $24,658 at age 65 — nearly twice as much as the cash-value amount of the whole life policy.

With the decreasing term policy, the protection decreases each year. At the same time the savings account builds up. If the person dies at any point the beneficiary will receive insurance and will have the savings account. If the person lives past 65 the decreasing term policy will terminate. The insured will have a larger retirement fund by buying term and saving the difference, $24,658. This plan assumes that the consumer has the discipline to systematically save the difference and to leave the savings account untouched until retirement.

Combination Package. The best arrangement for consumers who do not have the discipline to buy term and/or save may be a mixture of both term and cash-value insurance. A term policy can be used to take care of the high coverage needed during the early years of a growing family, and a cash-value policy can be used to supplement retirement income in later years. For example, as an employee, the consumer would probably have a group policy which could be supplemented with a renewable term policy to provide high coverage during the early years of the family. In addition the home mortgage could be covered with a decreasing term policy for the life of the mortgage. A whole life policy could be used to protect the insured after the heavy family responsibilities are over — between the ages of 50 and 65.

UNIVERSAL LIFE

A relatively new kind of insurance alternative is being sold by insurance companies. It is called universal life. The premiums you put into a universal life policy go into a fund after the insurance company makes two major deductions. The first is a charge for insurance protection—in reality, term insurance. The second charge is for company expenses and profits. The money that remains after the deductions earns interest for the policyholder. Cash value starts accumulating immediately. Unlike the traditional cash-value policy, the cash value grows at a variable rate, not a rate predetermined for the duration of the policy. Universal life policies offer significantly higher interest rates on cash value than traditional life insurance.

Some of the features of universal life that make it unlike other cash-value policies are:

—The policyholder can pay premiums when and in the amount desired, subject to certain minimums.

—The interest on the cash value is geared to market rates.

—The policyholder can withdraw funds from the cash value, as well as borrow against it, without canceling the policy.

—The face amount of insurance can be reduced or raised without rewriting the policy.

—The fees the company charges for the policy are clearly disclosed in the policy.

HEALTH INSURANCE

It's hard to think about accidents and illness when you are young and healthy, but it's too late after the accident or illness occurs. Medical and hospital costs are the fastest rising costs in the United States. At the beginning of the 1980s, according to the Health Insurance Institute, the average daily hospital cost was as high as $150 to $425 per day in some areas. Doctor's fees, dentist's bills, and the cost of eyeglasses all increased more rapidly through the 1970s than all other consumer items.

No one can afford to be without health insurance. In this section we will look at the different ways to purchase health insurance and the types of health insurance coverage.

The Role of Insurance

Health insurance, like life insurance, is based on the concept of sharing risks. A large number of people pay a small amount of money into a common fund from which the insurance company pays the expenses of those who have accidents or illnesses. It is estimated that approximately 80 percent of the American people have some type of health insurance. But even with health insurance, consumers pay 10 percent of all hospital costs, 40 percent of doctors' charges, 86 percent of dentists' bills, and 86 percent of prescription drug costs.

Group Health Insurance. Approximately 70 percent of all Americans buy health insurance coverage through a group plan. Most group plans are provided through an employer, union, or professional association. The cost of administering large group plans is low in contrast to individual plans. This means that group insurance can be as much as 15 to 40 percent less than similar coverage under individual insurance plans. Very often employers pay all or part of the premiums. With a group insurance plan the employee does not have to take a physical examination, there are no waiting periods, and the health insurance coverage cannot be canceled or the insured dropped. Group plans usually provide coverage for both employees and dependents. The disadvantage of group insurance is that coverage ends when the employee leaves the company or group. Although some group insurance can be converted to individual coverage when the employee leaves the group, the cost of the individual coverage is likely to be extremely high.

Individual Health Insurance. Individual health insurance plans are more expensive than group plans but are useful in supplementing the group plans or in providing for particular needs of an individual or family. Individual plans provide protection for persons who are not eligible for a group plan or who want protection between jobs. These policies usually require a physical examination or a statement of the condition of your health as well as a waiting period before the policy goes into effect.

Types of Insurers

Private firms that operate for a profit sell all kinds of insurance from property and liability insurance to life and health insurance. Nonprofit firms, notably Blue Cross/Blue Shield, run by medical organizations cover hospital and medical expenses. Blue Cross provides hospitalization coverage and Blue Shield covers medical and surgical expenses. More than 65 million people are covered by over 60 different Blue Cross and Blue Shield plans. Blue Cross/Blue Shield pays physicians and hospitals on a *service basis*; that is, the plan pays the doctor or hospital directly for the service provided. Private plans operate on an *indemnity basis* whereby the company pays either the insured, the physician, or the hospital.

Nonprofit associations, such as Blue Cross/Blue Shield, return over 90 percent of the premiums they collect in the form of benefits. By contrast, some individual plans written by private companies pay out only about half of what they take in as premiums. Blue Cross/Blue Shield base premiums and benefits on local experience; so if you live in a low-cost area, you pay less in premiums than someone living in an area where doctors and hospitals charge more for services.

Health Maintenance Organizations

As discussed in Chapter 11, health maintenance organizations (HMOs) are an alternative to traditional health insurance. An HMO is an organization of doctors, specialists, and hospitals which offer members a full range of health care services in exchange for a fixed monthly, quarterly, or yearly fee paid in advance. The Kaiser Permanente Medical Care Program in California is an early example of a voluntary program of prepaid health care. The basic theory behind HMOs is preventive health care; that is, to keep costs down by keeping people healthy and out of hospitals. Members are entitled to unlimited use of the medical center for checkups, emergency services, medical treatment, referral services, and family preventive health care services, such as eye and ear examinations.

Basic Types of Health Insurance Coverage

Group and individual policies provide six basic types of health insurance coverage. Remember that it is important to insure yourself and family members against the largest and most serious financial losses first. Minor medical expenses can be handled in the same manner as other routine family expenses.

Hospital Expense Coverage. Hospital expense coverage pays part or all of the bills for hospital rooms, operating rooms, laboratory tests, x-rays, drugs, and so forth. Usually the coverage is expressed as a given amount per day for room and board, nursing care, and medical services for a particular number of days.

As the cost of medical care continues to rise, no one can afford to be without health insurance.

Source: The Greyhound Corporation

Surgical Expense Coverage. Surgical expense coverage pays for the surgeon's fees for an operation. Policies often list the specific operations that the policy covers and states the maximum fee allowed for each operation. It is very important to update the amounts on both hospital and surgical coverage. Hospital and doctor expenses are climbing so rapidly that a policy which pays $50 to $75 a day for a semi-private room would be inadequate in an area where costs have risen to $225 to $275.

Major Medical Expense Coverage. This type of coverage, sometimes called *catastrophic insurance,* provides protection against the large expenses that result from serious injury or prolonged illness. Policies often range from $50,000 to $150,000 in benefits. Major medical coverage pays for the hospital room, doctor's fees, drugs, and almost all other expenses incurred both in and out of the hospital. It usually picks up where hospital and surgical coverage leaves off. Major medical policies contain two features which the insured should know about. The first feature, a *deductible provision*, requires that you pay a specified amount, such as $300 or $500 before the company pays the remainder. The second feature, a *co-insurance provision*, requires the policyholder to share in the expenses beyond the deductible amount. For example, the policy may be written "90-10." The insurance company pays 90 percent of the bill and the insured pay 10 percent. The amount of the deductible and the portion of the medical cost paid by the insured affects the premium for major medical insurance. The higher the deductible amount and the less the amount paid by the insurance company, the lower the premiums.

Physician's Expense Coverage. Physician's expense coverage pays the cost of nonsurgical medical care such as a visit to a doctor's office and a doctor's visit while a person is in the hospital. As a usual practice, benefits for other services, such as diagnostic x-rays and lab work, are paid for with this type of coverage. Physician's expense insurance, also called *medical expense insurance*, is often sold in combination with hospital and surgical insurance.

Dental Insurance. Dental insurance provides reimbursement for expenses of dental services and supplies and encourages preventive care. The coverage provides for oral examinations, fillings, extractions, inlays, bridgework and dentures as well as oral surgery and

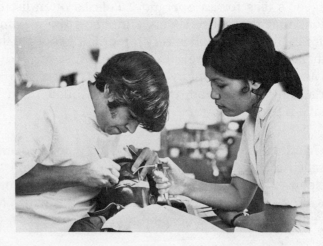

Dental insurance is as important as other types of coverage.

Source: The Seattle Times

root canal therapy. Dental coverage is generally available through insurance company group plans.

Disability (Loss of Income) Coverage. This kind of insurance coverage, also called *loss of income insurance,* compensates for loss of income when an employee or wage-earner cannot work because of illness or an accident. Some policies cover total disability only, while others cover partial disability. Disability may mean either the inability to perform your chosen occupation or an inability to perform any occupation. You should know which one your policy covers. Benefits usually supplement 40 to 60 percent of a wage-earner's regular salary.

WORKERS' COMPENSATION

Workers' compensation is a social insurance plan which provides disability benefits, medical care payments, and death benefits (a burial payment and an allowance for living expenses for survivors) for persons hurt or killed during the course of employment. Nearly eight out of ten workers are covered by workers' compensation. There are no costs to the employee for coverage because the employer pays the premium.

Workers' compensation provides income for persons who are hurt while on the job.
Source: Kerr-McGee Corporation

VOCABULARY REVIEW

Premium   Deductible provision

Beneficiary   Universal life

Face value   Co-insurance provision

Term insurance   Workers' compensation

Cash-value insurance

QUESTIONS FOR REVIEW

1. What is the primary purpose of life insurance?

2. What are the three rules for buying life insurance?

3. What determines that the premium for a 20-year-old person is less than that for a 35-year-old person?

4. Should a teenager have life insurance? Explain.

5. Why should burial or debit policies be avoided?

6. Why should low-cost mail-order policies be avoided?

7. How can a family determine the amount of insurance coverage the family needs?

8. Which type of insurance is commonly provided through employment?

9. What are the advantages of term insurance? Of cash-value policies?

10. What are the disadvantages of term insurance? Of cash-value policies?

11. What is the difference between group and individual health insurance? What source provides the lowest cost health insurance?

12. What are the six major types of health insurance coverage?

PROBLEM-SOLVING AND DECISION-MAKING PROJECTS

1. a. Using Table 18-1, Mortality Rates, about how many persons at age 16 die out of 1,000? At 15? At 20? At 55?

b. Use Table 18-2 (net income replacement chart) to find approximately what amount of insurance would be needed to replace a current gross earnings of $23,500 for a 35-year-old spouse with a 75 percent income replacement goal?

2. What kind of life insurance would you recommend for each situation?
   a. A man, 35 years old, who has just bought a new home with a mortgage on it and who already has a universal life policy.
   b. A businesswoman, 55 years old, who plans to retire in five years and therefore wants to build up as much retirement income as possible.
   c. A young adult who has no other insurance.

3. What is the proper health insurance for each situation described below?
   a. A man was hospitalized for six weeks for a back injury. Hospital care was at the rate of $250 a day.
   b. A woman had an appendectomy. Her physician charged $750 for the operation.
   c. An older person was in a serious automobile accident. This person experienced expenses beyond ordinary medical and hospital costs.
   d. A boy's father had been seriously ill for ten weeks. His father's employer continued to pay full wages for only three weeks after the illness.

COMMUNITY AND HOME PROJECTS

1. From a local insurance agent or the library, obtain a copy of the Life Insurance Fact Book, which is published by the American Council of Life Insurance. Answer the following questions.
   a. In the most recent year shown, how much life insurance was in force in the United States? Is this an increase or a decrease over the amount shown the previous year?
   b. What is the average size of ordinary life policy in force in the most recent year?
   c. What percent of families own life insurance coverage?

2. Obtain from home, or from a community life insurance agent, a copy of a life insurance policy. Analyze it by asking these questions:

a. What type of insurance policy is it?
b. What is the amount of the face value? Does it have current cash value?
c. Circle any terms or phrases that are unclear to you, and find out what these terms/phrases mean.

3. With the permission of your parents, find out what type of health insurance protection they have. Examine the policy for the following information:
a. Source of policy—group, individual, Blue Cross/Blue Shield, or HMO.
b. Type of coverage—basic hospital and physicians expenses, major medical, medical expense, disability, etc.
c. Special provisions such as deductible, co-insurance, exclusions, and the like. Explain what each provision means.

Unit **4**

CITIZEN
PARTICIPATION
IN THE
ECONOMY

Chapter **19**

The United States Economy

What do you think of when you hear the expression "the economy"? A United States Secretary of Commerce once observed, "If ignorance paid dividends, most Americans could make a fortune out of what they don't know about economics." In this chapter you will have an opportunity to visualize the vast mechanism called "the economy," examine the parts of the economy, and learn some of the important measurements that are used to describe what is happening in the economy.

PARTS OF THE ECONOMY

Everyone uses the expression "the economy." News commentators, politicians, the President, union leaders, workers, and consumers frequently talk about the economy. What they actually mean by the *economy* is the system that human beings use to provide for their material well-being and survival. You are probably familiar with other terms used to describe the American economy: free enterprise, capitalism, private enterprise, mixed enterprise, or market economy. We will discuss these other terms in Chapter 20.

The economy is a massive, intricate machinelike mechanism that solves the problems of production and distribution. Like any other machine, it has parts, relationships, and forces that make it function. And like most machines, the parts are so interrelated that tampering with one part causes changes throughout the whole. The American economic machine once was simple, but today it has become so complicated that it sometimes baffles the experts. Unlike real machines, the economy is not visible. You can understand it only by studying the parts that make it operate. There are four parts which make up the framework of the economy — consumers, business and industry, government, and international trade.

Consumer-Worker-Citizen

Every individual plays three roles in our economic system: the roles of a consumer, a worker, and a citizen. You are a consumer from the moment of birth to the moment of death. As you have seen throughout the preceding chapters, a consumer is a user of goods and services. As a consumer you are free to choose how much money to spend, how much to save and invest, whether to borrow, and how much to pay for goods and services. When you decide to spend part or all of your income, you spend to satisfy your wants by acquiring goods and services. When you decide to borrow money, you do so to consume more goods and services in the present and perhaps fewer in the future. When you decide to save, you give up immediate consumption for increased consumption later. When you decide to invest, you use your money or savings in order to increase future income.

As a *worker*, you produce goods or provide services, earn income, and fulfill personal needs. In our economy you will decide for whom you will work, develop skills according to your own interests and abilities, and take risks when you start your own business or change careers.

As a *citizen*, you join with other individuals to make group decisions. As citizens, we influence laws, pay taxes, vote for candidates, and strive to obtain for ourselves and for others the benefits of public goods and services. Problems such as pollution, discrimination, urban decay, poverty, energy shortages, wasted resources, and unemployment confront the citizens of today.

Business and Industry

Business and industry is the second component of the economy. Business and industry provides goods and services for consumers in return for a profit. Most business activity can be classified as either production, processing, distribution, or services. Production includes farming, mining, fishing, and forestry. Processing includes manufacturing, construction, processing foods, oil refining, publishing, and printing. Distribution includes wholesale and retail sales such as advertising, transportation, and communication. Services include finance, insurance, real estate; professional services, such as medicine and law; personal services, such as hairstyling or auto repair; and entertainment services, such as movies, music, sports, and television.

Government

The government is the third component of the economy. The role of the government has grown tremendously in the twentieth century. The government provides the legal framework (laws, rules, regulations, etc.) within which economic activity is carried out. Government also is a consumer of goods, a producer of goods, and an economic force in the economy.

In providing a *legal framework,* the government allows consumers and businesses the freedom to enter into contracts and make use of property. In other cases the government sets limits on the activities of consumers and businesses. For example, government controls narcotics, zones property, licenses occupations, passes laws to limit pollution of air and water, and enacts laws to protect consumers and workers.

As a *consumer,* the government is a buyer of billions of dollars worth of services and products. Government is a consumer when it buys building materials, office supplies, and other products.

As a *producer* the government resembles a private business in its effort to organize and offer services of value to consumers. Two of the government's important services are the Postal Service and highway systems.

As an *economic force,* the government has enormous influence. For example, the government can use its economic power to accomplish socially desirable goals such as providing income and health care to the elderly or disabled, and to exercise its spending and taxation powers to insure economic growth, stability, and full employment.

International Trade

The fourth component of the United States economy is international trade. Our country trades with other countries because we benefit by doing so. Consumers benefit when foreign nations produce articles that are better, different, or cheaper than Americans can get at home. Businesses and consumers benefit by international trade when foreign nations have resources that are essential to the production of goods and services in the United States.

In recent years we have learned the extent to which international interdependence exists between the United States economy and the other economies of the world. The Organization of Petroleum Exporting Countries (OPEC) oil embargo in 1973 shocked Americans into realizing that the United States depends on other countries for natural resources.

THE CIRCULAR FLOW OF ECONOMIC ACTIVITY

To understand how the economy works, it is necessary to see the interaction that takes place among the components of the economy. Economists use a device called the circular flow of economic activity to show the interaction that takes place among consumers, business and industry, government, and international trade.

Interaction in the Economy

The components — consumers, business and industry, government, and international trade — make up the framework of the economy. The interaction among these components sets the economy in motion. The interplay among those demanding goods and those supplying them takes place through the mechanism we call the economy. The circular flow diagram in Illus. 19-1 shows where the action and interaction takes place.

People Making Things . . . Producers. To visualize the "big circle," we start with the individual again. Individuals in our economy own the *factors of production:* land, labor, capital, and management expertise. Some combination of these factors is required to produce the goods and services that consumers want.

Land represents all types of property, including farm land, raw materials, mineral deposits, wildlife, timber, and fish. This broad term also includes oil and gas deposits, coal, water, solar energy, and even the natural richness of the soil. *Labor* consists of manual or mental efforts for which wages, salaries, or professional fees are received. *Capital* is property from which an income can be derived;

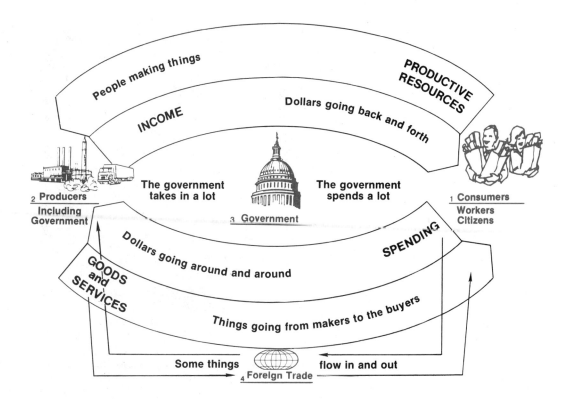

Illus. 19-1

The Big Circle—Putting it all Together

Economist E. Bowden suggests the following way to see the working of the system: "Maybe you could go up in a balloon, then lean out and look down. What would you see? People making things and getting money and buying things and spending money. *Things* going from the makers to the buyers. *Dollars* going back and forth and around and around. A person gets some dollars then spends them, then gets them again, then spends them again. It's all sort of like a big circle."

for example, factories and equipment which produce products or money invested in businesses through ownership of stocks and bonds. *Management*, sometimes called "entrepreneurship," involves the ability to organize and coordinate the other factors of production—land, labor, and capital—with maximum efficiency.

Government provides the legal framework within which economic activities take place. In our legal framework people in the United States own the productive resources—land, labor, capital, management. This means that all property, especially that which is

Factors of production include natural resources such as oil.

Source: Courtesy of Exxon Corporation.

used in production of goods and services, is privately owned. *Private property* is an important legal right in our economy. Some people prefer to use the term *private enterprise* to describe our economy because private ownership distinguishes our economy from economies in which government owns the factors of production.

Things Going from Producers to Buyers . . . Goods and Services. As you look at the big circle, you see things going from producers to buyers. These things are called *goods and services.* An economic *good* is any material object that is useful in satisfying wants and needs. An economic *service,* such as a medical treatment or a haircut, also satisfies a want or need, but it is not an object you can touch. Generally goods and services are classified according to their use; that is, as consumer goods or capital goods. *Consumer goods and services* are those used by consumers. They include such items as stereos, bicycles, houses, food, and clothing. Consumer services include legal representation, auto repairs, and education. *Capital goods* are products and equipment used by producers in the production of other goods. Machinery, equipment, and technology are examples of capital goods.

Goods and services are also classified according to the source of production—produced either by government or by private businesses. *Public goods and services* are those provided for by government agencies and paid for with taxes; for example, education and fire protection. *Private businesses,* also called the *private sector,* produce the myriad of products which consumers enjoy—televisions, stereos, groceries, clothing, and cars—to name a few.

Dollars Going Back and Forth and Around and Around...
Income. In exchange for the use of land, labor, and capital, the organizers of production must pay *income,* which is usually measured in money. Each factor of production earns its own type of income. Land earns *rent,* labor earns *wages,* and capital earns *interest.* Successful managers earn a *profit* for their company. People earn income from whatever factors of production they own.

A Person Gets Some Dollars and Spends Them, Then Gets Them Again and Spends Them...Spending.
As workers receive income with one hand, they as consumers spend it with the other hand. Consumers' choices are limited by their income and by the goods and services that producers are able and willing to supply. Consumer spending is often classified as spending on either durables or nondurables. *Durable goods* are long-lasting products, whereas *nondurable goods* usually have a short-time use. Durable goods include such items as automobiles, household appliances, and furniture. Nondurable goods include such items as food, clothing, and gasoline.

Business spending is called *capital spending.* Businesses spend money to invest in equipment to expand capacity, to improve the quality of existing goods and services, and to introduce new products. Examples of capital spending include spending for construction equipment, farm equipment, machine tools, engines, and electrical components. The amount of business or capital spending is important because it determines whether the economy will grow and the nation's standard of living will improve.

The Government Takes in a Lot of Money and Spends a Lot of Money... Taxes and Expenditures. About 7 percent of all spending on goods and services in the past century was government spending. Today, as we come to the end of this century, nearly 20 percent of all purchases of goods and services is *federal* government spending. As you can see, government plays a major role in the flow of economic activity. Government spending is classified as either *domestic* or *military-defense* expenditures. (Domestic spending is government spending on such expenses as social security, health care, unemployment, education, highways, or public transportation.)

One of the functions of government is to use its economic influence to accomplish socially desirable goals generally called *social welfare programs*. Expenditures on programs such as unemployment compensation, social security, public housing, and community development are examples of social welfare programs. Economists call these expenditures *transfer payments* because income is taken from people who are earning income and given to people who are not earning. Government also attempts to accomplish socially desirable results with expenditures called subsidies. A *subsidy* is some form of federal assistance, loan, grant, or guarantee given to a corporation, government agency, or nonprofit organization because its support is considered essential or desirable for the public welfare. These social goals include the protection of new or faltering industries and protection of industries essential to national security.

Federal, state, and local governments have the power to tax in order to raise revenues to pay for its services, expenses, and programs. Remember that the government does not own the productive resources, but it taxes citizens and businesses for its revenue. As government expenditures increase, taxes increase.

Some Things Flow In and Out of the Country... Foreign Trade Balance. Looking at the big circle, you see goods and services flowing in and out of the country. Those goods going out are called *exports*. Foreigners spend money on these exports, and money "flows" into the country. At the same time, U. S. consumers and producers want foreign products, and they *import* them; that is, goods flow in and money goes out. Economists watch this international flow of money known as the *foreign trade balance*. When consumers and producers in the United States buy more foreign products than foreigners buy from the United States, our nation has

Goods going out of the country are called exports.

Source: Colgate-Palmolive Company

a *negative* foreign trade balance. If foreigners buy more U. S. products than U. S. consumers buy from foreigners, we have a *positive* foreign trade balance.

The Circular Flow = Putting It All Together

Economists have a way of putting all this economic activity together. It's called *macroeconomics*. Macroeconomics is concerned with the big picture or the total of all economic activity.

You can probably see that if you wanted to know the output of all *goods and services* produced in one year, it would be enormously difficult to compile a list of all the tractors, cars, military equipment, eggs, blouses, shoes, stereos, and golf carts that are included in the outer circle of the diagram. It would be easier to add up the money spent on goods and services by consumers, producers, government, and foreigners.

One way that economists pull together the nation's economic activity is with a measurement known as the *gross national product.* GNP measures the economic performance of the whole economy.

When economists or politicians want to know how the economy is doing, they use this measurement. It tells the value of all goods and services produced in one year.

Gross national product is the spending by consumers for goods and services, spending by businesses for investment in capital goods, and spending by government plus or minus foreign trade. As a formula it looks like this:

$$GNP = C \left(\begin{matrix} consumer \\ spending \end{matrix}\right) + I \left(\begin{matrix} investment \\ spending \end{matrix}\right) + G \left(\begin{matrix} government \\ spending \end{matrix}\right) \pm F \left(\begin{matrix} foreign \\ trade \end{matrix}\right)$$

GNP is the total dollar value of products and services produced in the economy during one year. Also GNP tells how the economy is running; it can be used to compare one year with another and to know if economic activity is increasing or decreasing. Illus. 19-2 shows the amount of spending on each component part of the economy as a percent of the total GNP.

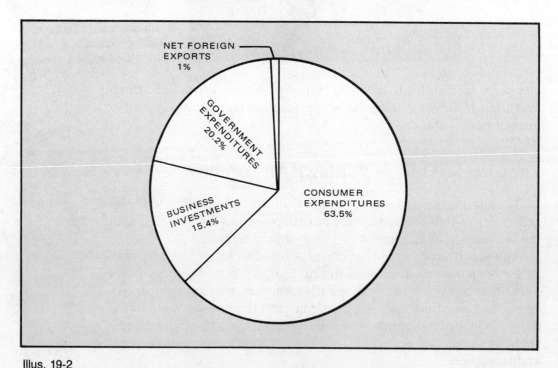

Illus. 19-2

Distribution of the Gross National Product

Source: Economic Indicators *(April, 1982), prepared for the Joint Economic Committee by The Council of Economic Advisors.*

In summary, instead of one big circle, the economy actually is two circles. (Refer to Illus. 19-3.) The outer circle is called *real output*, such as shoes, cars, and radios. Individuals provide producers with resources (land, labor, capital, management) and producers provide goods and services for individuals. The inner circle is called the *spending flow*, or the *flow of money*. The owners of the productive resources receive income, rent, wages, interest, and profit and spend it on the purchase of goods and services. Examine the diagram of the circular flow of economic activity and the subcomponents of each part of the economy.

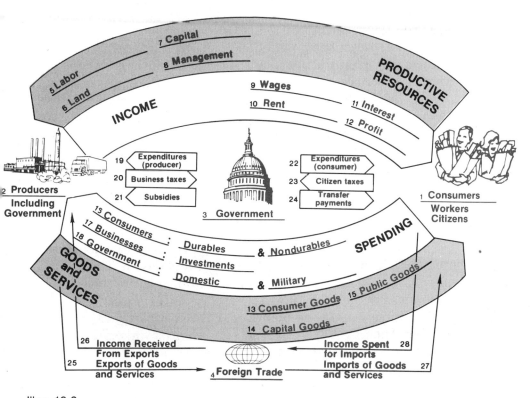

Illus. 19-3

The Big Circle — The Circular Flow of Economic Activity

MEASURING THE ECONOMY

It is important to understand the language of *economists*, the specialists who study the economy. One way to understand this language is to get acquainted with some of the economic measurements (figures and statistics) which describe what's happening in the economy. A brief explanation of some of the most commonly used economic measurements follows.

Economic Cycles

The economic condition or "health" of the economy is measured by the amount of economic activity during a period of time. The conditions in our economy rarely stand still. The state of our economy is usually described in a general way as either a period of prosperity, recession, or depression.

Prosperity describes a period characterized by high demand for products, by plentiful jobs, and by increased living standards. *Recession* describes a time of decline or a slowdown in economic activity. This cycle or period is characterized by increased unemployment, less take-home pay, and smaller profits for businesses. A *depression* is a period of little business activity and high unemployment. Consumers have little or no ability to purchase products and services.

The Consumer Price Index

The *Consumer Price Index* (CPI) is the chief economic measurement which makes headlines nearly every month. The CPI measures changes in the buying power of the dollar. Economists use the CPI to measure *inflation* (the general increase in prices).

The Bureau of Labor Statistics (BLS) compiles and publishes two CPIs. The CPI-W (wage-earners and clerical workers) represents the experience of urban wage-earners and clerical workers and includes approximately 40 percent of the population. The CPI-U is a broader index which covers about 80 percent of the population. The CPI-U (for all urban consumers) includes such diverse groups as salaried workers, the unemployed, the retired, and the self-employed. The BLS checks prices throughout the country of a "market basket" of goods and services. The market basket of some 400 items includes categories for everyday purchases such as housing, clothing, and professional services (health care, entertainment, and recreation).

The CPI measures the changes in the cost of the same market basket of goods and services over time; that is, items are compared this month against the cost a month ago, a year ago, or ten years ago. The index is expressed as a percent of change since 1967, the base year. At the end of 1981, as shown in Table 19-1, the CPI was computed as 281.5, meaning that goods and services costing $100 in 1967 now cost $281.50. Indexes are computed for individual items in the market basket such as food, transportation, and medical care. CPIs are computed also for major cities in the United States.

Table 19-1

Consumer Price Index – All Urban Consumers (1967 to 1981)

Year	All Items
1967	100.0
1968	104.2
1969	109.8
1970	116.3
1971	121.3
1972	125.3
1973	133.1
1974	147.7
1975	161.2
1976	170.5
1977	181.5
1978	195.4
1979	217.4
1980	258.4
1981	281.5

Source: Economic Report of the President, January, 1981.

Unemployment

The unemployment rate is one of the most closely watched measurements of the economy. The level of employment in the United

States tells the approximate number of individuals in the labor force currently working and the number unemployed.

In 1980 the United States labor force had a little over 100 million workers. The Labor Department finds out the unemployment rate by telephoning or visiting 65,000 randomly selected households. Each month the Bureau of Labor Statistics reports the unemployment rate, which represents the number of people out of work as a proportion of the total labor force. To be classified as unemployed, a person must have been without a job during the survey week, must have made specific efforts to find employment sometime during the prior four weeks, and must be presently available for work.

Income

One of the most important economic measurements for most individuals is level of income. Measurements commonly used to describe income are *mean income*, *median income*, and *real income*.

Mean Income. Mean household income is the average income of all households; that is, total income in the economy divided by the total number of households. One way of looking at income distribution is to divide the population into five equal income groups and look at the percent of income which goes to each group. Illus. 19-4 shows these percentages.

Median Family Income. Another commonly reported figure is median family income. Median family income is the amount that divides the income distribution in half—50 percent of all families having incomes above and 50 percent of all families having incomes below the amount. According to *Family Economic Review* (Spring, 1982), this figure was $21,023 in 1980. Probably more significant than median or mean income are the figures that show the percentage of households that earn specific levels of income, as shown in Table 19-2 on page 378.

Certain groups in the population appear to be more largely represented than other groups in the lower half or the upper half of the distribution. For example, the lower half of the distribution includes 70 percent of black families and 67 percent of Hispanic families. Seventy-five percent of the families in which the head of the household completed eight or fewer years of schooling have incomes

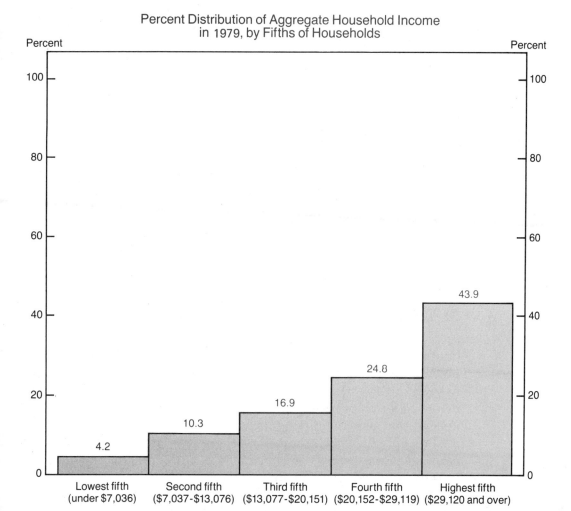

Percent Distribution of Aggregate Household Income
in 1979, by Fifths of Households

	Lowest fifth (under $7,036)	Second fifth ($7,037-$13,076)	Third fifth ($13,077-$20,151)	Fourth fifth ($20,152-$29,119)	Highest fifth ($29,120 and over)
Percent	4.2	10.3	16.9	24.8	43.9

Illus. 19-4

Money Income in 1979 of Households in the United States

Source: U. S. Department of Commerce, Bureau of the Census, Current Population Reports/Consumer Income, *Series P-60, No. 121 (June, 1981).*

below $17,000. Young and elderly families also are concentrated in the lower half of the distribution. On the other hand, 80 percent of families with householders having 16 or more years of education and 65 percent of two-earner families have incomes above the median.

Real Income. Measured in dollars, the gross (or total) average weekly earnings of employees and median income have more than

Table 19-2

Where Families Stand in Income

If Your Family Income Is	You Fall in This Bracket
More than $75,000	Top 2%
$50,000 or more	Top 7%
$35,000 or more	Top 20%
$25,000 or more	Top 39%
$20,000 or more	Top 53%
Less than $15,000	Bottom 33%
Less than $10,000	Bottom 19%
Less than $ 5,000	Bottom 6%

Reprinted from U.S. News & World Report, *Vol. XCI, No. 9 (August 31, 1981), p. 8. Copyright 1981, U.S. News & World Report, Inc.*

doubled in recent years. But what has been happening to the buying power of workers' income? Although gross pay increases from year to year, most workers in recent years have been no better off than before in terms of buying power. For this reason a measurement is needed that tells the buying ability of workers' earnings.

Probably the best indicator of progress for income earners is real earnings. *Real earnings* are average weekly earnings and median income adjusted to eliminate the effect of price changes. When an increase in income is matched by increases in prices, buying power remains the same. Real earnings provide a means of comparison of earnings in the current year with the buying power of earnings in previous years.

Poverty Income Level

Another important income measurement is the poverty income level. The *poverty income level* expressed in dollar terms is the minimum amount of income that is adequate for families to keep up with American consumption patterns. The Bureau of the Census reports that the poverty threshold for a nonfarm family of four persons was $8,414 in 1980. The poverty level is updated every year to reflect changes in prices. In 1980, 29.3 million persons were below the poverty level, representing 13.4 percent of the population. Some small changes in the size of the poverty population have occurred in recent years, but no long-term trend has been evident in either direction.

The *poverty rate* (the number below the poverty level) varies considerably among groups in our society. For example, persons in families maintained by women with no husband present had a higher poverty rate than families maintained by men. Persons who worked year around, regardless of race, had very low poverty rates. The poverty rate for the aged is somewhat higher than the overall U. S. poverty rate.

The Federal Debt

A measurement which worries many people is the federal debt. The debt of the federal government, often called the "national debt," reached nearly one trillion dollars in 1980. The federal debt is basically the result of government deficits; that is, the government spends more money than it collects in revenues.

The federal debt is made up of bills, notes, and bonds. Bills are usually of short length, notes range from one to five years, and bond issues are for longer periods. When the government borrows money, naturally it pays interest on the debt. The interest on the federal debt in 1981 was approximately 80 billion dollars or about 13 percent of total federal spending.

To whom does the government owe money? Approximately one third of the debt is held by government agencies such as the Federal Reserve System (a nationwide banking plan established by the federal government to assist banks in serving the public more efficiently). The rest, approximately two thirds, is held privately by individuals, businesses, financial institutions, and foreigners.

Productivity

Productivity is an economic measurement that indicates how efficiently resources are used to produce the goods and services people want. Like GNP and other indicators, productivity statistics are widely used by news reporters, union leaders, and business people.

Productivity is the measurement that shows changes (increases or decreases) in production in relation to number of hours worked.

For example, suppose a manufacturer of television sets has a 10-person crew working on an 8-hour shift. This shift produces 320 television sets a day.

The input of labor is 80 worker hours (10 workers × 8 hours) and the output per hour is 4 television sets (320 sets divided by 80 worker hours). If the company's research and development department or the workers could devise a way to improve production, workers could produce more television sets per day. Assume that because of newly developed technology, output should become 340 television sets per day. Output per worker hour (productivity) would then be 4.25. An increase in productivity means producing more goods with the same resources.

Productivity is an important measurement because output per worker hour is a crucial ingredient in the growth of the economy. Productivity in the United States economy rose at an annual rate of 3.2 percent from 1947 through 1967. From 1968 through 1978, however, the gains averaged only 1.6 percent. In recent years United States productivity has been declining. Economic growth and our standard of living depend to a large degree on the level of output (productivity). When productivity is improving, the economy is growing and the standard of living is improving.

Business Profitability

Profit is an economic measurement that creates a lot of misunderstanding. The word "profit" comes from a Latin word meaning "advance," "progress," or "go forward." Profit implies a reward for effort. Quite simply, profits are what remains after a company subtracts all the costs of doing business from total income.

From time to time, survey takers ask consumers to estimate corporate profits. Invariably, people guess profits to be 25 to 33 cents for every dollar of sales. The fact is that, for industry as a whole, the actual figure is closer to 5 cents for every dollar of sales. The profits of individual companies are often reported in the news as a percentage increase or decrease from the previous quarter or year.

Real GNP

Now we will return to the measure with which we began our discussion — GNP. Gross national product attempts to measure the current dollar value of all goods and services produced during the year, from shoe repairs and sidewalk construction to fighter planes and frozen pizzas. Since the value of the dollar changes from year to year, changes in the gross national product may reflect only price increases—not a change in actual output of products or services. As a result, a separate computation of GNP is made to determine the real GNP.

Real GNP is figured by using a "deflator" to eliminate changes in prices. To eliminate changes in prices, gross national product is divided by the consumer price index. The real GNP takes into account changes in the gross national product that result from rising prices. Therefore, real GNP makes it possible to compare the output of the current year with that of previous years. Real GNP is the figure economists consider the best indicator of the growth of the economy.

VOCABULARY REVIEW

Private property	Subsidies
Capital goods	Imports
Public goods	Gross national product
Durable goods	Consumer Price Index
Nondurable goods	Real earnings

QUESTIONS FOR REVIEW

1. What is meant by the expression "the economy"?

2. Name the four parts of the economy.

3. What three economic roles do all individuals have in the economy?

4. What are the four economic functions of government in the economy?

5. What are the four types of economic activity that flow from consumers to producers and from producers to consumers?

6. What are the basic factors of production needed to produce goods and services?

7. What are three terms used to describe the economic cycles of the economy?

8. What economic measurement tells how efficiently resources are being used when goods and services are produced? the current dollar value of all goods and services produced during the year?

PROBLEM-SOLVING AND DECISION-MAKING PROJECTS

1. Make a list of your activities that are examples of your role as a consumer, worker, and citizen.

2. Compile a list of government services that you utilize in your community.

3. Using the flow diagram presented in this chapter, trace the effect of each of the following conditions on the economy.
   a. a decrease in consumer spending on durable goods
   b. an increase in consumer purchases of foreign goods (imports) with no increase in foreign purchases of U. S. goods (exports)
   c. an increase in income payments (wages) for labor without an increase of goods and services
   d. a decrease in overall government expenditures and transfer payments
   e. an increase in overall expenditures and transfer payments without an increase of goods and services
   f. an increase in taxes collected from both businesses and citizens

COMMUNITY AND HOME PROJECTS

1. Your text identifies four types of business activity: basic production, processing, distribution, and services. Make a list of businesses in your community which are examples of each type of business activity.

2. Use *Economic Indicators* (a federal government periodical), *Statistical Abstracts of the United States* (published annually), or other reference material in your library to determine the current rate of unemployment, CPI, mean or median income, and GNP.

Chapter **20**

The Consumer in a Market Economy

In Chapter 19 you learned a method of visualizing the economy. You also learned some of the most common measurements of the performance of the economy. In this chapter you will study the forces that direct and coordinate all of the economic activity, and you will examine the role of the consumer in the economy.

A MARKET ECONOMY

Americans live in a market economy. In a *market economy* economic decisions are guided primarily by the interplay of consumers, producers, and government in the marketplace:

—Consumers seek the best value for the money they spend.
—Producers seek the best income from the products or services they provide.
—Governments (federal, state, and local) seek to promote safety and welfare of the public and to provide public goods and services in the community or national interest.

To understand how a market economy works, you will need to know about certain economic forces, such as scarcity, demand, supply, profit, competition, and prices, that influence buyers and sellers every time they come together in the marketplace.

Scarcity

Scarcity is a fundamental and universal economic problem. Half the world's population lacks sufficient supplies of necessities. For example, serious shortages exist in food, clothing, medical care, adequate shelter, and education. Even in our rich, affluent economy, many things are in short supply.

Scarcity results partially from shortages of the factors of production that are necessary to produce goods and services. It also results from unlimited human wants. People want more than is available. It seems that human desires expand as rapidly as production increases. The unlimited wants of people always result in more demand for items than the factors of production can produce.

As a result of scarcity, consumers must economize — that is, they must make choices. By making efficient decisions, consumers attempt to get maximum satisfaction from limited resources.

Demand

Consumers are free to make their choices from many products. Consumers influence producers through their demands whenever they make a purchase or decide not to make a purchase. We should distinguish between wants and demands. You may want an expensive car or an expensive home, but *demand*, sometimes called "effective demand," is backed up by your willingness and ability to spend your money for goods or services.

Changes in demand cause prices to fluctuate. In practice when demand for a product increases, the price of that item generally goes up. When demand for a product decreases, the price of that product generally goes down.

Supply

Consumers depend on suppliers or producers for goods and services. *Supply* is the amount of economic goods available for sale. The supply of a product will depend largely on the cost of producing it in relation to the price at which it can be sold. Prices change easily and respond quickly to the availability of a product. When the supply of an item is plentiful, the price of the product generally will decrease. If the supply of a product is scarce, the price of the product generally goes up.

Profit

Producers are not guaranteed an income when they start a business. Producers hope for profit. *Profit* is the difference between receipts and costs; that is, the amount it costs to produce an item is subtracted from the amount received from selling it. The idea of profit motivates people. Have you ever wondered what makes a person work for years in the basement, tinkering on an invention? What makes a person risk large sums of money on a business venture when the failure rate of new businesses is well over 50 percent? What makes a company spend millions of dollars on research and development of a new product? The *profit motive*, or self-interest, acts as a driving force to guide people to provide the goods and services that society is willing to pay for.

Profit is the incentive or reward for organizing the factors of production and for supplying products and services. The concept of profit also causes producers to shift their efforts from one product to another if there is more profit in another product. Profit also causes businesses to produce as efficiently as possible. Efficient producers will make more profit by producing at the lowest cost possible and selling at the highest price possible.

Competition

Competition is rivalry among sellers for consumers' dollars or rivalry among producers for the factors of production. Competition keeps producers from charging unreasonably high prices and getting excessive profit. Certain conditions have to exist for competition to work the way it's supposed to:

—There should be a large number of buyers and sellers.
—Buyers should have sufficient information regarding the nature of the product—particularly price and quality. They should also have alternatives, that is, substitutes and similar products to choose from.
—There should be easy entry into the market for new producers who are attracted by profits.

Competition works in this way. If profits for a business get too high, other businesses will move in and take away customers by offering a lower price or a better product. *Price competition* involves taking business away from a competitor by lowering prices. Actually price competition benefits consumers by forcing the price of products down to a level close to cost plus a reasonable profit.

There are many types of competition. Competition may take the form of efficient business management. It often causes producers to

Price competition involves taking business away from a competitor by lowering prices.

manage and operate their businesses in the most cost-efficient way. Competition makes them look for the best combination of the factors of production. For example, if a business person wishes to produce suits, then decisions must be made regarding the right combination of cloth, thread, sewing machines, designers, cutters, and machine operators. The most efficient managers will have the lowest cost product. The lowest cost product may make it possible to attract consumers away from less efficient producers.

There are other ways to compete for consumers' dollars. Winning business away from a competitor by product differentiation, advertising, high-quality customer service, or product design or improvement is called *nonprice competition*. Product improvement, such as the improvement of automobile gas consumption, can be beneficial to consumers. But some forms of nonprice competition may not benefit consumers. For example, product differentiation, which often involves excessive advertising to emphasize a minute product difference or to create an imaginary difference (as discussed in Chapter 4) may actually raise the cost of the product with no resulting advantage to consumers.

Prices

Every time a buyer and seller meet in the marketplace, the economic forces of scarcity, supply and demand, profit, competition, and prices interact. Prices are flexible. In other words, prices fluctuate as supply or demand changes, as the cost of production changes, and as competition increases or decreases. Prices fluctuate until they reach a balance with the existing forces. The price at this point of balance is known as the *equilibrium price* or *market price,* and it conveys the following information to both consumers and producers:

—Prices tell how much value a product has. The price that people are willing to pay reflects how much satisfaction or usefulness they expect from the product.
—Prices tell how scarce the product is.
—Prices tell the cost of production plus a reasonable profit.

Prices serve as a rationing device. High prices tell people to conserve or economize because the product is scarce and highly valued. At the same time, high prices motivate producers to direct their resources and efforts toward increasing the supply of certain products or services.

THE PHENOMENON OF PRICES*

Let me illustrate the function of prices in the market. This example comes from an article written by Leonard Reid. He said, "Nobody in the world knows how to make a pencil." He had in mind a simple pencil made out of wood with graphite in the middle and a piece of rubber on the end of it. It seems like a remarkable statement, "nobody knows how to make a pencil." A pencil is a simple, elementary thing, surely people know how to make a pencil, but of course they don't. To make a pencil, what must you do? You have to know how to grow the wood, which, when cut down, makes the shell of the pencil. You have to produce the saw that cut the wood. To produce a saw, you have to put up a blast furnace that will enable you to produce the iron and steel. But go even farther. To make a pencil, you have to know how to get the graphite, the inside of the pencil that we call lead. It isn't really lead, it's graphite; it comes from mines in South America. To make that pencil, you have to grow rubber. The rubber grows in Malaysia, perhaps. You can see that when you start to examine a lead pencil, thousands upon thousands of people have pooled their bits of knowledge and expertise to come together and produce the pencil.

When you go down to the store and pay 10 or 15 cents for the lead pencil, you are entering into a deal, an exchange, with thousands of people who have cooperated to produce the pencil. You are entering into a deal with the people in Malaysia who have grown the rubber, with the people in South America who dug the graphite, and with the people in the state of Washington who cut the Redwood trees. You have no idea who those people are; you couldn't name them; you never saw them.

Source: © Joanne Meldrum

Now how is this production brought about? How is it that you are able to step in and make this deal? How can you arrange for cooperation of all these people all over the world to produce that iron that goes into the saw that cut the wood and to produce the rubber? All this international cooperation is done through the *mechanism of prices*. The man in Malaysia does not know that you wanted a pencil; he has no idea you even exist. He may not even know what a pencil is. He is willing to grow the rubber because he knows that if he brings rubber to market in a certain town somebody will pay him for that rubber. The price that he will be paid for the rubber compensates him for growing it. The man in South America dug in the graphite mine for the same reason. Everywhere throughout the world prices bring people together.

Let there be an enormous craving for lead pencils. Imagine that for some reason a lead pencil fad exists and everybody has to have a dozen lead pencils. Demand for both graphite and rubber will increase. How will the fellow in Malaysia know that he should produce more rubber? How will the fellow in South America know that he should dig more graphite? They will know because they will suddenly discover when they go to market that a higher price will be paid for rubber or graphite. Prices serve as an extremely effective means of transmitting information.

A problem in social organization is that we somehow have to pool the knowledge of the fellow in Malaysia about how to grow rubber with the knowledge of the fellow from Washington on how to cut down a tree. Neither one knows about the other's existence. But somehow information must be transmitted between them. The price system is the fundamental means of transmitting information. Prices let people know what is happening. Now a crucial thing about prices is that they transmit precisely the information that is required; they do not transmit irrelevant information. The fellow in Malaysia doesn't really have to know why the demand for rubber has gone up. Whatever the cause for the increase in the demand for rubber, all that matters is that somewhere in the world people are willing to pay more for rubber.

Prices also transmit information to consumers. If for some reason graphite is scarce in South America because of a strike, people need to have this information. They don't need to know about a strike in South America, but they must be told that graphite is scarce. People must know that they should use something other than graphite or they should ration their use of graphite. How is such information transmitted to consumers? The strike in South America will cause a rise in the price of graphite. The users of pencils don't have to know the reason for a price increase; they will know from the price increase that they should limit their use of graphite. They get the signal when prices go up. Higher prices tell consumers to economize. In this way, prices serve as a means of transmitting information about a wide variety of matters whether about gas, food, or "pencils" to both consumers and producers.

*Source: Adapted from Dr. Milton Friedman, "The Phenomenon of Prices," Basic Economics, Lesson #4, 1981. Permission granted to reprint by Instructional Dynamics International, 666 North Lake Shore Drive, Chicago, Illinois 60611.

The Market Mechanism

Every society faces the problem of scarcity. You know that it takes productive resources to provide the goods and services people need and want—but these productive resources are too scarce for all the demands of the population. As a result, every society is confronted with two central economic questions:

—What is the best use of scarce resources?
—Who decides how the resources are going to be used?

What is the Best Use of Scarce Resources? The question is really threefold: (1) What goods and services should be produced and in what quantities? (2) How should goods and services be produced? (3) Who should get the goods and services? The answers to these questions will determine how society allocates resources; that is, how society makes the best use of land, labor, capital, and management.

Economists call the "what and how" questions the production problem, and the "who gets" question the distribution problem. Every economic system must solve the problems of production and distribution. Most modern economies use the market mechanism, or the market process, as the solution to the production and distribution problem. The *market mechanism* is a complex mode of organization in which the interaction of economic forces between buyers and sellers solves the problem of production and distribution. The components of the economy (consumers, business and industry, and government) are the complex mode of organization.

The market mechanism is the most efficient and powerful means of solving the problem of scarcity. The market process answers the questions "What?" "How?" and "Who Gets What?" The market process works automatically; it helps us conserve valuable resources; it provides the goods and services we want; and it allows a high degree of freedom for each of us to choose our products. In economic terms the market process *allocates scarce resources.* The market mechanism is the means we use in the United States to solve the central economic problem of scarcity.

Who Decides How the Resources are Going to be Used? In all modern economies the decisions about "What?" "How?" and "Who Gets What?" are made by three groups: (1) individuals as consumers and producers, (2) individuals as voters, and (3) central authorities.

When an individual consumer purchases a pair of boots or tennis shoes instead of blue suede shoes, a signal is given to producers to continue producing boots and tennis shoes. In this way *consumer choice* signals producers as to the satisfaction or dissatisfaction of consumers. When sales of products increase, merchants order more from the manufacturers. If the manufacturers are operating at full capacity and believe that consumer demand will continue, they may expand facilities, hire more workers, and obtain more raw materials. If consumers do not buy a product or buy a competitor's product, a signal is sent to the merchant and manufacturer to improve the product. When consumers stop buying a product, or when a significant number shift to a similar product, a signal is sent to producers to shift their efforts to producing products the consumer will buy.

Citizens also are asked to make decisions about the use of resources. We will call this *citizen-voter choice*. When citizens are asked to approve a school bond issue, they are asked whether they wish to use more resources for education. When citizens are asked to vote on the construction of a nuclear power plant in the community, they are being asked how to use resources. Citizen-voter choice often serves as an alternative to consumer choice. Transportation, for example, can be provided by private car or by public transportation.

Citizen-voter choice allows citizens to make decisions about the use of resources.

For public transportation to be available, voters must make the decision to provide the resources (taxes) for the public transit system.

Another source of decision making is *central authority*. The central authority may be a tribal chief, an absolute dictator, a central committee, Congress, or the President of the United States. By order or decree, the authority may allocate 25 percent of a nation's resources to military preparation, to investments in plant and equipment, or even to building a palace. There is an important distinction between voter choice and central authority decision making. Voter choice assumes that citizens are consulted directly or through their representatives, while a central authority gives relatively little consideration to citizen participation.

All modern economic systems use each of these three methods to some degree to arrive at the use of a nation's resources. For example, in most economies consumer choice determines such things as whether people wear white or brown shoes, eat beef or turkey, and go to a movie or read a book. In all economic systems central authorities decide whether to build a new missile system or a new aircraft carrier.

One economic system is distinguished from the other by the weight given to each of the three methods for arriving at resource allocation. In some economies the emphasis is on citizen-voter choice; in other economies, the emphasis is on central authority. When the emphasis is given to citizen-voter choice, the economic system is often referred to as *socialism*. Citizens vote directly or through elected representatives to determine resource allocation. Sweden, because of its extensive social legislation and welfare programs, is an example of an economy in which emphasis is given to citizen-voter choice. Some governments assume that a central authority can make better judgments than individuals. Such assumptions are typical of totalitarian governments. In Russia, Cuba, and China the emphasis is on central authority. Consumer choice is limited in these countries.

Consumer choice plays an important role in determining the use of resources in the United States. When consumers and producers make most of the decisions, the system is commonly referred to as a *free enterprise* or *private enterprise economy*. But even in the United States, many economic decisions are made by government agencies — partially through citizen-voter choice and the use of central authority.

THE CONSUMERS' ROLE IN THE ECONOMY

Adam Smith declared that "consumption is the sole end and purpose of production." Consumption may be the purpose of production, but the ultimate purpose of consumption is survival and satisfaction. In this process the consumer plays a crucial role in the economy. In our economic system individual economic decisions have power—*consumer power*.

Consumer Power

Consumer power is expressed each time a consumer spends money. When a consumer buys a product, the money spent is like a vote cast in favor of a product or service. In a market economy the consumer vote, represented by dollars spent in the marketplace, determines future growth patterns. If consumers vote for small high-mileage automobiles, if consumers vote for energy-efficient appliances, if shoppers vote for highly nutritious foods, then manufacturers will have no choice but to respond with desirable products. When consumers make efficient decisions and realize that their buying affects not only their pocketbooks, but the economy and the environment as well, they are demonstrating effective consumer power.

Opportunity Cost. Consumers increase their economic power by using the concept of *opportunity cost* or *real cost* as a tool for decision making. Because of scarcity and unlimited wants, consumers must *economize* — that is, make decisions and choices. People make choices on the basis of *cost*. Most people think of cost as money spent on goods and services. Actually money isn't the real cost. The real cost of something is the alternative product that you cannot have because you already spent your money. The real cost of a purchase is what you have to do without or what you could have bought instead.

The consumer has numerous opportunities to spend limited dollars. The consumer must make a decision between two things or among many things. You may want a concert ticket or a recent record album by a favorite artist. If you choose the ticket to the concert, you have to do without the new record. The real cost of the ticket is the

The real cost of any purchase is what you will have to do without in order to make that purchase.

Source: Chesebrough-Pond's Inc.

missed opportunity to have the record. You have to decide or choose on the basis of the highest or best value. When consumers use the real-cost concept to make decisions, they are ordering their priorities. That is, they will seek the highest or best use of their dollars. Different terms are commonly used for this real-cost concept such as opportunity cost or alternative cost. Perhaps the real cost of a purchase should be called the "best valued alternative opportunity."

As you learned in Chapter 3, the opportunity-cost principle is a decision-making tool. It helps you to sort out what is the highest or best value among alternative opportunities that you can get with your limited resources. When consumers use the opportunity-cost tool in making buying decisions, they attempt to get the highest or best value and maximum satisfaction.

Freedom to Choose and Refuse. Consumer power stems from your freedom to buy or not to buy. You hear a great deal about freedom to choose, but you seldom hear anything about freedom of rejection. We exercise both of these freedoms so regularly that we seldom think about them. It is assumed that consumers know what they need or do not need and that they can discern what will provide satisfaction and what will not. The market works most efficiently when consumers use this freedom with care and skill. The freedom to choose and refuse is the most powerful tool consumers have. As stated earlier, consumer choice is like a signal in favor of or against a product or service. If a product on the market is shoddy, unsafe, or harmful to the environment, the consumer's power to buy or not to buy will affect the continued production of the product.

WHAT'S IN A NAME?

The United States economy has many names—free enterprise, private enterprise, mixed enterprise, capitalism, and market economy. You also may hear laissez-faire economy, competitive economy, consumer economy, and a few others. Everyone seems to have a preference. Which term is correct? Actually each emphasizes a particular characteristic of the American economic system. Below are some definitions.

Free enterprise is an economic system in which the means of production are owned privately, and the owners and workers are free to use their resources, energies, tools, etc., as they desire.

Capitalism is an economic system in which the means of production (capital: the factories, tools, equipment, coal mines, oil wells, railroads, etc.) are owned by private individuals, not by the government.

Private enterprise is an economic system in which the means of production are owned and operated by individuals and privately owned organizations for the purpose of making profit, as opposed to government owned and controlled production.

Market economy is an economic system in which the market process organizes productive resources, the profit motive stimulates production, competition insures efficiency, and supply and demand directs the production and distribution of goods and services.

Mixed enterprise economy is a system in which resource allocation is determined by a mixture of consumer choice, voter choice, and central authority, for example, a combination of private decisions and government action shapes the overall economy.

Perhaps we can combine these into one definition. The United States economy is characterized by:

—private ownership

—a mixture of consumer choice, citizen-voter choice, and central authority to determine the use of resources

—the market process to organize the productive resources, the profit motive to stimulate production, competition to insure efficiency, and supply and demand to direct the production and distribution of goods and services

Using this comprehensive definition, it would be appropriate to call the United States economy a *private-mixed-market economy*. Unless you wish to use this mouth-filling term, the name you choose for the United States economy will probably emphasize only one of its characteristics.

Consumer Responsibility. In Chapter 1 you learned that consumers have certain rights in a market economy. Along with these rights consumers also have certain responsibilities to themselves, to the economy, to society, and to the environment.

Consumer Rights	Consumer Responsibilities
The Right to Safety	The responsibility to use products safely
The Right to be Informed	The responsibility to use information
The Right to Choose	The responsibility to choose efficiently
The Right to be Heard	The responsibility to express satisfaction or dissatisfaction about products and to participate in resolving consumer problems
The Right to Redress	The responsibility to seek a remedy to consumer problems
The Right to Consumer Education	The responsibility to be an educated consumer

The responsibility to use products safely means that consumers must learn about any physical risks associated with the use of the product before purchasing it. This responsibility requires the proper use of a product by reading and following the manufacturer's instructions. It means that consumers must use the product in a way that will not interfere with the personal or environmental safety of others.

In exercising the responsibility to use information, consumers need a wide variety of product and service information. To make the best choices, consumers need facts; they need to make a reasonable effort to understand the available information; and they need to weigh the personal benefits of a decision against potential social or environmental costs.

Consumers can choose from a variety of products and services at competitive prices. To make competition work, consumers have a responsibility to seek and demand low prices and high quality; to make choices based on an understanding of their needs and wants, values, and resources; to choose products which provide the greatest personal or family satisfaction; and to avoid products which are harmful to the environment.

The right to be heard carries with it the responsibility to express dissatisfaction when a product or service is poor quality or harmful to the environment or your health. This right implies the responsibility to communicate in an honest and fair manner in all marketplace activities. This responsibility is greater than merely complaining. The responsibility to be heard also means greater consumer participation at local, state, and national levels where government decisions are likely to affect consumers.

The responsibility to seek a remedy to consumer problems means that when consumers are dissatisfied, they need to know how to use the channels of redress. If a manufacturer or seller fails to solve a problem, consumers have a responsibility to know which of the consumer agencies and governmental agencies are most appropriate. Consumers with honest complaints represent not only themselves but also other consumers who are dissatisfied or mistreated.

The responsibility to become an educated consumer means that consumers must be able to make efficient decisions in light of their values. Educated consumers are aware that their decisions not only have personal consequences on their life-styles, but that the decisions also have social and global implications.

Consumer Impact on the Economy

The extent of the consumer's power and influence in the economy is easily measured by the GNP. As seen in Chapter 19, Illus. 19-2, consumer spending constitutes two thirds of total spending. A decrease in consumer spending increases unemployment and can cause a recession. Consumer confidence and consumer spending are vital to the health of the economy. Equally important to the economy is the consumer's decision to save rather than to spend. For new capital to be available for economic growth, someone must save. The more money that consumers save, the more there is available for investment. Saving and investing is the way productive capacity increases. Economic growth depends on the extent to which consumers save. Consumer spending makes the economy run, but consumer saving makes the economy grow.

VOCABULARY REVIEW

Demand	Consumer choice
Supply	Citizen-voter choice
Profit motive	Central authority
Competition	Mixed enterprise
Market price	Real cost

QUESTIONS FOR REVIEW

1. What is the central economic problem of all nations?

2. What are the six forces that interact in the market when buyers and sellers come together?

3. What is the incentive or reward for business persons who organize the factors of production?

4. What do prices tell consumers about products on the market?

5. What do prices tell producers about products on the market?

6. How do most modern economic systems solve the problem of scarcity?

7. In the United States economy who is responsible for determining the best use of the nation's resources?

8. How can an individual exercise consumer power?

9. What are the basic consumer responsibilities?

PROBLEM-SOLVING AND DECISION-MAKING PROJECTS

1. Assume that you are talking to a foreign visitor who knows very little about the U.S. economy. The visitor asks you why some people call the economy capitalism, others call it free enterprise, and still others call it a mixed enterprise or market economy. Explain.

2. Make a list of products toward which you feel consumers should express their dissatisfaction by withholding their purchases. Explain your reasons—unsafe, hazardous to health, scarce, causes harmful effects to environment, etc.

3. Sometimes consumers' freedom to choose causes manufacturers to shift their production to another product. Make a list of products which have been discontinued in favor of other products.

COMMUNITY AND HOME PROJECTS

1. There are several commonly used names to describe the U.S. economy—free enterprise, capitalism, market economy, private enterprise, and mixed enterprise economy. Prepare a questionnaire that you can use to survey which name is most commonly used. Ask the following people:

   a. five students who are not taking this course.
   b. five teachers in your school.
   c. five neighbors in the community.
   d. five persons who own or operate a business.

   Prepare a report on your findings. Which name do you prefer? Why?

2. Some economists say the consumer is king in the market. Others say the consumer is a pawn. One frustrated consumer expressed the role of the consumer in this way:

If one were to put the consumer on a chess board, some would put him in the role of king; others, the pawn. I would put the consumer in the role of knight who, with awkward movements, is able to avoid some frauds and misconceptions, but eventually will get taken.

Write an essay on how consumers can exercise their power in the economy.

3. Prepare a written report on Adam Smith and his book *Wealth of Nations*.

Chapter **21**

Consumer Problems and Remedies

Consumers need to know how to get what they deserve in today's marketplace —but the products and services offered are often complex. Relationships between buyers and sellers tend to be impersonal and complicated. The consumer is frequently the amateur buyer who must deal with a knowledgeable salesperson or a large corporation. Consumers also encounter rip-off artists and fraudulent schemes in the marketplace. Consumers who experience problems with a product or service often feel helpless. In this chapter we will look at some general problems of consumers, discuss a few fraudulent schemes and deceptive practices, and present ways in which consumers can resolve their problems.

TYPES OF CONSUMER PROBLEMS

Consumers must, of necessity, trust the persons with whom they deal in the marketplace. Consumers cannot be knowledgeable about enough products to evaluate the claims made by sellers. In general consumers assume that government does not permit false or misleading claims about products. The problems consumers experience fall into two categories: (1) problems concerning the product or service performance, and (2) problems of frauds or deceptive practices.

Product Quality

Consumers expect products to perform satisfactorily, to be durable, and to be safe. And regardless of the amount paid for a purchase, consumers have a right to quality and satisfaction. But in today's marketplace, consumers often experience frustrations and problems. In one national survey, 32.4 percent of the households reported that they had experienced consumer problems. Table 21-1 shows the types of problems consumers said they experienced.

Table 21-1

Most Prevalent Types of Consumer Problems

Type of Consumer Problem	Households Having This Type Problem	
	No.*	%
1. Store Did Not Have Product Advertised for Sale	203	24.9
2. Unsatisfactory Performance/Quality of Product (Construction, Ingredients)	182	22.4
3. Unsatisfactory Repair	165	20.3
4. Unsatisfactory Service (Unrelated to Repair)	127	15.6
5. Long Wait for Delivery	84	10.3
6. Failure to Receive Delivery	83	10.2
7. Overcharge or Excessive Price	78	9.6
8. Distasteful or Offensive Advertising	75	9.2
9. Product/Service Not as Ordered/Agreed On	72	8.8
10. Incorrect/Deceptive or Fraudulent Billing	70	8.6
11. Deceptive Advertising/Packaging/Pricing	66	8.1
12. Goods Received in Damaged Condition	65	8.0
13. Manufacturer/Dealer Didn't Live Up to Guarantee/ Warranty	58	7.1
14. Dealer/Salesperson Misrepresented Product/ Service	53	6.5
15. Failure to Receive Refund	43	5.3
16. Product Unsafe	30	3.7
17. Item Received Different from One Bought	27	3.3
18. Product Harmful to Environment	26	3.2
19. No Return from Repair or Service	19	2.3
20. Instructions for Use/Care Unclear/Incomplete	19	2.3
21. Credit Terms Misrepresented	14	1.7
22. Unauthorized Repair or Service	13	1.6
23. Other	10	1.2
TOTAL	1,582	

*Of the national sample (2,513) households, 32.4% (814) reported consumer problems that had occurred during the previous year. These households reported a total of 1,582 problems, for an average of 1.9 occurrences for households reporting problems.

Source: U.S. Office of Consumer Affairs, The National Consumer Survey: A Profile of Consumer Problems and Complaint Submission Trends, TARP Study, 1979.

Three of the four most prevalent problems dealt with basic deficiencies in the quality of products and services purchased. Many of the problems reported also concerned marketing and business practices. Eight products and services receive the greatest number of complaints from consumers. In order of frequency, the complaints are about automobiles, appliances (radios and televisions), all other major and minor appliances, postal service, clothing, telephone service, food, and household items. Many of the problems with automobiles and appliances were related to the services provided by repair shops.

Because of unsatisfactory service, American consumers lose an estimated $2 billion a year, for an average loss of $88 per household. Consumers are more likely to complain the greater the amount of the financial loss. However, even when large sums of money are involved, many consumers still don't complain. With amounts from $1 to $5, over 40 percent of the consumers who experience some problems do not take action. With amounts from $11 to $25, nearly 30 percent will not complain. Even with amounts from $100 to $500, 15 percent do not take action.

Consumers often fail to complain because they think it isn't worth the time or effort or because they don't know where to go or what to do. Interestingly, when consumers do complain and receive satisfaction, they usually remain loyal customers.

Consumer Fraud

Almost everyone has a story of "being taken," "ripped off," or "gypped" in the marketplace. But most consumer problems are difficult or impossible to pin down as consumer frauds. Six elements constitute a *fraud*. They are:

—A material representation must exist.
—The representation must be false.
—The representation is made with the knowledge of its falsity or must be made recklessly.
—The representation must be made with the intention to cause reliance on the representation.
—The reliance is justified.
—Injury must result.

In other words, you must be given information by someone who knows it is false and who intends for you to believe it. If you believe that the information is true and you suffer loss because of it, fraud can be claimed. But before courts can help the consumers in a fraud case, all the elements must be proved. Some common consumer frauds are described in the following paragraphs.

Referral Selling. "If your friends let me show them this product, you can earn a $25 commission for each person you refer who buys the product."

In a *referral sale* the seller suggests that the consumer will receive a rebate or commission by supplying the names of other buyers who, in turn, must purchase additional products. In the referral selling the salesperson sells a product, such as a vacuum cleaner or encyclopedia, for more than the regular price. For example, a vacuum cleaner may ordinarily sell for $100, but the consumer may be asked to pay $130. The purchase is made attractive by an agreement that if the consumer will give the salesperson the names of some friends, the salesperson will call on these friends. According to the agreement, the salesperson will give the consumer $5 for every demonstration that the salesperson gets to make and $10 for every sale resulting from the contacts with the persons whose names are supplied.

Referral selling is a fraud because the salesperson has no intention of contacting any of the people supplied by the purchaser. The customary answer from the salesperson or company is that no sales were made.

Home Study Courses. "Quick and easy correspondence school."

Ads for home study courses, which offer free career information, often appear in reputable newspapers and magazines. When consumers respond to the ads, they sometimes receive information about how the successful completion of this course will give them an edge over anybody who has not completed it. In addition the information may claim that many jobs are available in this particular field. By taking the course offered, a person will have no trouble finding a well-paying job.

While many respectable correspondence schools exist, there are also some that take advantage of the hopes and ambitions of the uninformed. Before buying a correspondence course, consumers should check with employers in the particular industry in which they are interested to determine the value of such a course.

Pigeon Drop. "Look, I just found an envelope filled with money. What should we do about it? We can split it if you won't call the police."

In this fraud you may be approached by a stranger who claims to have found some money. An offer is made to share it if you will not contact the police and if you will put up "good faith" money or other valuables until the money is divided. The scheme usually involves some requirement that you remove some amount from the bank in order to prove your good intentions. A person is defrauded when the promoter takes the good faith money and leaves the victim holding phony money or waiting to split the treasure. The following newspaper account exemplifies how the *pigeon drop* works.

> An elderly woman was approached by two young women. The victim was told that the two had found a large sum of money and that they could share it with her if she would put up some money in "good faith." The woman who had been approached gave the pair a $6,000 diamond ring and $2,800 she had withdrawn from a local bank. The victim was attempting to withdraw another large sum of money from another bank when she was warned about such schemes by bank officers. By the time the woman returned with police to where the pair had been waiting, they had disappeared with the ring and money.

Such frauds as the pigeon drop work because of the desire of most everyone to get "something for nothing."

Earn Money at Home. "Address envelopes, stuff envelopes, design Christmas cards, grow mushrooms, or write songs."

These are some of the typical "make easy money at home" schemes seen advertised. Most of these schemes require the consumer to buy something or make some type of payment before earning any of the easy money. In some cases when consumers send in the payment to a post office box, they never hear from the company again. Investigations usually reveal that the company has terminated the use of the post office box, changed names, and started over again in another location.

In other cases consumers are told to make "easy money" by running the same type of ad that hooked them. For example, one mail fraud involved an advertisement which claimed that for one dollar the promoters would send instructions on how to get rich.

For one dollar, the victim received a note saying, "Fish for suckers as we do."

Buying Clubs. "Fight inflation . . . Join a buying club."

A *buying club* is an organization that sells memberships by claiming that its members get brand-name products at prices lower than those found in retail stores. Unfortunately, a buying club may not save its members any money at all. They can even be more expensive than retail stores. When consumers join a buying club, they are asked to pay a large membership fee. Initiation fees range from $200 up to $600. This fee puts members "in the red." If people pay $500 to join a club and save 25 percent on everything they buy, they would have to spend $2,000 before breaking even.

Most buying clubs make the greatest part of their income from selling memberships rather than from selling merchandise. Another major drawback to buying clubs is the high number of clubs that go out of business.

Mail-Order Frauds. "Two digital watches and a bonus hand calculator for under $40."

Sounds too good to be true. Often the promotional material on mail-order products promises more than can be delivered. Illus. 21-1 represents one of the biggest mail frauds ever prosecuted. The operator of Teltronics was charged with mail fraud because he failed to furnish the product that was advertised. Primary use of the mail occurred when respondents mailed in their orders and payments. The scheme grossed $1,700,000, with about 100,000 orders being received. Not one watch was ever sent to persons placing orders. Another mail-order advertisement claimed to sell "the dirtiest book in the world" for $14.95. The buyer discovered that inside the hollowed-out book was a small bag of dirt.

Most mail-order business is legitimate. Ordering merchandise by mail can be convenient, and the consumer can save time, effort, and money. But mail-order purchases often cause consumers trouble because the merchandise arrives late or not at all. The Federal Trade Commission has a rule that gives consumers some rights when ordering by mail. The FTC mail-order rule provides for the following:

—Consumers must receive the merchandise when the seller says they will.

BUY DIRECT AND SAVE!
6-Function L.E.D. Watch

Teltronics manufactures and sells exclusively these quality-crafted solid state watches worldwide—over 1 million sold at much higher prices. Now, order direct and get tremendous savings, all these features:

- **6 functions** controlled by a single button: hour, minutes, seconds, month, date, and day. Accurate within 2 minutes per year.

- **Full year warranty** against defects in materials or workmanship, except battery. We will repair or replace any Teltronics watch developing such defect within 1 year of purchase.

- **30-day home trial,** if not completely satisfied with your watch, return it within 30 days for full refund of purchase price, no questions asked.

- **Ultra-thin case,** with stainless steel back. All watches shown are available finished in silver rhodium or gold plate with matching bracelets.

only
$**16**95
Silver rhodium finish

Yellow-gold plated, $17.95

FREE!

Order any *two* Teltronics L.E.D. watches and get this 8-digit 5-function electronic memory calculator, with battery and carry case, FREE!

TELTRONICS, 2400 E. Devon, Des Plaines, Ill. 60018

Illus. 21-1

Advertisement involved in mail fraud

Source: United States Postal Service

—The seller must ship the merchandise no later than 30 days after the order comes in.

—Consumers who do not receive the merchandise shortly after 30 days can cancel the sale and get the money back.

Telephone Sales. "Surprise! You've won our free telephone offer. Gift vacation for two. Have an exciting fun-filled holiday. Deluxe room accommodations for two days and three nights."

To receive the vacation certificates, deposits of $15 to $25 have to be made in advance. Some promoters sell vacation certificates without reserving any rooms. They issue counterfeit certificates that are not honored by the hotel, restaurant, or casino indicated. The promoters take in the money, go out of business overnight, and leave the "lucky winner" holding the bag.

Other companies which promote such vacation coupons make it impossible for consumers to use their certificates. They do this by repeatedly refusing consumers' requests for a specific vacation date. And when consumers do get a specific date, they have to pay travel costs and cost of meals. Their bonus coupon certificates for show tickets or golf may be limited to the hours of 2 A. M. to 5 A. M. Very often the consumers have to spend their own money first; then the promoter will provide the coupons. For example, one typical vacation certificate coupon requires consumers to spend as much as $50 to get a $13.50 value in coupons.

Health Quackery. "Burns away more fat each 24 hours than if you ran 14 miles a day."

People who are ill, are overweight, or have some concern about good health are often the victims of quack cures or gadgets. The products include weight reducers, blemish removers, hair-loss remedies, cancer cures, and many others. Consumers often trust the publications in which they see such "health cure" products. But many newspapers and magazines that carry mail-order health ads require no proof or substantiation of claims made. Many consumers believe that publishers make an effort to check the claims of advertisers. Consumers cannot rely on the magazine or newspaper printing an ad to judge the worth of a product. Consumers must rely on their own judgment to guard against mail-order health fraud.

Vocational Schools. "Don't waste time. Enter the career of your choice in six months."

Many people looking for a career become targets for misrepresentation by some private vocational schools. Reputable private vocational schools provide students with the skills necessary to get jobs. Some schools, however, promise students well-paying jobs and a bright future but cannot deliver the promise. As a result of unrealistic claims and exaggerations by some private vocational schools, the Federal Trade Commission has ruled that students in private vocational schools have the following rights:

—Students have 14 days after the school has accepted their enrollment application to change their minds about their choice.
—If students cancel within 14 days, they get all their money back even if the course has started.
—Schools must tell newly enrolled students in a separate written notice how many former students dropped out of the course before finishing.
—If the school makes claims about the demand for or potential earnings of their graduates, the notice must tell how many graduates were placed in jobs and how much they are earning.

Any person who is considering a private vocational school should get the names of five or six former students and find out if they were satisfied with the training and if it enabled them to get jobs.

Vanity Listings. "Congratulations—you're an outstanding young American."

Many teenage consumers receive a form letter telling them that they have been singled out for recognition for some achievement. The recipient of such a letter should ask "Who judged my qualifications?" "What are the requirements for such awards?" "What is the award worth in the real world?" "What's the catch?" Some are legitimate awards and honors; others are not. Some require the listed person to purchase a copy of the publication in order to be listed. For example, for only $5.99 you can get a handlettered scroll to tell the world about your honor, and for $24.99 you can get the "famous person book" that mentions your name.

Caveat Emptor: *Shoplifting*

Anyone may be a shoplifter. Grandfathers, teenagers, college students, executives, housewives, artists, and movie stars have been arrested for shoplifting. About the only thing most shoplifters have in common is that they seldom steal out of need. About one-third of shoplifters are between the ages of 12 and 17 and one in four is between 17 and 19. According to the Law Enforcement Assistance Administration, 75 percent of shoplifters are juveniles and 85 percent are females.

Shoplifting can have grave consequences for you. Shoplifting often results in a police record that can shadow you for the rest of your life. Law enforcement authorities estimate that 3 to 5 billion dollars worth of merchandise is stolen each year. Shoplifting is costly to consumers as well as to merchants. Generally, merchants have to increase the prices of items in the store to make up for the losses. Each time shoplifting takes place, it takes money out of your pocket. Buyer Beware.

Some merchants try to prevent shoplifting by attaching special tags to merchandise.

CONSUMER REMEDIES

What remedies do consumers have when they suffer losses after paying for defective products or misrepresented services? Obviously complaints to family and friends will do no good. Consumers have the right to *redress*. This is the right to register dissatisfaction and to be assured of an appropriate remedy for a wrongdoing. Consumers who expect to get their money's worth must know their rights and how to assert these rights. Competent consumers know the appropriate channels of redress and know how to complain effectively.

Effective Complaining

As a first step in effective consumer complaining, know what action you want. The goal of complaining should be more than an expression of anger, meaningless threats, sarcasm, or vague pleas for help. Effective complaining requires that you seek specific action such as the repair or replacement of a product or a refund of your money. The next step in effective complaining involves collecting all the data that pertain to the problem such as receipts, warranties, care instructions, or records of repair service. Once you begin the complaint process, keep a record of conversations, names of persons with whom you speak, and dates. Present accurate and specific information about your problem if you want it to be considered seriously.

A further step in complaining is to select the appropriate channel of appeal. Numerous agencies exist to help resolve consumer problems. Government offices play an important part in protecting consumers and assisting them with problems. Businesses, too, provide channels of appeal and support organizations which attempt to solve problems. Even media programs, such as action lines and hotlines, help consumers. A few of these channels of appeal will be discussed in the next section.

After selecting the appropriate channel of appeal, select your approach. You can appear in person, call on the phone, or write a letter. Usually the most effective approach is to write a letter of complaint. Most larger companies have complaint departments established for handling complaint letters. When writing a complaint letter, follow these simple procedures:

—Give all the facts
—Be honest and don't exaggerate
—Avoid threats, anger, and insults

—Let the company know what action you want (repair, replacement, or refund)
—Include copies of receipts, repair or service records, etc.
—Send a copy to a consumer protection agency, if appropriate

Illus. 21-2 shows the format and style of an effective complaint letter.

Your Address
Your City, State, Zip Code
Date

Appropriate Person
Company Name
Street Address
City, State, Zip Code

Dear Company President:

State Your Purchase — Last week I purchased (or had repaired) a (name of product with serial or model number or service performed). I made this purchase at (location, date and other important details of the transaction).

Name Product and Serial or Model Number or Service

Include Date and Location of Purchase: Other Details

State Problem — Unfortunately, your product (or service) has not performed satisfactorily (or the service was inadequate) because _____.

Give History of the Problem — Therefore, to solve the problem, I would appreciate your (here state the specific action you want). Enclosed are

Ask for Satisfaction — copies (copies—**NOT** originals) of my records (receipts, guarantees, warranties, cancelled checks, contracts, model and serial numbers, and any other documents).

Enclose Copies of All Documents

Ask for Action Within Reasonable Time — I am looking forward to your reply and resolution of my problem, and will wait three weeks before seeking third-party assistance. Contact me at the above address or by phone at (home and office numbers here).

Include Your Address, Work and Home Phone Numbers

Sincerely,

Your Name

Keep Copies of Your Letter and All Related Documents and Information

Illus. 21-2

Effective complaint letter

Channels of Appeal

To avoid wasting time, consumers will need to know which channel of appeal is the most appropriate for the problem. Illus. 21-3 on page 416 shows the steps to resolving a consumer complaint.

Suppliers First/Then Manufacturers. The first step in resolving a consumer problem is to go back to the business or person who sold the item or performed the service and calmly state the problem and the action the consumer would like taken. If this person is not helpful, ask to see the manager. Most consumer problems are resolved at this level.

When you have a complaint about a product or service, go first to the supplier or manufacturer.

If a company operates nationally or if a product is a national brand, write a letter to the president or the official in the company responsible for consumer affairs. Most large companies have a complaint department or department of consumer affairs that will hear grievances. These complaint departments have established procedures for dealing with consumer problems, and they try to work out satisfactory solutions to problems. Consumers can find the name of the president and the company address for most corporations in

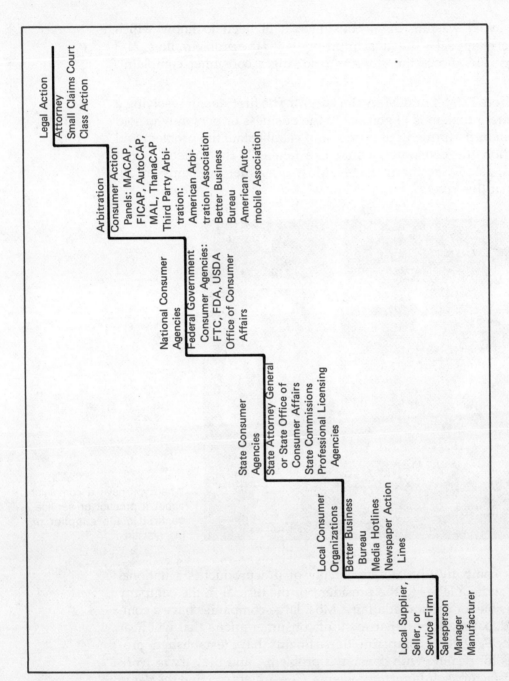

Illus. 21-3

Steps to resolving consumer complaints

Legal Action
 Attorney
 Small Claims Court
 Class Action

Arbitration
 Consumer Action
 Panels: MACAP,
 FICAP, AutoCAP,
 MAL, ThanaCAP
 Third Party Arbi-
 tration:
 American Arbi-
 tration Association
 Better Business
 Bureau
 American Auto-
 mobile Association

National Consumer
Agencies
 Federal Government
 Consumer Agencies:
 FTC, FDA, USDA
 Office of Consumer
 Affairs

State Consumer
Agencies
 State Attorney General
 or State Office of
 Consumer Affairs
 State Commissions
 Professional Licensing
 Agencies

Local Consumer
Organizations
 Better Business
 Bureau
 Media Hotlines
 Newspaper Action
 Lines

Local Supplier,
Seller, or
Service Firm
 Salesperson
 Manager
 Manufacturer

Standard and Poor's Register of Corporations, Directors and Executives.
For manufacturers, the *Thomas Register of American Manufacturers* lists
addresses of thousands of products and their manufacturers. These
reference books are available in most public libraries.

Local Consumer Organizations. At the local level, consumers can
receive a variety of assistance. Probably the best known local non-
government organization is the Better Business Bureau. Perhaps less
well known, but even more effective than the Better Business
Bureau, are media programs and consumer action groups.

Better Business Bureaus. Better Business Bureaus are nonprofit
organizations sponsored by private businesses. There are nearly 150
Better Business Bureau locations throughout the United States
today. Most offer a variety of services which include: providing
background information on local businesses and organizations and
providing information about companies' track records in handling
complaints. Better Business Bureaus do not judge individual products or brands, do not handle complaints about the prices of goods
or services, and do not give legal advice. Better Business Bureaus
vary from place to place, and the quality of consumer assistance
also appears to vary.

The Better Business Bureau requires all complaints to be in writing. Once a complaint is on file, a copy is mailed to the company in
question, and the company is given 15 days to respond. Generally
the Better Business Bureau sends a follow-up letter if the company
fails to answer. If the company still does not respond, the Better
Business Bureau may advise the consumer to consult a lawyer or a
local or federal agency. Companies that fail to respond or to resolve
consumer complaints can lose their rating with the Better Business
Bureau. Local businesses receive a rating from the BBB. Consumers
should check with the Better Business Bureau before dealing with an
unknown company. Such inquiries reduce the possibility of complaints arising.

Media Programs. Many local newspapers and radio and television stations throughout the United States have *action line* services
which solve problems of millions of consumers. When the consumer's personal efforts fail to resolve a problem, media action lines
may be able to get the results the consumer wants. Businesses fear
negative publicity; therefore, business people are inclined to resolve

At the local level, media action lines can help consumers solve problems.

a problem before it can be printed in the press or aired on radio or television. Some action lines, however, are not able to handle every complaint received. They may select only the severest problems or ones which are representative of a number of complaints.

Consumer/Community Action Groups. Local citizen-consumer advocacy organizations sometimes can help consumers. Examples of such groups are Native American organizations and tribal councils, women's groups, agricultural organizations, and single-issue groups. Many local community action groups focus their activities on energy, environment, housing, community development, health and safety, or consumer problems of special groups, such as senior citizens. Community action groups are seldom able to assist consumers with individual problems; instead, these organizations provide a way for individual consumers to work with other consumers and citizens for the improvement of the community and the marketplace. (See Chapter 22 on group citizen-consumer action.)

State Consumer Agencies. Numerous state government consumer agencies exist to help protect consumers. Generally the Office of the Attorney General and/or the Department of Consumer Affairs has broad authority for protecting the rights of consumers. The attorney general, for instance, can prosecute firms for violation of state consumer protection laws. Departments of consumer affairs police advertising practices and handle other types of consumer matters such as automobile repairs, credit problems, and door-to-door sales practices.

Equally important at this level are state commissions which regulate specific types of businesses within the state. Typically one or more of these commissions supervises financial institutions such as banks, savings and loans, and insurance companies. Many of these state agencies have broad regulatory power—even the power to license businesses to operate. These commissions see that businesses operate in a fair and responsible manner.

Other state agencies, known as occupational licensing boards, supervise various trades and professions such as hairstylists, accountants, doctors, and real estate agents. Because these occupations are important to the well-being of consumers, the practitioners are licensed by the state. Persons who desire to practice in these areas are required to attain and maintain a minimum level of competence. A person who fails to abide by established standards of conduct may be disciplined by the licensing board and subjected to the loss of a license to practice. Many of these state agencies publish consumer guides for utilizing the services of certain occupations.

National Consumer Agencies. Approximately 22 federal government agencies perform regulatory functions and have established programs designed to assist the consumer in dealing with problems and to involve consumers in the government decision-making process. In nearly all cases federal government agencies handle only problems associated with business conducted in two or more states (interstate trade). But because practically no product is created and sold solely within one state, most trade involves interstate commerce.

Most government agencies do not handle individual problems. For example, the FTC (see section below) will not likely intervene in a dispute over a malfunctioning stereo record player. However, if the problem involves the violation of the law, such as bait-and-switch tactics, the FTC will be interested. This is because the company you have a complaint against can be fined or penalized by the agency if it is violating a federal law or trade rule. When enough complaints occur, an agency can ask Congress to pass a law to stop a particular practice if no law exists. Following is a brief description of a few of the federal agencies which protect consumers through enforcement of federal legislation.

Federal Information Centers. Consumers who are interested in information on various aspects of the federal government, including programs and services, may visit, phone, or write to federal information centers located in most metropolitan areas of the country. If you want to know which federal agency can look into a consumer problem, this is a good place to begin. The Federal Information Center is listed in the phone book under U. S. Government.

Department of Agriculture. The Food Safety and Quality Service Division of the Department of Agriculture is responsible for assuring consumers that meat and poultry and products made from them are safe, wholesome, and truthfully labeled. In packing houses and food processing plants, the Department inspects meat and poultry products for sanitation, accurate labeling, and proper use of food additives. The Department investigates individual complaints concerning the freshness and quality of egg products and the grading of dairy products, eggs, poultry, and meat.

Consumer Product Safety Commission. The Consumer Product Safety Commission protects consumers against unreasonable risks from products used in and around the home, in schools, and in recreation areas. The Consumer Product Safety Commission has the authority to ban hazardous products, as well as to recall them from the market, and to set safety standards. CPSC also takes reports from consumers about product safety dangers and provides public information on the recall of unsafe products.

Federal Trade Commission. The Federal Trade Commission, one of the oldest consumer-oriented agencies, is charged with protecting consumers from unfair business practices and with promoting free and fair competition in the American marketplace. The FTC's principal functions are:

—To prevent price-fixing agreements and other unfair methods of competition

—To safeguard the public by preventing false or deceptive advertising

—To bring about truthful labeling of certain consumer products so as to prevent consumer deception and to facilitate value comparisons

—To insure the disclosure of the true cost of credit

—To protect consumers against inaccurate or obsolete information on credit reports

Food and Drug Administration. The Food and Drug Administration protects consumers by enforcing laws and regulations which prevent distribution of adulterated or misbranded foods, drugs, medical devices, and cosmetics. The FDA's principal functions are to assure consumers that:

—Prescription and over-the-counter drugs are safe and effective when used according to their directions.

—Drugs not safe for self-treatment are restricted to sale by prescription.

—New drugs are approved by the FDA before they can go on the market.

—Foods are pure and wholesome, safe to eat, and produced under sanitary conditions.

—Chemicals added to foods are safe before they are allowed to be used.

—Devices intended for medical use are safe and effective when used according to directions.

—Cosmetics are safe.

—Labeling of foods, drugs, medical devices, and cosmetics are truthful and informative.

Office of Consumer Affairs. The Office of Consumer Affairs in the Department of Health and Human Services coordinates and advises other federal agencies on issues of interest to consumers. The primary function is to represent the interests of consumers in the proceedings of federal agencies, to develop consumer information materials, and to assist other agencies in responding to consumer complaints. Although the OCA receives many specific consumer complaints, it is not authorized to act on them. The OCA does refer consumer problems to other appropriate agencies and uses complaints from consumers to promote legislation.

U. S. Postal Service. The Inspection Service of the U. S. Postal Service is responsible for dealing with consumer problems pertaining to illegal use of the mail. Mail fraud, false mail-order advertising, and unsatisfactory mail-order transactions come under the jurisdiction of the Inspection Service. Some examples include chain letters, work-at-home schemes, and direct-mail advertising.

Arbitration. Arbitration is often an efficient and effective way of resolving consumer complaints. *Arbitration* means that the different sides in a dispute agree to let an impartial person or panel decide on a fair solution to the problem. Third-party arbitration can clear up a problem more quickly and less expensively than can legal action. In a dispute between buyers and sellers the case is submitted to the third party, or arbitrator, who makes a decision that is binding on some or all of the parties. Once an arbitrator reaches a decision, it cannot be changed. More and more, local government agencies, trade associations, and other groups are setting up arbitration procedures to settle complaints. Some of the groups which offer third-party arbitration include: American Arbitration Association, American Automobile Association, and Better Business Bureaus.

Consumer Action Panels. At the national level several business and industry associations have established consumer action panels as another means of arbitration between consumers and manufacturers. A *consumer action panel* (CAP) is a special complaint-handling board of impartial business and consumer representatives who review and resolve consumer complaints. When consumers have problems with cars, furniture, or appliances, they can get help from a consumer action panel. A CAP should be contacted only after attempts to settle the problem with the dealer or manufacturer have failed.

When a consumer initiates a complaint to a consumer action panel, the CAP will ask the manufacturer to reinvestigate the problem and notify the CAP of action taken. If the consumer is not satisfied with the manufacturer's action, the panel will hear the facts of the case and will recommend the action that the manufacturer should take. Although manufacturers are not legally required to accept panel recommendations, they usually do. The following consumer action panels now exist: Auto Consumer Action Panel (Auto CAP), Furniture Industry Consumer Action Panel, Major Appliance

Consumer Action Panel, Magazine Action Line (MAL), and Thana CAP (funeral industry).

Legal Channels. Sometimes consumer problems cannot be settled directly by those involved and it becomes necessary to use a court of law. Under such conditions, consumers are faced with two choices: a private lawyer or a small-claims court.

Private Lawyer. Private lawyers handle legal and business transactions for their clients. Lawyers can manage a consumer's legal affairs, give legal advice, and present the consumer's case in court. However, lawyers usually do not take cases that involve small sums of money because their fees might well be more than is involved in the entire dispute. In such cases the small-claims court is an alternative to a private attorney.

Small-Claims Court. A small-claims court is a court of law for people who want to settle problems involving small amounts of money. In a small-claims court people can file a suit without a lawyer, tell the problem in their own words, and seek justice from the court for matters usually involving less than $1,000. The maximum amount that can be claimed or awarded differs from court to court with the average being around $500.

The small-claims court may be the best channel of appeal for consumers who have not been able to resolve a problem any other way. Court procedures are simple, inexpensive, quick, and informal. Court filing fees range from about $2 to $15, and a consumer usually gets the filing fee back if the case is won. If the party bringing the suit (the complainant) wins the case, the party who lost (the defendant) often will follow the court's decision without additional legal action. If the losing party does not obey the court's decision, the complainant can go back to the court and ask for the order to be enforced.

VOCABULARY REVIEW

Buying clubs	Redress
Mail-order frauds	Action lines
Health quackery	Arbitration
Vanity listings	Consumer action panels

QUESTIONS FOR REVIEW

1. What are two reasons that consumers encounter problems in the marketplace?

2. Approximately what percentage of consumers encounter problems when purchasing products in the marketplace?

3. Why do many consumers fail to complain when they encounter problems?

4. What six conditions must exist in order to prove fraud?

5. What precaution should one take before signing up for a correspondence course?

6. Why is shoplifting a problem for consumers and merchants?

7. What are the four steps in effective complaining?

8. When consumers experience a problem with a product or service, what is the first and most appropriate channel of appeal or redress?

9. When a consumer needs an address of a company, what source of information for corporation addresses is available in most libraries?

10. At the state level, what consumer agencies handle general consumer problems?

11. What kind of services do federal government agencies perform for consumers?

12. After complaining about the inadequacy of a product to a manufacturer who has neglected to answer your letters, name the three most appropriate channels of appeal which you would pursue.

13. When a consumer's problem involves a relatively small amount of money, what legal recourse is available?

PROBLEM-SOLVING AND DECISION-MAKING PROJECTS

1. Assume that you have purchased an AM/FM radio from a shopping center department store, and that the radio will not receive

the FM station in your area. The radio was advertised as capable of receiving both AM and FM stations. (a) First, decide what action you want taken. (b) Decide what information you have available to help you prove your case. (c) Decide which channel of appeal is the most appropriate in order to resolve the problem. (d) Assume that your first channel of appeal fails to respond to your complaint. What would be the next step in solving this problem?

2. Assume that you are involved in the situation described in this case:

You purchased a sweater from Harper's Department Store on December 15. The label in the sweater tells you it was made by Joseph & Company. You paid $30 for the sweater. Care instructions were included on a label in the sweater. Those instructions stated "Hand wash, lukewarm water, mild soap. Do not twist or wring. Lay flat to dry." After a couple of wearings you hand laundered the sweater according to directions and you noticed that the colors ran, streaked, and faded. When the sweater dried, you noticed that the color was now very uneven, and the sweater was ruined.

You return it on January 7 to Harper's Department Store and explain to the manager of the department what happened. The manager cannot do anything for you; it was obvious you did not follow the care instructions. Harper's refuses to give you either a refund or a replacement.

You want to write a complaint letter to help solve this problem. Write an effective complaint letter using the format shown in the illustration on page 414. When necessary, make up names and addresses and any other information you might need to complete the letter.

COMMUNITY AND HOME PROJECTS

1. Look through several magazines and note any "make money at home schemes," "correspondence schools," or "health claims" which appear suspicious. If possible clip them out and assemble them for an in-class analysis of the claims.

2. What consumer organizations exist in your community? Make a survey of local consumer organizations and their service or actions in the community. For example, find the following information: Which local or state agency is responsible for consumer frauds? What public citizens' groups, buying clubs, co-operatives does your community have? Which county or municipal court handles small claims?

3. With the assistance of your teacher, compile a community consumer resource directory. Use the following headings: name, address, type of service, and phone number.

Chapter 22

Consumer Action

Throughout the previous chapters you have seen how individual consumers can act effectively to find solutions to consumer problems. But consumer problems are not always *individual* problems. The rights of many people are often involved. For this reason, certain consumer problems call for collective (group) action.

Today, "consumer issues" cannot always be separated from national issues. The consumer's role cannot always be separated from the role of the citizen. Competent and concerned citizen-consumers can work together to influence their world. Citizen-consumers can help create a better way of life for everyone. In this chapter we will take a look at the social movement called "consumerism"—its history, its impact on the marketplace, and how consumers can use group action to further the interests of all consumers.

THE ROLE OF GROUP ACTION

Consumers influence the marketplace when they know how to make changes which create a better climate for all consumers. In the United States these changes are made through a variety of government and legal channels.

Our political system gives all citizens the right to work for such changes. However, past experience has shown consumers that *group action* is the most effective way to work for change. Many of the most impressive achievements in consumer protection came about because of strong and effective action by groups of consumers. Women's clubs fought for the first Pure Food and Drug Act in 1906. Neighborhood consumer groups pushed for and got local laws giving renters more protection in the 1970s. In each instance group action accomplished what individuals could not.

One for All, All for One

Consumers have strength in numbers. American workers of the late 1800s found that the best way to fight for their rights was to organize unions. Similarly, consumers in recent years have discovered that group action is the best way to effect changes in the marketplace.

Individual consumer action solves problems and makes changes when the outcome is under the consumer's direct control. Suppose that the action you want involves:

—getting a refund for a product you bought from a door-to-door salesperson

—being allowed to see your credit records

—having your car repaired under a warranty

Your individual actions should be enough to get a satisfactory solution to each of these problems because each situation is covered by a consumer protection law. But suppose these situations were not covered by consumer protection laws. Then group action would be necessary. Group action is in order when individual action is ineffective. For example, individual consumers cannot go out and purchase clean air; cannot assure that foods are safe; or that medicines work; or that television sets don't give off harmful amounts of radiation. Group action has helped to solve these consumer problems. Today the Food and Drug Administration inspects plants where food, drugs, television sets, medical devices, and cosmetics are made. These inspections assure that products are safe for consumer use.

By working together, consumers can do much to improve the climate of the marketplace; that is, the conditions, the products, the means of redress, and even the relationship between buyers and sellers. Legislators and business people alike are more apt to hear the voices of a group through such approaches as letter-writing campaigns, boycotts, "block" voting, and so on. Thus, the skills of a consumer must go beyond buying products; competent consumers need the skills required for effective group action.

The Citizen-Consumer

More and more of the events that influence the lives of consumers take place outside the traditional "buying-selling" marketplace. Consumers influence decisions that are made in legislatures, in corporate board rooms, and at public utility hearings. Therefore, the traditional definition of the consumer as a buyer and user of goods and services is not adequate because it does not cover consumer action. The consumer's role is also a political role. It is often impossible to see where the actions of consumers end and the actions of *citizens* begin.

In the following situations, are the people involved acting as consumers or as citizens?

> A high school student circulates a petition demanding that the city council pass a law banning the local sale of "throwaway" bottles.

> A family reluctantly makes a decision to buy a subcompact car. The car will save energy for them and for the nation as a whole.

> Members of a consumer group ask local citizens to boycott a supermarket chain which charges higher prices in its inner-city stores than in its suburban stores.

You will probably agree that it is all but impossible to divide these actions into "citizen" or "consumer" categories. A close relationship exists between consumer and citizen actions. Many of the most important "consumer issues" of the past 20 years involved the future of all our nation's citizens: protection of the environment, conservation of energy, the social responsibility of private business, and so on.

Circulating a petition can be both a consumer action and a citizen action.

THE CONSUMER MOVEMENT

The *consumer movement*, as it is called, encompasses public and private agencies, policies, laws, and regulations designed to protect consumer rights and enhance consumer interests. The consumer movement can be looked at from the early centuries through the 1980s. The ancient Romans had their own consumer motto: "Caveat emptor" — "Let the buyer beware." It was not until the mid-1960s that "Caveat emptor" changed to "Caveat venditor" — "Let the seller beware," and businesses were finally convinced that "consumerism" was a force to be reckoned with in the marketplace.

Earlier Centuries

In 1481 King Louis XI of France issued the following warning:

> Anyone who sells butter containing stones or other things (to add to the weight) will be put into our pillory, then said butter will be placed on his head until entirely melted by the sun. Dogs may lick him and people offend him with whatever defamatory epithets they please without offense to God or King. If the sun is not warm enough, the accused will be exposed in the great hall of the gaol in front of a roaring fire, where everyone will see him.

Most early consumer protection laws concerned the buying and selling of food. In ancient Greece and in medieval Europe, merchants were punished for mixing water with wine, grinding tree bark into pepper, and selling undersized "pound" loaves of bread. Groups of honest merchants often hired special inspectors to seek out unscrupulous business practices.

America's first consumer laws were the standards of weights and measures developed by Thomas Jefferson in the 1790s. Many of today's local consumer protection offices grew out of long-established government "weights and measures" offices.

Late 1800s

The Industrial Revolution of the 19th century radically changed consumer problems. Before this change most consumers lived in rural communities or small towns. They dealt with merchants they knew for simple goods such as food, lumber, and cloth. But as more and more of the American population moved into cities, many consumers had to buy from merchants they did not know. Processed food and pre-made clothing appeared on the scene. Consumers found it harder to judge the quality of what was purchased. Urban consumers faced the problems of city sanitation, crowded living conditions, and corrupt city politics.

Early 1900s

Unhealthy or dangerous foods were the most important consumer issue at the turn of the century. So-called "muckraking" journalists investigated filthy conditions in the food canning and meat packing factories. Dr. Harvey W. Wiley, the nation's pioneer consumer advocate, and chief chemist of the U.S. Department of Agriculture, found that food companies were using a number of dangerous chemicals in processing food. Dr. Wiley called for the passage of a federal pure food and drug law. He was joined in this effort by the American Medical Association, the National Consumer's League, and other groups.

In 1906 journalist Upton Sinclair published *The Jungle*, a book which confirmed the American consumer's worst fears about foods. Below is part of Sinclair's description of a meat packing plant:

> These rats were nuisances, and the packers would put poisoned bread out for them and they would die, and then rats, bread and meat would go into the hoppers together . . . Men who worked in the tank rooms full of steam . . . fell into the vats; and when they were fished out, there was never enough of them to be worth exhibiting — sometimes they would be overlooked for days, till all but the bones of them had gone out to the world as Durham's Pure Leaf Lard!

Sales of meat dropped 50 percent after publication of *The Jungle*. And later that year, Congress passed both the Pure Food and Drug Act and a meat inspection act authorizing stricter government inspection of the meat packing houses.

The 20s, 30s, 40s, and 50s

The next burst of consumer activity came in the late 1920s because consumers were concerned about rising prices and advertising

Consumer action was responsible for the passage of a meat inspection act.

Source: USDA Photo

campaigns for new and unfamiliar products. In the 1927 book *Your Money's Worth,* Stuart Chase and F. J. Schlink proposed forming a consumer organization which would test and rate products. Reaction to the idea was so good that Chase and Schlink founded Consumers' Research in 1929. Both Consumers' Research and its offshoot, Consumers Union, organized by Colston Warne, are alive and well today.

The Depression of the 1930s stepped up consumer interest in money-saving techniques. But an important issue of the 30s was that of dangerous drugs and cosmetics. One hundred people died from an "elixir" sold over the counter (sold lawfully without a prescription). Women were blinded by mascara dyes. Consumer indignation forced the passage of a strong Food, Drug and Cosmetics Act in 1938.

The years through World War II and the economic boom of the 1950s produced little consumer action. Nonetheless, subscriptions to product rating magazines like *Consumer Reports* increased from

50,000 in 1944 to 500,000 in 1950. The consumer event of the 50s was publication of Vance Packard's *The Hidden Persuaders*, a book outlining the manipulative selling techniques used by some advertisers and businesses.

The 60s

The 1960s was a decade of considerable consumer action. President Kennedy's "Consumer Bill of Rights" appeared in 1962 (see pages 9-10 of Chapter 1). Also in 1962 came the publication of Rachel Carson's *The Silent Spring* which created new consumer interest in protecting the environment. A Democratic landslide in the 1964 Congressional elections opened new doors for social and economic reformers concerned with consumer interests. Hundreds of consumer-related organizations sprang up—everything from small town food "co-ops" to Washington-based consumer action groups.

Without doubt, however, much of the force behind the consumer movement came from the energy of a few strong-minded individuals. They called themselves "consumer advocates," meaning that they advocated (spoke for) the consumer's interests. *Consumer advocacy* means recognizing, promoting, or protecting the causes or interests of consumers. Consumer advocates worked for the passage of consumer laws. They organized letter-writing campaigns on consumer issues. They helped set up national and local consumer action groups. They published books and articles letting consumers know what they could do to help themselves. The most famous consumer advocate of the 1960s and 1970s was Ralph Nader. Ralph Nader's campaign against unsafe cars resulted in passage of the National Traffic and Motor Vehicle Safety Act of 1966.

The 70s

As the 1970s progressed, it became clear that the new consumer movement was not a short-term interest. *Consumerism*, the search for the consumer's interest in the marketplace, established itself as a phenomenon in American economic and political life. In the 70s the American consumer was protected by many laws and regulations. Consumers were more concerned with how to use these existing laws and less concerned about working for more change.

The 1980s and Beyond

Because of high inflation and energy shortages, much consumer interest in the 1980s appears to focus on *conservation;* that is learning how to survive in a world of limited resources. The future of consumerism may lie in learning to consume less and to live more efficiently. Today American citizen-consumers will help decide how our nation copes with inflation, energy shortages, environmental problems, and so on. Thanks to the efforts of the past two decades, consumers have a better chance of being heard by their government. Through the 1980s consumers will work to maintain the protection and rights they gained in the past. The days of "consumer action" are not over yet.

CONSUMER LAWS

Year Passed	Law	Major Provisions
1906	Pure Food and Drug Act	Guarded against unhealthy and adulterated food and drugs.
1906	Meat Inspection Act	Required inspection of red meat products sold in interstate and foreign commerce and established strict sanitation for meat and poultry processing plants.
1914	Federal Trade Commission Act	Established the FTC and declared "unfair methods of competition" to be illegal.
1938	Food, Drug and Cosmetic Act	Expanded the 1906 Act to include cosmetics and established certain standards of identity for foods.

Consumer Laws (Continued)

Year Passed	Law	Major Provisions
1958	Food Additives Amendment	The "Delaney Clause" amended the 1938 Food Act to require food additives to be judged safe for human consumption.
1962	Kefauver-Harris Amendment	Required that all drugs be tested for safety and effectiveness before being sold to the public.
1966	Fair Packaging and Labeling Act	Required manufacturers to provide certain information on packages: who made it, what it contains, how much it contains, and so forth.
1966	National Traffic and Motor Vehicle Safety Act	Set up national safety standards for automobiles and new and used tires.
1966	Cigarette Labeling Act	Required health warning labels on cigarette packages.
1967	Wholesome Meat Act	Required state meat and poultry inspection programs to be "at least equal to" the Federal program.
1968	Consumer Credit Protection Act	"Truth-in-Lending" required lenders to make full disclosure of annual interest rates and other costs of credit.

Consumer Laws (Continued)

Year Passed	Law	Major Provisions
1969	Child Protection and Toy Safety Act	Provided for a ban on toys and other articles used by children which posed electrical, mechanical, or other dangers.
1970	Fair Credit Reporting Act	Set up rules governing the maintenance and reporting of consumer credit records.
1970	Poison Prevention Packaging Act	Required child-proof packaging of certain dangerous substances.
1970	Consumer Credit Protection Act Amendment	Prohibited companies from issuing unsolicited credit cards; limited consumer liability to $50 if card is stolen; provided for consumer access to credit files.
1972	Consumer Product Safety Act	Established Consumer Product Safety Commission empowered to oversee the safety of consumer products.
1975	Federal Trade Commission Improvement Act	"Magnuson-Moss Warranty Act" allowed the FTC to make rules for consumer warranties, provided for consumer redress including the class action suit.

Consumer Laws (Continued)

Year Passed	Law	Major Provisions
1975	Fair Credit Billing Act	Allows consumers to dispute alleged errors in credit statements. Sets up a step-by-step procedure for lenders and borrowers to follow in seeking resolution of problems.
1976	Equal Credit Opportunity Act	Prohibited credit discrimination on the basis of age, sex, race, religion, etc.
1976	Anti-Trust Improvement Act	Allows state attorneys general to sue on behalf of state residents to prevent price fixing.
1978	Fair Debt Collection Practices Act	Prohibits unfair debt collection tactics by agencies, such as harassment by phone.
1978	National Consumer Cooperative Bank Act	Set up a national bank empowered to provide funding for consumer cooperative and self-help groups.
1980	Depository Institutions Deregulation and Monetary Control Act of 1980	Allowed banks and other "depository" institutions to offer interest on checking accounts; also permitted raising of interest rates on some smaller savings accounts.

Articles used by children were made safer by the Child Protection and Toy Safety Act.

Source: Photo Courtesy Gerber Products Company

CONSUMER-CITIZEN ACTION IN THE MARKETPLACE

Today's consumers have a better chance of being heard by government and business because more groups are speaking effectively on behalf of the consumer. The groups are now apparent on advisory committees, regulatory commissions, and boards. The consumer activism of the 1960s and 1970s resulted in consumer protection in many areas. But economic, political, and social problems still affect consumers. You can help by joining a consumer-citizen action group and volunteering time and skills, or by signing your name to a petition in support of consumer laws or citizen initiatives. Consumer-citizen action comes in many forms.

Local and State Action

In your city or town the consumer's "voice" may be represented by a *local or state consumer protection office*, or perhaps by the *Office of the State Attorney General*. Consumers also have access to local *legal aid societies, community action programs*, newspaper and broadcast *"Action Lines,"* and *consumer representatives on local utility or licensing boards*. Many local communities also have *independent consumer groups* — some focused on one issue, such as food buying, others on political action.

One or more of these groups would be a starting place for consumer action — especially action involving local or state issues. These groups can provide information, organizational help, and even funds. But local groups also affect national issues. Representatives may participate in regulatory hearings in Washington D. C., or provide valuable data to national groups seeking information on a specific consumer problem such as auto repair fraud. Local issues, given much media publicity, may come to the attention of the nation as a whole. Local and state consumer groups are often vital to the success of Congressional letter-writing campaigns and other consumer "lobbying" efforts.

Also found in large businesses and corporations are *consumer affairs professionals*. In hopes of creating a better climate for the consumer from *within* industry, a consumer affairs professional tries to keep the consumer's interest fresh in the minds of corporation executives.

National Consumer-Citizen Action

Consumer representatives at the national level do many of the same things done by local or state consumer advocates; that is, provide information, organizational and legal help, and publicity. These national consumer representatives also get involved in some of the most complicated issues of the day. For example, consumer fact-finding organizations such as Ralph Nader's *Public Citizen* and *Common Cause* initiate and carry out in-depth research projects on such topics as product safety, energy usage, and government spending. The information provided is used in Congressional debates and federal regulatory meetings and is made available to the public.

Washington-based consumer organizations like the *Consumer Federation of America* or the *National Consumers League* work for the consumer's interest by testifying before Congress, or by helping state and local consumer groups learn how to lobby for consumer issues. Some national consumer organizations help in bringing lawsuits on behalf of consumers. *Consumers Union, Public Citizen,* and *Common Cause* have been especially active in pursuing legal action for consumers.

A few national groups act as clearinghouses for special information. For example, the Council of Public Interest Law will put individual consumers in touch with more than 100 centers specializing in legal help for *groups* of consumers with special problems.

In the executive branch of the government, the *Office of Consumer Affairs* in the White House is "the consumer's rep" in Washington. The OCA provides information, referrals, and many kinds of consumer action advice. The office is called upon many times each year to testify in hearings before Congress and federal agencies.

In addition many of the government's *regulatory agencies* are charged with helping create a better marketplace for consumers. The

Pollution is one of the concerns of some national consumer-citizen organizations.
Source: EPA-DOCUMERICA-Alexander

Federal Trade Commission, the *Food and Drug Administration,* the *Environmental Protection Agency,* and many other agencies must enforce consumer laws passed by the Congress. They have the power to make regulations which affect the consumer's life, and they seek out the advice and participation of individual consumers and consumer groups during rule-making procedures.

Regulation of business and marketplace activities has become controversial in recent years, with business and other interests complaining of "busybody" rules which do more harm than good. Americans are becoming more aware that each regulation means a trade-off. For example, safer cars ultimately cost more when purchased. Yet, the great majority of government regulations have done much good for consumers. The good may be seen in such things as food inspection standards, drug testing requirements, and advertising codes.

CONSUMER ACTION AND THE LAW

While consumer action may take many forms and have a variety of goals, the heart of consumer progress in the United States has always been the passage and enforcement of laws which benefit consumers. For this reason, competent consumers must learn how they can involve themselves in the legislative process. Consumers, as well as business persons, can lobby for their own interests and for "the public interest."

To most of us, the Congress may seem very far away. But as the following guidelines show, reaching your Congressional representatives is not impossible. With your cause in hand, approach the lawmakers in this way:

1. *Learn about the Congress.* Read the *Congressional Record;* write for selected Senate or House hearing transcripts. Become familiar with such things as the kinds of laws being passed and where the powerful people are.
2. *Research your cause.* Find out what your program will cost, who could manage it, and why it is needed. Discover some experts in the area, and keep them in reserve for later use as witnesses.
3. *Know your representatives.* Find out about their legislative voting records, committee assignments, family and career backgrounds, mutual acquaintances, and so forth.

4. *Start lobbying early.* Bills are studied and shaped by Congressional committees before they are discussed in the Congress. Committee hearings are a good time to send letters and to present testimony, if asked. Most laws are passed in virtually the same form as decided on by the committee.

5. *Let your representative know YOU.* If you or your group has received any publicity for your cause, send letters and press clippings to your representative or to key politicians in the debate on the issue. If possible, arrange a face-to-face visit. Most Congressional representatives have district offices, and they're often "in" on weekends. As an alternative, invite the representative to attend a question-and-answer session with your consumer action group.

6. *Remember to use resources available to you.* Look around. You are surrounded by useful lobbying tools. For a small sum you can send a Public Opinion Message (a kind of telegram) to your representative. An effective letter *will* reach the desk of your representative, and it costs no more than the cost of paper and a stamp. Local consumer journalists are often glad to publicize the efforts of local consumer activists.

7. *Remember the next election.* In your contacts with lawmakers be polite, practical, realistic, and helpful. But as a last resort, you can always let your representatives know that you will remember their actions next election day. Groups who vote as a "block" can make a difference in a reelection campaign.

8. *Always say "Thank you."* You don't have to limit your legislative contacts to the times when you have a problem or complaint. Be sure to thank your representatives for work well done. Keep up the contacts you have made by writing occasionally to praise or to comment on a recent vote. You may need to ask your representatives' help again.

The concerned citizen-consumer *can* help shape laws and influence the marketplace. Individual consumers *can* deal effectively with lawmakers. Individuals *can* lobby strongly in the face of wealthier and more powerful interest groups. But there's no doubt about one thing: Group consumer action is usually more effective than individual consumer action.

BUSINESS LOBBYING

Consumers can work with lawmakers to create a better consumer climate, but in the American political process, there is another group involved: the business lobby. A *lobby* or *special interest* is a group of persons who work to influence the decisions made by elected officials. By one count, there are nearly 15,000 full-time business lobbyists in Washington D. C. These lobbyists want to talk to elected representatives about issues that concern certain industries or interest groups such as oil, tobacco, sugar, and medicine.

Business lobbies now spend at least $1 billion every year to influence the laws and policies of the government. Although there is nothing illegal about it, some consumerists believe business lobbies are too powerful. But consumer groups have just as much right to lobby for their interests.

All lobbyists attempt to influence the legislative process. They work in the following way.

—The most important part of a lobby's influence is its ability to help finance election campaigns. In recent years corporations have used newly legal Political Action Committees (PACs) to solicit donations from employees. The money is then contributed to the company's favored candidate.

—Washington lobbyists get the chance to meet politicians face-to-face, to entertain them, and to perform favors. Lobbyists help Congress collect and analyze information relating to proposed legislation. The major oil lobby, the American Petroleum Institute, supplies much of the information Congress uses in considering laws for the oil industry.

—Business lobbies have adopted the consumer-style letter-writing campaign. Using computer lists of members, for instance, the National Rifle Association can mobilize its people by the thousands to write letters to Congress opposing gun control.

The problem is not that lobbying exists. It is a real and vital part of our political system. The problem is that most citizens, even most citizens' groups, do not have as much time, as much money, or as much "clout" to make sure their voice is heard above the voices of business lobbyists. What can you do? Learn to lobby too!

VOCABULARY REVIEW

Group action

Citizen-consumer

Consumer advocacy

Consumerism

Conservation

Consumer Federation of America

Consumers Union

Regulatory agencies

Consumer affairs professional

Lobby

QUESTIONS FOR REVIEW

1. What are the two ways by which consumers can influence the marketplace?

2. What is the consumer movement?

3. Give an example of consumer action from each of the following periods—earlier centuries, late 1800s, early 1900s, 1920s, 1930s, 1940s, 1950s, 1960s, 1970s.

4. What appears to be the primary concern of consumers for the 80s?

5. How can you as a consumer help create a better climate in the marketplace for all consumers?

6. What has been the "heart" of consumer progress in the United States?

7. List the steps which are proper when trying to get your elected representatives to hear your views.

8. How do lobbyists influence elected representatives?

PROBLEM-SOLVING AND DECISION-MAKING PROJECTS

1. For one full week collect every article in the daily newspaper that pertains to consumer problems, actions, legislation, complaints, etc. From this information, identify consumer problems or issues which are most appropriately solved by individual actions and which are solved by group actions.

2. Identify a consumer or citizen issue on which you feel some

action should be taken. Prepare a report which summarizes the following:

a. the current state of the issue before Congress, your state legislature, or local governing board
b. the issues involved in your cause: what action should be taken, who or what group is responsible, who are the experts on the issue, who is opposed and why
c. the identity of your elected local, state, and federal representatives who you feel should support the issue
d. the identity of other groups or individuals who are involved in group action on the same cause or issue

After you have finished your summary, outline any activities which would be most effective in getting action taken on this particular issue.

COMMUNITY AND HOME PROJECTS

1. With the permission of your teacher, compile a list of community action, consumer, or citizen groups. Identify their causes, issues, and leaders.

2. Using your school or public library, survey recent periodicals, newspapers and other references for articles on consumer issues. Prepare a report entitled, "Who is speaking for consumers?" Include in your report the activities of such organizations or agencies as National Consumers League, Consumer Federation of America, Common Cause, Public Citizen, Office of Consumer Affairs, Consumers Union, and national or local consumer advocates.

Glossary

A

Achievers: consumers who work for success and who spend money, time, and energy to display success

Action lines: services provided by local newspapers, radio, and television stations for resolving consumer grievances, particularly with business organizations

Ad substantiation: data which support the claims about the safety, performance, efficiency, quality, or prices of products

Advertised specials: specific items which are on sale at prices lower than normal prices

Annual percentage rate: the cost of a loan over a full year expressed as a percentage

Arbitration: a means of solving consumer problems by getting two sides in a dispute to agree to letting an impartial person or panel decide on a fair solution

Auto broker: a firm that does not maintain dealership showrooms or salespeople and that specializes in selling new cars directly to consumers, often at a low cost

B

Bait and switch: advertising that lures a customer to a store with a low price for a product; then a salesperson switches the customer to a higher priced product

Bankruptcy: a legal process that declares persons unable to pay their debts

Basic food groups: a guide to food selection consisting of five groups — vegetable-fruit, bread-cereal, milk-cheese, meat-poultry-fish-beans, and miscellaneous

Belongers: consumers who like to conform to group values

Beneficiary: a person named in an insurance policy to receive the insurance benefits (usually an amount of money)

Blend: the threadlike structure created by the combination of natural and synthetic fibers

Bodily injury liability insurance: coverage that pays for the expenses of others when you are responsible for an injury-related accident

Budget: a spending and savings plan that helps you gain control over your income

Buying clubs: membership organizations that offer brand-name products at prices lower than those in retail stores

C

Calories: the measurement of food energy

Capital goods: the products and equipment used by producers in the production of other goods

Capital spending: money spent by businesses on equipment to expand capacity, to improve quality of goods and services, or to introduce new products

Care labels: tags on clothing that give the consumer information about caring for a garment

Cash discount: a reduction in the cost of a product because the purchase was for cash instead of credit

Cash-value insurance: a type of life insurance policy that protects the insured and accumulates a savings fund known as the cash surrender value

Caveat emptor: let the buyer beware

Caveat venditor: let the seller beware

Central authority: a tribal chief, dictator, central committee, Congress, or the President of the United States who determines the use of resources

Certificate of deposit: a savings plan that requires a deposit for a period of time during which the saver cannot withdraw money from the plan without penalty

Check: an order written by a depositor requesting a bank to pay out money

Check register: used for recording all of the transactions that occur in your checking account

Citizen-consumer (or consumer-citizen): each individual engages in political actions and marketplace activities

Citizen-voter choice: the decisions of citizens as voters that determine the use of resources

Closing costs: the expenses which buyers normally have when completing the purchase of real estate

Co-insurance provision: a provision in health insurance coverage that requires the policyholder to pay a part of the medical expenses

Collateral: security for a loan in case the borrower cannot pay back the amount borrowed

Collision insurance: coverage that pays for repairs to your car if it is damaged

Common stock: a certificate reflecting ownership in a company that has no stated dividend rate

Competition: rivalry among sellers for consumer dollars

Compound interest: interest added to the total invested before interest is calculated

Condominium: individual ownership of one unit and joint ownership of common areas in a multiple unit building

Conservation: preserving or using resources efficiently

Consumer: a user of goods and services

Consumer action panels: established by business and industry associations as a means of solving problems between consumers and manufacturers

Consumer advocacy: the recognition, promotion, and protection of the causes and interests of consumers

Consumer affairs professional: a person within business or industry who works to keep consumer interests fresh in the minds of corporation executives

Consumer Bill of Rights: the basic rights of all consumers to be heard, to be safe, to choose, and to be informed

Consumer choice: the buying decisions of consumers that signal producers as to the satisfaction or dissatisfaction of consumers with goods or services

Consumer education: the study of a body of knowledge about choosing, spending, and conserving resources, goods, and services

Consumer Federation of America: a Washington-based consumer-citizen action organization that lobbies and testifies before Congress on behalf of consumers

Consumerism: the search for the consumer's interest in the marketplace

Consumer Price Index: an economic indicator that measures changes in the dollar's buying power

Consumer sovereignty: implies that consumers direct the use of resources by spending dollars for the products or services wanted most

Consumers Union: a not-for-profit consumer organization which tests and rates products, publishes *Consumer Reports* magazine, and speaks out on behalf of consumer interests

Contingency fee: a means of billing by attorneys (usually a percentage of the settlement if the lawyer wins the case for you)

Convenience foods: food items sold for quick and easy preparation

Cooling-off-period: a Federal Trade Commission rule giving consumers three days to cancel any purchase of $25 or more made in their homes

Cooperative: a form of ownership of a unit in a building that requires the purchase of stock in a company that owns the multi-unit building

Corporate bonds: certificates indicating a long-term loan of money to a corporation

Corrective advertising: used to correct misleading or incorrect advertising

Cosigner: a person who guarantees to pay a debt if the person who obtained the loan cannot do so

Cost-per-check fees: a checking account that requires payment of a fee for each check written

Coupons: 1) printed pieces of paper entitling the holder to a price reduction on a product; 2) pieces of paper which most be clipped from a bond and taken to a designated bank or other location for payment

Credit insurance: will pay the unpaid balance of a loan if the debtor dies or becomes disabled

Creditor: the lender of money, or the one to whom money is owed

Credit union: a cooperative lending and savings association which accepts savings deposits and makes small loans to its members

Credit worthiness: an individual's ability to repay debts

Cremation: the process of reducing a corpse to ashes

D

Debit card: a plastic card that is used to authorize an electronic transfer of funds for paying bills or for purchasing goods and services

Debt consolidation: a type of loan that combines many separate monthly payments (other loans) into one loan with a smaller single monthly payment stretched out over a longer period of time

Debtor: a person who buys goods and services or borrows money with a promise to pay later

Decision making: the act or process of establishing a goal, evaluating information, considering alternatives, and making a decision

Deductible clause (provision): a requirement that the insured pay a specified amount before the insurance company pays the balance

Deductions: money subtracted from gross salary for such items as FICA tax, insurance, federal and state income taxes, union dues, and pension payments

Demand: the willingness and ability of consumers to spend money for goods and services (The demand principle in economics suggests that when demand for a product increases, the price of the item generally goes up.)

Depreciation: a decrease in the value of property as it becomes older and is used more

Discount rate: a method of expressing the cost of credit; the finance charge is subtracted from the amount borrowed

Discretionary income: the amount of take-home income left after an individual pays for the basic needs of food, clothing, and shelter

Down payment: the part of the purchase price of an item that is paid at the time of a purchase

Downplaying: hiding, omitting, or disguising information that advertisers do not want consumers to think about before buying a product

Drawer: the person who signs the check requesting that payments be made

Durable goods: long-lasting products such as automobiles, household appliances, and furniture

E

Efficiency apartment: a relatively inexpensive one-room apartment which serves as a kitchen, living room, and bedroom

Electronic fund transfers: the use of the computer to transfer dollars from buyer to seller or from employer to employee without the use of cash or check

Emulators: consumers who spend money in order to be respected or to be like famous or wealthy people

Endorsement: 1) an advertising claim by a famous person; 2) a signature on the back of a check that transfers ownership of the check

Excise tax: a federal tax on specific products (such as gasoline, tobacco, and liquor) generally included in the price of the product

Exports: products made in a country that are sold outside of the country

Express warranty: a written or oral promise that informs the consumer of the seller's or manufacturer's responsibility for repairing or replacing a defective product (same as guarantee)

F

Fabrics: cloth formed by knitting, weaving, or bonding fibers together

Face value: 1) in insurance, the amount that an insurance policy will pay in the event of death; 2) on bonds, the amount printed on the front of a bond certificate

Factors of production: the combination of raw materials, labor, capital, and management required to produce the goods and services that consumers want

Fads: clothing trends which last for a brief period of time

False price comparisons: a deceptive advertising practice in which a false original (former) price of a product is stated so that the current lower price is more appealing

Family accounting: the principles of business financial planning applied to an individual or family

Fashion: the prevailing manner of dress accepted by the majority of a group at any given time

Fee-for-service: payment for services rendered at the time of the service or after the service is performed

FICA tax: employees and employers pay a percentage of the wages earned into a fund that entitles the employee to social security benefits

Finance charge: the total dollar amount that it costs a consumer to use credit

Financial planning: the process of identifying individual financial priorities and tailoring activities and resources toward achieving those priorities

Financial responsibility law: a state law that requires a driver who is at fault in an accident to pay for property damage or injury to other persons

Finish: a process applied after a fabric is woven or knitted to improve or change its performance, feel, or appearance; for example, waterproofing, preshrinking

Fixed costs: 1) expenses that occur regularly such as rent, mortgage payments, or loan payments; 2) the expenses that result from owning and operating a car, such as depreciation, insurance, finance charges, taxes, license, and registration fees

Flame resistant: a chemical finish which reduces the risk of flammability but which does not make a fabric fireproof

Fraud: a deliberate plan to cause a person to lose money or property

Fringe benefits: financial rewards for work which are in addition to salary, such as paid vacations, life and health insurance, retirement plans

Full warranty: a promise that a product will be repaired or replaced if it becomes defective during the warranty period

G

Garnishment: a legal procedure that allows a creditor to have a portion of a person's wages in payment of an overdue debt obligation

General sales tax: imposed as a percentage of the price of any item sold

Generic labels: food labels that state only the common name of the product sold

Grade: a seal or stamp on food that indicates the quality in terms of appearance and uniformity of size

Gross national product: an indicator that measures the total value of all goods and services produced in a country during a year

Gross salary: the total amount earned before deductions from the paycheck

Group action: the actions of citizens working together for changes to improve the environment, the marketplace, or society in general

Group insurance: low cost insurance provided through a wage-earner's place of employment

H

Health foods: foods that are regarded as wholesome, safe, and nutritious

Health maintenance organization: a group of physicians who stress preventive medicine and who offer group health care for a fixed monthly or yearly fee

Health quackery: false claims about a health product from a person who pretends to practice medicine or to be a health expert

High-balling: a high figure is quoted for the trade-in automobile but at the time to close the sale, the sales manager claims that the offer was a mistake

Human services: the useful work performed by individuals which contributes to the welfare of other consumers

I

Implied warranty: an unwritten promise that a product is fit for the purpose for which it was sold

Implied warranty of habitability: a law passed in some states that requires apartment building owners to rent a dwelling that is suitable for living

Imports: goods and services bought from another country

Impulse buying: unplanned buying of products that are often unneeded

Income tax: a tax on individual earnings from wages, salary, tips, interest, dividends, and capital gains

Indemnity basis: reimbursement for medical expenses whereby the insurance company pays either the insured, the physician, or the hospital

Inflation: a general overall increase in the prices of goods and services

Inner-directed consumers: consumers who buy to meet their own needs and wants

Installment contract: a legal agreement involving a loan which is repaid with interest in a series of small payments

Installment credit: a type of debt used primarily for large, expensive purchases and repaid in a series of small payments

Institutional advertising: advertising that promotes groups of businesses or an industry such as milk producers or florists

Insured: the person for whom risk is assumed by an insurance company (also called policyholder)

Intensifying: the use of bragging, emphasizing, or exaggerating to make a product appealing to the consumer

Interest: 1) the amount of money paid to rent or use someone else's money; 2) the money savers get for letting someone else use their money

Internist: a physician with training in all areas of medicine except surgery, obstetrics, and pediatrics

In-the-garage tests: the final step in examining the condition of a used car (involves a diagnostic check by a qualified mechanic)

Investing: the process of putting money to work

Iron dealers: small business operations that sell old cars which are usually in poor condition

K

Knock-offs: cheaply made products that look like name-brand merchandise

L

Lawyer referral service: a list of attorneys who may be willing to handle a case

Lease: a rental agreement that spells out the rights and responsibilities of the renters and the property owners

Life cycle: the stages of life that have unique characteristics, requirements, and expectations

Life-style: a person's typical way of life as influenced by resources, roles, values, goals, needs, and wants

Limited warranty: a promise to repair or replace a product that has specific restrictions on what will or will not be paid for by the manufacturer

Loan credit: a way of borrowing money for personal and family needs (also called personal or consumer loans)

Lobby: a person or group of people who work to influence the decisions made by elected public officials

Loss leaders: products sold at or near cost to attract customers to a store

M

Magazine seals: promises to replace the product or refund the purchase price if the product advertised in certain magazines is found to be defective

Mail-order frauds: false claims and promotions about products or services that are delivered through the mail

Manufacturer's suggested retail list price: the maximum price suggested by the manufacturer for the sale of a new product

Market mechanism: the complex mode of organization in which the interaction of economic forces between buyers and sellers solves the problem of production and distribution

Marketplace: the environment where buyers (consumers) and sellers meet

Market price: the price of a product that represents a balance between the forces of scarcity, supply and demand, profit, and competition

Materialism: a belief that comfort, pleasure, and wealth are the highest values and goals in life

Meal plan: the food items needed for a weekly menu

Mean income: the average income of all households

Mechanic's lien: a claim made against a homeowner for unpaid services, labor, or materials put into a home

Median income: the midpoint or middle level of income; that is, one half of all income received is above this point and one half is below this point

Memorial society: a nonprofit organization that arranges for a simple funeral for its members for about one third the cost of the average funeral

Minimum balance account: a checking account that requires the customer to maintain a certain daily balance; otherwise, a charge is imposed

Mixed enterprise: an economic system characterized by the use of consumer choice, citizen-voter choice, and central authority in the allocation of resources

Money market fund: a mutual fund that pools the money of small savers for investment in high-interest-earning corporate or U. S. Treasury securities

Mortgage: a legal claim against real property given by a borrower to a lender as security for a loan if the principal and interest on money borrowed are not paid as agreed

Mortgage insurance: a life insurance policy that assures the payment of debts on real property if the insured dies

Municipal bonds: a certificate indicating a long-term loan of money to a state, city, or other local government body

Mutual fund: a business that pools the money of people for investment in stocks or bonds of many corporations

N

Natural fibers: the threadlike fibers found in nature or grown—such as cotton or silk

Natural foods: foods that are unrefined and free from additives, preservatives, artificial color, and flavorings

Need-driven consumers: consumers who place a high value on security and survival

No-fault insurance: a type of insurance coverage (also called first-party coverage) that pays the financial loss of the insured regardless of who is at fault in an accident

Nondurable goods: products, such as food, clothing, and gasoline, that have a short-time use

NOW account: an interest-earning checking account

Nutrients: the substances in food which furnish fuel for energy, regulate body processes, and provide materials for building and maintaining body tissues

Nutrition: the process by which the human body acquires and converts food into energy for the maintenance and regulation of body functions

Nutritional labeling: a statement attached to a food product giving information about the nutritional value of the contents

O

Odd lot: the purchase of less than 100 shares of ownership in a company

Odometer: an instrument in a car for measuring the distance traveled

Odometer disclosure statement: a signed statement indicating the mileage registered on the odometer at the time of sale

On-the-lot tests: a method of examining specific aspects of a car in a used-car lot to determine the car's condition

On-the-road tests: a way of checking on the condition of a used car while driving the car

Opportunity cost: the real cost of a product; that is, spending money for one item will affect an individual's ability to obtain other items

Organic foods: foods that are unsprayed and raised with natural fertilizers

Outer-directed consumers: consumers who buy for outward appearances

P

Payee: the person to whom a check is made payable

Personal values: the ideas and principles which an individual, group, or society considers correct, desirable, or important

Persuasion: the act of influencing a person with an appeal to reason or emotion

Point-of-purchase information: information displayed with a product or on the package or label of a product

Postpurchase information: describes responsibilities of consumers and sellers if a product fails to perform properly

Premium: the amount of money the insured pays for insurance

Preneed funeral plan: a means of prepaying and making funeral arrangements before death

Prepaid legal services: members of a group pay for legal services at a set fee paid in advance of any need for legal help

Prepurchase information: helps consumers select products based on the expected performance of products

Primary care physician: a doctor who can take care of 85 percent of a person's health problems and refer the person to a specialist if necessary

Private property: a legal right which allows individuals to own the productive resources — land, labor, capital, and management

Private services: human services provided by privately owned businesses; for example, personal care and grooming, food preparation, household services, automobile repairs

Product-test ratings: the results of independent, objective testing performed by organizations that determine the overall quality of products

Professional advertising: advertising that is aimed at persons who provide professional services, such as doctors, dentists, teachers, architects

Profit motive: the force, incentive, or reward that guides people to provide the goods and services that society is willing to pay for

Progressive taxation: as earnings increase, taxes take a proportionately larger share of personal income

Property damage liability insurance: insurance coverage that pays for the damage done to property up to an amount stated in the policy

Property tax: a tax based on the value of residential, commercial, or industrial property

Prospectus: a printed statement that discloses all relevant facts needed for carefully evaluating a new stock issue or similar investment

Public goods: the goods or services provided by government agencies and paid for with taxes

Public-issue advertising: a type of advertising that advocates an idea or position regarding some public concern

Public services: human services provided by governmental agencies

Public utilities: businesses that perform essential services to the public at prices usually determined by government regulation rather than by competition

Puffery: an exaggerated statement about the quality and value of a product

Push money: a cash payment given to a salesperson by the manufacturer as an incentive to sell the manufacturer's product

Q

Quantity buying: buying a large number of nonperishable sale items in order to save money

R

Real cost: the alternative product which an individual must do without in order to purchase something else

Real earnings: an economic measurement that tells the actual buying power of wages or salary earned by eliminating the effect of price changes

Recession: the part of the business cycle characterized by a slowdown in economic activity

Recommended dietary allowances: the nutrients, protein, vitamins, carbohydrates, fats, minerals, and water needed for daily nutrient intake

Reconciliation (checkbook): the process of finding the correct ending balance of a checking account

Redress: a means to correct or compensate for some wrongdoing

Regressive tax: a tax that takes a higher percentage of income from lower income individuals than from individuals with higher incomes

Regular charge account: the seller allows the customer to purchase products or services during a fixed period, such as 30 or 60 days, and expects payment in full at the end of the period

Regulatory agencies: the government agencies which are charged with enforcing laws passed by the Congress and are charged with helping create a better marketplace for consumers

Rental agreement: a contract that spells out the rights and responsibilities of a tenant and the owner of the property

Resource allocation: the process of determining the use of resources

Resources: the human and material assets which are used by consumers in implementing their decisions; for example, knowledge/ability; money/property

Revolving charge account: a type of credit that allows the purchase of products or services with the agreement that the balance will be paid in full or that a finance charge will be paid on the unpaid balance

Risk: the chance of any unforeseeable events occurring such as injury, death, fire, or theft

S

Safety seals: indicate that equipment, materials, and products meet specific standards of performance

Sales credit: used to purchase goods or services in exchange for a promise to pay for them later

Saving: putting aside money for future use

Scarcity: 1) the economic problem of people wanting more than is available;

2) shortages in the factors of production that are necessary to produce goods and services

Security deposit: an amount of money that a tenant must give to a landlord/landlady to cover any damage done to an apartment

Self-help health care: the idea that individuals are responsible for their own health care decisions and actions

Self-regulation: the attempts of an industry, such as advertising, to set standards or a code of ethics for members of the industry

Service basis: medical insurance coverage that pays the doctor or hospital directly for reasonable and customary medical charges

Service contract: an agreement which provides for the cost of repairs after a warranty has expired

Shoplifting: the stealing of goods from a store

Social cost: the impact of individual decisions and actions when considered collectively

Specials: products advertised at a reduced price

Sticker price: the suggested manufacturer's retail list price for a new car; usually posted on the window

Sublet clause: a provision in a rental agreement that sets the conditions for renting your apartment while you are away

Subsidies: some form of federal assistance, loan, grant, or guarantee given to a corporation or other organization because it is considered essential or desirable for the public welfare

Supply: the amount of economic goods available for sale (The supply principle in economics suggests that when the supply of an item is plentiful, the price of the product generally will decrease.)

Synthetic fiber: the threadlike structure manufactured from such materials as petroleum, air, water, coal, and wood pulp; examples are Dacron and rayon

T

Take-home pay: the amount of earnings that remains after deductions are subtracted from gross salary

Tax: a compulsory contribution of money to local, state, and federal governments

Tax audit: an examination of your tax return by the Internal Revenue Service

Tax liability: the amount of tax owed on income received during the year

Term insurance: a low-cost insurance that protects the insured for a specified period of time

Trade advertising: advertising that is directed to wholesalers and retailers

U

Unit price: shows the cost of one standard measure of a product for a comparison of brands and sizes

Universal life: an insurance plan that provides flexible life insurance coverage and a fairly high rate of interest on the cash value

U. S. Recommended Daily Allowances: levels or amounts of essential nutrients needed by individuals for good health

V

Value conflicts: a clash of values; for example, an interest, idea, or desire in opposition to another interest, idea, or desire

Value priorities: values ranked from the highest or greatest importance to the least importance

Vanity listings: publications that falsely claim that a person has reached some degree of achievement

Variable costs: 1) costs which occur infrequently, are for widely differing amounts, and are often difficult to estimate; 2) the expenses that result from operating a car; for example, gas, oil, maintenance, tires, etc.

W

Wage Earner Plan: an alternative to declaring bankruptcy since the debtor is allowed to set a monthly amount to repay all debts

Waterproof: a chemical finish that fills the pores of a fabric so water cannot pass through it

Water repellent: a chemical finish that causes the fabric to shed water in normal wear but does not make the fabric completely waterproof

Weasel claim: a meaningless word or statement about a product

Workers' compensation: a social insurance plan which provides various types of insurance coverage for workers injured on the job or in job-related accidents

Y

Year-to-date-totals: a summary that appears on a paycheck giving the amount earned and the amount deducted from January to the current date

Index

Sources for Chapter Opener Photographs

Chapter 3.	H. Armstrong Roberts
Chapter 5.	© Greg Zajack 1980
Chapter 6.	© Tressa Traeger
Chapter 7.	© Gregory Heisler 1980
Chapter 8.	© 1979 Steve Salmieri
Chapter 10.	© 1979 Tim Olive ALL RIGHTS RESERVED
Chapter 11.	Burt Glinn/Magnum Photos, Inc.
Chapter 12.	H. Armstrong Roberts
Chapter 13.	H. Armstrong Roberts
Chapter 18.	© Steve Kahn, 1979
Chapter 19.	© Jay Dorin 1981/New York Convention and Visitors Bureau
Chapter 20.	Used with the permission of Alexander & Alexander Services, Inc.
Chapter 22.	© Peter Menzel, STOCK, BOSTON